13test ed 02/07

796.
083
MAL

Perspectives for a New Century

edited by

Robert M. Malina
Research Professor
Tarleton State University
Stephenville, TX

Michael A. Clark
Total Evaluation of Athletic Management (Team)
East Lansing, MI

Proceedings of a conference hosted by the Institute for the Study of Youth Sports
at Michigan State University, 23-26 May 1999.

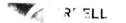

COACHES
CHOICE™

ISBN: 1-58518-861-1
Library of Congress Catalog Number: 2003106621
Cover design: Kerry Hartjen
Text design: Jeanne Hamilton
Front cover photo: Scott Halleran/Allsport

Coaches Choice
P.O. Box 1828
Monterey, CA 93942
www.coacheschoice.com

CONTENTS

Community Issues in Youth Sports

The Future

PREFACE

The timeliness of an integrated volume dealing with organized sport in the lives of children and adolescence is quite apparent. Much has changed in the world of youth sports, and issues related to the participation of youth in organized sports appear in the media on a regular basis. The contributions to this book represent invited lectures at a conference—Youth Sports in the 21st Century: Organized Sport in the Lives of Children and Adolescents—sponsored by the Institute for the Study of Youth Sports of Michigan State University in May 1999. The volume offers a comprehensive and critical examination of the many dimensions of youth sports—psychological, social, biological, and clinical. It also places these critical discussions in the context of the community, the unit in which youth sports programs operate and to which youth sports programs owe their existence. The proceedings represent a balanced overview of biological and health-related, social and psychological, and community issues in organized youth sports. An introductory and a closing chapter have been added to assist in putting the works in perspective. A chapter dealing with the trainability of youth also has been incorporated. We believe that these 19 chapters will fill a significant void in the youth sports literature by bringing together views from many disciplines.

The conference was organized to celebrate 20 years of service to the State of Michigan by the Institute for the Study of Youth Sports of Michigan State University. About 160 individuals participated in the conference, including 19 invited speakers and participants from 28 different countries. The conference had a distinct international flavor, emphasizing the reality that participation in organized sport by children and adolescents is a worldwide phenomenon.

The Institute for the Study of Youth Sports was established by a state legislative mandate in 1978. The groundwork for the Institute was laid in 1975 in Senate Concurrent Resolution No. 39: "A concurrent resolution creating a special study committee to investigate and study youth sports activities programs, particularly the actual educational benefits that youth receive from these programs, the medical and legal problems that result from these programs, to consider plans to improve these programs so that youth will be protected while enjoying these recreational programs." Thus, the Joint Legislative Study Committee on Youth Sports Programs came into being. The Joint Committee commissioned a two-year survey of the status of youth sports program in the State of Michigan. Results of the survey lead to the establishment of the Institute for the Study of Youth Sports at Michigan State University in 1978, with Dr. Vern Seefeldt as the director.

The Institute was established with three mandates, which continue to the present: research on youth sports, outreach in the form of coach education, and preparation of educational materials related to youth sports. In 1985, members of the Institute organized a conference on youth sports: Effects of Competitive Sports on Children and Youth. The most recent conference continues this effort, with many attendees returning to Michigan State University some 14 years later. But Youth Sports in the 21st Century also expands the view of what impacts those involved in youth sports.

The Institute acknowledges the generous financial support of the Skillman Foundation, our primary backer for the conference. The Skillman Foundation was founded December, 1960, by Rose P. Skillman, widow of Robert H. Skillman, vice-president and director of Minnesota Mining and Manufacturing Company. The Foundation is a private grant-making foundation with a budget of $20 million. Headquartered in Detroit, its geographic grant-making area is Wayne, Oakland and Macomb Counties. The Foundation makes grants in the areas of child and family welfare, child and family health, education, juvenile justice, youth development, basic human needs, culture and the arts, and strengthening community and civic institutions. The generosity of the Skillman Foundation is greatly appreciated.

The Institute also acknowledges the financial support of the Gatorade Sports Sciences Institute. The assistance of the Gatorade Sports Science Institute helped to cover the expenses associated with two of the speakers. General financial support for the conference was also provided by the Committee on Institutional Cooperation— Kinesiology. The CIC represents support from departments at 10 of the 11 Big Ten conference universities and the University of Chicago.

— Robert M. Malina and Michael A. Clark

CHAPTER 1

Current Status and Issues in Youth Sports

Robert M. Malina and Sean P. Cumming
Tarleton State University, and
University of Washington

INTRODUCTION

Sport is perhaps the most visible form of physical activity, and is the primary source of activity for many children and adolescents. Mass participation in sports at the community level is a major feature of daily living for American children. More than one-half of American children, for example, have their first experiences in organized sport by 8-9 years of age (Institute for the Study of Youth Sports, 1978). Participation rates increases during childhood, but subsequently decline during the transition into adolescence, i.e., after about 12-13 years of age (Institute for the Study of Youth Sports, 1976). The distribution of participants has the shape of a broad based pyramid, with numbers of participants decreasing as sport becomes more demanding and specialized, and as interests of children and early adolescents change. The decline in youth sports participation after 12-13 years parallels declining rates of participation in physical activities in general across adolescence (Malina, 1995).

ESTIMATED PARTICIPATION IN YOUTH SPORTS IN THE UNITED STATES

Organized youth sport implies the presence of a coach, who is quite often a volunteer, and regular practices and competitions during the course of a season, and. Estimates of the number of participants in the United States for the mid-1990s suggest that approximately 22 million youth 5-17 years of age participate in sport programs sponsored by community organizations, e.g., Kiwanis, Police Athletic League, American Youth Soccer Organizations, Little League Baseball, Pop Warner Football, and so on. About 2.4 million youth participate in club sports which are generally fee-based as in gymnastics, figure skating, swimming, and more increasingly in soccer. An additional 14.5 million youth are estimated to be involved in municipal recreational sports programs, which emphasize participation for everyone, whereas only a small number, about 450,000, participate in intramural sports programs in middle and high schools. Expressed as percentages of the United States population 5-17 years of age in 1995 (about 48.4 million), 45%, 5%, 30% and 0.1% participate in agency, club, recreation and intramural sports, respectively (Ewing et al., 1996). Within the more restricted age range of high school students, about 5.8 million youth (40% of the high school age population) participate in interscholastic high school sports (Ewing et al., 1996).

It is difficult to estimate historical statistics for participation in youth sports due the lack of specific and uniform information by age, gender, and sport.

It is reasonable to assume that the number of participants in youth sports has increased over time. A relevant question, however, is how has the number of participants in organized sports changed relative to the general increase in the youth population? This can be estimated for participants in interscholastic sports at the high school level. Absolute numbers of participants in high school sports by sex and the number of high school students in grades 9 through 12 in the United States from 1971 to 1998 are shown in Figure 1. Although the number of students enrolled in high school declined from the late 1970s to 1990, the numbers of high school athletes have fluctuated between 3.3 and 3.5 million among males and increased slightly from 1.7 to 1.9 million among females. Since 1990, the numbers of male athletes have increased from 3.4 to 3.7 million, while corresponding numbers for female athletes have increased from 1.9 to 2.6 million. As a percentage of total students in grades 9-12, the numbers of male athletes have remained rather stable, with few exceptions, between 24% and 26% from 1971 to 1998 (Figure 2). In contrast, the numbers of female athletes as a percentage of total students in grades 9-12 have increased from 2% in 1971 to 10% in 1975, and then more gradually from 12% in 1978 to 18% in 1997 and 1998 (Figure 2). However, the number of female high school athletes as a percentage of the number of male high school athletes continues to increase, reaching about 69% in the 1998-1999 school year.

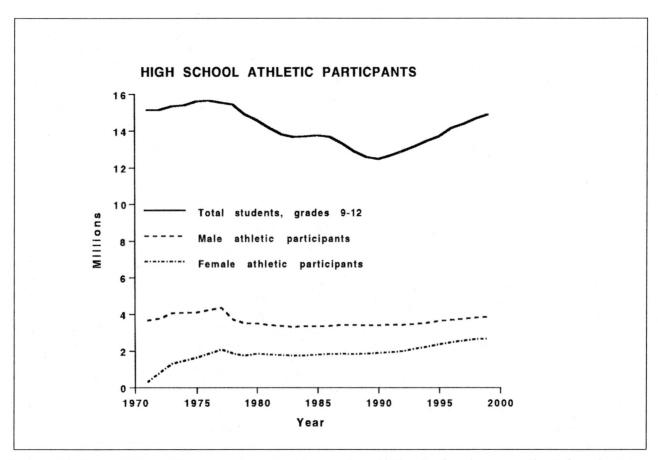

Figure 1. Participants in high school sports by sex and the number of high school students in grades 9 through 12 in the United States from the early 1970s through the late 1990s. Drawn from data reported by the National Federation of State High School Associations (1999) and the U.S. Department of Education (1998).

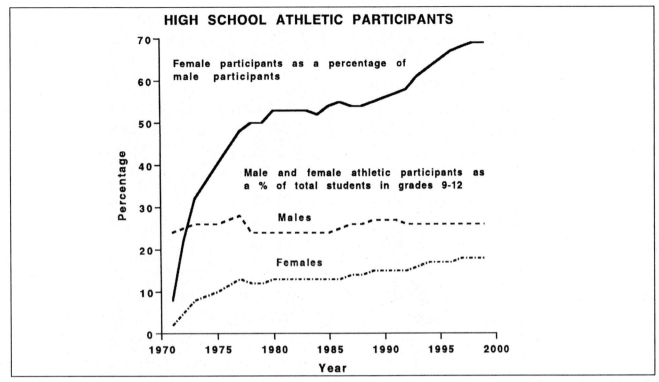

Figure 2. Participants in high school sports as a percentage of total students in grades 9-12, and the number of female high school athletes as a percentage of the number of male high school male athletes from the early 1970s through the later 1990s. Calculated from data reported by the National Federation of State High School Associations (1999) and the U.S. Department of Education (1998).

The numbers are estimates and some youth participate in more than one type of program. Using estimates for high school athletes as a guide, absolute numbers have increased in the 1990s, and the increase has been greater in females than in males. Corresponding estimates for other countries are difficult to compare to the United States, given the lack of interscholastic sports in most countries. The structure of youth sport programs also varies among countries (De Knop et al., 1996), which makes it difficult to estimate participation rates. Nevertheless, significant numbers of children and adolescents are involved in organized sport throughout the world. Given these levels of participation, questions and concerns often arise about the role of organized sports in the lives of children and adolescents. Perhaps a primary question is the following: What role does sport play among the many demands placed upon youth as they progress from childhood through adolescence into adulthood?

UNIVERSAL TASKS OF CHILDHOOD AND ADOLESCENCE

All children and adolescents have three primary tasks (Table 1): to GROW—increase in the size of the body as a whole and of its parts, to MATURE—progress towards the biologically mature state, which is an operational concept because the mature state varies with the body system, and to DEVELOP—acquisition of cognitive, affective and behavioral competence or the learning of appropriate behaviors expected by society. These terms are often treated as the same; yet, they are three distinctive, interacting tasks that dominate the daily lives of children and adolescents for approximately the first two decades of life. Growth and maturation are biological concepts, while development is primarily a psychological and behavioral concept and is specific to the culture—the amalgam of symbols, values and behaviors that characterize the population in which children and adolescents are raised.

GROWTH:	MATURATION:	DEVELOPMENT:
Size	Skeletal	Cognitive
Proportions	Sexual	Emotional
Physique	Somatic	Social
Composition	Neuroendocrine	Moral
Systemic	Neuromuscular	Motor
	SELF-ESTEEM	
	BODY IMAGE	
	PERCEIVED COMPETENCE	

Adapted from Malina (1993) and Malina et al. (2003)

Table 1. Growth, maturation and development.

The three processes—growth, maturation and development—do not occur in isolation of each other. Rather, they occur simultaneously and interact. They interact to influence the child's self-concept, self-esteem, body image, perceived competence, and in the context of sport, level of performance. Those involved with youth sports (parents, coaches, trainers, physicians) must be aware of these demands and interactions. How a youngster is coping with his/her sexual maturation or adolescent growth spurt, for example, may influence his/her beliefs, behaviors and performance. The demands of youth sports in general, or those of a specific sport, are superimposed upon the demands associated with normal growth, maturation and development. A mismatch between demands of a sport and those of normal growth, maturation and development may be a source of stress among some young athletes, and also may be a risk factor for injury.

MOTIVATION FOR SPORT

American children and adolescents participate in sport to have fun, to improve skills and to learn new skills, to be with friends or to make new friends, for thrills and excitement, to become physically fit, and to succeed or win, among others (Ewing and Seefeldt, 1989). Data for a survey conducted in the late 1980s are summarized in Table 2. Fun, skill learning and socialization are central to the why children participate in sport. On the other hand, changing interests, lack of fun or enjoyment in sport, and several coach-related behaviors are associated with stopping or "dropping out" of sport participation (Table 2). Changing interests and attempts at new and different activities are related to normal behavioral development as youth enter and progress through puberty.

Data for American youth indicate no consistent pattern of variation in motivation for sport or for discontinuation in sport that is associated with ethnicity (Ewing and Seefeldt, 1988). Recent data for urban Mexican youth in 1998 (Siegel, 1999) are consistent with those for American youth collected in the late 1980s (Ewing and Seefeldt, 1989). However, among reasons for discontinuing sport, Mexican youth appear to be more concerned about their studies than American youth, and this is

Reasons for Participating	Reasons for Discontinuing Participation
1. To have fun	1. I lost interest
2. To improve my skills	2. I was not having fun
3. To stay in shape	3. It took too much time
4. To do something I am good at	4. Coach was a poor teacher
5. For the excitement of competition	5. Too much pressure (worry)
6. To get some exercise	6. Wanted a non-sport activity
7. To play as a part of a team	7. I was tired of it
8. For the challenge of competition	8. Needed more study time
9. To learn new skills	9. Coach played favorites
10. To win	10. Sport was boring

Adapted from Ewing and Seefeldt (1989)

Table 2. Ten most important reasons for participating in sport and for discontinuing participation in sport among American youth 10-18 years of age.

apparent more so for females than for males (Siegel, 1999).

Presently available data on motivation for participation in sport and for discontinuation in sport are general, tend not to consider specific sports, and do not account for changes in descriptive terms with age. For example, the meaning of "what is fun in sports" differs by age (Harris and Ewing, 1992; Shi and Ewing, 1993). Systematic data are not extensive on the specific factors related to continuation or discontinuation in a sport. Important considerations include, among others, type of program, structure of the sport organization, level of competition, intensity of training and competition, individual differences in growth, maturation and development, and status of the individual within a team or club (Weiss and Petlichkoff, 1989; Weiss and Chaumeton, 1992). An important role for coach behaviors and quality of coaching in motivation to continue or discontinue in a sport is indicated (Black and Weiss, 1992, see also Table 2).

READINESS FOR SPORT

A question that often surfaces among parents when a child expresses interest in participating in an organized sport is whether or not the child is ready for sport. The concept of readiness relates to the ability of the individual to successfully handle the demands of instructional, learning, practice and competitive situations. The concept of readiness also refers to the needs of the individual and their responsiveness to the specific stimuli. The concept of readiness is not unique to sport; it also applies to a variety of disciplines, including school and the visual and performing arts. Talent identification is a corollary of readiness. Can talented youngsters in music, ballet, mathematics, and sport be identified among children at young ages, often 5-7 years? Are they ready to benefit from early experiences in these domains?

Readiness for sport can be viewed at two levels: the readiness of children to satisfactorily handle the demands of a sport, and the identification of potentially talented youngsters for early training in specific sports.

Many issues surface when individual readiness for a sport is considered. For example, what are the criteria of readiness for a given sport, and are the criteria applicable to other sports? Quite often, body size, biological maturity, motor skill, strength and aerobic characteristics are emphasized. More comprehensive approaches include social, emotional and cognitive characteristics. Is there a best time for entrance into competitive sports? Moreover, given the broad range of individual differences in growth, maturation and development, there is no single answer.

Recommendations as to the appropriate ages for beginning participation in organized sport range from 7-8 years (Passer, 1988) to 10 or 13 years (Roberts, 1980). Most researchers agree, however, that children should be discouraged from participating in competitive sport until there is an appropriate match between the demands of the activity and their growth and developmental status. It is also suggested that children should not be encouraged to participate in competitive sport until their parents are socially, emotionally and psychologically ready for the demands of sport (Malina, 1986).

The Readiness Equation

Readiness is a functional concept that emphasizes the relationship between the ability of an individual and the demands of a sport. Readiness for sport can be defined as the match between a child's ability and the task demands of a sport. An important corollary of the match between ability and demands is the social context in which it occurs. Readiness occurs when a child's ability is commensurate with or exceeds the task demands of a sport; when a child's ability is exceeded by the demands of a sport, he/she is not ready (Malina, 1986, 1993). Thus,

READINESS = ABILITY > DEMANDS OF A SPORT

UNREADINESS = ABILITY < DEMANDS OF A SPORT.

Success or failure in sport is thus dependent upon the balance between the child's ability and the task demands of a sport. An objective of youth sports programs is to teach sport-related skills. Hence, participation in programs that focus on instruction and practice of skills basic to a sport have the potential to enhance a child's readiness.

The readiness equation has two components, the ability of the child and the demands of a sport. Ability is a biocultural matrix of the growth, maturational and developmental characteristics of the individual (Table 1). The demands include sport specific objectives, tasks, techniques, tactics, and rules. Obviously, the decision making required to implement specific strategies with the tasks of a sport is an ongoing process that varies with level of behavioral competence, experience and coaching, and during the course of a contest.

Applicability of sport specific demands to children and youth is complex. This is perhaps due to the fact that the objectives, tasks and rules of most sports have been largely developed for and by adults. Children and youth, of course, are not miniature adults. How can tasks and rules be adjusted to meet the changing needs of growing, maturing and developing individuals? This has been accomplished for several sports, most notably Little League baseball, youth soccer and youth basketball.

Features of Readiness

Readiness has both temporary and permanent features. The temporary feature refers to a child's readiness for a specific task at a given point in time, e.g., is the child ready to learn the skills needed to participate in a sport at 5 or 6 years of age? The permanent feature refers to the individual's continuous readiness to meet the demands of tasks throughout his/her sporting career. Readiness is also functional and dynamic. The factors that influence readiness change, first, as the child grows, matures and develops, and second, as the child adapts to the demands of a sport. The child's ability as reflected in growth, maturation and development interacts with the demands of a sport.

Readiness for sport is not entirely a child-sport issue. The readiness of parents for their child's participation in sport, and the readiness of coaches to instruct and train children in the context of a sport are important considerations, which need further systematic study. The readiness question can also be extended to a sport or sport organization, i.e., when is a sport ready for children in contrast to when are children ready for a sport?

Readiness and Perceived Competence

Growth, maturation and development interact to mold self-concept, which in turn influences the child's perception of their own readiness for sport. The child's perception of his/her readiness for sport has not been systematically studied and merits equal concern with other issues in youth sports research. Some data suggest that youth involved in sport demonstrate greater levels of perceived physical and social competence compared to those who are not involved in youth sport (Weiss and Chaumeton, 1992; Cumming and Ewing, 1999). Further, currently active young athletes and those with more experience report higher levels of perceived physical and social competence than those who have dropped-out and who have less or no experience in sport (Feltz and Petlichkoff, 1983; Roberts et al., 1981; Cumming and Ewing, 1999).

The relationship between perceived and actual competence merits examination. In one of the first studies to address this issue, Ulrich (1987) considered the relationship between perceived competence and demonstrated competence in basic motor abilities and sports skills in children about 5 to 10 years of age. Children in the lowest tertile of perceived competence, on average, did not perform as well as children in the other tertiles in basic motor ability tasks and more specialized sports skills. The trends in the mean values suggest a dose-response effect, i.e., children with the highest perceived competence tend to show better levels of motor competence, more so in specialized sport skills than in basic motor ability items. The results suggest that 5-10 year old children have a reasonably accurate perception of their motor competence. They emphasize the need for developmentally appropriate programs of instruction and practice at these ages. Providing opportunities for success in motor activities at young ages may facilitate perceptions of competence when youngsters are involved in organized sports.

Other related questions need attention. For example, what are the determinants of perceived competence? Are they the same for motor skill and for sport? Are higher levels of perceived competence a result of participation and/or success in motor activities and sport? Or, do motor activities and sport attract children with high levels of perceived physical competence more so than other activities? Do children with lower levels of perceived competence shy away from sport activities, particularly those involving competition? Are they the children who drop out of sport or who have never been involved in sport? Preliminary data suggests that current youth sports participants reported a significantly greater desire to participate in sport in the context of adult organized competition compared to youth who dropped out of sport and who had never been involved in organized sport. On the other hand, the three groups did not differ in terms of desire to participate in the context of recreational sport, group instruction and individual participation (Cumming and Ewing, unpublished). What strategies can be used to encourage youth who have dropped out of sport or who have never been involved in sport to become or remain active in sport and other physical activities?

ACCESS TO SPORT

Although participation of youth in organized sport is extensive, a major limiting factor to organized sport participation is the availability of local resources, in particular human resources in the form of adults to coach and supervise programs. The majority of coaches at this level are volunteers, who have little or no experience in teaching and the principles of training. Parental support in terms of time and finance is also very important. In a study of young British athletes, parents played the main role introducing children into sport; further, most of these parents had participated in sport themselves when younger (Rowley, 1992).

Most community-based sport programs emphasize mass participation. Age and willingness to participate are the primary criteria for participation. Some programs, on the other hand, have as their objective the identification and subsequent training of young athletes with potential for success in national and/or international competition—high performance sports (see below). Such programs are often affiliated with professional clubs and/or sport governing bodies.

Economic resources are important considerations in youth sports. They can be a limiting factor in securing access to programs, facilities, expert coaches, and related requisites for success. Young athletes often have to travel considerable distances to get to a training facility and are dependent on their parent for transport. The cost of regular training can be considerable and in the most part is met almost exclusively by parents (Rowley and Baxter-Jones, 1995). Systematic training in sports such as gymnastics, swimming, diving, tennis and figure skating, and occasionally ice hockey and soccer, are often limited to private clubs and require a substantial economic investment by parents and possibly sponsors. Potential exploitation of youngsters, especially those from minority and economically impoverished backgrounds, is a factor in some sports, specifically interscholastic basketball and football in many United States communities. High school athletes in the United States are often the objects of rigorous and competitive selective recruiting practices by collegiate and university level athletic coaches. Thus, by the time an adolescent becomes an intercollegiate athlete, he/she has been the product of selective practices beginning in late childhood or early adolescence. Potential exploitation of youth by adults and sport clubs also occurs in many developing countries, where young males are scouted for their talents in soccer (European football), in some areas for their talents in baseball, and increasingly for their talents in basketball.

TALENT IDENTIFICATION AND SELECTION

Select or high performance programs emphasize the elite and have as their objective the identification, selection and training of individuals with potential for success in the national and international arena. Much discussion in this area has focused on the apparent success of sport systems in several Eastern European countries, former members of the Communist bloc. Many of these practices have been extended, with modification, to some sports in Western countries, and have been incorporated into those of other countries, with China, perhaps, presently the most visible example. The objective of such selection programs is quite clear: "Priority is given to selection of those children and young people thought most likely to benefit from intensive sports training and to produce top-class results in national and international competition" (Hartley, 1988, p. 50).

Although there is variation by sport, the general pattern of identification and selection refined in many Eastern European countries includes initial evaluation of physical and behavioral characteristics. The timing of evaluation varies by sport and the process involves several stages. For example, the primary selection phase for several sports, e.g., gymnastics, diving, swimming, and figure skating occurred between 3-8 years. Secondary selections vary by sport, e.g., 9-10 years for gymnastics, figure skating and swimming, and 10-15 years for girls and 10-17 years for boys in other sports in Romania (Bompa, 1985). Potential rowers, basketball players and weight lifters were not selected until after puberty in the former Soviet Union and German Democratic Republic (Hartley, 1988). Ballet, though considered primarily as an art form, also has rigorous, selective criteria that rival those of some sports; emphasis is commonly on extreme linearity and thinness (Hamilton, 1986). Physical, motor and behavioral requisites obviously vary among sports. The process of refining and perfecting talent after initial selection is ongoing as the youngsters adapt to the instructional and training programs, as well as to the social and emotional demands of the special programs. Many youngsters are excluded after initial selection.

Selection is based on the assumption that the requisites for a given sport can be identified at a young age and subsequently perfected through specific training. Identifying and selecting the potentially talented youngster at an early age is the first step in a relatively long-term process. The perfection of talent is another matter, which requires long hours of systematic and often repetitive training under the scrutiny of demanding coaches and often separation from parents and other family members. Much time and effort has been spent trying to identify the particular physical and psychological characteristics, which contribute to the selection and development of talent. The term "natural selection" has been occasionally used in discussing the exclusion or "weeding out" process in sport (Bompa, 1985), including ballet (Hamilton, 1986). The use of the term "natural selection" in this context has no relevance to natural selection in the Darwinian sense (Malina, 1991,1998a).

Selection programs raise ethical issues regarding the decision making process. Does the child have a voice? Are parents involved? Accounts in the electronic and print media often highlight parents who are seemingly more interested in their child's success than is the child. Are decisions made independently by coaches or other sports authorities? What kind of guidance is available for the child, or parents, when he/she is selected? What are the implications of being labeled "talented" for individual and parental expectations?

Selection programs are exclusionary. They initially involve the elimination of many individuals and subsequently cutting of others as competition becomes more specialized and rigorous. The merit of selection programs is usually cast in the context of the number of successful athletes (gold medals). Little, if anything, is ever indicated about the individuals who do not make it through the process, and they are by definition the vast majority.

Selection practices in some sports include discrimination along maturational lines, especially during the transition into puberty and adolescence. Advanced in biological maturity status is associated with better performances among boys. In contrast, differences in the performances of girls of contrasting maturity status are not marked, and in some tasks better performances are attained by girls who are later in biological maturation (Malina et al., in press).

Two groups of youth are often not represented among those who experience success in sport during early and mid-adolescence. The first is late maturing boys, who are generally at a size and strength disadvantage particularly in the early stages of their sport experiences. Many sports available for youth favor the larger, stronger, early maturing boy. The second group is early maturing girls whose physique and body composition may be a limiting factor in performance and who may be socialized away from sport by peers and/or the sport systems (Malina, 1996, 1998b). Such trends emphasize the need to provide opportunities for youngsters at the extremes of the maturation continuum.

POTENTIAL BENEFITS ASSOCIATED WITH PARTICIPATION IN YOUTH SPORTS

Growth and Maturation

It has been historically postulated that regular physical activity is important to support normal growth and maturation, and perhaps may even stimulate it (Rarick, 1960). However, currently available data indicate that regular participation and training for sport during childhood and adolescence does not influence size-attained, growth rate, and the timing and tempo of somatic, sexual and skeletal maturation in presumably healthy girls and boys. Data for young athletes in a variety of sports appear to emphasize a primary role for constitutional factors (structural, functional, behavioral) in the selection and sorting processes of young athletes of both sexes (Malina, 1994, 1998b, 2000).

In contrast to growth in height and the timing and tempo of biological maturation, regular training for sport can influence body mass and composition. Training is associated with a decrease in fatness in both sexes and occasionally with an increase in fat-free mass in boys. Changes in fatness depend on continued, regular activity or training (or caloric restriction, which often occurs in sports like gymnastics and ballet in girls and wrestling in boys) for their maintenance. When training is significantly reduced, fatness tends to accumulate. On the other hand, it is difficult to partition effects of training on fat-free mass from expected changes that occur with growth and sexual maturation per se. Regular training for sport during childhood and adolescence is associated with increased bone mineral content. The beneficial effects are more apparent in weight bearing than non-weight bearing activities. Of particular importance is the observation that bone mineral established during childhood and adolescence is a determinant of adult bone mineral status (Malina, 2000).

Regular Physical Activity and Improved Physical Fitness

Participation in organized sport provides an opportunity for regular physical activity in a safe, supervised setting. Youth active in sport expend more energy in physical activity than those who are not active in sport, and spend less time watching television, i.e., being inactive (Katzmarzyk and Malina, 1998). There is also the possibility that those with a history of participation in youth sports may be more physically active as adults, but data to this effect are limited (Engstrom, 1986, 1991; Kuh and Cooper, 1992). Instruction and practice associated with sports programs contribute to development and refinement of a variety of sport specific motor skills, which provide the foundation for other skills and for an active life style. However, children should be given a voice or a choice in their sport participation. Being forced to exercise during childhood may have potentially negative consequences for later activity (Taylor et al., 1999).

Participation in sport has potential physiological benefits. Regular training is associated with enhanced physical fitness, specifically motor skill, muscular strength and aerobic power, and possibly metabolic fitness (Malina, 2000).

Self-Concept and Self-Worth

Self-concept refers to perception of self, while self-worth refers to the value placed on one's self-concept. In many studies, however, the terms are used interchangeably. The specific domains or competencies of self-worth have implications for physical activity and sport. Among children and youth 8-15 years, first physical appearance and then social acceptance have an important impact on self-worth, while more specific competencies, i.e., scholastic and athletic, though important, contribute relatively less to self-worth at these ages (Harter, 1989). Most studies of self-concept or self-worth do not include actual measures of physical or athletic competence, and do not include measures of size, physique and maturity status. Nevertheless, physical appearance and social acceptability have more impact on a child's sense of self-worth than specific competencies during middle childhood and early adolescence. This is a period of change in size, physique and body composition and in sexual maturity as youth make the transition from childhood to adolescence. It would seem logical to include more direct measures of these biological parameters in assessments of self-concept. Several studies have looked at the relationship between the ponderal index (height divided by the cube root of weight) and self-concept, but results vary with age and are inconsistent among studies (Malina, 1992). Given concern for physical appearance among children and youth, training for sport has the potential to contribute to self-concept or self-worth.

The literature dealing with the influence of participation in organized youth sports on perception of self or self-concept is limited. Information on the role of systematic physical activity on self-concept/self-worth may have relevance for organized sports. Results of a meta-analysis of 27 experimental studies suggest that participation in directed play and physical activity programs positively influences the development of self-concept (Gruber, 1985). More specifically, physical fitness and aerobic programs have a greater influence on self-concept (effect size [ES] = 0.89) than programs of sport skills (ES = 0.40), creative dance (ES = 0.32) and perceptual-motor skills (ES = 0.29) (Gruber, 1986). There is no clear pattern of age and sex differences, but some evidence indicates greater gains in younger children. The programs for young children generally focus on motor skill development, which is an important developmental task at these ages, and also an important objective for youth sports programs. The results also suggest that the effect of such intervention programs may be greatest for children who are emotionally disturbed, economically disadvantaged, mentally retarded or perceptually disabled (Gruber, 1985). However, it is not clear exactly how participation in physical activity leads to developments in self-concept. Is it the activity per se or the overall personal and social context of the activity? What are the important components of the context of activity programs that are of specific relevance to the development of self-concept? In order to develop more effective programs for children and adolescents, it is important to identify and understand the mechanisms that govern these relationships in the contexts of physical activity and/or sport programs.

A shortcoming of experimental studies of physical activity and self-concept is that the persistence of activity-related effects is not considered. Are the changes permanent? Do changes associated with activity programs interact with normal processes of growth and maturation? It is reasonably well documented that self-worth or self-esteem declines in girls during the transition into puberty, and early maturing girls do not fare well compared to girls average (on time) and late in maturation (Brooks-Gunn and Peterson, 1983; Simmons and Blyth, 1987). There is also ethnic variation. Longitudinal data from the National Heart, Lung and Blood Institute Growth and Health Study indicate that the developmental pattern for self-esteem differs for American Black girls compared to American White girls (Brown et al., 1998). Global self-worth declines in White girls but is stable in Black girls from 9 to 14 years, and adjusting for stage of sexual maturation, body mass index (BMI) and household income does not alter the trends.

Further, as the BMI increases, scores for global self-worth, physical appearance and social acceptance decrease, but the decreases in physical appearance and social acceptance scores with an increase in the BMI are less in Black than in White girls (Brown et al., 1998). Implications of these results for participation in youth sports and perceived competence in sport need to be addressed.

Social Competence

Sport participation occurs within a social context. It can, therefore, have potentially significant implications for the development of social competence. Sport activities do not socialize per se. They provide a medium in which the socialization process occurs. The process has three primary components: socializing agents or significant others, social environments or situations, and role learners.

Socialization occurs through experiences and interactions in social environments and in the adoption of specific social roles. The individual is socialized into a specific role, i.e., an active participant in sport or a spectator, or both. On the other hand, the individual is socialized through these roles into the learning of more general attitudes, values, and so on. It is in the context of socialization through sport that the presumed social benefits of participation are often discussed.

Sport activities provide a variety of social experiences or interactions. The question of interest, of course, is whether these experiences contribute to the development of socially competent behaviors. Systematic study of the effects of participation in sport on social development or the development of social competence is rather limited. The literature tends to focus on specific social behaviors, values and characteristics of those who are proficient in motor skills or those who are involved in sport. It is often argued, for example, that the child who is proficient in motor skills usually possesses social status among his/her peers. In the world of children and youth, the peer group is central, and physical activities occur within the framework of the group and/or through peer sanction and support. Children generally have multiple peer groups (e.g., school, church, team, sport club, neighborhood, etc.), each with its own social demands and experiences.

The internal structure of the sport team and particularly skill may be important mediating factors in peer relations (Bigelow et al., 1989), while fourth and fifth grade boys and girls (about 9-10 years) involved in sport tend to be rated higher in social competence than those not involved in sport (Roberts et al., 1981). The relationship between sport participation and social status in girls may be mediated by society's perceptions of sport as an appropriate activity for females. Social status is positively related to membership in traditional sports—but not in non-traditional female sports — (Kane, 1988). These data are somewhat dated, and there is a need to examine current trends in female sports participation in the context of Title IX legislation in the United States and the relatively recent national and international exposure of women's sports. Title IX is associated with increased participation of females in interscholastic sports (Figures 1 and 2). It is not clear, however, to what extent increased interest in and exposure to women's sports via television has altered society's perceptions of sport as gender appropriate or inappropriate.

Variation in the timing and tempo of the growth spurt and sexual maturation enters the matrix of factors which influence social status and the socialization process during adolescence. Individual differences in biological maturation and associated changes are a major component of the backdrop against which youth evaluate and interpret their social status among peers. Physical performance and success in sports is an important aspect of the evaluative process, particularly among boys, and biological maturation has significant correlates in physical skills and the value attached to these skills by the peer group (Jones, 1949; Malina et al., 2003). Early maturation in boys is also associated with success in many youth sports (Malina, 1998b), with resulting advantages in social status.

The situation is different for girls. Differences in strength and performance among girls of contrasting maturity status are not as apparent as among boys during the transition into adolescence and do not persist into adolescence as in boys (Malina et al., 2003). Further, it is often the late maturing girl who performs better, who has success in sports, and who persists in sports through adolescence (Malina, 1983, 1996, 1998b). This raises several questions that merit systematic study. For example, how do individuals differences in the timing of sexual maturation impact sport participation and persistence in sport? Are late maturing girls socialized into sport, or are early maturing girls socialized away from sport?

Data on the socialization of young girls into sport and on the social status of young female athletes are not extensive. The status of the young teenage girl in her social group is often linked to her femininity, and until recently, sport has generally failed to consider femininity. With the increased acceptance of women as athletes and with more opportunities for young girls to participate in sport, this perception is changing. Many pre-adolescent and adolescent boys accept and value female peers who are skilled in sport, given the opportunity to do so. This may be one of the major benefits of co-educational youth sports programs.

Other Potential Behavioral Benefits

If sports are taught correctly, they can be a vehicle for social and moral development. Progress toward social and moral development includes the ability to recognize right from wrong, fair play, rules of the game, and more importantly, abiding by the rules of the game during practices and competitions. However, the potential influence of sport participation on the development of emotional control and moral reasoning needs to be established. Other benefits have been attributed to regular participation in interscholastic sports, including greater likelihood of staying in school, fewer absences from school (Marsh, 1993), reduced likelihood of being involved in delinquent behavior (Segrave and Hastad, 1982), and fewer risk-taking sexual behaviors and pregnancies foradolescent females (Sabo et al., 1998; Savage and Holcomb, 1999). These associations need to be more critically evaluated in the context of the many factors known to influence adolescent behaviors.

POTENTIAL RISKS INVOLVED WITH PARTICIPATION IN SPORT

Participation in sport has associated risks. These are usually set in the context of concern for compromised growth and maturation, psychological stress, and injury.

Growth and Maturation

In the past decade or so, concern has been expressed on a more or less regular basis about potential negative influences of intensive training for sport on growth, i.e., size attained, and maturation, i.e., timing and tempo of progress to the mature state, particularly in young female athletes. It has been suggested that intensive training during childhood and puberty may stunt growth and delay sexual maturation of girls (Laron and Klinger, 1989; American Medical Association/American Dietetic Association, 1991; Tofler et al., 1996). On the other hand, potential negative influences of training for sport on the growth and maturation of boys is only marginally expressed, usually in the context of young wrestlers who may severely modify their diets to meet specific body mass criteria.

In adequately nourished individuals, growth in stature and skeletal, somatic and sexual maturation are largely mediated by genotype (Malina et al., 2003). Linearity of physique is associated with later maturation in both sexes, and some sports select for this characteristic of body build. Dietary practices associated with an emphasis on thinness or an optimal weight for performance may possibly influence growth and maturation, especially if they involve energy deficiency for prolonged periods. The demands of training may compete with those of growth and maturational processes for available energy. Disordered eating behaviors are related factors. Psychological and emotional stresses associated with training and competition are

additional concerns, especially high levels of coach-athlete or parent-athlete stress and/or competitive stress. Thus, if intensive training for sport influences growth and maturation, it most likely interacts with, or is confounded by, other factors so that the specific effect of training per se may be impossible to extract. Given the presently available data, intensive training for sport has no effect on growth and maturational processes in young athletes. In the few athletes that may present problems related to growth and maturation factors other than training must be more closely examined before attributing the observations to training for sport (Malina, 1998b).

Psychological Stress

Discussions of potential psychological risks in sports for children and youth are usually set in the context of competitive stress. Stress may be accentuated in individual sports such as gymnastics, figures skating, diving, and distance running, sports in which athletes compete and perform as individuals, often in a one-on-one format. In contrast, team sports involve a greater number of particpants interacting at one time. The greater number of athletes involved and the highly interactive nature of activities in team sports tend to diffuse responsibility so that the performance of any individual athlete is generally less conspicuous and performance evaluation is less of a threat. In other words, team sports have the buffer of the team members which may alleviate stress associated with mistakes and losing.

Potential consequences of competitive stress, and specifically negative outcomes associated with it, include low self-esteem, elevated anxiety, aggressive behavior, possibly increased risk for injury, and "burn out". The latter is a term that is presently very common in high performance sports and refers to withdrawal from sport related to chronic stress. Signs of chronic stress include behavioral alterations such as agitation, sleep disturbances, and loss of interest in practice. Other manifestations include depression, lack of energy, skin rashes and nausea, and frequent illness

(Weinberg and Gould, 1995). Unfortunately, specific data on the prevalence of such conditions associated with participation in youth sports are not available.

Many factors are involved in competitive stress and "burn out." Two especially important factors negative performance evaluations, which are usually critical rather than supportive, and inconsistent feedback from coaches and officials, which often translates into mixed messages for the young athlete. An important contributing factor is overprotection by coaches, trainers, parents and sport officials, which limits exposure of young athletes to new situations and thus opportunities to develop coping mechanisms. Another factor is the young athlete's perception of not being able to meet expectations imposed by self and/or others. Other contributing factors include a training environment that is not supportive and intensive competition per se. These sport-related stresses are superimposed on and interact with normal stresses of adolescence, e.g., school, boy friends and girl friends, economic independence, and so on.

Among growing, maturing and developing young athletes there is also the need to be a child or adolescent. All too often, many young athletes find themselves in the microcosm of a sport organized and operated by and for the satisfaction of adults. It thus should come as no surprise that another factor in stress and "burn out" may be the conflicting demands between sport and the universal tasks of childhood and adolescence.

Risk of Injury

Risk of injury is a given in sport and many other activities of childhood and adolescence. The injury-related literature in youth sports focuses largely on risk factors related both to the host or young athlete (internal), and to the sport environment (external) (Caine and Lindner, 1990; Mandelbaum, 1994; Micheli, 1983, 1985; Stanitski, 1988), and to a lesser extent on the prevalence and incidence of injuries. The latter are limited in part by the lack of suitable exposure data for practices and competitions to accurately estimate rates. A confounding factor is the definition of an injury, which is quite variable. Injuries in youth sports are commonly classified as overuse, i.e., microtrauma, usually at joint surfaces, associated with excessive repetition of specific sport activities; or acute, especially injuries to the growth plate in youth.

Risk factors for injury related to the young athlete (internal) include the following:

- Physique—the child may not have the body build suitable for a specific sport

- Lack of flexibility

- Lack of muscular strength or strength imbalance

- Marginal and/or poor skill development

- Behavioral factors, including risk taking and inability to cope with stress

- Injury history, specifically inadequate rehabilitation from prior injury

- Adolescent growth spurt -individual differences in timing and tempo, strength imbalance—"outgrows his strength," reduction in flexibility, adolescent awkwardness

- Maturity-associated variation—maturity mismatches in size and strength, late maturation

Risk factors associated with the sport environment (external) include the following:

- Inadequate rehabilitation from prior injury

- Training errors—improper technique, lack of adequate instruction, use of inappropriate drills, lack of conditioning

- Playing conditions—structural hazards goal posts, fences, sprinklers; surfaces uneven, wet, foreign materials; environment lighting, heat/cold, lightening; proximity to spectators

- Equipment—availability, improper equipment, "hand-downs", ill fitting

- Age groups—size/maturity and experience mismatches

- Coach behaviors—inappropriate drills and techniques, poor instruction

- Parent behaviors—unrealistic expectations, pushing a child too fast

- Sport organizations (administrators, coaches, and officials)—increased tolerance for aggression and body contact with age in some sports (ice hockey, soccer, American football, basketball).

The contribution of specific risk factors to injuries in youth sports is neither known with certainty nor specified in available studies. Some are seemingly obvious, e.g., poor playing conditions and equipment; others need more systematic specification. The ability to "diagnose" a psychological predisposition to athletic injury is important in the prevention of injury (Geigle-Bentz and Bentz, 1994). There is a need for more specific information on the unique aspects of internal risk factors associated with the characteristics of the participants. For example, given the association among age, growth and maturation, and experience, can age of participants per se be partitioned as a risk factor? What is it about the adolescent spurt that places the adolescent sport participant at risk? What is the extent of maturity mismatches as a source of injury? Is lack of skill a risk factor, or are the skilled more able to avoid the risk of injury?

Data on the prevalence and incidence of injuries in youth sports are variable and limited. Data are especially limited for local, agency sponsored, club and recreational sports; in contrast, injury data are more systematically available for interscholastic sports. Many studies of young participants are limited to clinical observations and do not include suitable exposure data for practices and competitions. Surveys of young participants generally lack suitable exposure data for practices and competitions. Sources of data are also variable and include accident reports from a variety of sources (Zaricznyj et al., 1980), records from hospitals, emergency rooms and sport injury clinics (Ellison and Mackenzie, 1993; Tursz and Crost, 1986; Kvist et al., 1989; Kujala et al., 1995; Watkins and Peabody, 1996), interviews (Bijur et al., 1995), and retrospective questionnaires (Backx et al., 1989). These studies provide estimates of age-, sex- and sport-associated variation in the occurrence and type of injuries, but the specific context of injuries is not considered.

Available data for children and adolescents suggest several trends in sport-related injuries. The number of injuries increases with age, and peak ages of occurrence vary among studies, 11.0 to 14.9 years among girls and 13.0 to 16.9 years in boys. Injuries occur more often in boys than in girls, but not all studies control for sex differences in the number of participants. Youth who participate more often in sports are at higher risk for injury, which is probably related to greater exposure and perhaps to overtraining. And previous injury and lack of recovery from an earlier injury are risk factors for subsequent injury. There is a need for better exposure, incidence and prevalence statistics for injuries in youth sport, particularly at the level below interscholastic sport, and also a need for sport-specific data.

OVERVIEW

Involvement in sport has the potential to provide both positive and negative experiences and outcomes. The line between potential benefits and risks may be quite fine. Nevertheless, participation in organized sports is a satisfying experience for most children and adolescents. Experiences vary with a number of factors, including age, level of competition, motivation, expectations, parental involvement, quality of coaching, sport organizations, among others. Cultural variation and expectations are additional factors. The specific contributions comprising this volume provide a comprehensive overview of the biological, clinical, psychosocial and community dimensions of organized youth sports at the beginning of the 21st century.

REFERENCES

American Medical Association/American Dietetic Association. (1991). *Targets for Adolescent Health: Nutrition and Physical Fitness.* Chicago: American Medical Association.

Backx, F.J.G.; Erich, W.B.M.; Kemper, A.B.A.; & Verbeek, A.L.M. (1989). Sports injuries in school-aged children: An epidemiologic study. *American Journal of Sports Medicine* 17: 234-240.

Bigelow, B.J.; Lewko, J.H.; & Salhani, L. (1989). Sport involved children's friendship expectations. *Sport and Exercise Psychology* 11: 152-160.

Bijur, P.E.; Trumble, A.; Harel, Y.; Overpeck, M.D.; Jones, D.; & Scheidt, P.C. (1995). Sports and recreation injuries in US children and adolescents. *Archives of Pediatric and Adolescent Medicine* 149: 1009-1016.

Black, S.J. & Weiss, M.R. (1992). The relationship among perceived coaching behaviors, perceptions of ability, and motivation in competitive age-group swimmers. *Journal of Sport and Exercise Psychology* 14: 309-325.

Bompa, T.O. (1985). *Talent Identification. Sports: Science Periodical on Research and Technology in Sport, Physical Testing GN-1.* Ottawa: Coaching Association of Canada.

Brooks-Gunn, J. & Peterson, A. (1983). *Girls at Puberty: Biological and Psychosocial Perspectives.* New York: Plenum.

Brown, K.M.; McMahon, R.P.; Biro, F.M.; Crawford, P.; Schreiber, G.B.; Similo, S.L.; Waclawiw, M.; & Striegel-Moore, R. (1998). Changes in self-esteem in black and white girls between the ages of 9 and 14 years: The NHLBI Growth and Health Study. *Journal of Adolescent Health* 23: 7-19.

Caine, D.J. & Lindner, K. (1990). Preventing injury in young athletes. Part 1: Predisposing factors. *Canadian Association for Health, Physical Education and Recreation Journal*, March-April, pp. 30-35.

Cumming, S.P. & Ewing, M.E. (1999). *The Influence of Achievement Orientations and Perceptions of Physical Self-Competence Upon Desire to Participate in Youth Sports.* Paper presented at the Association for the Advancement of Applied Sport Psychology Conference. Banff, Canada (abstract).

Ellison, L.F. & Mackenzie, S.G. (1993). Sports injuries in the database of the Canadian hospitals injury reporting and prevention program—an overview. *Chronic Disease* Canada 14: 96-104.

Engstrom, L.M. (1986). The process of socialization into keep fit activities. *Journal of Sports Science* 8: 89-97.

Engstrom, L.M. (1991). Exercise adherence in sport for all from youth to adulthood. In Oja, P. & Telama, R. (Eds.) *Sport for All.* Amsterdam: Elsevier Press (pp. 473-483).

Ewing, M.E. & Seefeldt, V. (1988). *Participation and Attrition Patterns in American Agency-Sponsored and Interscholastic Sports: An Executive Summary.* East Lansing, MI: Michigan State University, Institute for the Study of Youth Sports.

Ewing, M.E. & Seefeldt, V. (1989). *American Youth and Sports Participation.* North Palm Beach, FL: American Footwear Association.

Ewing, M.E.; Seefeldt, V.; & Brown, T.P. (1996). *Role of Organized Sport in the Education and Health of American Children and Youth.* New York: Carnegie Corporation.

Feltz, D.L. & Petlichkoff, L.M. (1983). Perceived competence among interscholastic sport participants and dropouts. *Canadian Journal of Applied Sport Sciences* 8: 231-235.

Geigle-Bentz, F.L. & Bentz, B. (1994). Psychological aspects of sport. In Stanitski, C.L.; DeLee, J.C.; & Drez, D. (Eds.) *Pediatrics and Adolescent Sports Medicine.* Philadelphia: Saunders (pp. 77-93).

Gruber, J.J. (1986). Physical activity and self-esteem development in children: a meta-analysis. In Stull, G.A. & Eckert, H.M. (Eds.) *Effects of Physical Activity on Children (American Academy of Physical Education Papers No. 19).* Champaign, IL: Human Kinetics (pp. 30-48).

Hamilton, W.G. (1986). Physical prerequisites for ballet dancers: selectivity that can enhance (or nullify) a career. *Journal of Musculoskeletal Medicine* 3: 61-66.

Harris, A. & Ewing, M.E. (1992). *Defining the Concept of Fun: A Developmental View of Youth Tennis Players.* Paper presented at the Association for the Advancement of Applied Sport Psychology Conference. Colorado Springs, CO (abstract).

Harter, S. (1989). Causes, correlates, and the functional role of global self-worth: A life-span perspective. In Kolligian, J. & Sternberg, R. (Eds.) *Perceptions of Competence and Incompetence Across the Life-Span.* New Haven, CT: Yale University Press (pp. 67-97).

Hartley, G. (1988). A comparative view of talent selection for sport in two socialist states—the USSR and the GDR—with particular reference to gymnastics. In The National Coaching Foundation (Ed.) *The Growing Child in Competitive Sport.* Leeds: The National Coaching Foundation (pp. 50-56).

De Knop, P.; Engstrom, L.M.; Skirstad, B.; & Weiss, M.R. (Eds.) (1996). *Worldwide Trends in Youth Sport.* Champaign, IL: Human Kinetics.

Kuh, D.J.L. & Cooper, C. (1992). Physical activity at 36 years: Patterns and childhood predictors in a longitudinal study. *Journal of Epidemiology and Community Health* 46: 114-119.

Institute for the Study of Youth Sports. (1976). *Joint Legislative Study on Youth Sports Programs: Agency Sponsored Sports, Phase I.* East Lansing, MI: Michigan State University, Institute for the Study of Youth Sports.

Institute for the Study of Youth Sports. (1978). *Joint Legislative Study on Youth Sports Programs: Agency Sponsored Sports, Phase II.* East Lansing, MI: Michigan State University, Institute for the Study of Youth Sports.

Jones, H.E. (1949). *Motor Performance and Growth.* Berkeley: University of California Press.

Kane, M.J. (1988). The female athletic role as a status determinant within the social systems of high school adolescents. *Adolescence* 23: 253-64.

Katzmarzyk, P.T. & Malina, R.M. (1998). Contributions of organized sports participation to estimated daily energy expenditure in youth. *Pediatric Exercise Science* 10: 378-386.

Kujala, U.M.; Taimela, S.; Antti-Poika, I.; Orava, S.; Tuominen, R.; & Myllynen, P. (1995). Acute injuries in soccer, ice hockey, volleyball, basketball, judo, and karate: Analysis of national registry data. *British Medical Journal* 311: 1465-1468.

Kvist, M.; Kujala, U.M.; Heinonem, O.J.; Vuori, I.V.; Aho, A.J.; Pajulo, O.; Hintsa, A.; & Parvinen, T. (1989). Sports-related injuries in children. *International Journal of Sports Medicine* 10: 81-86.

Laron, Z. & Klinger, B. (1989). Does intensive sport endanger normal growth and development. In Laron, Z. & Rogol, A.D. (Eds.) *Hormones and Sport.* New York: Raven (pp. 1-9).

Malina, R.M. (1983). Menarche in athletes: A synthesis and hypothesis. *Annals of Human Biolgoy* 10: 1-24.

Malina, R.M. (1986). Readiness for competitive sport. In Weiss, M.R. & Gould, D. (Eds.) *Sport for Children and Youths.* Champaign, IL: Human Kinetics, pp 45-50.

Malina, R.M. (1991). Darwinian fitness, physical fitness and physical activity. In Mascie-Taylor, C.G.N. & Lasker, G.W. (Eds.) *Applications of Biological Anthropology to Human Affairs.* Cambridge: Cambridge University Press (pp. 143-184).

Malina, R.M. (1992). Physical activity and behavioural development during childhood and youth. In Norgan, N.G. (Ed.) *Physical Activity and Health.* Cambridge: Cambridge University Press (pp. 101-120).

Malina, R.M. (1993). Youth sports: Readiness, selection, and trainability. In Duquet, W. & Day, J.A.P. (Eds.) *Kinanthropometry IV.* London: E & FN Spon (pp. 285-301).

Malina, R.M. (1994). Physical growth and biological maturation of young athletes. *Exercise and Sport Sciences Reviews* 22: 389-433.

Malina, R.M. (1995). Physical activity and fitness of children and youth: Questions and implications. *Medicine, Exercise, Nutrition, and Health* 4: 123-135.

Malina, R.M. (1996). The young athlete: biological growth and maturation in a biocultural context. In Smoll, F.L. & Smith, R.E. (Eds.) *Children and Youth in Sport: A Biopsychosocial Perspective.* Dubuque, IA: Brown and Benchmark (pp. 161-186).

Malina, R.M. (1998a). Physical activity, sport, social status and Darwinian fitness. In Strickland, S.S. & Shetty, P.S. (Eds.) *Human Biology and Social Inequality.* Cambridge: Cambridge University Press (pp. 165-192).

Malina, R.M. (1998b). Growth and maturation of young athletes—is training for sport a factor. In Chan, K.M. & Micheli, L.J. (Eds.) *Sports and Children.* Hong Kong: Williams and Wilkins Asia Pacific (pp. 133-161).

Malina, R.M. (2000). Growth and maturation: Do regular physical activity and training for sport have a significant influence? In Armstrong, N. & van Mechelen, W. (Eds.) *Oxford Textbook of Paediatric*

Exercise Science and Medicine. Oxford: Oxford University Press (in press).

Malina, R.M.; Bouchard, C.; & Bar-Or, O. (2003). *Growth, Maturation, and Physical Activity*, 2nd edition. Champaign, IL: Human Kinetics.

Mandelbaum, B.R. (1994). Sports injuries in the immature athlete. *Sports Medicine Digest* 16: 1-2.

Marsh, H.W. (1993). The effects of participation in sport during the last two years of high school. *Sociology of Sport Journal* 10: 18-43.

Micheli, L.J. (1983). Overuse injuries in children's sports: The growth factor. *Orthopedic Clinics of North America* 14: 337-360.

Micheli, L.J. (1985). Preventing youth sports injuries. *Journal of Physical Education, Recreation and Dance* 56(8): 52-54.

National Federation of State High School Associations (1999). *1999 High School Athletics Participation Survey.* National Federation of State High School Associations, http://www.nfhs.org.

Passer, M.W. (1988). Psychological issues in determining children's age readiness for competition. In Smoll, F.L.; Magill, R.A.; & Ash, M.J. (Eds.) *Children in Sport, 3rd edition.* Champaign, IL: Human Kinetics (pp. 67-78).

Rarick, G.L. (1960). Exercise and growth. In Johnson, W.R. (Ed.) *Science and Medicine of Exercise and Sports.* New York: Harper and Brothers (pp. 440-465).

Roberts, G.C. (1980). Children in competition: A theoretical perspective and recommendations for practice. *Motor Skills: Theory Into Practice* 4: 37-50.

Roberts, G.C.; Kleiber, D.A.; & Duda, J.L. (1981). An analysis of motivation in children's sport: The role of perceived competence in participation. *Journal of Sport Psychology* 3: 201-216.

Rowley, S. (1992). *Training of Young Athletes Study (TOYA): Identification of Talent.* London: The Sports Council.

Rowley, S. & Baxter-Jones, A.D.G. (1995). *Training of Young Athletes Study (TOYA): Identification of Talent II.* London: The Sports Council.

Sabo, D.; Miler, K.; Farrell, M.; Barnes, G.; & Melnick, M. (1998). *The Women's Sports Foundation Report: Sport and Teen Pregnancy.* East Meadows, NY: Women's Sports Foundation.

Savage, M.P. & Holcomb, D.R. (1999). Adolescent female athlete's sexual risk-taking behaviors. *Journal of Youth and Adolescence* 28: 595-602.

Segrave, J.O. & Hastad, D.N. (1982). Delinquent behavior and interscholastic athletic participation. *Journal of Sport Behavior* 5: 96-111.

Shi, J. & Ewing, M.E. (1993). *Definitions of fun for youth soccer players.* Paper presented at the North America Society for the Psychology of Sport and Physical Activity Conference. Brainerd, MN (abstract).

Siegel, S.R. (1999). *Patterns of Sport Participation and Physical Activity in Urban Mexican Youth.* Doctoral dissertation, Michigan State University, East Lansing, MI.

Simmons, R.G. & Blyth, D.A. (1987). *Moving into Adolescence: The Impact of Pubertal Change and Social Context.* New York: Aldine de Gruyter.

Stanitski, C.L. (1988). Management of sports injuries in children and adolescents. *Orthopedic Clinics of North America* 19: 689-697.

Taylor, W.C.; Blair, S.N.; Cummings, S.S.; Wun, C.C.; & Malina, R.M. (1999). Childhood and adolescent physical activity patterns and adult physical activity. *Medicine and Science in Sports and Exercise* 31: 118-123.

Tofler, I.R.; Stryer, B.K.; Micheli, L.J.; & Herman, L.R. (1996). Physical and emotional problems of elite female gymnasts. *New England Journal of Medicine* 335: 281-283.

Tursz, A. & Crost, M. (1986). Sports-related injuries in children. *American Journal of Sports Medicine* 14: 294-299.

U.S. Department of Education (1998). *Digest of Education Statistics, 1998: Chapter 1. All Levels of Education.* National Center for Education Statistics, http://nces.ed.gov/.

Ulrich, B.D. (1987). Perceptions of physical competence, motor competence, and participation in organized sport: Their interrelationships in young children. *Research Quarterly for Exercise and Sport* 58: 57-67.

Watkins, J. & Peabody, P. (1996). Sports injuries in children and adolescents treated at a sports injury clinic. *Journal of Sports Medicine and Physical Fitness* 36: 43-48.

Weinberg, R.S. & Gould, D. (1995). *Foundations of Sport and Exercise Psychology*. Champaign, IL: Human Kinetics.

Weiss, M.R. & Chaumeton, N. (1992). Motivational orientations in sport. In Horn, T.S. (Ed.) *Advances in Sport Psychology*. Champaign, IL: Human Kinetics (pp. 61-99).

Weiss, M.R. & Petlichkoff, L.M. (1989). Children's motivation for participation in sport and withdrawal from sport: Identifying the missing links. *Pediatric Exercise Science* 1: 195-211

Zaricznyj, B.; Shattuck, L.J.M.; Mast, T.A.; Robertson, R.V.; & D'Elia, G. (1980). Sports-related injuries in school-aged children. *American Journal of Sports Medicine* 8: 318-324.

CHAPTER 2

Auxological Issues in Youth Sports

G. P. Beunen and A. L. Claessens
Faculty of Physical Education and Physiotherapy
Katholieke Universiteit Leuven

INTRODUCTION

Growth refers to measurable changes in size, physique, and body composition and various systems of the body, whereas maturation refers to the progress towards an adult state. Maturation varies not only among the systems considered, whether endocrine, reproductive, skeletal, digestive or immunological, but also in timing, i.e. chronological age at reaching maturational milestones, and tempo, i.e. rate of progress. Cellular processes underlie growth and maturation: increase in cell number or division (hyperplasia), increase in cellular volume (hypertrophy) and accretion of intercellular substances (Malina, 1998a). Chronological age (CA) has limited utility as an indicator of biological maturation. All children are characterized by their individual growth and maturation process and there is considerable variation in growth and maturation. Some early maturing girls reach age at menarche at 10.5 years CA, whereas others attain this milestone of sexual maturation as late as at 16.0 years. Especially during the pubertal period, i.e., the period of becoming sexually mature, considerable variability in tempo and timing is observed. The processes of growth and maturation are interrelated, and both influence physical performance (Beunen and Malina, 1996).

Sport is perhaps the most visible form of physical activity, and is a major source of physical activity in most children. In several countries, mass participation in sports at the local club level is a major feature of daily living in a majority of children and adolescents. Participation rates increase until puberty and decline thereafter, which parallels the declining rates of participation in physical activities across adolescence (Malina, 1998b).

Some youth compete in several sports at national or international levels. The selection and guidance of these youngsters is not without problems, especially in those sports in which boys and girls begin to specialize at relatively young ages such as diving, figure skating, gymnastics, and swimming. The process of identifying talented youth begins early in these sports, and there are concerns about the treatment of young athletes and the training process at young ages. Some of the techniques used by top coaches may well fall within the bounds of child abuse.

The purpose of this review is to synthesize the available evidence about the growth and maturation of youth competing in a variety of sports, especially with regard to concern about potentially negative influences of training and competition. Additionally the role of somatic and performance characteristics in the prediction of future success is assessed.

GROWTH AND MATURATION OF YOUNG ATHLETES

Since several recent reviews have been published concerning the growth and maturation of young athletes, this overview will be based on these excellent sources of information (Beunen and Malina, 1996; Beunen et al., 1999; Claessens, 1999; Malina, 1994, 1998b, 1999). The reader is referred to these publications for chronological references. It should also be mentioned that no uniform definition of an athlete or an elite athlete has been used in the studies reported. The definition of a sample as athletes was accepted as reported. Most studies include youngsters that can be classified as select, elite, junior national, or national caliber.

SIZE ATTAINED AND GROWTH VELOCITY

Stature or standing height and body mass are the two most common somatic characteristics that are considered in growth studies. Consequently, the focus is on these dimensions. In an extensive review of the growth of children and adolescents in a variety of sports, Malina (1994) plotted the means/medians of the athletic samples against US reference data. Athletes of both sexes in team sports (basketball, soccer, volleyball and ice hockey) have, on the average, statures that equal or exceed reference medians. Similarly, in individual sports (diving, tennis, track and field including sprint and distance runs, and swimming), the average statures of young athletes of both sexes equal or exceed those of the US reference group. Moreover, when verifying the growth curves of those athletes it is noteworthy that these curves closely parallel those of the US reference. Gymnastics is the only sport that consistently presents a profile of short stature in both sexes (means or medians varying between percentile 10 and percentile 50 of the US reference). More recent samples of elite gymnasts, are, on the average, shorter and closer to the 10th

percentile of the reference group than those of 20 years ago (Malina, 1994; Claessens, 1999). Although data are limited, figure skaters of both sexes also present shorter statures.

Body mass presents a similar pattern. Young athletes in most sports have, on the average, a body mass that equals or exceeds the reference medians. Only gymnasts, figure skaters, and ballet dancers have consistently lower body mass. Gymnasts and figure skaters, however, have adequate body mass for their stature, but ballet dancers have low body mass for stature.

Although longitudinal data on young athletes followed over the adolescent period are limited and samples sizes are most often quite small (n < 20), the estimated mean peak height velocity (cm/year) during adolescence in male athletes in several sports (basketball, cycling, ice hockey, rowing, track and field, and soccer) varies between 8.7cm/year and 10.1cm/year. These values are well within the boundaries of estimated peak height velocities reported in European longitudinal growth studies, 8.3cm/year to 10.3cm/year. The peak height velocities of physically inactive and active adolescents also fall within these ranges (Beunen and Malina, 1996; Beunen et al., 1999; Malina, 1998b). Longitudinal data for female athletes are limited to Polish girls active in several individual and team sports. The average peak height velocities for these Polish girls active in sports vary between 7.8cm/year and 8.0cm/year and compare favorably with the velocities reported for European longitudinal studies (7.0cm/year to 9.0cm/year).

A few short-term longitudinal studies of female gymnasts have been reported in the 1990s. The statures of 25 female Swiss gymnasts (n = 25), selected for the National team and training for 13 hours/week, were at the start of the study well within the normal range of the Swiss reference data, and the average stature did not deviate from the reference (Tönz et al., 1990). After four years of study the average stature was 0.85 SD below the mean of the Swiss population. Growth velocity was also within the normal range at the start of the study; it then slowed, but at the end of the study there was a clear catch up. This is characteristic of a slow or late maturation process and is confirmed by the late biological maturation of the female gymnasts. Of interest is that gymnasts who stopped training before 14 years were taller and heavier at the start of the study than those who continued training. They had also an earlier skeletal age and age at menarche, and their mothers were also taller than those who continued training. Surprisingly, the statures and body mass at the end of the study did not differ between those who stopped training before 14 years and those who continued training until 16.3 to 19.0 years (Tönz et al.,1990). In contrast, Theintz et al. (1993) demonstrated that 22 female Swiss gymnasts who trained, on the average, 22 hours/week and were followed over a short period (range 2.0 to 3.7 years) had significantly lower growth velocities than 21 female swimmers who trained 8 hours/week. Further, the height SD scores of the gymnasts deviated more and more with time and a marked stunting of estimated leg length was indicated in the gymnasts. Concomitantly, predicted adult height of the gymnasts decreased significantly with time. Considering the short time period during which these female gymnasts were followed, it is difficult to ascertain a smooth velocity curve and define accurately the timing and maximal velocity of the growth spurt.

Additionally, Claessens et al. (1999) demonstrated that the sitting height/stature ratio of world-class female gymnasts did not differ from those of a matched reference group.

More recently Baxter-Jones and Helms (1996) summarized the data from the Training of Young Athletes (TOYA) study in which 81 female gymnasts were followed over three years. The gymnasts had below-average statures, particularly from 12 to 16 years, compared to the British reference data. However, at 17 years of age, the average stature of the gymnast was similar to the average of the reference group. This study confirms the lag in adolescent growth in female gymnasts and subsequent catch-up.

BIOLOGICAL MATURATION

The biological maturity status of athletes has been studied quite extensively, especially the age at menarche (Beunen and Malina, 1996; Malina, 1994, 1998b). Later mean ages at menarche are reported in athletes in many but not in all sports (Beunen and Malina, 1996, Malina, 1998b). It is also often suggested that training delays menarche. The term delay is, however, misleading since it implies a causal effect; i.e., training before reaching menarche causes a later occurrence of this maturational event. From the available evidence this is a precocious conclusion not warranted by the available evidence. Part of the confusion associated with later ages at menarche in athletes stems from the methods used to estimate age at menarche. The most precise, valid and reliable estimations are obtained with the prospective method in which subjects are followed and interrogated at regular intervals to obtain age at menarche. Also the status quo method, in which large samples of girls in the age range 9 through 18 years are asked whether or not they already experienced a first menstruation, result in adequate estimates. Such data need to be analyzed properly with probits or logits. The least precise estimates are obtained with retrospective studies in which sexually mature females are interrogated about the age at which the first menstruation occurred. The vast majority of data for age at menarche in athletes are retrospective.

In Table 1 prospective and status quo estimates of age at menarche in female athletes from several sports are summarized. With the exception of ballet dancers, divers and gymnasts, the mean or median ages at menarche fall well within the range of European and US reference data. Female gymnasts in particular show very late ages at menarche with both methods. It should be noted that the variability in the reported mean/median ages at menarche is most probably due to sampling bias, population differences and competition level. Within a sport mean ages tend to be later in athletes who are at a higher competitive level. This probably reflects selective drop out of early maturing girls and selective success in sport of late maturing girls.

Sport	Prospective—Mean	Status quo—Median
Individual sports		
Ballet dancers	15.4 years	13.6 − 14.1 years
Divers		13.6 years
Gymnasts	14.3 − 15.1 years	15.0 − 15.6 years
Rowers	12.7 years	
Swimmers	13.3 years	12.7 − 13.1 years
Track and field	12.3 years	12.6 years
Tennis	13.2 years	
Team sports		
Soccer		12.9 years
Team sports		12.7 years
European girls[a]	12.1 − 13.5 years	
US girls[b]	12.8 years	

Note: For some studies not all girls reached already menarche

[a,b] Status quo estimates for European girls from the mid-1960s through the 1980s. All except two of the 39 ages were between 12.5 and 13.5 years. In Europe there is a North-South gradient with earlier age at menarche in the South (Eveleth and Tanner, 1990).

Table 1. Prospective and status quo ages at menarche in adolescent athletes. After Malina (1998b)

Other indicators of biological maturation such as secondary sex characteristics, age at peak height velocity, and skeletal maturation are less well documented, but, in general, lead to similar conclusions.

The pubertal progress of girls active in sport is similar to non-active girls with the exception of gymnasts and ballet dancers. Explanatory factors are, among others, selection and eating habits. Rigid selection criteria which place emphasis on thinness and linearity of physique, both of which are associated with later maturation partly explain this late maturation. Furthermore, eating habits are another confounding factor. In both sports the diets of the young gymnasts are closely monitored and perhaps manipulated. Disordered eating and a negative energy balance are present in a significant number of these athletes (Malina, 1998b).

In male athletes indicators of sexual and skeletal maturation indicate that young athletes competing in a variety of sports are characterized by average or early biological maturation (Beunen and Malina, 1996, Malina, 1998b). Age at peak height velocity (PHV) is an indicator of somatic maturation. Estimation of PHV requires longitudinal data, and methods to determine PHV are based on mathematically modeling of the growth curve and derivation of the velocity curve and biological parameters, such as onset and maximum or peak of the growth spurt, that characterize the growth process. The limited longitudinal observations for male athletes are consistent with the data for skeletal age, i.e., age at PHV tends to be average or earlier in male athletes as compared to controls or reference data (Table 2).

Sport	N	Age at PHV in years mean ± SD
Team sports		
Basketball	8	14.1 ± 0.9
Ice hockey	16	14.5 ± 1.0
	11	12.8 ± 0.5
Soccer	32	14.2 ± 0.9
	8	14.2 ± 0.9
Individual sports		
Cycling	6	12.9 ± 0.4
Distance running	4	12.6
Rowing	11	13.5 ± 0.5
Several sports and boys active in sports	7-32	13.1 – 14.6 (± 1.1 – 1.5)
Non-athletes[1]		13.8 – 14.4

[1]Non athletes: the range of mean ages at PHV, based on a variety of graphical and mathematical curve fitting techniques, reported in European longitudinal studies; 18 of the 20 estimated ages at PHV for boys are between 13.9 and 14.2 years.

Table 2. Estimated ages at peak height velocity (cm/year) in adolescent male athletes (Malina, 1998b).

Summarizing the available evidence it is clear that the growth and maturity of most athletes competing in a variety of sports closely parallels the growth and maturity process of their non-athlete peers. Male athletes are generally taller and heavier than the reference population and tend to be average or early in their biological maturation process. Female athletes also have statures and body mass that equal or exceeds the average values of reference populations. Gymnasts of both sexes consistently show short statures and low body mass, although adequate for their statures. Female athletes are in general late maturing especially in ballet, diving, figure skating and gymnastics. At least two formal hypotheses have been formulated to explain this sexual dimorphism, more precisely with regard to the later age at menarche in female athletes. The first hypothesis states that training 'delays' menarche. The second is a two-part biocultural hypothesis stating that the characteristics of physique associated with later maturation are more suitable for successful athletic performance, and that early maturing girls are socialized away from sport or, in contrast, late maturing girls are socialized into sport (Beunen and Malina 1996). The training hypothesis is commonly accepted in popular literature, but has been severely criticized on methodological, experimental and statistical considerations. The genetic disposition hypothesis stresses the importance of selection for the appropriate physique that is made by the coach, parents and/or child herself. A variety of confounding factors need, however, to be considered such as the monitoring of the diet, the desire for thinness and associated risks for disordered eating and negative energy balance. Furthermore, it should be stressed that in well-nourished populations biological maturation and growth characteristics are under strong genetic control, which is, for example, suggested by the mother-daughter correlation for age at menarche. Finally other biocultural factors need to be considered such as family size. Although data are limited, athletes tend to come from bigger families and family size is related to biological maturation; children from large families tend to be late maturers (Beunen and Malina, 1996, Malina 1998b).

PREDICTION OF ATHLETIC SUCCESS

The prerequisites of athletic success in most sports rely to a considerable extent upon biological traits such as somatic dimensions, physique, body composition, proportions and physical abilities. Studies of Olympic and world-class athletes consistently show evidence of morphological and physical performance differences among sports and even within sports.

With regard to selection and talent identification, even at a young age, the question remains whether these morphological and performance characteristics are already present at that young age and, moreover, whether characteristics seen in late adolescence or early adulthood track over time. In other words, are those who excel at a young age within their age group the same as those who excel at adult age. Further, it can even be questioned if adult performance levels can be accurately predicted. The focus of this section is on morphological and performance characteristics, and

does not imply that other factors in the perceptual, cognitive, emotional and behavioral domains do not contribute to athletic success.

During the last decades, a number of scientific studies have focussed on the identification and selection of future athletes (e.g., Bloomfield et al., 1992; Fisher and Borms, 1990; Komadel, 1988; Malina, 1993, 1997; Marfell-Jones, 1996; Matsudo, 1996; Régnier et al., 1982, 1993, Zaciorskij et al., 1974). Talent identification, guidance and development, can be done very differently, ranging from the simplest way where the coach "detects" most talented children on the basis of his/her "eye," to the more sophisticated based on an extended battery of tests, which are scientifically designed and validated. Extreme examples of such "batteries" were used in former East European selection programs (see Fisher and Borms, 1990; Malina, 1993, 1997; Régnier et al., 1993).

Well-developed "screening programs" or "detection batteries" consist of different items among which "morphological" characteristics are of real importance in addition to health-related, physiological, motor-functional, and psychological features (Bloomfield, 1992, Hebbelinck, 1989; Hübscher and Wutscherk, 1980; Komadel, 1988). An overview of items used for talent detection and development is given in Table 3.

- Health status
- Genetic basis
- Time spent in sport
- Maturity
- Physical capacities
    - ✓ Morphological assessment
        - Somatotype
        - Size / body composition
        - Proportionality
    - ✓ Posture
    - ✓ Basic motor abilities (flexibility, strength, power, speed)
- Functional capacity : physiological and motor function tests
- Psychological profile

(adapted from Bloomfield, 1992; and Komadel, 1988)

Table 3. List of items necessary within the talent identification and talent developmental process.

The importance of morphological and performance characteristics within the total process of talent development is based on the fact that: (1) sports performance in youth is, to a large extent, related to physical and maturational characteristics (Beunen, 1996; Beunen & Malina, 1996, Malina, 1994; Malina and Beunen, 1996a), and (2) these parameters show a relatively high degree of heritability and predictability (Bouchard et al., 1997, Claessens et al., 1986; Maes et al., 1996; Malina, 1990; Malina and Bouchard, 1986; Ponnet, 1993). Both aspects are important within the talent detection and developmental process. Also, from a medical point of view, a "suitable physique" for specific sports is often stressed, based on the fact that "physique," in addition to other factors, may be an "etiological" factor in some sports injuries (Backx, 1996). This is clearly illustrated in a study on elite female gymnasts in which heavier, taller and more robust girls are more characterized by a positive ulnar variance (ulnar overgrowth) leading to wrist pain, compared to their less heavy and smaller peers (Claessens et al., 1996). Also, the American College of Sports Medicine (1993) stresses the importance of a suitable build for sport: "...if possible, a child or adolescent should be counseled toward sports that are realistic given the individual's body type" (p.3).

Genetic factors that explain variation in morphological and performance characteristics are briefly discussed. Tracking of somatic dimensions, physical abilities, and sport skills is analyzed, and prediction of somatic dimensions, physical abilities, and skills is considered.

GENETIC FACTORS

It is beyond the scope of this account to review the genetics of somatic characteristics and fitness. Recently, Bouchard, Malina and Pérusse (1997) thoroughly reviewed the methods used in genetic epidemiology and the present knowledge of genetics of fitness, physical activity, performance and related factors. A significant fraction of the variation in body size, proportions, physique, skeletal lengths and breadths, limb circumferences, and bone mass is genetically determined. The available evidence stems largely from twin, family and sibling studies. Heritability estimates, which are sample or population specific parameters, vary and are generally higher for twin than for family studies. For most dimensions, heritabilities vary between $h^2 = 0.70$ and $h^2 = 0.95$. Studies relating somatic dimensions to specific genes are very limited. Indicators of obesity, adiposity, and fat distribution are also under relatively strong genetic influence but less so than skeletal dimensions. Heritability estimates for fat and the body mass index (BMI) reach about $h^2 = 0.25$ to $h^2 = 0.40$. The search for genes associated or linked with obesity, adiposity and fat distribution has exploded over the last five years. Genes located on all chromosomes except the Y-chromosome are associated or linked with indicators of fatness (Pérusse et al. 1999).

Heritability estimates for aerobic, strength and motor performances are largely derived from studies of younger subjects and twins. Some of the earlier studies obtained unrealistic high estimates due to small sample sizes. The genetic contribution to strength and motor performance is difficult to quantify given the large variability in reported estimates. Heritability estimates for maximal oxygen uptake corrected for body mass range from $h^2 = 0.25$ to $h^2 = 0.40$. Response to training, i.e., genotype x environment interaction, has also been demonstrated. Maes et al. (1996) reported inheritance of performance characteristics based on a sample of 105 10-year-old twins and their parents. Using path analytical techniques, it was demonstrated that genetic and specific environmental factors explain the phenotypic variance and that the genetic component explained between 25% to 85% of the phenotypic variance in performance characteristics.

In summary, morphological characteristics and to a lesser but significant extent performance characteristics are under genetic control giving support to the notion that an 'athlete is born and then made.'

TRACKING AND STABILITY

Tracking is defined as the maintenance of the relative rank or position within a group over time. Longitudinal observations are needed to study the tracking (Malina, 1996). Stability is usually used as a synonym, but it refers more to the underlying characteristic. If individuals tend to track in body dimensions over time, the body dimensions are then stable characteristics. Although various statistical techniques can be used to study tracking, inter-age correlations or auto-correlations are used most often in estimating the tracking of morphological and performance characteristics.

In general, tracking coefficients decline with increasing time or age interval between observations, and also with the age period considered, e.g. infancy and childhood or adolescence. Furthermore, measurement error, biological variation, e.g., variation in the timing of the growth spurt, and significant changes in environmental conditions, e.g., physical training, can influence inter-age correlations.

Longitudinal data from several large European and North American longitudinal studies permit the study of tracking across the growth period. Similar long-term follow-up studies are not available for performance characteristics.

Tanner and Whitehouse (1982) report inter-age correlations for several somatic dimensions followed from birth to adulthood in the Harpenden growth study. In general, the tracking coefficients are low between body dimensions taken near birth and at adult age, about 0.1 to 0.3. But at subsequent ages the inter-age correlations (with adult values) increase considerably to about 0.70 to 0.80, and remain fairly stable until the onset of puberty. Due to the time spreading of the adolescent growth spurt in most body dimensions, the auto-correlations decrease temporarily and then increase as adulthood is approached.

For indicators of overweight and adiposity, auto-correlations are much lower than for other somatic dimensions. In most studies, overweight in the form of a high BMI and adiposity or subcutaneous fat are considered. Subcutaneous fat does not track very well from birth to about 5 to 6 years, it is very labile in infancy and early childhood. Inter-age correlations between measurements taken at 7 years and at subsequent ages, and measurements taken at adulthood are moderate but fairly constant. Auto-correlations between skinfolds taken at adjacent ages are, however, fairly high, about 0.7 to 0.9. Also, tracking at the extremes, i.e., the 25% or 20% fattest, is considerably higher. The fattest children, after age 6 have a higher risk remaining fat at subsequent ages and in adulthood (Malina and Bouchard, 1991).

Inter-age correlations for the three somatotype components taken separately vary between 0.45 and 0.85 in the age range 12 to 17 or 13 to 18 years in both boys and girls (Malina and Bouchard, 1991).

Measures of performance (aerobic maximal power, isometric strength, explosive strength, muscular endurance, flexibility, speed) track significantly across childhood and adolescence, but correlations are low to moderate. Correlations aver three years periods or longer time spans vary mostly between about 0.25 and 0.70 (Malina 1996). Inter-age correlations from the Leuven Longitudinal Study on Lifestyle, Fitness and Health (Beunen et al. 1997) cover the adolescent and adult periods. Correlations between fitness components observed at 13 years and subsequent ages, and observations made at 30 years are reported in Figures 1 and 2. With the exception of flexibility, the correlations between fitness components at 13 years and at 30 years are low to moderate, about 0.3 to 0.5; thereafter, correlations tend to increase to about 0.5 to 0.7 between observations made at 18 and 30 years. Flexibility shows considerable tracking, about 0.7 to 0.8, over the whole age span.

For track and field events such as the high jump, shot put and 60m sprint, Ponnet et al. (1994) report inter-age correlations between observations at 12 and 15 years of about 0.55 to 0.75.

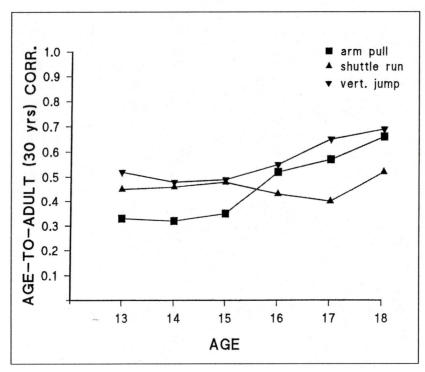

Figure 1. Inter-age correlations between adolescent ages and 30 years of age (n=173) for measures of performance-related physical fitness (Adapted from Beunen et al, 1992).

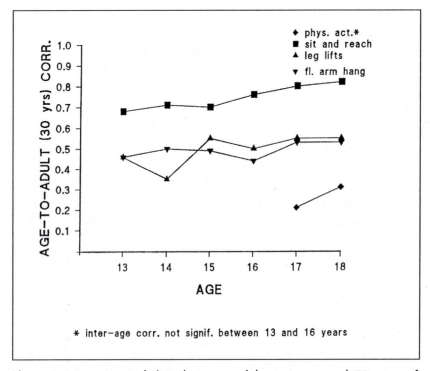

Figure 2. Inter-age correlations between adolescent ages and 30 years of age (n=173) for measures of health-related physical fitness and physical activity (Adapted from Beunen et al, 1992, and Vanreusel et al, 1993).

In summary, most somatic dimensions show considerable tracking after three years of age even over long time spans. Indicators of fatness and adiposity track moderately from 6 years onwards, but those at risk, i.e., the fattest children and adolescents have a higher risk of remaining fat at later ages. Performance-characteristics track at lower levels. Auto-correlations between observations made in adolescence and at 30 years are also fairly low to moderate (about 0.3 to 0.7).

PREDICTION OF ADULT CHARACTERISTICS

Stature prediction has caught considerable interest over the last 55 years. Several prediction methods have been developed, but the most commonly used and, more importantly, the most accurate, are those of Bayley and Pinneau (1952), Roche, Wainer and Thissen (RWT) (1975), and Tanner et al. (1983). In each of these methods stature at 18 years is accepted as a proxy of adult stature mainly because choice of an older age would reduce available sample sizes considerably. Although the median increase in stature after 18 years is small, 0.8cm for boys and 0.6cm for girls, the increase exceeds 1cm at the 90th percentile. This late growth is related in part to the rate of maturation (Roche, 1984). The predictor variables used in the three methods are: (1) present stature, (2) present skeletal maturation, and (3) present chronological age. Also, age at menarche, mid-parent height, and body mass are used in some of the methods. Rate of skeletal maturation over one year and height velocity over one year increase the accuracy of the adult stature prediction (Tanner et al., 1983). The accuracy of the predictions varies with chronological age. For the method of Tanner et al. (1983), the residual standard deviations decline from 4.7 cm at 6 years to 1.4 cm at 18 years in boys and from 3.7cm at 5 years to 1.1cm at 16 years in girls. Similar residual standard deviations are found in the RWT method (Roche et al., 1975). This means that from 5 to 6 years onwards fairly accurate adult stature predictions can be made. An important drawback, however, is that in all of the accurate methods, skeletal age is an important predictor especially during the adolescent years. Beunen et al. (1997b) demonstrated that in boys aged 13 through 16 years adult stature measured at 30 years could be predicted with nearly the same accuracy as with the method of Tanner et al. (1983) using present stature, sitting height, the subscapular and triceps skinfolds, and chronological age as predictors. On the other hand, Khamis et al. (1994) showed that the original RWT method can be substituted by using only present stature, body mass, and mid-parent stature in the absence of skeletal age. The accuracy is, however, less during the period of the adolescent growth spurt.

The chief reason for the inclusion of physique and somatotype photographs in the Harpenden Growth Study was the desire to evaluate the claim of Sheldon et al. (1940) that the human somatotype does not change with age, at least under reasonably favorable environmental conditions. The inter-age correlations for somatotype components—endomorphy, mesomorphy and ectomorphy, were respectively, 0.72, 0.83, and 0.82. These values are similar in magnitude to those for height (Walker and Tanner, 1980). Lower stability of somatotype components was, however, reported in other longitudinal studies (Malina and Bouchard, 1991)

Few attempts have been made to verify if inter-individual variability in adult physical fitness can be explained by morphological and fitness characteristics observed during childhood and or adolescence. Beunen et al. (1992) demonstrated that the amount of explained variance in adult fitness increased significantly when other characteristics such as other fitness scores, skeletal maturation and body dimensions observed during adolescence entered the regression or discriminant functions.

Apart from fitness scores, anthropometric dimensions, skeletal maturity and behavioral characteristics added significantly to the prediction of adult fitness scores. At 13 years the multiple correlations for predicting fitness scores observed at 30 years varied between 0.50 for pulse recovery

Event	Domain	Explained Variance	Dimensions/test
High jump	Somatic	31%	Ecto, breadths, skel. age
	Motor	50%	High, broad jump
	Somatic + Motor	75%	High, broad jump, breadths, circ., skinf., meso
60 m spring	Somatic	30%	Skinf., sitt. ht.
	Motor	71%	Sprint, plyom. jump, bench press, endur. run, bent arm hang, leg lifts
	Somatic + Motor	74%	Sprint, plyom. jump, bench press, endur. run, bent arm hang, leg lifts
Shot put	Somatic	28%	Sitt. ht., skel. age, circ.
	Motor	51%	Shot put, endur. run, leg lifts
	Somatic + Moto	53%	Shot put, endur. run, leg lifts, circ

Table 4. Prediction of track and field events at 17 years from characteristics observed at 12 years.

after a step test to 0.68 for flexibility. With the exception of pulse recovery, the multiple correlations increased for all fitness items and varied between 0.46 and 0.87 for predictions made from observations at 18 years. Similar results were obtained with discriminant analysis when extreme performance groups were contrasted at 30 years.

Although much have been published about talent identification and theoretical models of talent identification, little is known about the prognostic value of anthropometric dimensions and fitness characteristics in the prediction of later athletic success. Based on a longitudinal study of 144 boys aged 10 to 18 years, Ponnet et al. (1994) demonstrated that somatic dimensions measured at 12 years explained 28%, 30%, and 31% of the variation respectively, in the shot put, 60m sprint and high jump at 17 years (Table 4). Motor abilities explained 50% to 71% of the variance in the three track and field items, and anthropometric dimensions and motor abilities combined explained 53% of the variance in the shot put, 74% of the variance in the 60m sprint, and 75% of the variance in the high jump.

OVERVIEW

In conclusion evidence from cross-sectional and longitudinal studies indicates that physical training, even at high intensities, does not have harmful effects on the growth and maturation process of successful young athletes. Further studies are needed to document if intensive training has a potentially harmful influence, but in these studies the effect of training has to be carefully partitioned from constitutional factors and other components of the overall sport-specific environment, before causality can be established. With regard to the athlete-coach environment, caution is needed with the emphasis on thinness in sports in which aesthetic factors or in which body mass plays an important role.

It is well documented that genetic factors explain considerable amounts of variation in anthropometric dimensions and biological maturation, and to a lesser but still significant extent in physical performance. Inter-age correlations as indicators of tracking are high for somatic dimension from 2 to 3 years of age onwards. They are low to moderate for most fitness items and motor skills over longer periods (five years or longer). But, anthropometric and fitness components observed in early adolescence explain considerable amounts of variation in motor abilities and sports skills observed at adult age. Consequently, morphological and fitness characteristics may be useful criteria for talent identification at a young age.

For ethical reasons it is highly unlikely that a true experimental growth study with random assignment to experimental groups and different training regimes to test the effects of physical activity and training for sport on growth, maturation and development will ever be undertaken. It would indeed be unethical to impose training regimens to children and adolescents comparable to those of elite athletes. Furthermore, as stressed above, elite athletes are highly selected and do not represent a cross section of the general population. Consequently, we should rely our knowledge on longitudinal studies of young athletes competing in a variety of sports. Mixed or multiple longitudinal designs, covering fairly short intervals (e.g. 3 to 5 years) with overlapping age levels are required in combination with pure longitudinal studies covering longer age periods but with less high frequency of observation. Since the effects of strenuous exercise are multiple and a large number of confounding factors may interfere there is a need to include a variety of dimensions and measurements in these longitudinal studies, e.g., growth factors and hormonal secretions sampled at regular intervals during the day, anthropometric dimensions, biological maturation, body composition, physical performance, daily physical activity, nutritional habits, clinically ascertained disordered eating, personality characteristics and detailed recordings of the training regimens (frequency, intensity, hours of training and type of training).

In order to increase our understanding about the possible positive or negative health consequences of intensive training, there is also a need to design longitudinal studies during which former athletes are followed over the life span.

In all these studies, it remains to be verified if there is a level of physical activity resulting in optimal growth, maturation and development. Moreover, are some children and adolescents more susceptible to the beneficial or harmful effects of physical activity?

REFERENCES

American College of Sports Medicine. (1993). The prevention of sport injuries of children and adolescents (current comment from the American College of Sports Medicine). *Medicine and Science in Sports and Exercise* 25: 1-7.

Backx, F.J.G. (1996). Epidemiology of paediatric sports-related injuries. In: Bar-Or, O. (Ed.) *The Child and Adolescent Athlete. Volume VI. The Encyclopedia of Sports Medicine, An IOC Medical Commission Publication.* Oxford: Blackwell Scientific Publications (pp. 163-172).

Baxter-Jones, A.D.G. & Helms, P.J. (1996). Effects of training at a young age: A review of the training of young athletes (TOYA) study. *Pediatric Exercise Science* 8: 310-327.

Bayley, N. & Pinneau, S.R. (1952). Tables for predicting adult height from skeletal age: Revised for use with the Greulich Pyle hand standards. *Journal of Pediatrics* 40: 432-441.

Beunen, G.; Lefevre, J.; Claessens, A.L.; Lysens, R.; Maes, H.; Renson, R.; Simons, J.; Vanden Eynde, B.; Vanreusel, B.; & Van Den Bossche, C. (1992). Age-specific correlation analysis of longitudinal physical fitness levels in men. *European Journal of Applied Physiology* 64: 538-545.

Beunen, G. (1996). Physical growth, maturation and performance. In: Eston, R. & Reilly, T. (Eds.) *Kinanthropometry and Exercise Physiology Laboratory Manual.* London: E. & F.N. Spon (pp. 51-71).

Beunen, G. & Malina, R.M. (1996). Growth and biological maturation: Relevance to athletic performance. In: Bar-Or, O. (Ed.) *The Child and Adolescent Athlete. Volume VI. The Encyclopedia of Sports Medicine, An IOC Medical Commission Publication.* Oxford: Blackwell Scientific Publications (pp. 3-24).

Beunen, G.; Ostyn, M.; Simons, J.; Renson, R.; Claessens, A.L.; Vanden Eynde, B.; Lefevre, J.; Vanreusel, B.; Malina, R.M.; & Van 't Hof, M.A. (1997a). Development and tracking in fitness components:

Leuven longitudinal study on lifestyle, fitness and health. *International Journal of Sports Medicine* 18: S171-S178.

Beunen, G.P.; Malina, R.M.; Lefevre, J.; Claessens, A.L.; Renson, R.; & Simons, J. (1997b). Prediction of adult stature and noninvasive assessment of biological maturation. *Medicine and Science in Sports and Exercise* 29: 225-230.

Beunen, G.P.; Malina, R.M.; & Thomis, M. (1999). Physical growth and maturation of female gymnasts. In: Johnston, F.E.; Eveleth, F.; & Zemel, B. (Eds.) *Human Growth in Context*. London: Smith-Gordon (pp. 281-289).

Bloomfield, J. (1992). Talent identification and profiling. In: Bloomfield, J.; Fricker, P.A.; & Fitch, K.D. (Eds.) *Textbook of Science and Medicine in Sport*. Melbourne: Blackwell Scientific Publications (pp. 187-198).

Bloomfield, J.; Fricker, P.A.; & Fitch, K.D. (Eds.) (1992). *Textbook of Science and Medicine in Sport*. Melbourne: Blackwell Scientific Publications.

Bouchard, C.; Malina, R.M.; & Pérusse, L. (1997). *Genetics of Fitness and Physical Performance*. Champaign, Ill.: Human Kinetics.

Claessens, A.L. (1999). Elite female gymnasts: A kinanthropometric overview. In: Johnston, F. E.; Eveleth, P.; & Zemel, B. (Eds.) *Human Growth in Context*. London: Smith-Gordon.

Eveleth, P.B. & Tanner, J.M. (1990). *Worldwide Variation in Human Growth*. Cambridge: Cambridge University Press.

Fischer, J. & Borms, J. (1990). *The Search for Sporting Excellence (ICSSPE Sport Science Studies 3)*. Schorndorf, Germany: Verlag Karl Hofmann.

Hebbelinck, M. (1989). Detection and development of talent in sports: Kinanthropometric aspects. *Sport (Bloso)* 31(2): 2-9.

Hübscher, J. & Wutscherk, H. (1980). Die Bedeutung der Anthropometrie für die Eignungsdiagnostik im Kindes- und Jugendalter. *Theor und Prax Körperk* 29: 603-608.

Khamis, H.J. & Roche, A.F. (1994). Predicting adult stature without skeletal age: The Khamis-Roche method. *Pediatrics* 94: 504-507.

Komadel, L. (1988). The identification of performance potential. In: Dirix, A.; Knuttgen, H.G.; & Tittel, K. (Eds.) *The Olympic Book of Sports Medicine*. Oxford: Blackwell Scientific Publications (pp. 275-285).

Maes, H.M.; Beunen, G.P.; Vlietinck, R.F.; Neale, M.C.; Thomis, M.; Vanden Eynde, B.; Lysens, R.; Simons, J.; Derom, C.; & Derom, R. (1996). Inheritance of physical fitness in 10-yr-old twins and their parents. *Medicine and Science in Sports and Exercise* 28: 1479-1491.

Malina, R.M. (1990). Tracking of physical fitness and performance during growth. In: Beunen, B.; Ghesquiere, J.; Reybrouck, T.; & Claessens, A.L. (Eds.) *Children and Exercise*. Stuttgart: Enke Verlag (pp. 1-10).

Malina, R.M. (1993). Youth sports: Readiness, selection and trainability. In: Duquet, W. & Day, J.A.P. (Eds.) Kinanthropometry IV. London: E. & F.N. Spon (pp. 285-301).

Malina, R.M. (1994). Physical growth and biological maturation of young athletes. *Exercise and Sport Sciences Reviews* 22: 389-433.

Malina, R.M. (1996). Tracking of physical activity and physical fitness across the lifespan. *Research Quarterly of Exercise and Sport* 67: 48-57.

Malina, R.M. (1997). Talent identification and selection in sport. *Spotlight on Youth Sports* 20(1): 1-3.

Malina, R.M. (1998a). Growth and maturation of young athletes—is training for sport a factor? In: Chan, K.-M. & Micheli, L.J. (Eds.) *Sports and Children*. Hong Kong: Williams and Wilkins (pp. 133-161).

Malina, R.M. (1998b). Physical activity and training for sport as factors affecting growth and maturation. In: Ulijaszek, S.J.; Johnston, F.E.; & Preece, M.A. (Eds.) *The Cambridge Encyclopedia of Human Growth and Development*. Cambridge: Cambridge University Press (pp. 216-219).

Malina, R.M. (1999). Growth and maturation of elite female gymnasts: Is training a factor. In: Johnston, F.E.; Eveleth, P.; & Zemel, B. (Eds.) *Human Growth in Context*. London: Smith-Gordon (pp. 291-301).

Malina, R.M. & Beunen, G. (1996). Matching of opponents in youth sports. In: Bar-Or, O. (Ed.) *The Child and Adolescent Athlete*. Oxford: Blackwell Scientific Publications (pp. 202-213).

Malina, R.M. & Bouchard, C. (Eds.) (1986). *Sport and Human Genetics*. Champaign, IL: Human Kinetics.

Malina, R.M. & Bouchard, C. (1991). *Growth, Maturation and Physical Activity*. Champaign, IL: Human Kinetics.

Marfell-Jones, M.J. (1996). Talent identification down under. *ISAK—Kinanthreport '96* 9(2): 1-3.

Matsudo, V.K.R. (1996). Prediction of future athletic excellence. In: Bar-Or, O. (Ed.) *The Child and Adolescent Athlete*. Oxford: Blackwell Scientific Publications (pp. 92-109).

Pérusse, L.; Chagnon, Y.C.; Weisnagel, J.; & Bouchard, C. (1999). The human obesity gene map: The 1998 update. *Obesity Research* 7: 111-129.

Ponnet, P. (1993). *Determinants of specific athletic abilities in male adolescents*. (Doctoral dissertation, in Dutch). Leuven, Belgium: Faculty of Physical Education and Physiotherapy, Katholieke Universiteit Leuven.

Ponnet, P.; Lefevre, J.; Beunen, G.; & Claessens, A.L. (1994). Die Prognose von leichtathletischen Leistungsfähigkeit bei untrainierten Adolescenten. In: Blaser, P.; Witte, K.; & Stuche, C. (Eds.) *Steuer- und Regelvorgänge der menschliche Motorik*. Sankt Augustin: Academia Verlag (pp. 195-200).

Régnier, G.; Salmela, J.H.; & Alain, C. (1982). Strategie für die Bestimmung und Entdeckung von Talenten im Sport. *Leistungssport* 12(6): 431-440.

Régnier, G.; Salmela, J.; & Russell, S.J. (1993). Talent detection and development in sport. In: Singer, R.N.; Murphey, M.; & Tennant, L.K. (Eds.) *Handbook of Research on Sport Psychology*. New York: McMillan Publishing Company (pp. 290-313).

Roche, A.F. (1984). Adult stature prediction: A critical review. *Acta Medica Auxologica* 16: 5-28.

Roche, A.F.; Wainer, H.; & Thissen, D. (1975). Predicting adult stature for individuals. *Monographs in Pediatrics* 3: 1-114.

Sheldon, W.H.; Stevens, S.S.; & Tucker, W.B. (1940). *The Varieties of Human Physique*. New York: Harper and Brother.

Tanner, J.M. & Whitehouse, R.H. (1982). *Atlas of Children's Growth: Normal Variation and Growth Disorders*. New York: Academic Press.

Tanner, J.M.; Whitehouse, R.H.; Cameron, N.; Marshall, W.A.; Healy, M.J.R.; & Goldstein, H. (1983). *Assessment of Skeletal Maturity and Prediction of Adult Height (TW2 Method)*. London: Academic Press.

Theintz, G.E.; Howald, H.; Weiss, U.; & Sizonenko, C. (1993). Evidence for a reduction of growth potential in adolescent female gymnasts. *Journal of Pediatrics* 122: 306-313.

Tönz, O.; Stranski, S.M.; & Meiner, G.Y.K. (1990). Wachstum und Pubertät bei 7- bis 16-jährigen Kunstturnerinnen: Eine prospektive Studie (Growth and puberty in 7 to 16 year old gymnasts: a prospective study). *Schweizerische Medizinische Wochenschrift* 120: 10-20.

Walker, R.N. & Tanner, J.M. (1980). Prediction of adult Sheldon somatotypes I and II from rating and measurements at childhood ages. *Annals of Human Biology* 7: 213-224.

Zaciorskij, V.M.; Bulgakowa, N.S.; Ragimow, R.M.; & Segijonko, L.P. (1974). Das Problem des Talents und der Talentsuch im Sport: Richtungen und Methodologien der Undersuchungen. *Leistungssport* 4: 239-251.

CHAPTER 3

Pubertal Alterations in Growth and Body Composition and Neuroendocrine Mechanisms

Alan D. Rogol, MD., Ph.D. and James Roemmich, Ph.D.
University of Virginia

GROWTH

Normal growth and development are testimony to the overall good general health of a child or adolescent. On the other hand, children who have virtually any subacute or chronic illness may grow more slowly than their age-appropriate peers. What constitutes the normal range varies with the gender, age and genetic background of the individual child. Linear growth is merely the outward manifestation of the complex interplay of genetic background, nutrition, total energy as well as macro- and micronutrients and hormones. We have traditionally considered linear growth only, but reparative and hypertrophic growth are also relevant (see below) as are alterations in the compartments of body composition. Growth in a number of dimensions shows a significant family resemblance. Adult stature, *tempo* of growth, *timing* and *rate* of pubertal maturation, and skeletal maturation (bone age) are all significantly influenced by genetic factors (Sinclair, 1978) with estimates of genetic transmissibility ranging from 41% to 71% (Tanner, 1989).

Of paramount importance to the expression of normal growth are adequate nutrition and good general health. Statural growth is a continuous, but not linear process over time. After the very rapid growth of the fetus, the child's linear growth occurs in at least three phases; infantile, childhood and pubertal – each with its own distinctive pattern. The infantile phase is characterized by a very rapid but continuously decelerating rate during the first 2 years of life; overall growth is approximately 25 cm over the first year and half of that during the second year. During this period the infant may cross percentile lines on the growth chart (as many as 2 or 3) as he/she grows toward the genetic potential and is further displaced in time from the excesses or constraints of the intrauterine environment. Birth length and ultimate adult height have a correlation coefficient of only 0.25 compared to 0.80 by 2 years of age (Tanner, et al., 1956). As children stand and walk, they attain a more linear habitus, become more muscular and experience a dramatic reduction in percentage body fat.

During childhood, the growth rate is relatively constant and averages approximately 5-6 cm/yr. A wide range of normal exists for linear growth rate and the actual velocity depends upon which percentile a child is tracking. Those children growing along the 3rd percentile of the linear growth curve average 5.1 cm per year and boys growing the 97th percentile grow 6.4 cm/yr and girls 7.1 cm/yr during the childhood phase to maintain that trajectory (Baumgartner et al., 1986; Roche and Himes, 1980; World Health Organization, 1983). During childhood the changes in body proportions reflect a descending pattern of growth priority; maturation of the head precedes that of the trunk, which, in turn, occurs before the limbs. The more distal portions of the limbs tend to mature before the more proximal parts (Sinclair, 1978). The hormonal control of childhood growth depends on the thyroid hormones and the growth hormone/insulin-like growth factor (GH/IGF-I) axis (see below). The percentage body fat slowly decreases in boys, but is relatively constant in girls. The total fat mass increases modestly in both genders.

The third phase, that of puberty, is a dynamic period of development marked by rapid changes in body size, shape, and composition, all of which are sexually dimorphic. It is characterized by the greatest sexual differentiation since fetal life and the most rapid rate of linear growth since infancy. The onset of puberty corresponds to a skeletal (biological) age of approximately 11 years in girls and 13 years in boys (Tanner et al., 1975). On average, girls enter and complete each stage of puberty earlier than boys, but there is significant inter-individual variability.

One of the hallmarks of puberty is the adolescent growth spurt. As puberty approaches the growth velocity slows to a nadir ("preadolescent dip"), before its sudden acceleration during mid-puberty. The timing of the pubertal growth spurt occurs earlier in girls, typically during Tanner breast stage 2 to 3, and does not reach the magnitude of that in boys. Girls average a peak height velocity of 9 cm/yr at age 12, and a total gain in height of 25 cm during the pubertal growth period (Kelch and Beitins, 1994; Marshall and Tanner, 1969). Boys attain a peak height velocity of 10.3 cm/yr, on average, 2 years later than girls during Tanner genital stage 4, and gain 28 cm in height (Kelch and Beitins, 1994; Marshall and Tanner, 1970). The longer duration of prepubertal growth combined with a greater peak height velocity results in the average adult height difference of 13 cm between men and women (Tanner, 1989). Following a period of decelerating height velocity, growth virtually ceases due to epiphyseal fusion, typically at a skeletal age of 15 years in girls and 17 years in boys (Tanner, 1989).

Puberty is also a time of significant weight gain; 50% of adult body weight is gained during adolescence. In boys peak weight velocity occurs at about the same time as peak height velocity (age 14) and averages 9 kg/yr. In girls, peak weight velocity lags behind peak height velocity by approximately 6 months and reaches 7.8 kg/yr at about age 12.5 years (Barnes, 1975; Tanner, 1975). The rate of weight gain decelerates in a similar manner as height velocity during the latter stages of pubertal development.

Sexual maturation occurs during puberty under the influence of gonadal steroid hormones (predominantly testosterone in males and estradiol in females) and the adrenal androgens, primarily dehydroepiandrosterone sulfate (DHEAS). Development usually occurs in a defined sequence within each gender, but individual variation does occur normally. Adrenarche, the production of adrenal androgens, generally occurs 1 to 2 years before the other hormonal changes of puberty, although visible evidence is generally not apparent until after thelarche in girls or testicular enlargement in boys (Kelch and Beitins, 1994). In both genders adrenarche results in the appearance of sexual hair, adult-type body odor, occasionally acne and is a separate and distinct process from the centrally-mediated gonadarche.

In boys gonadarche is heralded by testicular enlargement and a thinning and reddening of the scrotal skin. On average, this occurs between age 11.5 and 12 years, but a broad range of normal exists. The onset of these changes prior to age 9 is considered precocious and later than age 14, delayed. The testes undergo enlargement from the prepubertal volume of 3 mL or less to 4 mL at the onset of puberty, and undergo a 10-fold increase in size by the end of pubertal development (Marshall, 1975). Approximately 75% of boys will reach their peak height velocity during genital stage 4 and the remainder during stage 5. Sperm production and ejaculatory capability are present early during sexual development (biological age of 13.5-13.7 years) and do not correlate well with testicular size or other physical signs of sexual maturation (Kelch and Beitins, 1994).

The first evidence of gonadarche in girls is the appearance of breast buds (thelarche). This sign typically occurs between age 8 and 13 years with an average of 11 years. Development prior to 8 years is considered precocious and later than 13 years delayed (Tanner, 1989; Mirlesse et al., 1993), although more recent data suggest that normal development may begin months earlier. The pace of adolescent pubertal development correlates with the levels of sex steroid hormones during early puberty (De Ridder et al., 1992). In girls, the duration of pubertal development is usually 3-3.5 years, but may be completed within 2 years or take up to 6 years (Mirlesse et al., 1993). Menarche usually follows the onset of breast development by about 2.5 years. In North America the average age of menarche in girls of European descent is 12.8-13.3 years, but slightly earlier in girls of African origin (12.5 years) (Tanner, 1989; Mirlesse et al. 1993; Zacharias et al., 1970). Menstrual cycles are anovulatory in more than one-half of girls for up to 2 years beyond menarche, resulting in irregular intermenstrual intervals (Finkelstein, 1980).

BODY COMPOSITION

Two-compartment models

Direct measures of body composition require chemical analysis of the body tissues. Human body composition assessments are indirect estimates usually based on a two compartment model where the body is divided into the fat mass and fat-free mass (FFM) compartments based on the chemical comparison of human adult cadavers. The fat compartment is assumed to have a density of 0.9 g/mL and the FFM 1.1 g/mL. The density of the whole body is then function of the densities and proportional contributions of the two components. The body density is usually estimated by underwater weighing using Archimedes' principle. Following the assumptions presented by Siri (1961) the two-compartment model assumes that a density of less than 1.1 g/mL is due to the addition of fat to the body. However, the density of the FFM of children and adolescents is less than 1.1 g/mL, so the two compartment model consistently overestimates their percentage body fat.

There is an air displacement method that measures body volume through changes in air pressure (McCrory et al., 1995; Dempster and Aitkens, 1995). We have validated this air displacement technique in a group of children and adolescents and found that it generally overestimates the body density resulting in an underestimation of the percentage body fat (unpublished data). However, it may still have a niche in pediatric research because underwater weighing is generally difficult to perform in children younger than 8 years and those with disabilities. The difficulty arises from the child having to remain underwater for several seconds after exhaling all but the residual volume of air from the lungs.

Multi-compartment models

Several multicompartment models attempt to correct for maturational differences in the proportional composition (density) of the FFM. A criterion four-compartment approach divides the body into the FM and the FFM. The fat free mass is subdivided into its constituent parts; water, mineral, and protein (Lohman, 1992). Hydrometry and DXA (dual x-ray absorptiometry) are used to correct for the water and mineral fractions of the FFM, respectively and the protein fraction is determined by subtraction. The four-compartment model is currently the most accurate practical body composition model.

Three-compartment models combine two constituents of the FFM into a single compartment.

In the water-density model, the body density is adjusted for the total body water and protein and mineral are combined as solids. In the mineral-density model, the density is adjusted for bone mineral and the water and protein are combined to form the lean soft tissue compartment (Lohman, 1992). In a group of children and adolescents the mineral-density model did not perform well on an individual basis overestimating by as much as 7.5% body fat and underestimating by as much as 5% body fat. The water-density model performs very well on an individual basis and has a small mean bias of 0.75 % body fat. (Roemmich et al., 1997).

Field methods

In many field and clinical settings, underwater weighing can not be performed so other methods must be used to estimate the body composition. The most common field methods include bioelectrical impedance and auxologic variables such as skinfold thicknesses and body girths. Models using these methods attempt to estimate the body composition that was already estimated by underwater weighing. Often these field models are valid for only a specific population such as nonobese, caucasian, pubertal boys and girls and they generally predict well for a group of subjects, but there may be a large error for any individual.

Alterations in body composition at puberty

Marked changes in body composition, including alterations in the relative proportions of water, muscle, bone and fat are a hallmark of pubertal maturation and result in typical female-male differences. Under the influence of the gonadal steroid hormones and growth hormone, increases in bone mineral content and muscle mass occur and the deposition of fat is maximally sexually dimorphic. The changes in the distribution of body fat (central vs peripheral, subcutaneous vs visceral) result in the typical android and gynoid patterns of fat distribution of the older adolescent and adult (Cheek et al., 1974). Differential growth of the shoulders and hips and differences in lean tissue

accrual between males and females are also evident.

Under the influence of testosterone boys have a significant increase in the accrual of bone and muscle with simultaneous loss of fat on the limbs (Tanner, 1965). The maximal reduction in percent fat and increase in muscle mass in the upper arms correspond to the timing of peak height velocity. In some boys the increase in the amount of lean body mass can exceed the total gain in weight due to the concomitant loss of adipose tissue. As height velocity declines, fat accumulation continues in both genders, but twice as rapidly in girls (Rallison, 1986). As adults, males have 150% of the lean body mass of the average female and twice the number of muscle cells (Cheek et al., 1974). Both androgens and estrogens promote deposition of bone mineral; more than 90% of peak skeletal mass is present by age 18 in adolescents who have undergone pubertal development at the usual time. In girls, nearly one-third of total skeletal mineral is accrued in the 3 to 4 year period immediately after the onset of puberty (Bonjour et al., 1991; Slemenda et al., 1994). Adolescents with delayed puberty or secondary amenorrhea may fail to accrue bone mineral normally and have reduced bone mineral density as adults (Drinkwater et al., 1984; Finkelstein et al., 1992; Smith et al., 1982)

The changes in fat mass, FFM, percentage body fat and the proportional composition of the FFM have been reviewed by Roemmich and Rogol (1999), Van Loan (1996), and Malina and Bouchard (1991). From infancy through childhood boys have slightly more FFM than girls. The gender difference in FFM increases steadily from about 1 kg at 4 years of age to 3 kg by 9 years of age. Boys and girls have similar amounts of fat mass from infancy until about 7 years at which time girls start accruing greater amounts of fat. The percentage body fat is greater in girls than in boys from 1 year of age onward. Girls are about 1% fatter at age 5 and 6% fatter at age 10 (Van Loan, 1996). Boys and girls have similar amounts of FFM around age 11 to 12 years due to the earlier growth spurt in FFM in girls. During male puberty boys accrue FFM at a greater rate and for a longer time than girls, such that a young adult amount of FFM is attained at 15 to16 years for girls and 19 to 20 years for boys (Malina and Bouchard, 1991). Pubertal girls increase their percentage body fat and accrue FM at a rate of 1.14 kg per year. Pubertal boys decrease percentage body fat by 1.15 kg per year while the FM increases more modestly than for girls (Van Loan, 1996).

THE NEUROENDOCRINE AXES AND PUBERTAL GROWTH

Pubertal changes in physique, sexual maturation and body composition are controlled, in large part, by the growth hormone (GH)-insulin-like growth factor-I (IGF-I) and hypothalamic-pituitary-gonadal (HPG) axes.

GH is the primary hormone responsible for somatic growth, having, in addition, potent actions on protein, carbohydrate and lipid metabolism. Many of the effects of GH are indirectly mediated through insulin-like growth factors, primarily IGF-I, which can be locally synthesized by target tissues or by the liver, the predominant locus of circulating IGF-I. GH has direct end organ effects as well, initiating complex cellular processes that result in cell differentiation and proliferation. At the growth plate, IGF-I-induced epiphyseal cartilage proliferation and differentiation of stem cell chondrocytes increase the formation of cartilage and elongation of bone (Roemmich and Rogol, 1995).

The neuroendocrine regulation of GH production and pulsatile GH release is subject to various influences as a child's biological age advances toward reproductive maturity (Rogol, 1995; Westphal, 1995). Prepubertally, resting GH secretion is modulated primarily through GH-releasing hormone (GHRH) originating from the arcuate nucleus of the hypothalamus, and through somatostatin released from the preoptic and paraventricular nuclei. From infancy to childhood genetic determinants and environmental influences, such as diet, nutrition, or chronic disease may influence GH-IGF-I axis thereby affecting the growth potential. The IGF-I levels may decline with poor nutrition or chronic illness opening up the feedback loop to increase GH release. The net result is relative GH "resistance."

At the onset of puberty a marked acceleration in growth velocity results from a complex network of interactions between the GH-IGF-I and HPG axes. Total GH secretion increases two to three-fold, modulated through increased amplitude of secretory bursts, independent of pulse frequency (Veldhuis et al., 1997). Increases in circulating IGF-I and insulin-like growth factor-binding protein 3 (IGF-BP-3) parallel the augmented GH secretion.

Increases in the mass and rate of GH released per secretory burst during puberty may be modulated by the increasing concentrations of sex steroid hormones. Once believed to be primarily androgen-dependent (Veldhuis et al., 1997), the activation of the HPG and GH/IGF-I axes are now thought to be controlled by rising estrogen concentrations. Data suggest that estrogen may control feedback amplification of GH secretion during puberty, even in the male (Veldhuis et al., 1997; Mauras et al., 1996). Ultrasensitive measurements demonstrate the pattern of rising estrogen concentrations in boys during their progress through puberty (Klein et al., 1996) growth. Thus, estrogen in girls, or aromatization of testosterone to estrogen in boys, may likely be the initial trigger of amplified GH secretion in puberty (Veldhuis et al., 1997). Estrogen may act synergistically with increasing testosterone and GH concentrations to mediate skeletal growth in boys and girls at low concentrations; at higher concentrations they may induce epiphyseal fusion in both sexes. Recently, osteoporosis, unfused epiphyses, and continuing linear growth in adulthood were described in a man with an estrogen-receptor mutation rendering him unresponsive to estrogens. Previously thought to be lethal, the estrogen receptor mutation in a living human provides valuable clinical evidence supporting the hypothesis that estrogen is responsible for normal male and female skeletal growth and development (Smith et al., 1994). Identification of aromatase deficiency (the enzyme that converts androgenic precursors to biologically effective estrogens) in a man revealed a similar clinical presentation to that of the mutated estrogen receptor phenotype. Epiphyseal closure occurred only after estrogen therapy (Carani et al., 1997). In addition, boys with androgen insensitivity have female characteristics in timing and duration of pubertal growth, if there is no therapeutic response to androgen administration (Ritzen, 1992; Zachman et al., 1986). These findings and other supporting studies are contrary to previous hypotheses that pubertal growth is mediated by an androgen-dependent process.

In summary, the complex interrelationship of the GH/IGF-I and HPG axes governs normal growth and puberty. Recent advances have further characterized the neuroendocrine alterations controlling GH secretion at puberty. Our greater understanding of the physiology of pubertal growth will soon lead to improved therapeutic options in pathologic conditions, and will heighten awareness of potential positive and negative influences from additional factors, such as exercise.

NEUROENDOCRINE AXES AND BODY COMPOSITION

Growth hormone

Growth hormone therapy reduces the total adiposity and abdominal visceral fat of growth hormone-deficient children and adults (Bengtsson et al., 1992; Gregory et al., 1993; Vaisman et al., 1994). The relationship between endogenous growth hormone release and body composition in normal adolescents is less clear. Body composition-growth hormone studies of children have used the body mass index as a crude marker of adiposity. Most (Albertson Wikland et al., 1994; Martha et al., 1992; Rose et al., 1991), but not all (Costin et al., 1989), have reported an inverse relationship between body mass index [BMI, wt(kg)/ht2(m2)] and growth hormone release. Future studies should utilize an ultrasensitive growth hormone assay to accurately measure pulsatile growth hormone release and the lack of accurate estimates of body composition to

better investigate this relationship. Using a four-compartment body composition model and measures of abdominal visceral fat, we recently found that growth hormone release and the percentage body fat were modestly inversely related in pubertal boys and girls. However, in contrast to adults (Vahl et al., 1996), growth hormone release was not related to the amount of abdominal visceral fat. (Roemmich et al., 1998).

Leptin

Leptin, the protein product of the obesity (ob) gene, has been the focus of many recent studies in humans. Secreted from adipocytes into the blood stream, leptin may be an important hormonal link between the peripheral fat depot mass and the central control of metabolism (Lonnquist and Schaling, 1997). Extensively studied in normal and ob/ob mice, leptin deficiency is associated with a decreased metabolic rate, increased appetite, decreased energy expenditure, obesity, and infertility. These abnormalities are reversed after leptin administration (Dryden and Williams, 1997). Leptin treatment also accelerates pubertal onset in normal and ob/ob mice (Cameron, 1997). The mechanisms by which leptin regulates body weight and integrates adiposity with other neuroendocrine axes remain unclear (Lonnquist and Schaling, 1997). Congenital leptin deficiency has been reported in two severely obese children and in adults (Strobel et al., 1998) all of whom have a markedly increased fat mass, but low serum leptin concentration (Montague et al., 1997). These findings support the hypothesis that leptin is an important regulator of energy balance in humans and may be the first genetic evidence that leptin deficiency can cause obesity in humans.

Leptin may affect the timing and tempo of puberty since it is involved in energy balance and reproduction in small lab animals, although this has not yet been proven in humans (Cameron, 1997). Leptin may be one of the factors through which exercise training and reduced adiposity affects the neuroendocrine axes (Rogol, 1995). In effect, leptin may be one of several molecular signals linking nutritional status to the activation of the HPG axis (Apter, 1997). Leptin has been hypothesized to be a possible trigger for the onset of human puberty because leptin concentrations rise (approximately two-fold) prior to the pubertal increase in testosterone in males (Mantzoros et al., 1997) and prior to activation of the HPG axis in females (Garcia-Mayor, 1997). However, the physiologic mechanisms for the leptin surge remain unknown. Others have also reported increases in leptin concentrations in the prepubertal to pubertal transition of girls and boys and then pubertal reductions in leptin concentrations in boys (Clayton et al., 1997; Blum et al., 1997).

The relationships between gender, leptin concentration, and body fat mass accumulation during puberty remain unclear. Recently Roemmich et al. (1997a) described that the gender difference in leptin concentration of boys and girls was related to differences in the amount of subcutaneous fat and greater androgen concentrations of boys. Leptin concentrations were more highly related to the subcutaneous fat than the total fat mass as measured by a criterion 4-compartment model. The gender differences in leptin concentration remained after correcting for the amount of subcutaneous fat or total fat mass. Although previously hypothesized to increase energy expenditure and physical activity by others (Selbe et al., 1997), serum leptin concentrations were inversely related to the total energy expenditure (measured by $^2H_2^{18}O$ dilution), when adjusted for the amount of fat-free mass. Energy expenditure may reduce leptin concentrations by reducing the subcutaneous fat and total fat mass (Roemmich et al., 1997a). Nagy et al. (1997a) also found that body fat distribution (subcutaneous and intraabdominal adipose tissue measured by computed tomography) could account for gender differences in serum leptin concentrations.

Other investigators have found significant gender effects on leptin concentrations in children after correcting for the adiposity but using non-criterion estimates of body composition (Blum et al., 1997; Caprio et al., 1996; Ellis and Nicolson, 1997).

Thus, gender differences in leptin concentration may be due to differences in leptin synthesis, bioactivity, clearance rates and other biokinetic properties (Ellis and Nicolson, 1997). Pubertal increases in testosterone concentration may also reduce the leptin concentration in adolescent males (Blum et al., 1997; Wabitsh et al., 1997; Lahlou et al., 1997). Therapy with long acting testosterone esters reduces leptin concentrations in adolescent boys with delayed puberty (Arslanian and Suprasongin, 1997). The fat mass also decreased in those subjects; however, the authors did not report the effects of testosterone treatment on leptin concentrations independent of the change in fat mass. More detailed studies in children and adolescents are required to elucidate the role of leptin in pubertal development and to further define the relationship among gender, sex steroid hormone levels, body composition, body fat distribution, energy expenditure and leptin concentrations.

Sex Steroid Hormones

Under the influence of testosterone boys have a significant increase in the growth of bone and muscle with a simultaneous loss of fat in the limbs (Tanner, 1965). The maximal loss of fat and increase in muscle mass in the upper arms correspond to the time of peak height velocity. In boys the significant increase in the amount of lean body mass exceeds the total gain in weight due to the concomitant loss of adipose tissue. As height velocity declines, fat accumulation resumes in both genders, but is twice as rapid in girls. As adults, males have 150% of the lean body mass of the average female and twice the number of muscle cells (Cheek et al., 1974). The increase in skeletal size and muscle mass lead to increased strength in males. Both androgens and estrogens promote deposition of bone mineral, and more than 90% of peak skeletal mass is present by age 18 in adolescents, who have undergone normal pubertal development at the usual time. In girls, nearly one-third of total skeletal mineral is accumulated in the 3 to 4 year period immediately after the onset of puberty (Bonjour et al., 1991; Slemenda et al.,

1994). Increases in both height and weight (to limits) are the strongest correlates of skeletal mineralization during childhood and adolescence. Boys have a marked age-related delay in skeletal mineralization compared to girls. The former continue to accrue substantial bone mineral between the ages of 15 and 18 years. Increases in bone mineral density continue after the pubertal growth spurt. Adolescents with delayed puberty of secondary amenorrhea may fail to accrue bone mineral normally and have reduced bone mineral density as adults (Finkelstein et al., 1992). The pubertal accretion of bone mineral may account for more than one-half of the variability in bone mass in the elderly (Hui et al., 1990).

During pubertal development the *interactions* between GH and the sex steroid hormones are striking and pervasive. Numerous studies of adolescent boys have shown that the rising levels of testosterone during puberty play a pivotal role in augmenting spontaneous GH secretion and production (Martha et al., 1992; Mauras et al., 1989; Rose et al., 1989). The ability of testosterone to stimulate pituitary GH secretion, however, appears to transient, expressed only peripubertally, since GH and IGF-I levels decrease significantly during late puberty and into adulthood despite continued high concentrations of gonadal steroid hormones (Martha et al., 1989). In contrast to testosterone, estrogen modulates GH secretory activity in a disparate manner; low doses of estrogen stimulate IGF-I production through enhanced GH secretion, but higher doses inhibit IGF-I production at the hepatic level (Ho et al., 1987).

Many of the growth-promoting effects of the gonadal steroid hormones are mediated through estrogens rather than androgens, either via direct secretion of estrogen or conversion of androgens to estrogen by peripherally located aromatase. Individuals with complete androgen insensitivity (formerly denoted testicular feminization) demonstrate that androgens are not necessary to support the normal adolescent growth or to achieve pubertal levels of GH and IGF-I, if sufficient levels of estrogen are present (Zachmann et al., 1986).

Implications for Training

How might athletic training affect the genetically programmed timing and tempo of pubertal development? One might easily postulate that there would be acquired alterations of the hypothalamic-pituitary axes for GH and the gonadotropins as one might expect in anorexia nervosa or other form of severe stress. In fact, there are no convincing neuroendocrine studies to confirm this postulate. Although such studies of the pulsatile release of GH or LH are simple to conceive, they have not been done because of their invasive nature in a group of athletes that is trying to increase their performance. Tied closely to the effects of endurance or resistance training are alterations in diet, especially total energy intake and multiple dietary alterations in terms of macronutrients as well as dietary supplements including the "hormonally active" ones such as DHEA, androstenedione and testosterone. The issues concerning genetic influence, energy expenditure, reaction to stress and a myriad of others simply cannot be disentangled.

Those studies that have been done showing single hormonal levels or growth rates or alterations in body composition are difficult to interpret because of the expected alterations at puberty. Several have shown striking alterations, for example, in scholastic wrestlers in season versus out of season (Roemmich and Sinning, 1997 a and b) because proper control groups of non exercising boys were followed in the same manner.

Delay in growth and sexual maturation is well documented among certain groups of *elite* female athletes, most notably gymnasts, dancers and long distance runners; however the underlying mechanisms are not entirely clear nor have the factors of selection bias (genetic) been well accounted. Delayed menarche favors the continuation of sports such as gymnastics, suggesting that elite gymnastics are selected, in part, for this attribute. Continued participation, in turn, leads to more intense training and blurring of cause and effect. It is likely that specific neuroendocrine axes, e.g., those for ACTH-cortisol, GH-IGF-I and gonadotropins-gonadal steroids transduce the altered activity to delayed puberty.

CONCLUSION

Growth at puberty represents integrated information from the genetic, nutritional and neuroendocrine (hormonal) spheres. It is important to realize that all of the univariate correlations with growth velocity, body composition and the regional distribution of body fat are not unique. Redundancy of information is prominent as a mechanism to ensure the unfolding of processes as fundamental as growth and reproduction. Many factors including the role of intermediary metabolism and the effects of physical training and illness may modify these physiologic processes during the transition from childhood to adulthood.

RESEARCH NEEDS FOR THE FUTURE

The physical changes in body composition and adolescent development are quite well described over a range of racial and ethnic diversity. What has not been well studied and are prime research topics are longitudinal studies of the effects of endurance and resistance training protocols on the various aspects of body composition, including the regional distribution of body fat, and adolescent development, especially its timing and tempo. These studies, although important descriptive ones, would not evaluate the mechanism(s) of such alterations. The neuroendocrine alterations are postulated to drive physical changes. As noted above proper studies are difficult to perform because of the research (clinical) facilities needed, but they are critical especially if coupled to functional alterations in strength, agility and power. When done longitudinally and anchored to precise biological events such as peak height velocity one can then ascribe specific alterations to changes in neuroendocrine (and paracrine) axes and likely multiple interactions among them.

REFERENCES

Albertsson-Wikland, K.; Rosberg, S.; Karlberg, J.; & Groth, T. (1994). Analysis of 24-hour growth hormone profiles in healthy boys and girls of normal stature: Relation to puberty. *Journal of Clinical Endocrinology and Metabolism* 78: 1195-1201.

Apter, D. (1997). Leptin in puberty. *Clinical Endocrinology* 47: 175-176.

Arslanian, S. & Suprasongsin, C. (1997). Testosterone treatment in adolescents with delayed puberty: Changes in body composition, protein, fat, and glucose metabolism. *Journal of Clinical Endocrinology and Metabolism* 82: 3213-3220.

Barnes, H.V. (1975). Physical growth and development during puberty. *Medical Clinics of North America* 59: 1305-1317.

Baumgartner, R.N.; Roche, A.F.; & Himes, J.H. (1986). Incremental growth tables. *American Journal of Clinical Nutrition* 43: 711-722.

Bengtsson, B.-A.; Brummer, R.-J.M.; Eden, S.; Rosen, T.; & Sjostrom, L. (1992) Effects of growth hormone on fat mass and fat distribution. *Acta Paediatrica Supplement* 383: 62-65.

Blum, W.F.; Englaro, O.; Hanitsch, S.; Juul, A.; Hertel, N.T.; Muller, J.; Skakebaek, N.E.; Heiman, M.L.; Birkett, M.; Attansio, A.M.; Kiess, W.; & Rascher, W. (1997). Plasma leptin levels in healthy children and adolescents: dependence on body mass index, body fat mass, gender, pubertal stage, and testosterone. *Journal of Clinical Endocrinology and Metabolism* 82: 2904-2910.

Bonjour, J.; Theintz, G.; Buchs, B.; Slosmman, D.; & Rizzoli. R. (1991). Critical years and stages of puberty for spinal and femoral bone mass accumulation during adolescence. *Journal of Clinical Endocrinology and Metabolism* 73: 555-563.

Cameron, J.L. (1997). Search for the signal that conveys metabolic status to the reproductive axis. *Current Opinion in Endocrinology and Metabolism* 4: 158-163.

Caprio, S.; Tamborlane, W.V.; Silver, D.; Robinson, C.; Leibel, R.; McCarthy, S.; Grozman, A.; Belous, A.; Maggs, D.; & Sherwin, R.S. (1996). Hyperleptinemia:

An early sign of juvenile diabetes. Relations to body fat depots and insulin concentrations. *American Journal of Physiology* 271: E626-E630.

Carani, C.; Qin, K.; Simoni, M.; Faustini-Fustini, M.; Serpente, S.; Boyd, J.; Korach, K.S.; & Simpson, E.R. (1997). Effect of testosterone and estradiol in a man with aromatase deficiency. *New England Journal of Medicine* 337: 91-95.

Cheek, D.B.; Grumbach, M.M.; Grave, G.D. et al. (Eds.). (1974). *Control of the Onset of Puberty*. New York: John Wiley & Sons (pp. 424).

Clayton, P.E.; Gill, M.S.; Hall, C.M.; Tillmann, V.; Whatmore, A.J.; & Price, D.A. (1997). Serum leptin through childhood and adolescence. *Clinical Endocrinology* 46: 727-733.

Costin, G.; Kaufman, F.R.; & Brasel, J.A. (1989). Growth hormone secretory dynamics in subjects with normal stature. *Journal of Pediatrics* 115: 537-544.

Dempster, P. & Aitkens, S. (1995). A new air displacement method for the determination of human body composition. *Medicine and Science in Sports Exercise* 27: 1692-1697.

DeRidder, C.M.; Thijssen, J.H.H.; Bruning, P.F.; Van Den Brande, J.L.; Zonderland, M.L.; & Erich, W.B.M. (1992). Body fat mass, body fat distribution, and pubertal development: A longitudinal study of physical and hormonal sexual maturation of girls. *Journal of Clinical Endocrinology and Metabolism* 75: 442-446.

Drinkwater, B.L.; Nilson, K.; Chestnut, C.H. III: Bremner, W.J.; Shainholtz, S.; & Southworth, M.B. (1984). Bone mineral content of amenorrheic and eumenorrheic athletes. *New England Journal of Medicine* 311: 277-281.

Dryden, S. & Williams, G. (1997). Leptin as a neuromodulator of feeding and energy balance. *Current Opinion in Endocrinology and Metabolism* 4: 124-129.

Ellis, K.J. & Nicolson, M. (1997). Leptin levels and body fatness in children: Effects of gender, ethnicity, and sexual development. *Pediatric Research* 42: 484-488.

Finkelstein, J.S.; Neer, R.M.; Biller, B.M.K.; Crawford, J.D.; & Klibanski, A. (1992). Osteopenia in men with a history of delayed puberty. *New England Journal of Medicine* 326: 600-604.

Finkelstein, J.W. (1980). The endocrinology of adolescence. *Pediatric Clinics of North America* 27: 53-69.

Garcia-Mayor, R.V.; Andrade, M.A.; Rios, M.; Lage, M.; Dieguez, C.; & Casanueva, F.F. (1997). Serum leptin levels in normal children: Relationship to age, gender, body mass index, pituitary-gonadal hormones, and pubertal stage. *Journal of Clinical Endocrinology and Metabolism* 82: 2849-2855.

Gregory, J.W.; Greene, S.A.; Jung, R.T.; Scrimgeour, C.M.; & Rennie, M.J. (1993). Metabolic effects of growth hormone treatment: An early predictor of growth response. *Archives of Disease in Childhood* 68: 205-209.

Ho, K.Y.; Evans, W.S.; Blizzard, R.M.; Veldhuis, J.D.; Merriam, G.R.; Samojlik, E.; Furlanetto, R.; Rogol, A.D.; Kaiser, D.L.; & Thorner, M.O. (1987). Effects of age and sex on the 24-hour profile of growth hormone secretion in man: Importance of endogenous estradial concentrations. *Journal of Clinical Endocrinology and Metabolism* 64: 51-58.

Hui, S.L.; Slemenda, C.W.; & Johnston, C.C. (1990). The contribution of bone loss to postmenopausal osteoporosis. *Osteoporosis* 1: 30.

Johnston, F.E. (1992). Developmental aspects of fat patterning. In: Hernandez. M. & Argente, J. (Eds.), *Human Growth: Basic and Clinical Aspects*. BV, Elsevier Science Publishers (pp. 217-226).

Kelch, R.P. & Beitins, I.Z. (1994). Adolescent sexual development. In: Kappy, M.S,; Blizzard, R.M.; & Migeon, C.J. (Eds.), *The Diagnosis and Treatment of Endocrine Disorders in Childhood and Adolescence (4th Edition)*. Springfield, IL: Charles C. Thomas (pp. 193-234).

Klein, K.O.; Martha, P.M. Jr.; Blizzard, R.M.; Herbst, T.; & Rogol, A.D. (1996). A longitudinal assessment of hormonal and physical alterations during normal puberty in boys. II. Estrogen levels as determined by an ultrasensitive bioassay. *Journal of Clinical Endocrinology and Metabolism* 81: 3203-3207.

Lahlou, N.; Landais, P.; De Boissieu, D.; & Bourgneres, P.F (1997). Circulating leptin in normal children and during the dynamic phase of juvenile obesity: Relation to body fatness, energy metabolism, caloric intake, and sexual dimorphism. *Diabetes* 46: 989-993.

Lohman, T.G. (1992) *Advances in Body Composition Assessment*. Champaign, IL: Human Kinetics.

Lonnqvist, F. & Schaling, M. (1997). Role of leptin and its receptor in human obesity. *Current Opinion in Endocrinology and Metabolism* 4: 164-171.

Malina, R.M. & Bouchard, C. (1991). Models and methods for studying body composition. In: *Growth, Maturation, and Physical Activity*. Champaign, IL: Human Kinetics (pp. 87-100).

Mantzoros, C.S.; Flier, J.S.; & Rogol, A.D. (1997). A longitudinal assessment of hormonal and physical alterations during normal puberty in boys. V. Rising leptin levels may signal the onset of puberty. *Journal of Clinical Endocrinology and Metabolism* 82: 1066-1070.

Marshall, W.A. (1975). Growth and sexual maturity in normal puberty. *Clinical Endocrinology and Metabolism* 4: 3-25.

Marshall, W.A. & Tanner, J.M. (1969). Variations in patterns of pubertal changes in girls. *Archives of Disease in Childhood* 44: 291-303.

Marshall, W.A. & Tanner, J.M. (1970) Variations in patterns of pubertal changes in boys. *Archives of Disease in Childhood* 45: 13-23.

Martha, P.M. Jr.; Gorman, K.M.; Blizzard, R.M.; Rogol, A.D.; & Veldhuis, J.D. (1992). Endogenous growth hormone secretion and clearance rates in normal boys, as determined by deconvolution analysis. Relationship to age, pubertal status and body mass. *Journal of Clinical Endocrinology and Metabolism* 74: 336-344.

Martha, P.M. Jr.; Rogol, A.D.; Veldhuis, J.D.; Kerrigan, J.R.; Goodman, D.W.; & Blizzard, R.M. (1989). Alterations in the pulsatile properties of circulating growth hormone concentrations during puberty in boys. *Journal of Clinical Endocrinology and Metabolism* 69: 563-570.

Mauras, N.; Rogol, A.D.; Haymond, M.W.; & Veldhuis, J.D. (1996). Sex steroids, growth hormone, insulin-like growth factor-I: Neuroendocrine and metabolic regulation in puberty. *Hormone Research* 45: 74-80.

Mauras, P.M. Jr.; Rogol, A.D.; Veldhuis, J.D.; Kerrigan, J.R.; Goodman, D.W.; & Blizzard, R.M. (1989). Alterations in the pulsatile properties of circulating growth hormone concentrations during puberty in boys. *Journal of Clinical Endocrinology and Metabolism* 69: 563-570.

McCrory, M.A.; Gomez, T.D.; Bernauer, E.M.; & Mole, P.A. (1995). Evaluation of a new air displacement plethysmograph for measuring human body composition. *Medicine and Science in Sports and Exercise* 27: 1686-1691.

Mirlesse, V.; Frankenne, F.; Alsat, E.; Poncelet, M.; Hennen, G.; & Evain-Brion, D. (1993). Placental growth hormone levels in normal pregnancy and in pregnancies with IUGR. *Pediatric Research* 34: 439-442.

Montague, C.T.; Farrqi, I.S.; Whitehead, J.P.; Soos, M.A.; Wareham, N.J.; Sewter, C.P.; Digby, J.E.; Mohammed, S.N.; Hurst, L.A.; Cheetham, C.H.; Earley, A.R.; Prins, J.B.; & O'Rahilly, S. (1997). Congenital leptin deficiency is associated with severe early-onset obesity in humans. *Nature* 387: 903-908.

Nagy, T.R.; Gower, B.A.; Trowbridge, C.A.; Dezenberg, C.; Shewchuk, R.M.; & Goran, M.I. (1997). Effects of gender, ethnicity, body composition, and fat distribution on serum leptin concentrations in children. *Journal of Clinical Endocrinology and Metabolism* 82: 2148-2152.

Rallison, M.L. (1986). *Growth Disorders in Infants, Children, and Adolescents*. New York: John Wiley & Sons, Inc.

Ritzen, E.M. (1992). Pubertal growth in genetic disorders of sex hormone action and secretion. *Acta Paediatrica Supplement* 383: 22-25.

Roche, A.F. & Himes, J.H. (1980). Incremental growth charts. *American Journal of Clinical* Nutrition 33: 2042-2052.

Roemmich, J.N.; Clark, P.A.; Berr, S.S.; & Rogol, A.D. (1997a). Leptin and criterion estimates of body composition and body fat distribution. *Current Opinion in Endocrinology Metabolism*

Roemmich, J.N.; Clark, P.A.; Mai, V.; Berr, S.S.; Weltman, A.; Veldhuis, J.D.; & Rogol, A.D. (1998). Alterations in growth and body composition during puberty, III. Influence of maturation, gender, body composition, body fat distribution, aerobic fitness and total energy expenditure on nocturnal growth hormone release during puberty. *Journal of Clinical Endocrinology and Metabolism* 83: 1440-1447.

Roemmich, J.N.; Clark, P.A.; & Rogol, A.D. (1997b). Alterations in growth and body composition during puberty: I. Comparing multicompartment body composition models. *Journal of Applied Physiology* 83: 927-935.

Roemmich, J.N. & Rogol, A.D. (1995). Physiology of growth and development: Its relationship to performance in the young athlete. *Clinical Sports Medicine* 14: 483-502.

Roemmich, J.N. & Sinning, W.E. (1997a). Weight loss and wrestling training: Effects on nutrition, growth, maturation, body composition, and strength. *Journal of Applied Physiology* 82: 1751-1759.

Roemmich, J.N. & Sinning, W.E. (1997b). Weight loss and wrestling training: Effects on growth-related hormones. *Journal of Applied Physiology* 82: 1760-1764.

Rogol, A.D. (1995). Growth and development: Editorial overview. *Current Opinion in Endocrinology and Metabolism* 2: 79-82.

Rose, S.R.; Kibarian, M.; & Gelatto, M. (1989). Sex steroids increase spontaneous growth hormone secretion in short children. *Journal of Pediatric Endocrinology* 3: 1-5.

Rose, S.R.; Municchi, G.; Barnes, K.M.; Kamp, G.A.; Uriarte, M.M.; Ross, J.L.; Cassorla, F.; & Cutler, G.B., Jr. (1991). Spontaneous growth hormone secretion increases during puberty in normal girls and boys. *Journal of Clinical Endocrinology and Metabolism* 73: 428-435.

Selbe, A.D.; Nicolson, M.; & Ravussin, E. (1997). Total energy expenditure and the level of physical activity correlate with plasma leptin concentrations in five-year old children. *Journal of Clinical Investigations* 99: 592-595.

Sinclair, D. (1978). Human Growth after Birth. *Oxford University Press* (pp. 1-15, 140-259).

Siri, W.E. (1961). Body composition from fluid spaces and density: Analysis of methods. In: Brozek, J. & Henschel, A. (Eds.). *Techniques for Measuring Body Composition*. Washington, DC: National Academy of Science.

Slemenda, C.W.; Reister, T.K.; Hui, S.L.; Miller, J.Z.; Christian, J.C.; & Johnston, C.C. (1994). Influence on skeletal mineralization in children and adolescents: Evidence for varying effects of sexual maturation and physical activity. *Journal of Pediatrics* 125: 201-207.

Smith, E.P.; Boyd, J.; Frank, G.R.; Takahasi, H.; Cohen, R.M.; Specker, B.; Williams, T.C.; Lubahn, D.B.; & Korach, K.S. (1994). Estrogen resistance caused by a mutation in the estrogen-receptor gene in a man. *New England Journal of Medicine* 331: 1056-1061.

Smith, M.A.; Wilson, J.; & Price, W.H. (1982). Bone mineralization in patients with Turner's syndrome. *Journal of Medical Genetics* 19: 100-103.

Strobel, A.; Isaad, T.; Camoin, L.; Qzata, M.; & Strosberg, A.D. (1998). A leptin missense mutation associated with hypogonadism and morbid obesity. *Nature Genetics* 18: 213.

Tanner, J.M. (1965). Radiographic studies of body composition. In: J. Brozek (Ed.) Body Composition. *Symposia of the Society for the Study of Human Biology* 6: 211-236.

Tanner, J.M. (1989). *Fetus Into Man: Physical Growth From Conception to Maturity*. Cambridge, MA: Harvard University Press.

Tanner, J.M.; Healy, M.J.R.; Lockhart, R.D.; et al. (1956). Aberdeen growth study: I. The prediction of adult body measurement from measurements taken each year from birth to five years. *Archives of Disease in Childhood* 31: 372-381.

Tanner, J.M.; Whitehouse, R.H.; Marshall, W.A.; & Carter, B.S. (1975). Prediction of adult height, bone age, and occurrence of menarche, ages 4 to 16 with allowance for midparental height. *Archives of Disease in Childhood* 50: 14-26.

Vahl, N.; Jorgensen, J.O.L.; Jurik, A.G.; & Christiansen, J.S. (1996). Abdominal adiposity and physical fitness are major determinants of the age associated decline in stimulated GH secretion in healthy adults. *Journal of Clinical Endocrinology and Metabolism* 81: 2209-2215.

Vaisman, N.; Zadik, Z.; Akivias, A.; Voet, H.; Katz, I.; & Yair Ashkenazi, A. (1994). Changes in body composition, resting energy expenditure, and thermic effect of food in short children on growth hormone therapy. *Metabolism* 43: 1543-1548.

Van Loan, M.D. (1996). Total body composition: Birth to old age. In: Roche, A.F.; Heymsfield, S.B.; & Lohman, T.G. (Eds.), *Human Body Composition*. Champaign, IL: Human Kinetics (pp. 205-215).

Veldhuis, J.D.; Metzger, D.L.; Martha, P.M. Jr.; Mauras, N.; Kerrigan, J.R.; Kennan, B.; Rogol, A.D.; & Pincus, S.M. (1997). Estrogen and testosterone, but not a nonaromatizable androgen, direct network integration of the hypothalamosomatotrope (growth hormone) insulin-like growth factor I axis in the human: Evidence from pubertal pathophysiology and sex-steroid hormone replacement. *Journal of Clinical Endocrinology and Metabolism* 82: 3414-3420.

Wabitsch, M.; Blum, W.F.; Muche, R.; Braun, M.; Hube, F.; Rascher, W.; Heinze, E.; Teller, W.; & Hauner, H. (1997). Contribution of androgens to the gender differences in leptin production in obese children and adolescents. *Journal of Clinical Investigations* 100: 808-813.

Westphal, O. (1995). Normal growth and growth disorders in children. *Acta Odontologica Scandinavica* 53: 174-178.

World Health Organization. (1983) *Measuring change in nutritional status*. Geneva: World Health Organization.

Zacharias, L.; Wurtman, R.J.; & Schatzoff, M. (1970). Sexual maturation in contemporary American girls. *American Journal of Obstetrics and Gynecology* 108: 833-846.

Zachmann, M.; Prader, A.; Sobel, E.H.; Crigler, J.F. Jr.; Ritzen, E.M.; Atares, M.; & Fernandez, A. (1986). Pubertal growth in patients with androgen insensitivity: Indirect evidence for the importance of estrogens in pubertal growth of girls. *Journal of Pediatrics* 108: 694-697.

CHAPTER 4

Cardiac Characteristics of the Child Endurance Athlete

Thomas W. Rowland, M.D.
Baystate Medical Center

The functional capacity of the heart has long been recognized as a critical determinant of aerobic fitness. According to the traditional paradigm, performance by an endurance athlete in events such as distance running, cycling, or swimming is strongly related to the peak ability of his or her exercising muscle to utilize oxygen, measured as maximal aerobic power (VO_2max). VO_2max, in turn, is primarily defined by the limits of oxygen transport—the maximal capacity of the heart to generate cardiac output.

Consistent with this concept, elite-level adult endurance athletes demonstrate values for VO_2max which are usually 60% greater than those of sedentary individuals. Correspondingly, maximal cardiac output in a typical trained adult male cyclist is approximately 35 L min^{-1} compared that of about 25 L min^{-1} in a nonathlete (Gledhill et al., 1994). Understanding the factors which are responsible for this superior level of cardiac function should provide insight into the physiological mechanisms that separate endurance athletes from nonathletes. Such information might prove useful in defining training regimens that would most effectively alter the determinants of cardiac functional capacity and consequently optimize endurance performance.

Interest in the cardiac features of child athletes has been triggered by the increasing participation of young competitors in elite-level intensive endurance training regimens. Several issues are particularly pertinent to this age group:

- Evidence from studies of both animals and adult ultramarathoners indicates that high levels of prolonged exercise can transiently depress cardiac function (Maher et al., 1972; Niemela et al., 1984). Can the potential recurrent cardiac stresses of intensive endurance training interfere with normal development of the growing heart?

- Previous reports in nonathletic children indicate that the magnitude of improvement in VO_2max with endurance training is less than that observed in adults (Rowland, 1985). Are there maturational changes in cardiac responses to repetitive exercise that would indicate a need to modify training regimens for child endurance athletes?

- Can the physiological features of the competitive child athlete be interpreted as a model for the effects of endurance training on immature individuals? Whether these characteristics reflect the effects of training or genetic endowment cannot be easily differentiated. However, it should be expected that physiological features of child endurance athletes must *include* the influence of training. Physiological characteristics of these young competitors might, therefore, provide insight into maturational influences on responses to endurance training.

- The superior cardiac capacity of the adult endurance athlete is associated with a set of clinical features termed the "athlete's heart" (ventricular enlargement, bradycardia, electrocardiographic changes). Recognizing the "athlete's heart" as a physiologic manifestation of extensive endurance training is important, since these features may mimic those of individuals with heart disease. Should child endurance athletes also be expected to demonstrate these characteristics?

With the use of safe, noninvasive means of measuring cardiac responses to exercise, information in young athletes is becoming increasingly available. This review examines the current body of information regarding the cardiac responses to exercise in trained child endurance athletes as well as the prevalence of clinical findings of the "athlete's heart" in this age group. Specific attention is focused on comparisons of these findings with those observed in nonathletic children and the identification of qualitative and/or quantitative differences which might exist between child and adult endurance athletes. The discussion focuses on young athletes in the prepubertal or early pubertal age groups and addresses only those involved in endurance sports. Presently, most of this information describes male athletes, and possible gender differences in cardiac features of child endurance athletes has not been systematically examined.

CARDIAC RESPONSES TO ACUTE EXERCISE

An exploration into the cardiac responses to a bout of progressive exercise in child athletes can begin with their well-documented high levels of maximal aerobic power. VO_2max in young male distance runners and cyclists is typically 60-65 ml kg^{-1} min^{-1}, compared to an average value of approximately 52 ml kg^{-1} min^{-1} on treadmill testing in the pediatric age group (Rowland, 1996). Improvements in VO_2max in the general pediatric population with short term (3-month) periods of aerobic training are typically small (5-10%). The 20% greater maximal aerobic power in the child endurance athlete might, therefore, be presumed to reflect 1) a genetic pre-selective influence on the determinants of VO_2max (such as an inherently larger heart size), and/or 2) a magnified physiological response to aerobic training.

While their levels of VO_2max are high, aerobic fitness in child endurance athletes does not match that of adult distance runners, rowers, and cyclists, whose VO_2max values typically reach 70-80 ml kg^{-1} min^{-1} (Faria et al., 1989). Several explanations have been offered for the lower VO_2max in child compared to adult athletes:

- Most child endurance athletes have been involved in intensive training programs for no more than 3-5 years. A long duration of high-level endurance training may be necessary to achieve the levels of maximal aerobic power observed in adult athletes. This argument is weakened by the observation that the magnitude of change in aerobic fitness is inversely related to pre-training fitness level, and VO_2max typically is not observed to change appreciably with training in either child or adult endurance athletes.

- A biological "ceiling" exists for VO_2max which cannot be exceded prior to puberty. This explanation implies that the mechanisms for generating a high VO_2max are influenced by maturation and do not become "turned on" until the hormonal influences of puberty.

- Reports of the very high levels of VO_2max in elite adult endurance athletes describe only those selected individuals with exceptional genetic endowment and extensive training, while those with lesser talents and lower aerobic fitness are not included (i.e., have already been excluded by the selective demands of endurance sports). Studies of groups of child athletes have not undergone this "filtering" process. This possibility is suggested by observations of individual child endurance athletes with VO_2 max values comparable to those seen in adults (Rowland et al., 1999).

What physiological factors are responsible for the higher VO_2max in child endurance athletes compared to nonathletes? Does the same explanation account for the differences in maximal aerobic power between child and adult athletes? The answers to these questions must lie within the Fick equation, which dictates that VO_2max is the product of maximal heart rate, stroke volume, and peripheral oxygen extraction (the arterial venous oxygen difference). The available data indicate that maximal stroke volume is the sole physiological factor responsible for VO_2max differences between athletic and nonathletic children, who do not differ in maximal heart rate and arterial venous oxygen difference. Adult male endurance athletes have a greater arterial venous oxygen (AV O_2) difference than child athletes, and this, plus a greater maximal

stroke volume, accounts for the higher values of VO_2max in adults.

Maximal Heart Rate

In adult endurance athletes, no significant differences have been observed in maximal heart rate during progressive exercise testing compared to nonathletes. Typically, however, the average maximal heart rate for the athletes is 3-5 beats lower than that of the nonathletes (Rowell, 1986). Maximal heart rate, then, does not contribute to the 60% greater VO_2max values usually observed in the adult endurance athlete.

A similar picture is seen in comparisons of child athletes and nonathletes (Table 1). Most studies have indicated that the average maximal rate in young endurance athletes is 2-3 beats lower than nonathletes, but the difference is not statistically significant. Because maximal heart rate in individuals over 16 years old declines with age, the maximal rate of the trained adult endurance athlete is expected to be lower than that of the child athlete.

Study	Sport	Athletes	Nonathletes
Resting			
Sundberg and Elovainio (1982)	Runners	96(9)	83(14)
Rowland et al. (1987)	Swimmers	65(7)	74(8)
Rowland et al. (1994)	Runners	71(6)	73(8)
Obert et al. (1998)	Swimmers	69(7)	83(13)
Rowland et al. (1998)	Runners	67(10)	90(14)
Rowland et al. (2000)	Cyclists	71(12)	85(15)
Maximal			
Mayers and Gutin (1979)	Runners	203(5)	205(5)
Van Huss et al. (1988)	Runners	197	201
Vaccaro and Clark (1978)	Swimmers	197(11)	199(5)
Rowland et al. (1998)	Runners	190(13)	192(10)

Table 1. Heart rates in child endurance athletes versus nonathletes. Values are means (bpm) and standard deviations in parentheses.

These observations indicate that maximal heart rate is not responsible for either the higher VO_2 max in child athletes compared to nonathletes, or for the differences in maximal aerobic power between child and adult endurance athletes. Moreover, it is clear that physiologic responses to endurance training do not influence the mechanisms responsible for defining the limits of the sinus node response to exercise.

Maximal Arterial Venous Oxygen Difference

The increased oxygen demands of contracting muscle cells can be satisfied either by increasing the flow of oxygen supply (improved cardiac output), or by extracting more oxygen from a given unit of blood, thereby increasing the difference between arterial and venous oxygen content (AV O_2 difference). AV O_2 difference is thus measured as a rate, ml of oxygen extracted per 100 ml of blood flow passing the cell. Maximal values appear to be defined principally by the arterial oxygen content, and arterial O_2 content, in turn, is determined mainly by the blood hemoglobin concentration.

Both adult male athletes and nonathletes demonstrate a significantly higher maximal AV O_2 difference than their respective female counterparts, since the blood hemoglobin concentration of the adult male is typically 15% greater than that of the adult female (Hossack and Bruce, 1982). However, little or no differences in maximal AV O_2 difference have been observed between adult endurance athletes and nonathletes of the same gender when hemoglobin concentrations are similar (Gledhill et al., 1994; Rowell, 1986).

Limited data have indicated that values for the maximal AV O_2 difference in child endurance athletes and nonathletes are similar, but less than in adult athletes. Rowland et al. (1999) reported that highly-trained 10-12 year old child cyclists and nonathletes had average calculated maximal AV O_2 differences of 13.1±0.8 and 13.0±2.5 ml 100 ml^{-1}, respectively. A mean AV O_2 difference of 13.1±1.0 ml 100 ml^{-1} was also described in the same laboratory in a study of child distance runners (during cycle testing) (Rowland et al., 1998), while adult untrained men had an average value of 17.2±4.5 ml 100 ml^{-1} (Rowland et al., 1997) (Figure 1).

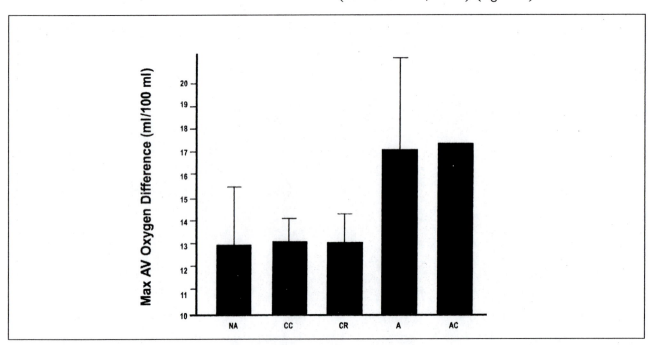

Figure 1. Maximal arteriovenous oxygen difference in different groups. Data from Rowland et al. (1998) and Rowland et al. (2000). NA = nonathletic male children CC = male child cyclists CR = male child runners A = nonathletic adult men AC = adult male cyclists (n=2).

Maximal AV O_2 difference does not, therefore, appear contribute to variations in VO_2 max between trained child endurance athletes and nonathletes. Peripheral oxygen extraction is greater in adult male compared to male child athletes, however, presumably because of the greater blood hemoglobin concentration in the former. The adult male has a 2 gm dl^{-1} greater hemoglobin concentration than a prepubertal boy. The subsequent 30% greater values for AV O_2difference in male adult compared to child endurance athletes partially explains the higher VO_2max values in mature athletes.

These data also indicate that the limits of the AV O_2 difference is not influenced by aerobic training in children, which is consistent with the observation of Eriksson (1972) that no changes in maximal AV O_2 difference were seen after a 16-week aerobic training program in a group of 11-13 year old boys. This implies that the AV O_2 difference is determined principally by blood hemoglobin concentration, and that the minimum content of oxygen in skeletal muscle venous effluent is independent of training status or aerobic fitness.

Maximal Stroke Volume

Differences in the maximal ability of the heart to generate stroke volume explains the greater VO_2 max in child athletes compared to nonathletes and, to a large extent, the variations in maximal aerobic power observed between child and adult athletes. Rowland et al. (2000) found that the average maximal stroke index was 76±6 ml m^2 in a group of 8 child cyclists compared to 60±11 ml m^2 in nonathletes (Figure 2). Respective values for VO_2max for the two groups were 60±6.0 and 47.0±5.8 ml kg^{-1} min^{-1}, and for the maximal cardiac index were 13.94±1.37 and 11.95±2.28 L min^{-1} m^2. Child distance runners had a mean maximal stroke index of 68±8 ml m^2 compared to 58±10 ml m^2 in nonathletes, and values for the maximal cardiac index were 13.09±1.54 and 11.05±2.11 L min^{-1} m^2, respectively (Rowland et al., 1998).

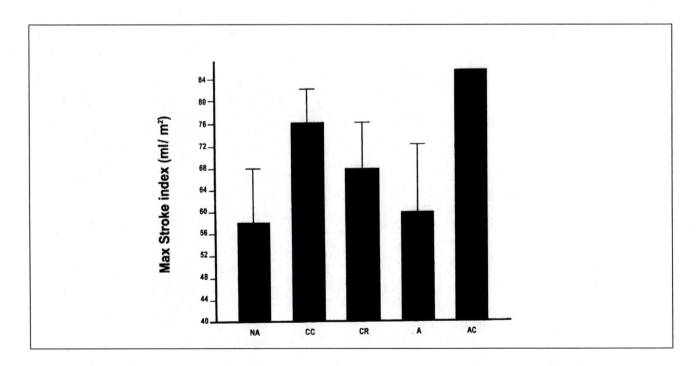

Figure 2. Maximal stroke index in different groups. Data sources and abbreviations as indicated in Figure 1.

The high stroke index at maximal exercise in these child athletes is less than those observed in elite adult endurance athletes, in whom values in the range of 85 to 100 ml m^{-2} have been described (Ekblom and Hermansen, 1968). Adult endurance athletes demonstrate a maximal stroke index which is typically 40-50% greater than nonathletes. The greater VO$_2$ max in adult endurance athletes compared to child athletes can, therefore, be explained physiologically by their approximately 30% greater stroke index and 30% higher AV O$_2$ difference.

Changes in stroke volume with exercise, and ultimately the maximal stroke volume, result from an extremely complex interplay of factors which influence ventricular preload (diastolic filling), heart rate, intrinisic myocardial contractility, and afterload (peripheral vascular resistance). Understanding the intricacies of the stroke volume response to exercise is confounded by the fact that each of these factors is composed of multiple determinants, many of which are inter-related, and which change dramatically in the course of a progressive exercise test. Not surprisingly, then, the variables and mechanisms responsible for the differences in maximal stroke volume between athletic and nonathletic individuals are not well understood. It is evident, though, that insights into this question are likely to pay important dividends in understanding the physiological uniqueness of the endurance athlete.

Some investigators have suggested that an analysis of the *pattern* of stroke volume response to progressive exercise may provide clues to factors influencing maximal values in athletes. In order to discuss this, a brief overview of the normal cardiovascular responses to an incremental cycle test is useful (Rowland et al., 2000a).

As upright exercise begins in a progressive test, stroke volume rises, reaching values about 40% greater than resting levels with mild-moderate exercise intensities. The initial rise in stroke volume is associated with increases in systemic venous return, the left ventricular end-diastolic dimension, and the left ventricular shortening fraction, along with a dramatic fall in peripheral vascular resistance. The most likely explanation for these changes observed at the onset of upright exercise is an initiation of skeletal muscle pump function (increasing ventricular preload) with an associated fall in ventricular after-load resulting from peripheral vasodilatation.

With increasing workloads beyond the early exercise stages, the stroke volume remains essentially unchanged, even to levels of exhaustion. During this time, systemic venous return continues to rise, heart rate increases, the left ventricular end-diastolic dimension remains essentially stable, and the end-systolic dimension declines, with resulting increase in the left ventricular shortening fraction. This scenario is presumably a reflection of a rise in heart rate to match the volume of systemic venous return, maintaining a stable ventricular preload (end-diastolic size). As exercise work increases, there is evidence of increased contractility (from adrenergic stimulation as well as continuing fall in afterload) while stroke volume remains unchanged. This can best be explained by the need of the ventricle to express the same stroke volume in a shorter ejection period as heart rate increases.

Somewhere in this complex scenario are factors which differentiate stroke volume responses in the highly trained endurance athlete from those of the nonathlete. The data reviewed above also suggest that the magnitude of such differences is less in children than in adults.

In general, two different patterns of stroke volume response to progressive exercise have been described in adult endurance athletes. In the first, the value for resting stroke volume is greater than that of the nonathlete, and the response is exactly the same, but with higher values in the athlete (Rubal et al., 1986). That is, the stroke volume curve of the adult endurance athlete rises early, then plateaus, always paralleling that of the nonathlete. This type of response would suggest that variables influencing resting stroke volume, particularly those affecting diastolic filling, are important in distinguishing the cardiac responses of endurance athletes from those of nonathletes. By this interpretation, factors such as plasma volume, resting heart rate (autonomic tone), and inherent left ventricular size are important in defining resting and maximal stoke volume, maximal cardiac output, and VO$_2$ max, and ultimately contributing to endurance performance.

Alternatively, some reports have indicated that the cardiac response to exercise by the trained adult endurance athlete is characterized by a failure of stroke volume to plateau at high exercise intensities, rising progressively to exhaustion (Gledhill et al., 1994). This pattern suggests that factors operating *during* exercise are critical in defining the high levels of stroke volume in athletes. Potential determinants include effectiveness of the skeletal muscle pump, better diastolic ventricular filling properties, larger fall in peripheral resistance, and augmented intrinsic contractility.

The two studies describing the stroke volume responses to exercise using Doppler echocardiography in child athletes have demonstrated both of these patterns. The 7 cyclists described by Rowland et al. (1999) demonstrated an identical rise and plateau pattern as nonathletic controls, with the curve displaced upwards (Figure 3). No difference was seen in the ratio of maximal to resting stroke volume in the two groups. The mean left ventricular end-diastolic dimension supine at rest was greater in the cyclists (3.81±.16 and 3.64±31 BSA$^{-0.5}$ for the athletes and nonathletes, respectively), although the difference was not statistically significant.

In a group of child runners, however, no significant difference was observed in resting upright stroke volume between athletes and nonathletes (Rowland et al., 1998) (Figure 4). With increasing work load, the runners demonstrated a progressive rise in stroke volume, while values in the nonathletes reached a typical plateau. The ratio of maximal to resting stroke volume was 1.57±.29 in the runners and 1.35±.23 in the nonathletes (p<.05).

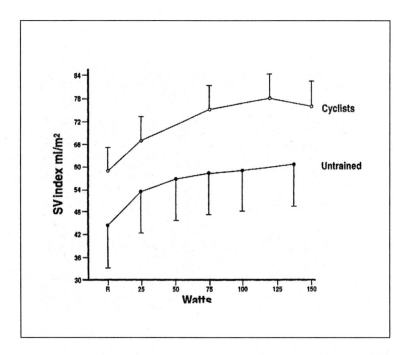

Figure 3. Stroke index response to progressive exercise in child cyclists and nonathletes. Reprinted with permission from Medicine and Science in Sports and Exercise.

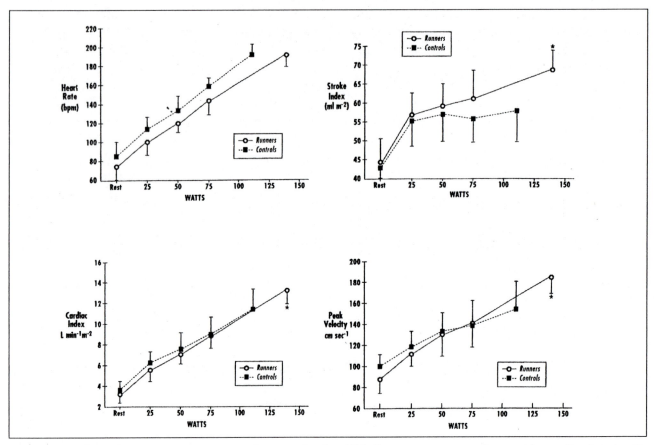

Figure 4. Stroke index response to progressive exercise in child distance runners and nonathletes. Reprinted with permission from the International Journal of Sports Medicine.

In summary, maximal stroke volume is the sole physiological factor responsible for the greater VO$_2$max in child endurance athletes compared to nonathletes. Adult endurance athletes demonstrate a higher VO$_2$max than child athletes, which may be due to biological, selection, and/or training factors. Both a higher maximal stroke volume and greater AV O$_2$ difference contribute to these differences. Understanding the mechanisms responsible for the differences in maximal stroke volume in athletes and nonathletes would provide valuable insights into the nature of endruance fitness. However, the current understanding of these factors is clouded.

CARDIAC FEATURES WITH ENDURANCE TRAINING: THE "ATHLETE'S HEART"

The highly-trained adult endurance athlete demonstrates a set of predictable clinical findings known collectively as the "athlete's heart" (George et al., 1991; Maron, 1986; Rost and Hollman, 1983). These features were recognized as early as 1899, when Henschen concluded, using only percussion of the chest, that "skiing [training] causes an enlargement of the heart and this enlarged heart can perform more work than the normal one. There is therefore a physiological enlargement of the heart due to athletic activity: the athlete's heart" (Rost, 1990, p. 340). While the findings of the "athlete's heart" were recognized as associated with (and perhaps required for) superior endurance performance, many of these features also mimicked those of heart disease. Earlier concern that these characteristics of the trained athlete might be pathological have now been essentially dispelled. It remains important, however, that clinicians be capable of separating findings which represent physiological adaptions in such athletes from indicators of heart disease.

The essential features of the "athlete's heart" are cardiac enlargement, ventricular hypertrophy, sinus bradycardia, and electrocardiographic changes (such as left ventricular hypertrophy, atrioventricular block, and ST-T wave changes). There is evidence in adult athletes to suggest that the nature of athletic training—specifically, endurance versus resistance training—dictates the type of cardiac morphologic features observed (Morganroth, 1975).

Cardiac enlargement. Adult competitors in events such as distance running, swimming, and cycling typically demonstrate a greater left ventricular end diastolic volume compared to non-athletes. This enlargement is accompanied by a mild degree of adaptive wall hypertrophy as a means of minimizing wall tension according to LaPlace's law, termed *eccentric hypertrophy*. The degree of ventricular enlargement is typically not marked, usually falling just above the upper limits of the range of values seen in the nonathletic population. The range is about 40-52 mm, while values for elite male endurance athletes typically average 54-56 mm (Fagard, 1997). Occasionally, such highly-trained athletes can demonstrate a left ventricular size similar to those observed in patients with myocardial dysfunction (>60 mm).

Some findings indicate that athletes involved in resistance sports (power lifting, wrestling) have a disproportionately greater degree of ventricular hypertrophy than chamber enlargement (*concentric hypertrophy*). Competitors in sports which involve both endurance and resistance exercise (soccer, tennis, hockey) may show both ventricular dilatation and hypertrophy.

Sinus bradycardia. A resting heart rate <60 bpm is common in trained endurance athletes, and rates between 35 and 50 bpm are not unusual. The average resting heart rate of an adult endurance athlete is about 11 bpm slower than that of the nonathletic individual (Perrault and Turcotte, 1993). Such findings are consistent with the observed effect of endurance training in lowering resting heart rate in nonathletic individuals.

The mechanism for resting bradycardia in trained adult endurance athletes is unclear. A shift in autonomic tone—an increase in parasympathetic and decline in sympathetic activity—is an intuitively-attractive hypothesis, but autonomic blocking studies and investigations of heart rate variability have not always supported this concept. Others have suggested that sinus bradycardia might reflect changes in intrinisic sinus node function, an increased sensitivity of vagal receptors, or a response to augmented resting stroke volume.

Electrocardiographic changes. Sinus bradycardia and voltage criteria for left ventricular hypertrophy are the most common electrocardiographic features of the "athlete's heart." A variety of other findings have been described, including sinus arrhythmia, various forms of AV block, wandering atrial pacemaker, incomplete right bundle branch block, ST segment changes, and T wave inversion.

Murmurs and extra heart sounds. The large stroke volume in the resting endurance athlete has been associated with a high frequency of innocent flow murmurs. Third and fourth heart sounds (S3 and S4, respectively) are also commonly reported in athletes. For instance, Roeske et al. (1976) described an S3 in 96% of a sample of professional basketball players; 56% had an S4.

Mechanisms for the "Athlete's Heart"

The "athlete's heart" has been interpreted as representing 1) a genetic endowment of cardiac features which permits athletic excellence, 2) an expression of physiologic adaptations to long term repetitive bouts of intense exercise (i.e., athletic training), or c) both.

Studies examining the heritability of cardiac features have failed to reveal an impressive genetic influence on ventricular size. An early twin study suggested that the heritability of heart volume (assessed radiographically) was 25-30% (Klissouras, 1973). A significant parent-child association (r=0.23) was observed by Diano et al. (1980) for the left ventricular diastolic dimension. However, Bielen et al. (1991) found no evidence of a genetic contribution to the left ventricular end diastolic dimension in an echocardiographic study of monozygotic (MZ) and dizygotic (DZ) 6- to 8-year old twins. Fagard et al. (1987) reported the same finding in 18-31 year old twin pairs and concluded that "cardiac hypertrophy in athletes is secondary to training."

Evidence does suggest that genetic factors may be influential in determining the magnitude of cardiac responses to exercise. When Bielen et al. (1991) submitted pairs of MZ and DZ twins to submaximal exercise (heart rate 110 bpm), the genetic effect on the increase in left ventricular (LV) internal diameter was 24%. Landry, Bouchard, and Dumesil (1985) suggested a genetic influence on variability of the response of left ventricular size to a 20-week endurance training program in 10 pairs of sedentary MZ twins.

The relative roles of inheritance and training on the "athlete's heart" have been assessed by examining changes in LV size during periods of training and de-training. An analysis of 9 such studies indicated that the mean left ventricular end-diastolic dimension was 1.1 mm greater in the trained versus untrained condition (Fagard, 1997). Galanti et al., (1987) reported a decrease in the LV diastolic dimension (indexed to body size) from 28.1 mm to 26.6 mm in elite soccer players forced to rest 4-6 weeks with injury. The inactive dimension was still significantly greater than that of nonathletic control subjects (mean 25.3 mm).

Ehsani et al., (1978) described echocardio-graphic changes in 6 highly-trained members of a college cross-country team who volunteered to stop training for 3 weeks. Following cessation of training, the mean LV end diastolic dimension fell from 51.0 (3.0) mm to 46.3 (2.3) mm, while VO$_2$max declined from 62.3 to 56.7 ml kg^{-1} min^{-1}. Others, however, have failed to find evidence of regression of cardiac enlargement with cessation of training (Dart et al., 1992; Maron et al., 1993).

If the "athlete's heart" reflects a a response to training, physiological *triggers* during acute exercise (increased heart rate, augmented myocardial contractility, and perhaps ventricular stretch) should be expected to account for chronic *outcomes* (left ventricular enlargement, eccentric hypertrophy, and autonomic changes). The nature of this interplay between the training stimulus and long-term cardiac features at anatomic, cellular, and biochemical levels, however, remains obscure.

In the search for such mechanisms. many investigators have drawn parallels with cardiac enlargement observed in pathological conditions. The increased left ventricular dimension of the trained endurance athlete has been viewed as a response to recurrent volume overload of exercise training in the same way that patients with aortic or mitral valve insufficiency exhibit LV dilatation from volume overwork (Colan, 1997). In this condition, cardiac myocytes demonstrate longitudinal growth, a phenomenon well-documented with exercise training in animals, and this growth results in ventricular chamber enlargement (Moore and Palmer, 1999).

The trigger for such myocyte growth, however, is not altogether clear. The model of training-induced ventricular stretch from volume overload is tempered by the observation that little change is observed in left ventricular dimension during bouts of acute exercise. In addition, the responses to training are not accompanied by evidence of functional impairment seen in the disease state. Such evidence challenges the traditional concept that the "athlete's heart" is simply a reflection of repetitive hemodynamic volume overload, analagous to that of heart disease.

Other triggers during acute exercise may be responsible for features of the "athlete's heart." Several mechanisms have been postulated whereby the mechanical stress of increased contractility might stimulate adaptive cardiac changes. Such stress may stimulate upregulation of fetal genes reponsible for shifts in myosin isoforms as well as increases in angiotensin II, atrial naturetic factor, and brain natriuretic peptide (Baar et al., 1997; Moore and Palmer, 1997). These hormones play a role in regulation of blood volume, a key element in increasing left ventricular preload.

Acute exercise causes a rise in serum catecholamines, glucocorticoids, thyroxine, testosterone, and growth hormone, all endocrinologic influences with recognized effects of increasing cardiac size (George et al.,1991). Exercise training may serve to induce repeated "doses" of these anabolic agents to stimulate increases in ventricular size and perhaps function. Training may also enhance myocardial sensitivity to catecholamines and beta-adrenergic stimulation.

Besides a direct effect on growth of cardiac myocytes, endurance training might cause ventricular enlargement as a response to well-documented increases in plasma volume or by directly altering autonomic tone (Perrault and Turcotte, 1993). Endurance training is accompanied by a rise in plasma volume, and volumes of adult endurance athletes are typically 20-25% greater than those of nonathletes. As noted above, hormonal responses to repeated bouts of acute exercise could be responsible for modulating such changes.

Perrault and Turcotte (1993) suggested that the sinus bradycardia of the endurance athlete might contribute to increases in left ventricular dimensions. Using the data of DeMaria et al. (1979), they estimated that the difference is resting heart rate between adult athletes and nonathletes accounts for a difference of 1.4 mm in mean values for the left ventricular end diastolic dimension. However, the trigger by which endurance training might cause a reduction in sinus node firing rate (either by autonomic or primary mechanisms) is not clear.

Do Child Endurance Athletes Have the "Athlete's Heart"?

In light of the preceding discussion, an examination of the "athlete's heart" in child athletes not only has clinical pertinence but also may provide insights into underlying mechanisms. For example, the physiological triggers and hormonal responses to acute exercise may differ between prepubertal and adult athletes. Adrenergic responses may be less than in the child athlete (Lehmann et al.,1981; Rowland et al., 1996). The influence of elevated testosterone for inducing muscular hypertrophy is lacking in the prepubertal athlete, and the growth hormone response to intense exercise may be one-third that of the older adolescent (Marin et al, 1994).

In addition, insights into the relative contributions of heredity and training to findings of the "athlete's heart" may be gained by evaluating young athletes who are in the early stages of their sports involvement. Less evidence of the athlete's heart should be expected in child versus adult endurance athletes if training intensity and duration are important determinants.

Clinicians need to know if findings such as bradycardia, cardiac enlargement, and left ventricular hypertrophy on the electrocardiogram are to be expected in trained prepubertal athletes. If not, child athletes exhibiting these findings should be more suspect of having cardiac disease.

Studies of the "athlete's heart" in child endurance athletes have largely involved swimmers and distance runners, with a single study in cyclists. The findings indicate that some but not all of the features observed in adults are seen in child athletes. Certain sport-specific findings are intriguing and await explanation.

Sinus bradycardia. With one exception, all studies evaluating resting heart rate in child endurance athletes have found a significantly lower rate than untrained subjects (Table 1). Among these studies (which included swimmers, runners, and cyclists), the average difference was 15 bpm, similar to that found in comparisons of adult athletes and nonathletes. Among the reports, four included echocardiographic measurements of left ventricular dimensions. In three, the athletes had significantly larger end diastolic size than nonathletes, and in each of these reports the resting heart rate of the athletes was also lower. The one study in which no differences were observed in ventricular size also showed no difference in resting heart rates in child athletes and nonathletes. These limited observations thus suggest a relationship between resting heart rate and left ventricular diastolic dimensions.

Study	N	Age (yrs)	Sex	Sport	LVED(mm)	Controls(mm)
Obert et al. (1998)	9	10-11	M,F	Swimming	41.6*	39.0 (BSA.[33])
Rowland et al. (1987)	11	8-13	M	Swimming	39.5*	36.2 (BSA.[33])
Ozer et al. (1994)	82	7-14	M,F	Swimming	46.2*	40.4[a]
Lengyel and Gyarfas (1979)	9	14	M,F	Swimming	30.3*	27.9 (BSA)
Medved et al. (1986)	72	8-14	M	Swimming	45.2*	40.5[b]
Gutin et al. (1988)	8	8-11	M	Running	34.3	34.3 (BSA)
Shepherd et al. (1988)	13	5-12	M	Running	41.0	41.0[b]
Rowland et al. (1994)	10	11-13	M	Running	33.2	33.5 (BSA)
Telford et al. (1988)	48	11-12	M	Running	46.6	45.9[c]
	37	11-12	F	Running	45.7	45.9[c]
Nudel et al. (1989)	5	8-13	M,F	Running	44.4	40.1[d]
Rowland et al.(2000b)	7	10-13	M	Cycling	38.1	3.64 (BSA$^{0.5}$)

* = p<.05.   a = matched for weight.   b = matched for body surface area (BSA).
c = matched for lean body mass.   d = matched for body height.

Table 2. Echocardiographic measurement of mean left ventricular diastolic dimension in child endurance athletes. The far right column indicates body surface area (BSA) as the denominator used to normalize for body size.

Electrocardiographic changes: All studies which have analyzed resting electrocardiograms in child athletes have found no differences compared to nonathletes (with the exception of lower heart rates) (Nudel et al., 1989; Rowland et al., 1987, 1994, 1998). Specifically, there has been no evidence of ventricular hypertrophy, conduction delay, or dysrhythmias in the electrocrdiograms of young athletes, although most were studies in which no echocardiographic evidence of left ventricular enlargement compared to nonathletes was observed.

Left ventricular enlargement: Echocardiographic studies of left ventricular dimensions in child endurance athletes and nonathletes are listed in Table 2. While values for the left ventricular end diastolic dimension have been normalized to different indices, it is apparent that among the five studies involving swimmers, all indicated a significantly greater LV diastolic size in athletes compared to nonathletes. The average difference was 10.1±2.7%, comparable to research findings in adult endurance athletes, who demonstrate an increase in the diastolic dimension of approximately 10% compared to matched sedentary controls (Maron, 1986). On the other hand, among five studies of child endurance runners, only one (that of child marathon runners) showed an appreciably greater LV diastolic dimension compared to nonrunners.

Not included in Table 2 is the combined cross-sectional and longitudinal echocardiographic study of competitive child swimmers ages 8-11 years by Rost and Hollman (1993). Left ventricular diastolic diameters were greater in the swimmers compared to controls, and training exaggerated the differences.

No differences have been observed in resting systolic or diastolic function in child endurance athletes and nonathletes (Obert et al., 1998; Ozer et al., 1194). In the only study directly comparing males and females, Telford et al. (1988) found no gender differences in end diastolic dimension when subjects were matched for fat-free mass and skeletal age. (Both male and female runners in this study demonstrated no significant difference in left ventricular size compared to nonrunners.)

It may be concluded from the available data that 1) some but not all features of the "athlete's heart" are observed in child endurance athletes, 2) the mechanism for left ventricular enlargement may be more operant in child swimmers than child runners, and 3) the magnitude of left ventricular enlargement in child swimmers is similar to that seen in adults. Within these findings lie implications regarding maturational differences and similarities in the hormonal, autonomic, blood volume, and peripheral responses to endurance training, the understanding of which presents a challenge for future investigators.

One particularly intriguing observation is the apparent sport-specific increase in left ventricular dimensions in child swimmers in contrast to distance runners. This might reflect differences in the hemodynamics of these two sports. Swimming, for instance, is performed in the horizontal position with less gravitational demands on peripheral mechanisms for systemic venous return. This is not an adequate explanation, however, for similar swim-run training differences observed in rats. In reviewing studies of cardiac adaptation in rats to chronic exercise, Harpur (1980) concluded that "swimming programs are more successful [than running] for demonstrating an increase in heart weight, and the length of daily swim is important." Evidence also exists in adult humans to suggest that left ventricular cavity dimensions are larger in elite swimmers compared to distance runners (Morganroth et al., 1975; Pellicia, 1996).

Research Directions

This review of the cardiac characteristics of child endurance athlete reveals that initial insights are being achieved in understanding the cardiac contributions to aerobic fitness in this group. It is clear, however, that a great deal more needs to be learned:

- While previous research has focused primarily on cardiac systolic function, there is a growing awareness that diastolic function plays a critical role in defining cardiac functional capacity. The factors determining cardiac diastolic function and the contributions these may make to aerobic fitness and endurance athletic performance needs to be assessed.

- Present evidence indicates that improvements in VO$_2$max with endurance training are less in children than young adults. It is likely that this blunted response is related to a smaller relative rise in maximal stroke volume. Understanding the influence of biological maturation on factors responsible for augmented stroke volume with training would provide insight into child-adult variations in aerobic trainability.

- It is not clear if child endurance athletes have a sport-specific differential expression of findings of the "athlete's heart." Limited current information suggests that left ventricular enlargement, for instance, is observed with training child swimmers but not distance runners. Verification and explanation for these observations are needed.

- Whether extensive endurance training prior to puberty can have long-term negative or positive effects on heart function has not been examined. Limited reports have shown no clinical abnormalities from training or competition in child runners and swimmers. Additional research is needed to assure the safety of these athletes.

REFERENCES

Baar, K.; Blough, E.; Dineen, B.; & Esser, K. (1999). Transcriptional regulation in response to exercise. *Exercise Sport Science Review* 27: 333-379.

Bielen, E.C.; Fagard, R.H.; & Amery, A.K. (1991). Inheritance of acute cardiac changes during bicycle exercise: an echocardiographic study in twins. *Medicine and Science in Sports and Exercise* 23: 1254-1259.

Colan, S. (1997). Mechanics of left ventricular systolic and diastolic function in physiologic hypertrophy of the athlete's heart. *Cardiology Clinics* 15: 355-372.

Dart, A.M.; Meredith, I.T.; & Jennings, G.L. (1992). Effects of 4 weeks endurance training on cardiac left ventricular structure and function. *Clinical and Experimental Pharmacology and Physiology* 777-783.

DeMaria, A.N.; Neumann, A.; Schubart, P.J.; Lee, G.; & Mason, D.T. (1979). Systematic correlation of cardiac chamber size and ventricular performance determined with echocardiography and alterations in heart rate in normal persons. *American Journal of Cardiology* 43: 1-9.

Diano, R.; Bouchard, C.; Demesnil, J.; Leblanc, C.; Laurenceau, J.L.; & Perrault, J. (1980). Parent-child resemblance in left ventricular echocardiographic measurements. *Canadian Journal of Applied Sports Science* 5: 4 (abstract).

Ehsani, A.A.; Hagberg, J.M.; & Hickson, R.C. (1978). Rapid changes in left ventricular dimensions and mass in response to physical conditioning and deconditioning. *American Journal of Cardiology* 42: 52-56.

Ekblom, B. & Hermansen, L. (1968). Cardiac output in athletes. *Journal of Applied Physiology* 25: 619-625.

Eriksson, B.O. (1972). Physical training, oxygen supply, and muscle metabolism in 11-13 year old boys. *Acta Physiologica Scandinavica, Supplement* 384: 1-48.

Fagard, R.H. (1997). Impact of different sports and training on cardiac structure and function. *Cardiology Clinics* 15: 397-412.

Fagard, R.; Van Den Broeke, C.; Bielen, E.; & Amery, A. (1987). Maximum oxygen uptake and cardiac size and function in twins. *American Journal of Cardiology* 60: 1362-1367.

Faria, I.E.; Faria, E.W.; Roberts, S.; & Yoshimura, D. (1989). Comparison of physical and physiological characteristics in elite young and mature cyclists. *Research Quarterly of Exercise and Sport* 60: 388-395.

Galanti, G.; Toncelli, L.; & Comeglio, M. (1987). Morphological and functional effects on athletes' heart after a period of absolute inactivity. *Journal of Sports Cardiology* 4: 102-106.

George, K.P.; Wolfe, L.A.; & Burggraf, G.W. (1991). The 'athletic heart syndrome.' A critical review. Sports Medicine 11: 300-331.

Gledhill, N.; Cox, D.; & Jamnik, R. (1994). Endurance athletes' stroke volume does not plateau: major advantage is diastolic function. *Medicine and Science in Sports and Exercise* 26: 1116-1121.

Gutin, B.; Mayers, N.; Levy, J.A.; & Herman, M.V. (1988). Physiologic and echocardiographic studies of age-group runners. In Brown, E.W. & Branta, C.F. (Eds.) *Competitive Sports for Children and Youth.* Champaign, IL: Human Kinetics (pp. 117-128).

Harpur, R.P. (1980). The rat as a model for physical fitness studies. *Comparative Biochemistry and Physiology* 66A: 553-574.

Hossack, K.F. & Bruce, R.A. (1982). Maximal cardiac function in sedentary normal men and women: Comparison of age-related changes. Journal of Applied Physiology 53: 799-804.

Klissouras, V.; Pirnay, F.; & Petit, J.M. (1973). Adaptation to maximal effort: Genetics and age. *Journal of Applied Physiology* 35: 288-293.

Landry, F.; Bouchard, C.; & Dumesnil, J. (1985). Cardiac dimension changes with endurance training. *Journal of the American Medical Association* 254: 77-80.

Lehmann, M.; Keul, J.; & Korsten-Reck, U. (1981). The influence of graduated treadmill exercise on plasma catecholamines, aerobic and anaerobic capacity in boys and adults. *European Journal of Applied Physiology* 35: 299-303.

Lengyel, M. & Gyarfas, I. (1979). The importance of echocardiography in the assessment of left ventricular hypertrophy in trained and untrained schoolchildren. *Acta Cardiologica* 34: 63-69.

Maher, J.T.; Goodman, A.L.; Francesconi, R.; Bowers, W.D.; Hartley, L.H.; & Angelakos, E.T. (1972). Responses of rat myocardium to exhaustive exercise. *American Journal of Physiology* 222: 207-212.

Marin, G.; Domene, H.M.; Barnes, K.; Blackwell, B.J.; Casorla, F.G.; & Cutler, G.B. (1994). The effects of estrogen priming and puberty on the growth hormone response to standardized treadmill exercise and arginine-insulin in normal girls and boys. *Journal of Clinical Endocrinology and Metabolism* 79: 537-541.

Maron, B.J. (1986). Structural features of the athlete heart as defined by echocardiography. *Journal of the American College of Cardiology* 7: 190-203.

Maron, B.J.; Pellicia, A.; Spataro, A.; & Granata, M. (1993). Reduction in left ventricular wall thickness after deconditioning in highly trained Olympic athletes. *British Heart Journal* 69: 125-131.

Mayers, N. & Gutin, B. (1979). Physiological characteristics of elite prepubertal cross country runners. *Medicine and Science in Sports and Exercise* 11: 172-176.

Medved, R.; Fabecic-Sabadi, V.; & Medved, V. (1985). Relationship between echocardiographic values and body dimensions in child swimmers. *Journal of Sports Cardiology* 2: 28-31.

Moore, R.L. & Palmer, B.M. (1999). Exercise training and cellular adaptations of normal and diseased hearts. *Exercise Sports Science Review* 27: 285-316.

Morganroth, J.; Maron, B.J.; Henry, W.L.; & Epstein, S.E. (1975). Comparative left ventricular dimensions in trained athletes. *Annals of Internal Medicine* 82: 521-524.

Niemela, K.O.; Palatski, I.J.; Ikaheimo, M.J.; Takkunen, J.T.; & Vuori, J.J. (1984). Evidence of impaired left ventricular performance after an uninterrupted competitive 24-hour run. *Circulation* 70: 350-356.

Nudel, D.B.; Hassett, I.; Gurain, A.; Diamant, S.; Weinhouse, E.; & Gootman, N. (1989). Young long distance runners: Physiologic characteristics. *Clinical Pediatrica* 28: 500-505.

Obert, P.; Steecken, F.; Courteix, D.; Lecog, A.-M.; & Guenon, P. (1998). Effect of long-term intensive endurance training on left ventricular structure and diastolic function in prepubertal children. International Journal of *Sports Medicine* 19: 149-154.

Ozer, S.; Cil, E.; Baltaci, G.; Ergun, N.; & Ozme, S. (1994). Left ventricular structure and function by echocardiography in childhood swimmers. *Japanese Heart Journal* 35: 295-300.

Pelliccia, A. (1996). Determinants of morphologic cardiac adaptation in elite athletes: The role of athletic training and constitutional factors. *International Journal of Sports Medicine* 17: S157-S163.

Perraul, H.M. & Turcotte, R.A. (1993). Do athletes have "the athlete heart?" *Progress in Pediatric Cardiology* 2: 40-50.

Roeske, W.R.; O'Rourke, R.A.; Klein, A.; Leopold, G.; & Karliner, J.S. (1967). Noninvasive evaluation of ventricular hypertrophy in professional athletes. *Circulation* 53: 286-292.

Rost, R. (1990). The athlete's heart. What we did learn from Henschen, what Hensechen could have learned from us! *Journal of Sports Medicine and Physical Fitness* 30: 339-346.

Rost, R. & Hollman, W. (1983). Athlete's heart—a review of its historical assessment and new aspects. *International Journal of Sports Medicine* 4: 147-165.

Rowell, L. (1986). *Human Circulation. Regulation During Physical Stress*. New York: Oxford University Press,

Rowland, T.W. (1985). Aerobic response to endurance training in prepubescent children: A critical analysis. *Medicine and Science in Sports and Exercise* 17: 493-497.

Rowland, T.W. (1996). *Developmental Exercise Physiology*. Champaign, IL: Human Kinetics.

Rowland, T.W.; Delaney, B.C.; & Siconolfi, S.F. (1987). "Athlete's heart" in prepubertal children. *Pediatrics* 79: 800-804.

Rowland, T.; Goff, D.; Popowski, B.; DeLuca, P.; & Ferrone, L. (1998). Cardiac responses to exercise in child distance runners. *International Journal of Sports Medicine* 19: 385-390.

Rowland, T.W.; Maresh, C.M.; Charkoudian, N.; Vanderburgh, P.M.; Castellani, J.R.; & Armstrong, L.E. (1996). Plasma norepinephrine responses to cycle exercise in boys and men. *International Journal of Sports Medicine* 17: 22-26.

Rowland, T.; Popowski, B.; & Ferrone, L. (1997). Cardiac responses to maximal upright cycle exercise in healthy boys and men. *Medicine and Science in Sports and Exercise* 29: 1146-1151.

Rowland, T.; Potts, J.; Potts, T.; Sandor, G.; Goff, D.; & Ferrone, L. (2000a). Cardiac responses to progressive exercise in normal children: A synthesis. *Medicine and Science in Sports and Exercise*, 31: 253-259.

Rowland, T.W.; Unnithan, V.B.; MacFarlane, N.G.; Gibson, N.G.; & Paton, J.Y. (1994b). Clinical manifestations of the 'athlete's heart' in prepubertal male runners. *International Journal of Sports Medicine* 15: 515-519.

Rowland, T.; Wehnert, M.; & Miller, K. (2000b). Cardiac responses to exercise in competitive child cyclists. *Medicine and Science in Sports and Exercise*, 32: 747-757.

Rubal, B.J.; Moody, J.M.; Damore, S.; Bunker, S.R.; & Diaz, N.M. (1986). Left ventricular performance of the athletic heart during upright exercise: A heart rate-controlled study. *Medicine and Science in Sports and Exercise* 18: 134-140.

Shapiro, L.M. (1997). The morphologic consequences of systemic training. *Cardiology Clinics* 15: 373-379.

Shepherd, T.A.; Eisenman, P.A.; Ruttenberg, H.D.; Adams, T.D.; & Johnson, S.C. (1988). Cardiac dimensions of highly trained prepubescent boys. *Medicine and Science in Sports and Exercise, Supplement* 20: 53 (Abstract).

Sundberg, S. & Elovainio, R. (1982). Cardirespiratory function in competitive runners aged 12-16 years compared with normal boys. *Acta Paediatrica Scandinavica* 91: 987-992.

Telford, R.D.; McDonald, I.G.; Ellis, L.B.; Chennells, M.H.D.; Sandstrom, E.R.; & Fuller, P.J. (1988). Echocardiographic dimensions in trained and untrained 12-year old boys and girls. *Journal of Sports Science* 6: 49-57.

Vaccaro, P. & Clarke, D.H. (1978). Cardiorespiratory alterations in 9 to 11 year old children following a season of competitive swimming. *Medicine and Science in Sports* 10: 204-207.

Van Huss, W.; Evans, S.A.; Kurowski, T.; Anderson, D.J.; Allen, R.; & Stephens, K. (1988). Physiologic characteristics of male and female age-group runners. In Brown, E.W. & Branta, C.F. (Eds.), *Competitive Sports for Children and Youth*. Champaign, IL: Human Kinetics (pp. 143-158).

Wolfe, L.A.; Cunningham, D.A.; & Boughner, D.R. (1986). Physical conditioning effects on cardiac dimensions: A review of echocardiographic studies. *Canadian Journal of Applied Sport Sciences* 11: 66-79.

CHAPTER 5

Dehydration and Rehydration in the Exercising Child and Adolescent

Oded Bar-Or
McMaster University

Introduction

Exercise, particularly in hot/humid climates, is accompanied by major changes in body fluid balance. Such changes are manifested by water and electrolyte shifts among body fluid compartments. When total body fluid losses are greater than fluid intake, a person incurs a fluid deficit. In this text, dehydration is used to denote the process of progressive fluid deficit, whereas hypohydration is used to indicate the degree of this deficit at any given point in time. This review focuses on several issues regarding hydration during exercise in children and adolescents:

- Voluntary dehydration, its causes and sequelae,

- Voluntary dehydration in children,

- The means by which thirst and voluntary drinking can be enhanced in the exercising child,

- Cystic fibrosis as a model for the study of voluntary dehydration and rehydration,

- Practical implications to youth sports, and

- Issues that require further research.

Voluntary Dehydration: Causes and Sequelae

At the start of exercise plasma volume drops, mostly due to an increase in intracapillary hydrostatic pressure. When exercise intensity is very high, the drop in plasma volume occurs within a few seconds, reaching as much as 10-15% of resting plasma volume. This has been shown for young men who performed the Wingate anaerobic test (Rothstein et al., 1982). A similar magnitude of decline occurs in children who perform the same task (unpublished data from the Wingate laboratory in Israel). When exercise lasts several minutes, plasma volume decreases further, due to a rise in extravascular osmotic pressure, which results from the efflux of metabolites and K+ from the contracting muscle cells. More prolonged exercise (e.g., 30 min or more), particularly if not accompanied by sufficient fluid intake, will result in total body dehydration and a further decrease in plasma volume. Body fluid losses under these conditions are comprised mostly of sweat and, to a lesser extent, urine and respiratory water.

Such dehydration occurs even when the person is offered drink *ad libitum*, a phenomenon that has been called "voluntary dehydration" (Rothstein et al., 1947). The causes for voluntary dehydration are unclear. It is not known why a person's thirst perception underestimates the amounts of fluids lost from the body, nor is it known whether such underestimation provides any advantages during exertion. It is clear, though, that dehydration, whether voluntary or forced, is accompanied by adverse physiological responses. Indeed, at advanced levels dehydration may become a health hazard. Physiologic changes during dehydration include: a reduction in plasma volume, stroke volume, cardiac output, renal blood flow, glomerular filtration rate and liver glycogen content, and an increase in submaximal heart rate (Sawka and Pandolf, 1990). One outcome of the reduction in blood volume is a decrease in the ability to convect heat from the body core to the periphery. This, in turn, induces an excessive rise in core temperature, as discussed below. Dehydration is also accompanied by a reduction in physical performance. Items affected are muscular strength and muscle endurance (Bosco et al., 1968), the duration that strenuous activity can be sustained (Claremont et al., 1976; Saltin, 1964), and mental alertness (Leibowitz et al., 1972). Maximal O_2 uptake is not usually reduced when exercise is performed in a thermoneutral environment (Saltin, 1964), but it does decrease when hypohydration is marked (e.g., more than 5%) and exercise is performed in a hot environment (Sawka et al., 1996). Anaerobic performance, as measured by the 30-sec Wingate test, was not affected in one study (Jacobs, 1980) and reduced in another (Webster et al. 1990). These studies were conducted with adults. There are no data on the effect of hypohydration on the physical performance of children and adolescents.

In addition to water deficit, sweating without sufficient fluid and electrolyte replenishment may induce deficits in sodium (Na+), chloride (Cl-), potassiom (K^+), calcium, and magnesium. Hyponatremia is one outcome of insufficient Na+ replenishment (Armstrong et al., 1993; Geist and Barzilai, 1992), even though the concentration of NaCl in the sweat of children and early pubescents is lower than in adults (Araki et al., 1979; Dill et al., 1966; Meyer et al., 1992). The concentration of K^+ in children's sweat is higher than in adults (Meyer et al., 1992), but the consequences of insufficient K^+ replenishment in the exercising child have not been documented.

Voluntary Dehydration in Children

Does voluntary dehydration occur in children? In a study performed at the Wingate Institute in Israel, healthy 10- to 12-year-old boys performed intermittent cycling exercise at 45% VO_2max while exposed to 39°C at 45% relative humidity. Even though chilled water was provided *ad libitum*, voluntary water intake was insufficient to prevent progressive dehydration (Bar-Or et al., 1980). This pattern was subsequently confirmed in other studies (Bar-Or et al., 1992; Kriemler et al., 1999; Rodriguez et al., 1995; Wilk and Bar-Or, 1996). Even though there are no studies that directly compare the degree of hypohydration in children and adults, it seems to be similar in the two groups (Bar-Or et al., 1980). However, at any given level of hypohydration (described as a percentage of pre-exercise body weight), children have a higher rise in core body temperature (Bar-Or et al., 1980). This is one important reason why voluntary dehydration in children should be prevented.

Preventing Voluntary Dehydration in the Exercising Child

A person's wish to drink can be enhanced by increasing the palatability of a beverage, or through physiologic means.

Increasing Palatability. While water is the most readily available drink for fluid replenishment, many people do not consider water a palatable choice. In point of fact, water seems to quench thirst, rather than stimulate further drinking (Hubbard et al., 1984). Based on studies with adults, the two main means by which palatability of a beverage can be increased are the addition of flavor and chilling (Boulze et al., 1983; Hubbard et al., 1990; Szlyk et al., 1989).

Child-related data on the palatability of drinks are scarce. A project by Meyer et al. (1994, 1995) was designed to find out whether there are certain flavors that children consider more palatable than others. Nine- to 13-year-old girls and boys, residents of Southern Ontario, were asked to rate four drinks (apple, orange, grape and water) for sweetness, saltiness and sourness, as well as for the intensity of the drink (choosing between "too strong," "just right" and "not strong enough"). Rating was done at rest in a thermoneutral environment, during progressive mild dehydration in a hot environment, and during rehydration in a thermoneutral environment. The subjects also had to choose one of the four drinks following a maximal aerobic power test. Irrespective of the situation, the children preferred the grape flavor to all others. In addition, their spontaneous rate of rehydration was highest when given the grape drink (Meyer et al., 1994). This preference occurred irrespective of whether the children saw the color of the drinks or not. In spite of such consistency in response, rating may depend on culture, ethnic and socioeconomic background and on geographic location. For example, children from Puerto Rico, who are habitually exposed to a warm climate year-round, had no consistently preferred flavor when they were given the same testing protocol as described above for the Canadian children (Rivera-Brown et al., 1999). Furthermore, in some societies, grape-flavored drinks are considered to be "wine" and therefore children are not allowed to drink them.

Does the addition of flavor enhance the spontaneous drinking of a beverage by the exercising child? This question was addressed in a study by Wilk and Bar-Or (1996) in which 9- to 12-year-old boys were exposed to intermittent exercise in a hot climate. Their *ad libitum* drinking volume increased by some 44.5% when grape-flavored water was given instead of unflavored water. No studies are available which determine the effect of chilling a beverage on children's voluntary drinking during exercise.

Physiologic Means. There are two main physiologic triggers that stimulate thirst: a reduction in plasma volume and an increase in body fluid osmolality which, in turn, stimulates hypothalamic and extracerebral osmoreceptors (Greenleaf, and Morimoto, 1996). The latter process was demonstrated in animals and humans whose thirst was enhanced when they were given NaCl intravenously or by mouth. (Gisolfi, 1973; Morimoto et al., 1981; Nose et al., 1988).

To test whether the osmotic drive operates in children, 9- to 12-year-old boys were exposed for three hours to intermittent moderate-intensity exercise at 35°C, 45-50% relative humidity (Wilk and Bar-Or, 1996). Their voluntary fluid consumption increased from 290 to 395 ml/hour when 6% carbohydrate (2% glucose, 4% sucrose) plus 18 mmol/l NaCl were added to grape-flavored water. This enhanced intake was sufficient to prevent voluntary dehydration by the end of the session. In contrast, neither the consumption of unflavored water nor that of grape-flavored water was sufficient to prevent voluntary dehydration. This experiment took place in the Canadian winter, with subjects who were neither trained nor acclimatized to the heat, and whose sweating rate was low. As has been shown for adults, children's sweating rate increases through acclimation to heat (Inbar, 1978) and by aerobic training (Inbar et al., 1981). The question arises as to whether voluntary dehydration can still be prevented in children when their sweating is more profuse than that produced by the above-mentioned Canadian children. A recent study, performed in Puerto Rico (Rivera-Brown et al., 1999), included trained boys who were fully acclimatized to the heat. Even though their sweating rate was twice as high as in the non-acclimatized, non-athletic Canadian boys, voluntary drinking was enhanced and dehydration was prevented by the addition of a flavored NaCl-carbohydrate solution.

Another study (Wilk et al., 1998) has shown that the beneficial effect of a NaCl-carbohydrate drink is not merely due to its novelty. Ten- to 12-year-old boys attended over two weeks, six identical 70-min intermittent exercise sessions at 35°C, 50-55% relative humidity. When a grape-flavored solution with 18 mmol.l[-1] NaCl and 6% carbohydrate was provided, *ad libitum* drinking was consistently sufficient to yield a slightly positive fluid balance in each of the sessions.

The Cystic Fibrosis Model

Cystic fibrosis (CF) is the most common genetic disorder among Caucasian newborns. It affects several body systems, including the sweat glands. This is manifested by a very high concentration of NaCl in the child's sweat. Among healthy children and pubescents, sweat Na^+ and Cl^- concentration is usually lower than 40 mmol/l (Meyer et al., 1992). In contrast, the respective values among patients with CF may exceed 100 mmol/l (Bar-Or et al., 1992; Kessler, Andersen, 1951; Orenstein et al., 1983). The high NaCl loss, especially when combined with drinking of water, may result in a drop in serum Na^+, Cl^- and osmolality (Orenstein et al., 1983). In contrast, healthy individuals respond to exercise by an increase in serum NaCl and osmolality (Sawka et al., 1985), which triggers their enhanced drinking. We hypothesized that, because of the above pattern, CF patients may have a deficient osmotic trigger for thirst during prolonged exercise in the heat. This, in turn, would cause excessive voluntary dehydration. This hypothesis was confirmed when children and adolescents with CF were compared with healthy controls during a 3-hour intermittent exercise at 31-33°C, 43-47% relative humidity (Bar-Or et al., 1992). When presented with chilled water, the CF patients drank voluntarily only one-half of the amount consumed by the controls (0.80% vs 1.73% of initial body weight). The resulting hypohydration level in the patients was twice that of the controls (1.57% vs 0.78%).

Recently the question of whether one can enhance the thirst of children with CF by including a NaCl solution in their drink was addressed (Kriemler et al., 1999). The study protocol was identical to the Wilk and Bar-Or (1996) experiment with healthy boys. The one exception was that the NaCl concentration in the drink was 30 mmol/l instead of 18 mmol/l. This, however, did not trigger a higher drinking rate, compared with the water session. In a subsequent session, the NaCl concentration was raised to 50 mmol/l and this did induce a significant increase in voluntary drinking such that voluntary dehydration was prevented. Even though the experiments with the CF patients were not designed to identify the mechanism which underlies variability in drinking pattern, they strongly suggest that it is the NaCl that triggers an increase in thirst among children. It should be emphasized, though, that the drink provided in the study by Kriemler et al. (1996) included also 6% carbohydrate and it is not clear whether NaCl without carbohydrate would have had the same effect.

Practical Implications to Youth Sports

The knowledge that children and adolescents underestimate their fluid requirements during prolonged physical activity and that dehydration may impair performance and health has practical implications for young athletes. This is particularly relevant for endurance events such as running and cycling races that last 30 minutes or more, and for team sports such as soccer, football, rugby or basketball. Special attention must be given to individuals who take part in two or more games per day, such as in soccer tournaments that are often held in the summer. While the climatic heat stress during outdoor activities may be high due to solar radiation, it may also be high during indoor activities (e.g., a basketball game) due to a high humidity in the gymnasium.

Promotion of periodic drinking (e.g., every 15-20 minutes) can be achieved through education of the athletes, parents and coaches. Drinking can also be stimulated by improving beverage palatability and by including salt-and carbohydrate in the drink. Most commercially available sports drinks have the right combination of NaCl and carbohydrates. As an alternative, one can use home-made drinks which include 60 gram of sugar (7-8 heaped teaspoons) and a pinch of salt in one liter (2.2 pints) of flavored water. Ideally, one should identify and then select the specific flavor that is preferred by each individual athlete.

The amount of drink depends mostly on the sweating rate which, in turn, depends on the prevailing climate and on the duration and intensity of exercise. Because of large inter-individual differences in sweating rate one must determine fluid losses in each individual athlete. The best approach is to measure body weight before and after a "typical" training session. Ideally, one should use a scale accurate to 100 grams and take the measurement after the athlete has urinated at the start and at the end of the session. Each 100 grams of weight loss should be replaced by a 100 ml beverage. It is important to emphasize that sweating rate increases with the increase in aerobic fitness and with heat acclimatization. Therefore, one should repeat the weight measurements periodically during the season, to account for changes in fitness and acclimatization status.

Future Research

The following is a list of child-related research topics that, based on this author's interest, are worth pursuing:

- Is there a relationship between physiologic heat strain and hypohyration levels?

- What is the relative importance of carbohydrates and NaCl in triggering thirst?

- How much of an ingested fluid is actually absorbed into the vascular compartment and how much remains in the gastric or intestinal lumen? Studying this issue will require ethical methods to determine the rate of gastric emptying and of intestinal water absorption, at different climatic and metabolic heat stresses.

- Does cooling of a beverage enhance voluntary drinking?

- Is there an optimal combination of beverage flavor and temperature that will induce maximal voluntary drinking?

- Is there a relationship between a child's states of hunger and thirst?

- Are there gender-related differences in dehydration-rehydration patterns?

REFERENCES

Araki, T.; Toda, Y.; Matsushita, K.; & Tsujino, A. (1979). Age differences during sweating during muscular exercise. *Japanese Journal of Fitness Sports Medicine* 28: 239-248.

Armstrong, L.E.; Curtis, W.C.; & Hubbard, R.W. (1993). Symptomatic hyponatremia during prolonged exercise in the heat. *Medicine and Science in Sports and Exercise* 25: 543-549.

Bar-Or, O.; Blimkie, C.J.R.; Hay, J.A.; MacDougall, J.D.; Ward, D.S.; & Wilson, W.M. (1992). Voluntary dehydration and heat intolerance in cystic fibrosis. *The Lancet* 339: 696-699.

Bar-Or, O.; Dotan, R.; Inbar, O.; Rothstein, A.; & Zonder, H. (1980). Voluntary hypohydration in 10- to 12-year-old boys. *Journal of Applied Physiology: Respiratory, Environmental, and Exercise Physiology* 48: 104-108.

Bosco, J.S.; Terjung, R.L.; & Greenleaf, J.E. (1968). Effects of progressive hypohydration on maximal isometric muscular strength. *Journal of Sports Medicine and Physical Fitness* 8: 81-86.

Boulze, D.; Montastruc, P.; & Cabanac, M. (1983). Water intake, pleasure and water tempearture in humans. *Physioloical Behavior* 30: 97-102.

Claremont, A.D.; Costill, D.L.; Fink, W.; & Van Handel, P. (1976). Heat tolerance following diuretic induced dehydration. *Medicine and Science in Sports* 8: 239-243.

Dill, D.B.; Hall, F.G.; & Van Beaumont, W. (1966). Sweat chloride concentration: Sweat rate, metabolic rate, skin temperature, and age. *Journal of Applied Physiology* 21: 99-106.

Geist, M. & Barzilai, N. (1992). Dilutional hyponatremia and convulsions after strenuous exercise (in Hebrew). *Harefua* 122: 420-421.

Gisolfi, C.V. (1973). Work-heat tolerance derived from interval training. *Journal of Applied Physiology* 35: 349-354.

Greenleaf, J.E. & Morimoto, T. (1996). Mechanisms controlling fluid ingestion: Thirst and drinking. In: Buskirk, E.R. & Puhl, S.M. (Eds.), *Body Fluid Balance: Exercise and Sport*. Boca Raton, FL: CRC Press (pp. 3-17).

Hubbard, R.W.; Sandick, B.L.; Matthew, W.T.; Francesconi, R.P.; Sampson, J.B.; Durkoot, M.J.; Maller, O.; & Engell, D.B. (1984). Voluntary dehydration and alliesthesia for water. *Journal of Applied Physiology* 57: 868-875.

Hubbard, R.W.; Szlyk, P.C.; & Armstrong, L.E. (1990). Influence of thirst and fluid palatability on fluid ingestion during exercise. In: Gisolfi, C.G. & Lamb, D. R. (Eds.) *Perspectives in Exercise Science and Sports Medicine, Volume 3*. Fluid homeostasis during exercise. Carmel, IN: Benchmark Press (pp.39-86).

Inbar, O. (1978). *Acclimatization to Dry and Hot Environment in Young Adults and Children 8-10 Years Old*. Doctoral dissertation, Columbia University: New York, NY.

Inbar. O.; Bar-Or, O.; Dotan, R.; & Gutin, B. (1981). Conditioning versus exercise in heat as methods for acclimatizing 8- to10- year-old boys to dry heat. *Journal of Applied Physiology: Respiratory, Environmental, and Exercise Physiology* 50: 406-411.

Jacobs, I. (1980). The effects of thermal dehydration on performance of the Wingate anaerobic test. *International Journal of Sports Medicine* 1: 21-24.

Kessler, W.R. & Andersen, D.H. (1951). Heat prostration in fibrocystic disease of the pancreas and other conditions. *Pediatrics* 8: 648-656.

Kriemler, S.; Wilk, B.; Schurer, W.; Wilson, W.M.; & Bar-Or, O. (1999). Preventing dehydration in children with cystic fibrosis who exercise in the heat. *Medicine and Science in Sports and Exercise* 31: 774-779.

Leibowitz, H.W.; Abernathy, C.N.; Buskirk, E.R.; Bar-Or, O.; & Hennessy, R.T. (1972). The effect of heat stress on reaction time to centrally and peripherally presented stimuli. *Human Factors* 14: 155-160.

Meyer, F.; Bar-Or, O.; MacDougall, J.D.; & Heigenhauser, G.J.F. (1992). Sweat electrolyte loss during exercise in the heat: Effects of gender and maturation. *Medicine and Science in Sports and Exercise* 24: 776-781.

Meyer, F.; Bar-Or, O.; Salsberg, A.; & Passe, D. (1994). Hypohydration during exercise in children: Effect on thirst, drink preferences, and rehydration. *International Journal of Sports Nutrition* 4: 22-35.

Meyer, F.; Bar-Or, O.; & Wilk, B. (1995). Children's perceptual responses to ingesting drinks of different compositions during and following exercise in the heat. *International Journal of Sports Nutrition* 5: 13-24.

Morimoto, T.; Miki, K.; Nose, H.; Yamada, S.; Hirakawa, S.; & Matsubara, C. (1981). Changes in body fluid volume and its composition during heavy sweating and the effect of fluid and electrolyte replacement. *Japanese Journal of Biometeorology* 18: 31-39.

Nose, H.; Mack, G.W.; Shi, X.; & Nadel, E.R. (1988). Role of plasma osmolality and plasma volume during rehydration in humans. *Journal of Applied Physiology* 65: 325-331.

Orenstein, D.M.; Henke, K.G.; Costill, D.L.; Doershuk, C.F.; Lemon, P.J.; & Stern, R.C. (1983). Exercise and heat stress in cystic fibrosis patients. *Pediatric Research* 17: 267-269.

Rivera-Brown, A.; Gutierrez, R.; Gutierrez, J.C.; Frontera, W.R.; & Bar-Or, O. (1999). Drink composition, voluntary drinking, and fluid balance in exercising, trained, heat-acclimatized boys. Journal of Applied Physiology 86: 78-84.

Rodriguez, J.R.; Rivera-Brown, A.M.; Frontera, W.R.; Rivera, M.A.; Mayol, P.; & Bar-Or, O. (1995). Effect of drink pattern and solar radiation on thermoregulation and fluid balance during exercise in chronically acclimatized children. *American Journal of Human Biology* 7: 643-650.

Rothstein, A.; Adolph, E.F.; & Wills, J.H. (1947). Voluntary dehydration. In: Adolph, E.F. (Ed.), *Physiology of Man in the Desert*. New York: Interscience Publishers, (pp. 254-270).

Rothstein, A.; Bar-Or, O.; & Dlin, R. (1982). Hemoglobin, hematocrit, and calculated plasma volume changes induced by a short, supramaximal task. *International Journal of Sports Medicine* 3: 230-233.

Saltin, B. (1964). Aerobic and anaerobic work capacity after dehydration. *Journal of Applied Physiology* 19: 1114-1118.

Sawka, M.N.; Montain, S.J.; & Latzka, W.A. (1996). Body fluid balance during exercise-heat exposure. In: Buskirk, E.R. & Puhl, S.M. (Eds.), *Body Fluid Balance:*

Exercise and Sport. Boca Raton, FL: CRC Press (pp. 139-157).

Sawka, M.N. & Pandolf, K.B. (1990). Effect of body water loss on physiological function and exercise performance. In: Gisolfi, C.V. & Lamb, D.R. (Eds.), *Perspectives in Exercise and Sport Medicine: Fluid Homeostasis During Exercise*. Indianapolis, IN: Benchmark (pp. 1-30).

Sawka, M.N.; Young, A.J.; Francesconi, R.P.; Muza, S.R.; & Pandolf, K.B. (1985). Thermoregulatory and blood responses during exercise at graded hypohydration levels. *Journal of Applied Physiology* 59: 1374-1401.

Szlyk, P.C.; Sils, I.V.; Francesconi, R.P.; Hubbard, R.W.; & Armstrong, L.E. (1989). Effects of water temperature and flavoring on voluntary dehydration in men. *Physiological Behavior* 45: 639-647.

Webster, S.; Rutt, R.; & Weltman, A. (1990). Physiological effects of a weight loss regimen practiced by college wrestlers. *Medicine and Science in Sports and Exercise* 22: 229-234.

Wilk, B. & Bar-Or, O. (1996). Effect on drink flavor and NaCl on voluntary drinking and rehydration in boys exercising in the heat. *Journal of Applied Physiology* 80: 1112-1117.

Wilk, B.; Kriemler, S.; Keller, H.; & Bar-Or, O. 1998. Consistency of preventing voluntary dehydration in boys who drink a flavored carbohydrate-NaCl beverage during exercise in the heat. *International Journal of Sports Nutrition* 8: 1-9.

CHAPTER 6

Trainability During Childhood and Adolescence

Robert M. Malina and Joey C. Eisenmann
Tarleton State University, and
York University

INTRODUCTION

Systematic instruction, practice and training are basic to youth sport programs. Such programs are important for several essential components of athletic performance—motor skill, muscular strength, cardiovascular and muscular endurance, and anaerobic capacity. Specific instruction, practice and training programs for young sport participants are often discussed in the context of the concept of the trainability—the responsiveness of children and adolescents at different stages of growth and maturation to the stimulus provided by such programs. The concept of trainability of children and adolescents is first discussed briefly, followed by more detailed consideration of responses to specific motor skill, muscular strength, anaerobic and aerobic training programs.

CONCEPT OF TRAINABILITY

Trainability refers to the responsiveness of the individual to a specific training stimulus. Trainability is related to the concepts of readiness and critical periods. It is often suggested, for example, that youth are more responsive to the beneficial effects of training during periods of rapid growth and maturation.

Factors that may influence trainability include age, sex, variation in growth and maturity status, prior experiences (such as early opportunities to practice motor skills or levels of habitual physical activity), pre-instruction or pre-training levels of skill, strength, and anaerobic and aerobic power (current phenotype), genotype, and the interaction between genotype and environment. Genotype refers to the individual's genetic make-up, whereas the training stimulus is the environmental influence upon the organism. With the exception of studies of sedentary young adults to aerobic or strength training, these factors are not ordinarily controlled in studies of the responsiveness of children and adolescents to training.

Discussions of trainability deal with two related, but different, questions: (1) What are the responses of children and adolescents to systematic training programs? (2) How responsive are children and adolescents to specific training programs? The first deals with the effects of training programs, whereas the second deals with the trainability of children and adolescents.

Cross-sectional studies are often used to make inferences about the trainability of children and adolescents. Such studies compare groups which are variously labeled as trained and untrained, active and inactive, or athletes and non-athletes. This approach includes a selection bias. In addition to possible genetic pre-disposition of active, trained and/or athletic youth, some of the variation in a biological variable of interest may also be explained by environmental factors (i.e., exercise training) and genetic-environment interactions. In the context of trainability presented here, only interventional studies and longitudinal studies are considered to explore the trainability of youth.

The issue of trainability in the context of sport has been related largely to the development of muscular strength and aerobic power, but it applies as well to the effects of instruction and practice on the development of proficiency in motor skills and anaerobic power. The term training, as used in this discussion, includes instruction and practice.

MOTOR SKILLS

Improvement of motor skills in general and sport specific skills is often a primary objective of youth sports programs. Children and adolescents also indicate improvement in sport skills as a major motivation for participation in sport. Given the importance placed upon motor skill acquisition and improvement in youth sports programs, it is somewhat surprising that the literature in the area is not more extensive.

Early Motor Skill Development.

Most neural structures are near adult form and most fundamental movement patterns are reasonably well established by 6 to 8 years of age (Malina et al., 2003). It might be expected, therefore, that these ages would be ideal for specific instruction and practice in the basic motor skills. This is reasonably well established. Children refine established motor patterns and learn new motor skills and sequences of skills as they grow and mature, with practice associated with everyday activities, and with instruction as in organized youth sports programs. Planned instructional programs can enhance the development of basic motor skills in children 4 and

5 years of age and more complex skills in older children. Guided instruction by specialists, trained parents or qualified coaches, appropriate motor task sequences, and adequate time for practice are essential components of successful instructional programs at young ages (Haubenstricker and Seefeldt, 1986). Since the skills utilized in most sports are combinations and modifications of the fundamental movement patterns, a beneficial role for early instruction and practice for the transition into organized sport during middle childhood is suggested. More data are necessary in this area, and other issues need to be addressed. For example, the role of parental, sibling or peer modeling in the motor development merits consideration given the amount of time that these individuals spend with each other in a variety of activities. The role of coach education and coaching style in skill development also needs careful study.

Motor Skill during Childhood and Adolescence

Instruction and practice in basic movement skills per se and in combinations or modifications of these skills, as in the requirements for specific sports, are very beneficial during middle childhood and adolescence. It may be difficult, however, to partition learning effects from those associated with growth and maturation. Motor performance improves more or less linearly with age during middle childhood. It continues to improve during adolescence in males, but tends to reach a plateau or to improve only slightly in females after 14-15 years. Maturity-associated variation in performance may also influence the response to instruction and practice. Boys advanced in biological maturity status tend to perform better than those who are later in maturation. On the other hand, differences in the performances of girls of contrasting maturity status are not marked, but later maturing girls attain better performances in some tasks (Malina et al., 2003).

Genotypic Considerations in Motor Skill

The potential role of genotype in the learning and refinement of motor skills needs attention. Are improvements in motor skill associated with practice and learning dependent upon genetic characteristics? How does genotype interact with characteristics of the learner and the learning/training environment, including the adult component of the environment? Several relatively dated experimental studies have considered the pattern of learning of motor skills in adolescent twins (Bouchard et al., 1997). Except for a stabilometer task, which places a premium on dynamic balance and coordination, tasks used in these experimental studies tend to be fine motor skills that stress manual dexterity and precision of movement. The results suggest that the rate of learning a motor skill is more similar in monozygotic (MZ) than in dizygotic (DZ) twins. However, estimates of the genetic contribution to learning vary from task to task, emphasizing the specificity of motor learning. Estimates of the genetic contribution also vary over a series of practice trials or training sessions.

A study of Polish twins 9-13 years considered three parameters of the learning curves associated with practice of four tasks: plate tapping with the hand, tapping with one foot, mirror tracing, and a ball toss for accuracy (Sklad, 1975). The level of learning and rate of learning are more similar in MZ than in DZ twins, and intrapair correlations tend to be higher in male than in female MZ twins. The final level of skill attained, the third parameter of the learning curve, is, however, quite variable between twin types and sexes, and among the four tasks.

Factors that are potentially capable of influencing the trainability of motor skills are not considered in the available studies. The data suggest that the genotype is an important determinant of the ease or difficulty with which new motor skills are learned, or of the improvement in performance that occurs with practice. There is a need for more detailed study of the individuality of responses to specific training programs or to regular practice of motor tasks during childhood and adolescence.

NEUROMUSCULAR STRENGTH

Historically, resistance training for the development of strength was not recommended for prepubertal children (American Academy of Pediatrics, 1983). Resistance programs typically involve the use of weights or specially designed machines to provide the resistance against which a particular muscle group must work. It was generally believed that circulating androgenic hormones in sufficient quantities in prepubertal boys preclude strength improvement with such specific training. Secondary factors included risk of injury in unsupervised resistance training programs and potential for premature closure of epiphyses due to excessive loads.

Responses of Prepubertal Child to Resistance Training

The conservative view presented above suggests that prepubertal children are not as responsive to strength training as pubertal or postpubertal youth. This, however, is not true. Results of two studies of resistance training in prepubertal boys are summarized in Figures 1 and 2. In the first study of boys 6-11 years, 19 boys trained on a supervised circuit of exercises on 8 hydraulic resistive units plus sit-ups and stationary cycling, 3 times per week, for 14 weeks, while 10 control subjects did no formal training (Weltman et al., 1986). In the second study of boys 9-11 years, 27 boys trained with 8 different exercises on an apparatus, 3 times per week for 10 weeks, while 12 control subjects did no formal training (Blimkie et al., 1989). As expected, the trained boys made greater gains in strength than the control subjects in each study. However, the control subjects also improved to some extent in strength. This reflects, in part, a learning effect (how to perform the tests), the effects of normal day-to-day physical activities, and probably normal growth-associated changes in strength over the duration of the experiments.

Prepubertal children respond to resistance training programs with gains in muscular strength, but show minimal muscular hypertrophy. The data on hypertrophy are variable for several reasons. First, the training program may not have been sufficiently long or intense. Generally, gains in strength following programs less than 6 weeks are related primarily to

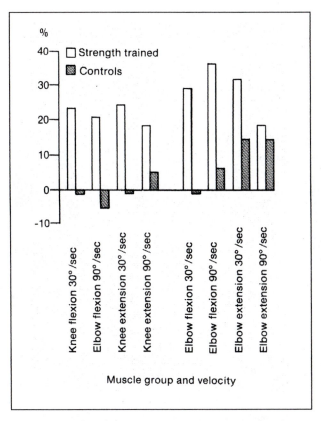

Figure 1. Relative changes in muscular strength after 14 weeks of resistance training in prepubertal boys 6-11 years. Drawn from data reported by Weltman et al. (1986).

neuromuscular factors (see below). Second, estimates of muscle size are often limited to limb circumferences or limb circumferences corrected for the thickness of skinfolds. Both estimates are only indirect indicators of muscle size. Third, ages of subjects in the experimental studies often span several years, e.g., 6-11 years (Weltman et al., 1986) or 5-11 years (Faigenbaum et al., 1999) so that chronological age per se is a potential confounding factor. Studies that are based on more narrowly defined age groups, e.g., 9-11 (Blimkie et al., 1989), or 7.0±0.3, 9.0±0.3 and 11.0±0.3 years (Fukunaga et al., 1992) show small but significant gains in estimated arm muscle area in both the older trained and control subjects. In the study of Fukunaga et al. (1992), the 7 year old groups of boys and girls showed no changes in estimated muscle area, but the two older groups of trained

boys and girls and the oldest group of control boys and girls show significant increases in muscle area.

Variation in biological maturation is another potentially confouding factor in strength training studies. In the study of Fukunaga et al. (1992), skeletal age was significantly related to the gains in estimated muscle area associated with resistance training (r=0.36). Thus, variation in maturity status may have a significant role in mediating the response to training.

Studies of the responses of children to resistance training simply classify them as prepubertal, which means that they do not show overt manifestation of secondary sex characteristics. Classification of subjects as prepubertal is not sufficiently sensitive to individual differences in biological maturation. Prepubertal children do in fact

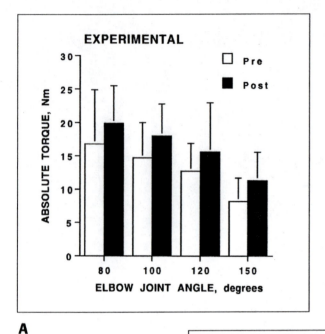

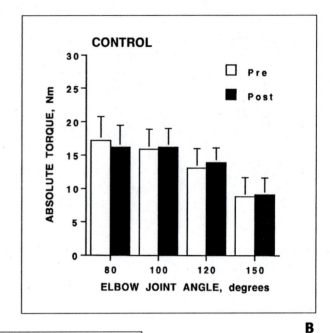

A

B

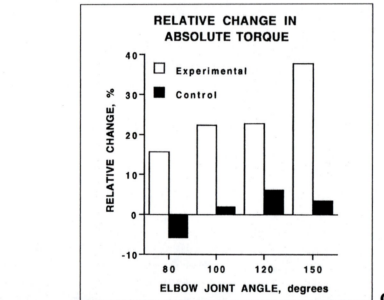

C

Figure 2. Absolute and relative changes in muscular strength after 10 weeks of resistance training in prepubertal boys 9-11 years: (A) absolute changes in the trained group, (B) absolute changes in the control group, (C) relative changes in the trained and control groups. Drawn from data reported by Blimkie et al. (1989).

differ in level of biological maturation. Skeletal age varies by as much as five years within samples of 6, 7 and 8 year old children (Malina et al., 2003). It is thus important to control for biological maturity in studies of the responses of young children to strength training, and at these ages, skeletal maturation is the only maturity indicator that is available.

It may also be important to consider more carefully other characteristics of children enrolled in resistance training studies. In the recent study of Faigenbaum et al. (1999) on children 5.2 to 11.8 years of age, the combined samples boys and girls who comprised two training groups were, on the average, significantly heavier than the control group by 7.7 kg and 12.1 kg, respectively. The training group was also taller, on the average, by 3.2 cm and 5.6 cm. If the mean values for height and weight are used to estimate the body mass index, the two experimental groups would be classified as obese at the start of the training program. Unfortunately, the body size differences among the groups at the start of the study were not controlled in the analysis.

As a group, prepubertal children respond positively to systematic resistance training programs. Unfortunately, intra-individual variation in responses to the training programs are not considered or reported. Do all children respond in a similar manner? Are there specific age- and maturity-related effects on the response to training? As noted above, some studies are based on samples that span a broad age range, e.g., 6-11 years (Weltman et al., 1986) or 5-11 years (Faigenbaum et al., 1999). The analyses do not control for age of the subjects. Do younger and older children in the range make similar gains with training? The data of Fukunaga et

al. (1992) suggest smaller absolute gains in younger children.

Prepubertal children as young as a 5 and 6 years of age are included in some of the studies of resistance training (Weltman et al., 1986; Faigenbaum et al., 1999). How important is strength training for 6-8 year old children? The answer is not known, but motor skill training is probably more important at these ages.

Variation by Sex and Pubertal Status

Other questions that arise in discussions of strength training deal with possible differences in the responses of boys and girls, and of differences among youth who vary in pubertal status. Several studies of prepubertal children include small numbers of girls. There is no or only a small sex difference in responses to resistance training among prepubertal children (Sale, 1989; Fukunaga et al.,

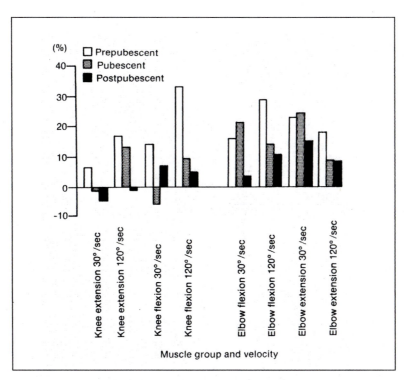

Figure 3. Relative changes in muscular strength after 9 weeks of strength training in prepubertal, pubertal and postpubertal boys. Drawn from data reported by Pfeiffer and Francis (1986).

1992; Blimkie and Sale, 1998), but data on strength training in girls are not extensive as for boys. In one of the few studies that focused exclusively on girls, three groups of 7-19 year old girls trained 3 times per week for 5 weeks in isometric knee extension, vertical jumping, or sprint running, while a fourth group served as a control (Nielsen et al., 1980). The responses were specific to the type of training program, particularly for isometric knee extension and vertical jumping, whereas responses to the sprint running protocol were small. Further, younger girls (<13.5 years) appeared to experience greater relative gains than older girls. Unfortunately, the maturity status of the girls was not controlled in the analysis. Thus, the evidence suggests increases in both static and functional strength in girls in response to several types of training programs.

Variation in response to training by pubertal status has received somewhat more consideration. Relative changes in strength in small samples (the total sample was 33) of prepubertal (G1, PH1), pubertal (G2 to G4, PH2 to PH4), and postpubertal (G5, PH5) boys after a 9-week resistive exercise program are summarized in Figure 3. Prepubertal boys made the largest relative gains, followed by the pubertal, and then the postpubertal boys. And, relative gains were greater in the upper extremity (Pfeiffer and Francis, 1986). Mean ages varied among the three groups, 10.3±1.2, 13.1±1.0, and 19.7±1.2 years. The range of variation in maturity status of the pubertal boys is another factor. The pubertal sample included those just beginning puberty (G2, PH2) and those in late puberty (G4, PH4). Age and variation in maturity were not considered in the analysis of gains associated with training in the three groups, and both are confounding factors in the interpretation of the results. The focus in this study was on relative gains. Absolute strength is probably less trainable in prepubertal than in pubertal and/or postpubertal youth (Sale, 1989; Blimkie and Sale, 1998).

Mechanisms

The relatively small increases in muscle size compared to gains in strength suggest that the response to the resistance training stimulus in prepubertal children is largely neural. The nature of the responses is not known with certainty, but probably includes enhanced motor unit recruitment and/or frequency of motor unit firing. The pattern of motor unit recruitment may also be altered, and changes in muscle activation and instrinsic contractile characteristics with strength training are also possibilities (Ozmun et al., 1994; Ramsey et al., 1990). Strength gains associated with resistance training among pubertal subjects are likely related to

Age	Maximal Strength		Muscular Endurance	
---	Trained	Control	Trained	Control
8	34.2%	0%	34.3%	2 . 6 %
10	29.6	13.5	45.6	3.5
12	23.3	-3.9	44.8	-3.9
14	6.5	-4.0	60.0	6.1

Table 1. Relative changes in muscular strength and endurance after five weeks of training on an arm ergometer in Japanese boys. (Adapted from Ikai, 1966).

neuromotor changes, but among boys advanced in puberty (G/PH 3 and 4) increased circulating levels of gonadal hormones are additional factors contributing to both muscular hypertrophy and strength (Malina et al., 2003; see also Rogol and Roemmich, this volume).

Effect of Training on Neuromuscular Endurance

The preceding studies focus on resistance training. Programs designed to improve neuromuscular endurance also result in strength increments. This is shown in Table 1, which indicates relative changes in muscular strength and endurance after a short-term training program on an upper body ergometer in small samples of boys 8 to 14 years of age. The boys exercised to exhaustion at one-third of maximum strength 6 days per week (except Sunday) for 5 weeks. As expected, trained boys made significant gains, whereas control subjects, who did not train, had more variable responses. Among the trained subjects, younger boys made greater relative gains in maximal arm strength, while the older boys made greater relative gains in muscular endurance. The results thus suggest possible differential responses to the type of training stimulus depending upon age.

Genotype in Responses to Strength Training

The role of genetic factors in the response to strength training of children and adolescents has not been investigated. Among 5 pairs of young adult MZ twins who did isokinetic strength training for 10 weeks, there were as many interindividual differences in the response to training within members of any given pair of twins as between pairs (Thibault et al., 1986). In a similar study, a 10 week resistance training program for the elbow flexors was used with young adult male twins (25 MZ and 16 DZ pairs). Twin resemblances for gains in strength with training within MZ twin pairs were significant only for 1 RM (maximal resistance that can be moved a single time through the full range of motion) and isometric strength, but the within pair correlations were at best moderate (0.46 and 0.30, respectively). Intrapair correlations for MZ

twins for other measures of strength were low and/or negative, and corresponding intrapair correlations for DZ twins were generally similar to those for MZ twins (Thomis et al., 1998). The limited results thus far suggest that the response to strength training in young adult males is independent of the genotype.

Persistence and Maintenance of Strength Gains

Two questions dealing with strength training in children and adolescence need further study. The first is the persistence of strength gains after the cessation of resistance training, and the second is the amount of training needed to maintain strength gains associated with training. Limited data for prepubertal children indicate that gains in strength associated with resistance training tend to revert to control values several weeks after the cessation of training, while information on the training requirements for the maintenance of strength gains is inconclusive (Blimkie and Sale, 1998). The preceding discussion focuses on prepubertal children; corresponding data for adolescents are lacking.

Transfer of Strength Gains to Other Performance Tasks

The observations on girls in the study by Nielson et al. (1980) have implications for the transfer of gains with one mode of training to other aspects of performance. The girls who did isometric strength training also improved in the vertical jump and acceleration in sprint running, and girls who did vertical jump training also improved in isometric strength and acceleration in sprint running. Gains were relatively greater in the domain that was specifically trained, i.e., girls who did isometric training made greater relative gains in isometric strength and girls who did vertical jump training made greater relative gains in the vertical jump. On the other hand, girls who did sprint training did not improve in acceleration in sprint running, but did make small relative gains in isometric strength and the vertical jump.

Other data dealing with transfer of strength training to other aspects of performance are limited. In a study of boys 6-11 years, 14 weeks of resistance training was associated with improvements in the vertical jump and the sit and reach (Weltman et al., 1986). On the other hand, a study of boys and girls 7-12 years, 8 weeks of strength training was associated with negligible changes in the vertical jump and the sit and reach (Faigenbaum et al., 1996). The results highlight the difficulty in partitioning the effects of a training program from expected changes associated with normal growth. They also indicate a need to consider the body size characteristics of the subjects in analyses of changes in performance associated with training.

A related question is the relevance of strength training for endurance training programs. For years, the endurance community advised athletes not to be involved in resistance exercise for fallacious reasons that were not supported by scientific evidence. This view has changed somewhat more recently, but still is not widely accepted. Data for adults indicate 5km performance time can be improved by replacing one-third of the total training volume with an explosive-type strength training consisting of plyometrics (jump training) and lower body resistance exercise (squats). The improvement was related to a change in running economy and measures of anaerobic capacity (maximal anaerobic treadmill speed, vertical jump, 20 meter sprint speed), while VO2max was maintained throughout the period of resistance exercise training (Paavolainen et al., 1999). The influence of training-related increases in muscular strength on endurance performance of children and adolescents has not been addressed.

ANAEROBIC POWER

Many youth sports are characterized by activities that involve short bursts that rely on anaerobic metabolism to provide energy, for example, a Little League baseball player sprinting to first base or a Pop Warner running back dashing towards the goal line. Anaerobic work capacity and performance are influenced by growth and maturation (Martin and Malina, 1998) and by specific anaerobic exercise training.

Limitations

Different measurements of anaerobic power and capacity make comparisons difficult. Anaerobic power and capacity have been ordinarily assessed using various whole-body tasks performed over a short-period of time at high-intensities – the vertical jump, 40 yard dash, 30 second all-out cycling, and treadmill time to exhaustion at high work loads. Maximal blood lactate level following short-term, high intensity work has also been used to assess anaerobic capacity. Current technology permits the of study skeletal muscle metabolism in a safe and non-invasive manner (in contrast to muscle biopsy) by the use of magnetic resonance spectroscopy (MRS). MRS may prove to be an effective means in establishing mechanisms in adult-child and between-child differences during short-term, high-intensity exercise bouts. An additional consideration is variation in the frequency, duration, intensity, and methods of training, which makes comparisons among studies difficult.

Trainability of Anaerobic Capacity in Children and Adolescents

Data on the trainability of anaerobic capacity in children and adolescents are limited. Two experimental studies suggest that anaerobic power is increased following a period of high-intensity training in youth. Peak power and mean power, measured by the Wingate test, increased by 14% and 10%, respectively, in 10-11 year old boys engaged in a 9 week interval training program (Rothstein et al., 1986) and by 3% to 4% in 11-13 year old boys following a 6 week high-intensity cycling or sprint program (Grodjinovsky et al., 1980). The small training effect in the latter study may be due to the length of the study and the relative duration of each training session—only 10-15 minutes per session as part of a physical education class. The lack of data emphasizes the need for study of the trainability of anaerobic power in children and adolescents. Such information may have a valuable impact on the efficacy of conditioning programs given the predominance of short-burst activities in many youth sports.

Mechanisms

Definitive mechanisms have not been established for growth-related changes in adaptive responses to short-term, high-intensity exercise programs (Inbar and Bar-Or, 1986). It appears that puberty is an important period in the development of anaerobic power, which probably reflects changes in body size, muscle mass, and glycolytic capacity. Neural factors may also contribute to training-induced changes in anaerobic tasks.

Genotype in Responses to Anaerobic Training

Data on the contribution of the genotype to the response to anaerobic training are quite limited. Among adults, the genotype is implicated in the response of short term anaerobic performance (10 second all out cycling) to a 15 week program of intermittent high-intensity exercise only when results are expressed per unit thigh muscle volume (Simoneau and Bouchard, 1998). Inter-individual differences in response to the high-intensity training program were considerable and suggest "high" and "low" responders to training (see also Bouchard et al., 1997).

Transfer of Anaerobic Power to Field Performances

There are moderately strong relationships between laboratory measures of anaerobic power and field performance in children and adolescents (Rowland, 1996). This suggests a transfer of training-related improvements in anaerobic power and short-burst activities during sports participation. However, association is not grounds for casual inference. For example, a 20% improvement in treadmill time to exhaustion (7 mph at 18% grade) following a 12 week program of high-speed activities did not result in a significant change in 40 yd dash time in 10-11 year old elite soccer players (Mosher et al., 1985).

Study	N	Methods	Main Findings
Mahon and Vaccaro (1989)	8 boys, 10-14 yrs	8 weeks run training	19.4% increase in VT (ml/kg/min) Increase in VT (%VO$_2$max) from 67 to 74%
Haffor et al. (1990)	5 boys, 11 yrs	Interval training 5 d per week,	6 weeks Increase in VT (%VO$_2$max) from 59 to 72%
Becker and Vaccaro (1983)	11 boys, 9-11 yrs	8 weeks cycle training at HR midway between VT and HR for 40 minutes, 3 days per week	Increase in VT (ml/min/kg and % VO$_2$max) in both training and control groups
Rothstein et al. (1986)	28 boys, 10-12 yrs	9 weeks interval training	Increase in running velocity and %VO$_2$max at blood lactate threshold

VT, ventilatory threshold; Vo2max, maximal oxygen consumption; HR, heart rate.

Table 2. Studies of the effects of training on the anaerobic threshold in children and adolescents.

Although sprint speed did not improve, changes probably occurred in the ability to resist fatigue during short-term, high-intensity intermittent bouts of sprints, i.e., repeated bouts of sprints.

Anaerobic Threshold

The anaerobic threshold (AT) corresponds to the exercise capacity at which lactic acid begins to accumulate in the blood. Other terms have been used to represent the AT such as lactate threshold and ventilatory threshold. Although each is assessed differently, the terms are related and generally represent the same concept. The anaerobic threshold is expressed as either VO_2 at AT ($L.min^{-1}$ or $ml.kg^{-1}.min^{-1}$) or as a percentage of peak VO_2 (i.e., 85% of peak VO_2). AT can be useful as an index of either anaerobic or aerobic fitness (Rowland, 1996).

Training-induced changes in AT are summarized in Table 2. The available data indicate that AT is trainable in youth either as increases in VO_2 at AT or as a percentage of peak VO_2. The limited number of studies include only males and small sample sizes, and vary in specific training protocols.

Potential mechanisms involved in training-induced changes of AT in youth have not been examined. Blood lactate depends on rates of production and clearance; hence, skeletal muscle morphology and function influence these processes.

Hormones (catecholamines) and pubertal status also influence skeletal muscle metabolism in youth. The development of the sensitivity of respiratory contol may be an additional factor. There are moderately strong relationships between AT and endurance performance in children and adolescents (Rowland, 1996), but no training study has specifically examined the transfer of AT to improvements in endurance performance.

AEROBIC POWER

Peak Oxygen Consumption

Relative changes in peak VO_2 per unit body weight ($ml.kg^{-1}.min^{-1}$) associated with training in children and adolescents are summarized in Table 3. The data include both boys and girls, although more data are available for boys. The samples are arbitrarily grouped into three age categories, < 10, 10-13, and 14+, and studies in which subjects were grouped across a broad age range, e.g., 8-13 or 10-15 years, were excluded. Sample sizes vary among studies as do the frequency, intensity and duration of the aerobic training programs.

The available data indicate relatively little trainability of maximal aerobic power in children under 10 years of age. Changes in peak VO_2 per unit body weight in children under 10 years are generally less than 5%, and in several studies negative

		Magnitude of Relative Changes in Peak VO2 in Specific Studies				
Age (yrs)	N	≤ 0%	+1 to +5%	+6 to +10%	+11 to +15%	>15%
≤ 10	13	4	8			1
10-13	12	1	2	3	2	4
14 +	3			1		2

Table 3. Relative changes in peak VO2 (ml/min/kg) associated with training during childhood and adolescence. Based on reviews of Mocellin (1975), Rowland (1985) and Pate and Ward (1990). N refers to the number of training studies in the indicated age range.

changes are apparent. It is not certain whether these results are the consequences of low trainability, i.e., a low adaptive potential to aerobic training, to inadequacies of the training programs, or to expression of VO2 per unit body mass (see below). For example, if it can be assumed that young children are habitually more physically active than adolescents and adults, a more intensive aerobic training program may be required to induce significant changes in maximal aerobic power. Further, anticipated changes should be less than in a sedentary individual, because young children are closer to maximal training status at the onset. When young subjects are rather sedentary at the start of the program, short-term training studies (several weeks to a few months) generally yield improvements in maximal aerobic power similar to those observed in young adults, and sex differences are small. Several studies report only absolute changes in peak oxygen uptake, and results are equivocal (McManus et al., 1997; Welsman et al., 1997). The results may be confounded, in part, by failure to control for changes in body mass during the training program.

Payne and Morrow (1993) used a similar, but more quantitative, approach to summarize information on trainability of peak VO_2. After screening 69 studies of children and adolescents were screened, 28 met the criteria for meta-analysis for inclusion—healthy children and adolescents ≤13 years, training and control groups, measurements of peak VO_2 before and after a systematic training program, and descriptive statistics (sample sizes, means, standard deviations) for peak VO_2 per unit body weight. The results suggest a gain of about 2 ml.kg-1.min-1 with training or <5% in children and adolescents ≤13 years, and indicate no differences by sex, mode of exercise testing (treadmill versus cycle), or quality of the training program (frequency, duration, intensity).

Among older children and adolescents, responses of aerobic power to training improve, but the results are variable among studies. The variability probably relates to individual variation in the timing and tempo of the growth spurt and sexual maturation so that it is difficult to separate training-associated increases in aerobic power from those associated with growth and maturation. In addition, maximal aerobic power (L.min^{-1}) shows a clear adolescent spurt that occurs close in time to peak height velocity (Malina et al., 2003). The variability also reflects sampling and methodological variation. Some studies, for example, have used young athletes as subjects, while others have used reasonably active or sedentary youngsters. And, youngsters training for a variety of sports, especially sports with a significant endurance component, usually have higher absolute and relative maximal aerobic power (Rowland, 1996). Young athletes tend to be a highly select group, and it is difficult to partition selection and training effects. In studies of adolescent non-athletes, training programs also vary, outside activity is difficult to control, and changes in body composition are not ordinarily considered.

Tolfrey et al. (1998) controlled for pre- and post-intervention values of habitual physical activity and percentage body fat by including these values in the analyses in an effort to identify independent effects of an exercise training program on prepubertal children. Age- and sexual maturity-matched controls were used. Subjects were in either stages 1 and 2 of breast and pubic hair (girls)and genital and pubic hair (boys) development. The results indicated that 12 weeks of stationary cycling exercise at 80% of maximum heart rate for 30 minutes, 3 times per week did not have a significant effect on peak VO2. Although sexual maturity status of the subjects did not change during the study, combining prepubertal (stage 1) and early pubertal (stage 2) subjects may have influenced the results. Prepubertal children do in fact vary in biological maturation, specifically skeletal maturation (Malina et al., 2003). Nevertheless, the approach of Tolfrey et al. (1998) is a good model for future exercise training studies in children.

Submaximal Oxygen Consumption (Economy of Movement)

Most activities of young children proceed at submaximal work rates, so that maximal aerobic power may not be an appropriate measure. It may be more appropriate to consider changes in submaximal economy in response to training. The effects of instruction and practice on the development of proficiency in running has been previously investigated to a limited extent. For example, submaximal running economy did not improve following an 11-week running training program in 10 year old children (Petray and Krahenbuhl, 1985).

Mechanisms

Improvements in peak VO_2 must involve structural and functional adaptations in the oxygen transport system (lung, heart, blood, vascular system, and/or oxidative capacity of skeletal muscle). Based on the Fick equation, improvements must reflect increases in heart rate, stroke volume, or arterio-venous O_2 difference or their respective determinants. Maximal heart rate does not change following exercise training. Several early studies indicate that maximal stroke volume, blood volume, and oxidative enzymes increase following exercise training of youth (Rowland, 1996, see also Rowland, this volume). Capillary density following exercise training of youth has been shown to be unchanged. Training-induced changes in other components of the oxygen transport system (pulmonary diffusing capacity, cardiac contractility, hemoglobin and myoglobin content, and mitochondrial volume density) remain to be determined. However, ethical limitations are apparent.

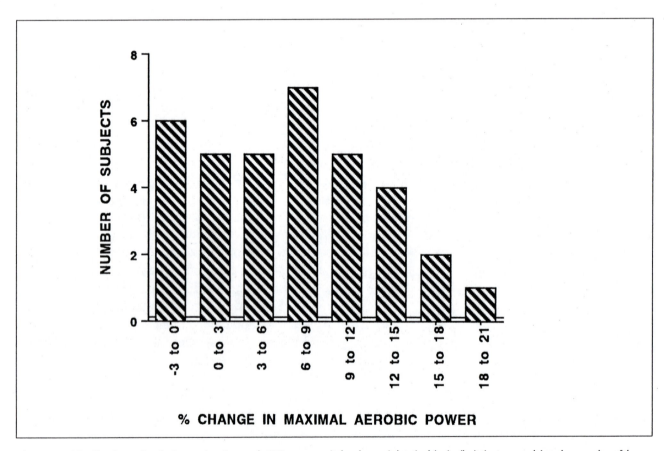

Figure 4. Distribution of relative gains in peak VO_2 per unit body weight (ml/min/kg) in a combined sample of boys and girls 10.9 to 12.8 years after a 12 week aerobic training program. Drawn after data from Rowland and Boyajian (1995).

Individual Differences in Response to Aerobic Training

As in studies of strength training, individual differences in response to aerobic training programs are not ordinarily reported. Do all children respond in a similar manner? Results from a study of 35 boys and girls, 10.9 to 12.8 years, who participated in a 12 week aerobic training program are shown in Figure 4. Although the mean change in peak VO_2 per unit body weight was 6.5%, the range was from -2.4% to 19.7% (Rowland and Boyajian, 1995). Individual differences in response to the aerobic training program are clearly evident. The results also indicate that mean values may be somewhat misleading. Potential age- and maturity-related effects on the response to the aerobic training program were not considered. Nevertheless, data for young adolescents (Figure 3) and also for young adults (Bouchard et al., 1997) indicate that some individuals exhibit a pattern of high response to the training program, while others present a pattern of no or minimal response, with a wide range of variation between the extremes. There are also "quick" or "slow" responders to training programs.

Genotype in Responses to Aerobic Training

Variation in responses among individuals suggests a potentially important role for the genotype in mediating responses to aerobic training. This issue was addressed in several studies of MZ twins. Individuals of the same genotype (within twin pairs) were more similar in the response of peak VO_2 to a standard training program than those with different genotypes (between twin pairs). Gains in peak VO_2 consistently showed more variation between DZ twin pairs than within MZ twin pairs, which is consistent with the view that the genotype conditions in part the response to aerobic training (Bouchard et al., 1997). Peak VO_2 in the sedentary state and the peak VO_2 response to exercise training also shows familial aggregation (Bouchard et al., 1998, 1999).

Specific genetic characteristics that contribute to individual differences in responses to training are as yet undetermined. The identification of genes and mutations responsible for the heterogeneity of peak VO_2 is currently an active area of research. Muscle-specific creatine kinase (Riveria et al., 1997), Na+-K+-ATPase (Rankinen et al., 2000), and angiotensin converting enzyme (Gangay et al., 1998) have been suggested as possible candidate genes.

Persistence of the Training Response

Experimental studies of the effects of systematic training on aerobic power are short term and ordinarily do not include a follow-up component. Thus, as in the case of strength training there is lack of information on the persistence of improvements in aerobic power after the cessation of training and on the amount of regular physical activity needed to maintain the improvements associated with training. Some data indicate a reversion to pre-training levels when the training programs cease (Eriksson et al., 1971).

Transfer of Aerobic Training to Endurance Performance

The study of endurance performance and oxygen consumption is more complex in youth given the important contribution of normal growth and maturation to the development of these processes. Endurance performance (e.g., 1 mile run time) improves with age regardless of training. At the same time, relative peak VO_2 ($ml.kg^{-1}.min^{-1}$) remains stable while running economy improves with age. Thus, when an exercise training intervention is introduced, what portion of change can be attributed to training? This is a difficult question to answer.

How changes in specific physiological parameters associated with exercise training influence endurance performance has received little attention. Age-related changes in peak VO_2 and running economy suggest that improvement in running economy leads to an improvement in endurance performance. This is suggested in two studies. A 7 year follow-up study of 10 yr old males indicated no change in peak VO_2 per unit body mass, a decline in the submaximal oxygen cost of locomotion—234 to 203 ml.kg^{-1}.km^{-1}, and an increase in the distance covered on a 9 minute run—1637 to 2115 m (Krahenbuhl et al.,1989). Daniels et al. (1978) showed similar results in young male distance runners in a mixed-longitudinal study that spanned 2 to 5 years. The trends are influenced, however, by the manner of expressing peak VO$_2$. When peak VO$_2$ is expressed per unit kg$^{-0.75}$, the opposite conclusion is suggested: peak VO$_2$ increases and running economy remains stable through childhood and adolescence. The endurance performance paradigm thus remains unclear.

Trainability of Aerobic Power in the Context of Growth and Maturation

Many physiological changes that occur in response to exercise mimic those that occur with normal growth and maturation. Therefore, a major obstacle is the partitioning of training effects from those associated with normal growth and maturation. The selection of appropriate control subjects is a critical element in the design of exercise training studies in youth (Rowland, 1996). Pre- and post-intervention levels of habitual physical activity, body size, and maturity status are also important considerations (Tolfrey et al., 1998).

A major question is as follows: "Are the growth-related improvements in physiological capacity a function of increasing body size or qualitative changes in the structural and functional capacity independent of body size or both?" To provide answers to this question, the confounding factor of body dimensions must be appropriately controlled. Until recently, growth- and training-related changes in peak VO$_2$ have been considered in absolute terms and expressed as a ratio standard, i.e., per kg of body mass (ml.kg^{-1}.min^{-1}). It is thus assumed that peak VO$_2$ is "normalized" and the influence of body mass is thus removed. Alternate statistical models, including analysis of covariance, allometric scaling, and multilevel modeling have been used to create a "size-free" expression of peak VO$_2$ in children and adolescents.

Among these models allometric scaling is the most widely used, although it remains to be demonstrated if allometric scaling in a small range of body size warrants such statistical manipulation. Scaling differences in body size within a small range to understand variation in biological function may thus be of limited value.

Armstrong and Welsman (1994) argue against the expression of peak VO$_2$ as a ratio standard for growth-related comparisons, stating that it clouds the understanding of growth and maturational changes in the oxygen transport system. A different interpretation of growth-related changes in peak VO$_2$ in a small sample of young athletes (n=8) is evident when it is expressed per kg$^{-0.75}$. Peak VO$_2$ remained stable during adolescence in the young distance runners when expressed as a ratio standard, but increased from 161 to 186 ml.kg$^{-0.75}$.min^{-1} (Sjodin and Svedenhag, 1992).

More recently, multilevel modeling has been used to investigate the effects of regular training during the transition into adolescence and through a good part of adolescence (Baxter-Jones et al., 1993). This approach attempts to partition the independent and multiplicative effects of age, body size, body composition, pubertal status, and exercise training on peak VO$_2$, the dependent variable. Two studies using multilevel modeling have demonstrated size-independent effects of sex and maturity status on peak VO$_2$ (Baxter-Jones et al., 1993; Armstrong et al., 1999). The biological interpretation of results derived from the multilevel modelling approach needs further clarification. Further, the approach has been used primarily with mixed-longitudinal data that do not span the adolescent phase of growth and maturation.

FUTURE DIRECTIONS

- The growth and maturation characteristics of subjects are generally not incorporated into studies of trainability. As a result, it is difficult to partition training effects from those associated with normal growth and maturation. Current statistical approaches, e.g., allometric scaling and multilevel modeling, need to be critically evaluated for their appropriateness and biological significance in examining interactions of growth and maturation on one hand, and training on the other.

- The presence of critical periods for trainability and related physiological mechanisms need further exploration.

- Appropriate animal models need to be developed to help understand structural and functional adaptations to training in young subjects. Many presently available technologies are invasive and thus have limitations in applicability to youth, but some current technology, e.g., magnetic resonance imagining and spectroscopy, may facilitate understanding of this area.

- Appropriate and effective training protocols for the development and maintenance of functional capacity at different stages of growth and maturation need to be established.

- There is a need for studies examining the effects of training on anaerobic power, anaerobic threshold, and submaximal economy, especially in girls.

- Results of trainability studies highlight the specificity of training and suggest transfer to other tasks. More studies need to examine the transfer of gains in functional capacity to field-related performances. Requirements for the maintenance of improvements associated with specific training protocols also need further study.

REFERENCES

American Academy of Pediatrics. (1983). Weight training and weight lifting: Information for the pediatrician. *Physician and Sportsmedicine* 11(3): 157-161.

Armstrong, N.; Welsman, J.; Nevill, A.; & Kirby, A. (1999). Modeling growth and maturation changes in peak oxygen uptake in 11-13 yr olds. *Journal of Applied Physiology* 87: 2230-2236.

Armstrong, N. & Welsman, J.R. (1994). Assessment and interpretation of aerobic fitness in children and adolescents. *Exercise and Sport Sciences Reviews* 22: 435-476.

Baxter-Jones, A.; Goldstein, H.; & Helms, P. (1993). The development of aerobic power in young athletes. *Journal of Applied Physiology* 75: 1160-1167.

Becker, D.M. & Vaccaro, P. (1983). Anaerobic threshold alterations caused by endurance training in young children. *Journal of Sports Medicine* 23: 445-449.

Blimkie, C.J.R.; Ramsay, J.; Sale, D.; MacDougall, D.; Smith, K.; & Garner, S. (1989). Effects of 10 weeks of resistance training on strength development in prepubertal boys. In Oseid, S. & Carlsen, H.-K. (Eds.), *Children and Exercise XIII*. Champaign, IL: Human Kinetics (pp. 183-197).

Blimkie, C.J.R. & Sale, D.G. (1998). Strength development and trainability during childhood. In Van Praagh, E. (Ed.), *Pediatric Anaerobic Performance*. Champaign, IL: Human Kinetics (pp. 193-224).

Bouchard, C.; Daw, E.; Rice, T.; Pérusse, L.; Gagnon, J.; Province, M.; Leon, A.S.; Rao, D.C.; Skinner, J.; & Wilmore, J.H. (1998). Familial resemblance for VO2max in the sedentary state: The HERITAGE family study. *Medicine and Science in Sports and Exercise* 30: 252-258.

Bouchard, C.; Malina, R.M.; & Pérusse, L. (1997). *Genetics of Fitness and Physical Performance*. Champaign, IL: Human Kinetics.

Bouchard, C.; Ping, A.; Rice, T.; Skinner, J.; Wilmore, J.H.; Gagnon, J.; Pérusse, L.; Leon, A.S.; & Rao, D.C. (1999). Familial aggregation of VO2max response to exercise training: Results from the HERITAGE Family Study. *Journal of Applied Physiology* 87: 1003-1008.

Daniels, J.; Oldridge, N.; Nagle, F.; & White, B. (1978). Differences and changes in VO$_2$ among young runners 10 to 18 years of age. *Medicine and Science in Sports* 10: 200-203.

Eriksson, B.O.; Engstrom, I.; Karlberg, P.; Saltin, B.; & Thoren, C. (1971). A physiological analysis of former girl swimmers. *Acta Paediatrica Scandinavica Supplement* 217: 68-72.

Faigenbaum, A.D.; Westcott, W.L.; Micheli, L.J.; Outerbridge, A.R.; Long, C.J.; LaRosa-Loud, R.; & Zaichkowsky, L.D. (1996). The effects of strength training and detraining on children. *Journal of Strength and Conditioning Research* 10: 109-114.

Faigenbaum, A.D.; Westcott, W.L.; LaRosa-Loud, R.; & Long, C. (1999). The effects of different resistance training protocols on muscular strength and endurance development in children. *Pediatrics* 104: 1-7.

Fukunaga, T.; Funato, K.; & Ikegawa, S. (1992). The effects of resistance training on muscle area and strength in prepubescent age. *Annals of Physiological Anthropology* 11: 357-364.

Gayagay, G.; Yu, B.; Hambly, B.; Boston, T.; Hahn, A.; Celermajer, D.; & Trent, R. (1998). Elite endurance athletes and the ACE I allele—the role of genes in athletic performance. *Human Genetics* 103: 48-50.

Grodjinovosky, A.; Inbar, O.; Dotan, R.; & Bar-Or, O. (1980) Training effect on the anaerobic performance of children as measured by the Wingate anaerobic test. In Berg, K. & Erisson, B.O. (Eds.), *Children and Exercise IX*. Baltimore: University Park Press (pp. 139-145).

Haffor, A.A.; Harrison, A.C.; & Catledge-Kirk, P.A. (1990). Anaerobic threshold alterations caused by interval training in 11 year olds. *Journal of Sports Medicine and Physical Fitness* 30: 53-56.

Haubenstricker, J. & Seefeldt, V. (1986). Acquisition of motor skills during childhood. In Seefeldt, V. (Ed.), *Physical Activity and Well-Being*. Reston, VA: American Alliance for Health, Physical Education, Recreation and Dance (pp. 41-101).

Ikai, M. (1966). The effects of training on muscular endurance. In Kato, K. (Ed.), *Proceedings of the International Congress of Sports Sciences*, 1964. Tokyo: University of Tokyo Press (pp. 145-158).

Inbar, O. & Bar-Or, O. (1986). Anaerobic characteristics in male children and adolescents. *Medicine and Science in Sports and Exercise* 18: 264-269.

Krahenbuhl, G.S.; Morgan, D.W.; & Pangrazi, R.P. (1989). Longitudinal changes in distance-running performance in young males. *International Journal of Sports Medicine* 10: 92-96.

Mahon, A.D. & Vaccaro, P. (1989). Ventilatory threshold and VO_2max changes in children following endurance training. *Medicine and Science in Sports and Exercise* 21: 425-431.

Malina, R.M.; Bouchard, C.; & Bar-Or, O. (2003). *Growth, Maturation, and Physical Activity*, 2nd edition. Champaign, IL: Human Kinetics.

Martin, J.C. & Malina, R.M. (1998). Developmental variations in anaerobic performance associated with age and sex. In Van Praagh, E. (Ed.), *Pediatric Anaerobic Performance*. Champaign, IL: Human Kinetics (pp. 45-64).

McManus, A.M.; Armstrong, N.; & Williams, C.A. (1997). Effect of training on the aerobic power and anaerobic performance of prepubertal girls. *Acta Paediatrica* 86: 456-459.

Mocellin, R. (1975). Jugend und sport. *Medizinische Klinik* 70: 1443-1457.

Mosher, R.E.; Rhodes, E.C.; Wenger, H.A.; & Filsinger, B. (1985). Interval training: The effects of a 12 week programme on elite prepubertal male soccer players. *Journal of Sports Medicine* 25: 5-9.

Nielsen, B.; Nielsen, K.; Behrendt-Hansen, M.; & Asmussen, E. (1980). Training of "functional muscular strength" in girls 7-19 years old. In Berg, K. & Eriksson, B.O. (Eds.), *Children and Exercise IX*. Baltimore: University Park Press (pp. 69-78).

Ozmun, J.C.; Mikesky, A.E.; & Surburg, P.R. (1994). Neuromuscular adaptations following prepubescent strength training. *Medicine and Science in Sports and Exercise* 26: 510-514.

Paavolainen, L.; Hakkinen, K.; Hamalainen, I.; Nummela, A.; & Rusko, H. (1999). Explosive-strength training improves 5-km running time by improving running economy and muscle power. *Journal of Applied Physiology* 86: 1527-1533.

Pate, R.R. & Ward, D.S. (1990). Endurance exercise trainability in children and youth. *Advances in Sports Medicine and Fitness* 3: 37-55.

Payne, V.G. & Morrow, J.R. (1993). Exercise and VO_2max in children: A meta-analysis. *Research Quarterly for Exercise and Sport* 64: 305-313.

Petray, C.K. & Krahenbuhl, G.S. (1985). Running training, instruction on running technique, and running economy in 10-year old males. *Research Quarterly of Exercise and Sport* 56: 251-255.

Pfeiffer, R.D. & Francis, R.S. (1986). Effects of strength training on muscle development in prepubescent,

pubescent, and postpubescent males. *Physician and Sportsmedicine* 14(9): 134-143.

Ramsay, J.A.; Blimkie, C.J.R.; Smith, K.; Garner, S.; MacDougall, J.D.; & Sale, D.G. (1990). Strength training effects in pre-pubescent boys. *Medicine and Science in Sports and Exercise* 22: 605-614.

Rankinen, T.; Pérusse, L.; Borecki, I.; Chagnon, Y.; Gagnon, J.; Leon, A.S.; Skinner, J.; Wilmore, J.H.; Rao, D.C.; & Bouchard, C. (2000). The Na+-K+-ATPase alpha2 gene and trainability of cardiorespiratory endurance: The HERITAGE Family Study. *Journal of Applied Physiology* 88: 346-351.

Rivera, M.; Dionne, F.; Simoneau, J.A.; Pérusse, L.; Chagnon, M.; Chagnon, M; Gagnon, J.; Leon, A.S.; Rao, D.C.; Skinner, J.; Wilmore, J.H.; & Bouchard, C. (1997). Muscle-specific creatine kinase gene polymorphism and VO2max in the Heritage Family Study. *Medicine and Science in Sports and Exercise* 29: 1311-1317.

Rogol, A.D. & Roemmich, J. (This volume). Pubertal alterations in growth and body composition and neuroendocrine mechanisms.

Rothstein, A.; Dotan, R.; Bar-Or, O.; & Tenenbaum, G. (1986). Effect of training on anaerobic threshold, maximal aerobic power and anaerobic performance of preadolescent boys. *International Journal of Sports Medicine* 7: 281-286.

Rowland, T.W. (1985). Aerobic response to endurance training in prepubescent children: A critical analysis. *Medicine and Science in Sports and Exercise* 17: 493-497.

Rowland, T.W. (1996). *Developmental Exercise Physiology*. Champaign, IL: Human Kinetics.

Rowland (This volume). *Cardiac Characteristics of the Child Endurance Athlete*.

Rowland, T.W. & Boyajian, A. (1995). Aerobic response to endurance exercise training in children. *Pediatrics* 96: 654-658.

Sale, D. (1989). Strength and power training during youth. In Gisolfi, C.V. & Lamb, D.R. (Eds.), *Perspectives in Exercise Science and Sports Medicine. Volume II. Youth, Exercise, and Sport.* Indianapolis, IN: Benchmark Press (pp. 165-216).

Simoneau, J.-A. & Bouchard, C. (1998). In Van Praagh, E. (Ed.), *Pediatric Anaerobic Performance.* Champaign, IL: Human Kinetics (pp. 5-21).

Sjodin, B. & Svedenhag, J. (1992). Oxygen uptake during running as related to body mass in circumpubertal boys: A longitudinal study. *European Journal of Applied Physiology* 65: 150-157.

Sklad, M. (1975). The genetic determination of the rate of learning of motor skills. *Studies in Physical Anthropology* 1: 3-19.

Thibault, M.C.; Simoneau, J.-A.; Cote, C.; Boulay, M.R.; Lagasse, P.; Marcotte, M.; Bouchard, C. (1986). Inheritance of human muscle enzyme adaptation to isokinetic strength training. *Human Heredity* 36: 341-347.

Thomis, M.A.; Beunen, G.P.; Maes, H.H.; Blimkie, C.J.; Van Leemputte, M.; Claessens, A.L.; Marchal, G.; Willems, E.; & Vlietinck, R.F. (1998). Strength training: Importance of genetic factors. *Medicine and Science in Sports and Exercise* 30: 724-731.

Tolfrey, K.; Campbell, I.; & Batterham, A. (1998). Aerobic trainability of prepubertal boys and girls. *Pediatric Exercise Science* 10: 248-263.

Welsman, J.R.; Armstrong, N.; & Withers, S. (1997) Responses of young girls to two modes of aerobic training. *British Journal of Sports Medicine* 31: 139-142.

Weltman, A.; Janney, C.; Rians, C.B.; Strand, K.; Berg, B.; Tippitt, S.; Wise, J.; Cahill, B.R.; & Katch, F.I. (1986). The effects of hydraulic resistance strength training in pre-pubertal males. *Medicine and Science in Sports and Exercise* 18: 629-638.

CHAPTER 7

Injury Profiles and Surveillance of Young Athletes

Steven J. Anderson
University of Washington

With increasing numbers of participants in youth sports comes an increasing risk for sports-related injury. Regular physical activity is being promoted for all young people because of the potential health benefits. However, injuries are an inevitable consequence of increasing activity and can offset the desired health benefits. To maintain the benefits of sports participation and physical activity, it is crucial to better understand and manage the risks.

Epidemiologic studies provide information on the frequency and types of sports injuries occurring in young people (Caine, et al, 1996; Mueller and Blyth, 1982; Rome, 1995; van Mechelin, et al., 1992). Unfortunately, limitations in the available literature often result in incomplete or biased concepts of injury risk. Deficiencies in our knowledge of the nature, frequency, and causes of youth sport injury limit efforts to enhance safety and/or prevent injuries.

Analysis of injury surveillance methods

Ideally, injury surveillance would provide clear information on which sports are safe (or unsafe), which participants are safe (or unsafe), and which factors (intrinsic and extrinsic) can be modified to improve safety. Analysis of surveillance methods reveals why clear answers are not always forthcoming.

Virtually every injury surveillance method has some basis for criticism (Atkinson and Nevill, 1998). Emergency department surveys of sports injuries tend to reflect a disproportionate number of acute and/or more severe injuries (Kvist et al., 1989; Tursz and Crost, 1986). Overuse injuries are underestimated in such surveys as well as injuries cared for in non-emergency settings. The injuries sustained in contact and collision sports such as football, wrestling, and hockey are more likely to be acute and hence, more likely to be seen in an emergency department. Conversely, sports such as swimming or distance running have a higher proportion of overuse injuries that rarely necessitate emergency care. Therefore, an emergency department survey of injury rates can make acute injuries appear to be more common than overuse injuries and make some contact-collision sports appear more dangerous than non-contact or endurance sports.

Similar biases may arise from examining insurance claims or medical costs for injuries (Kujala et al., 1995; Zaricznyj et al., 1980). Again, high visibility acute injuries are more likely to generate a medical evaluation when compared to injuries that are insidious in onset or are not severe enough to restrict activity. Acute injuries are also more likely to result in hospitalization or surgery and hence, are more likely to generate large medical bills. Acute injuries are also more easily linked with the sport that caused the injury. Since overuse injuries do not occur at a specific time or place, they are more difficult to connect with a particular sport. If overuse problems are not associated with a sport, surveys of sports-related injuries may under-report this category of injuries.

Injury surveys that require self-reporting are limited by patient recall and the patient's interpretation of what are often vague or non-specific symptoms (Backx et al., 1989; Baxter-Jones, et al., 1992; Bijur et al., 1995). Diagnostic accuracy and proper categorization of injuries may be difficult to verify. Self-reporting by children and adolescents is problematic as is reliance on the second-hand reports of parents or guardians.

Surveying injuries by the use of a field recorder can capture a broader range of injuries and injury severities (Garrick and Requa, 1981). Depending on the training of the recorder, diagnostic accuracy can also be enhanced by this method. Despite these benefits, the personnel and time commitment required for on-site injury surveillance limits the feasibility of such methods.

The information gathered by recorders is also limited by the diagnostic accuracy that can be achieved in a field setting (Atkinson and Nevill, 1998). If confirming a diagnosis requires X-rays or other special tests performed at outside locations, the quality of "on-site" information will be limited by the quality of "off-site" information and the degree to which this is communicated to the recorder.

Unless there are strict, objective criteria for defining injury, on-site surveillance carries the risk of producing inflated numbers of injuries. The convenience of having someone available to evaluate early or mild symptoms may result in a lower threshold for determining that an "injury" has occurred. Conversely, the inconvenience and cost of scheduling a formal medical appointment can raise the threshold for injury and decrease the apparent number of young athletes who get "injured."

Because of the inherent difficulties in yearlong field studies, some on-site injury surveys will focus on a specific sporting event or tournament (Maehlum, et al., 1986). With this format, the number and types of injuries recorded will be heavily influenced by the participants and the conditions at the time of the study. Information from such surveys is often generalized to the entire sport when, in reality, the information is applicable only to similar events or tournaments.

Cross-sectional studies examine injuries in a subset of the population over a defined time period. Unless the study population can be shown to be representative of the population at large, generalizations made from cross-sectional studies are not justified. Conditions at the time of the study may also limit extrapolations to the general population.

Defining injury

The definition of injury has significant bearing on the types and frequency of injuries recorded. The threshold for injury in most surveys requires time loss from the sport or a need to seek medical attention (Bijur et al., 1995; Kujala et al., 1995; Kvist et al., 1989; Tursz and Crost, 1986). If "time loss" is a criteria for injury, acute or severe injuries are more likely to be counted. Overuse injuries (e.g., tendinitis, periostitis, apophysitis) tend to limit, but not prevent, sports participation. As such, overuse injuries may not be equally recognized when the definition of injury requires "time loss."

When the threshold for injury is a medical contact or an insurance claim, the nature of the injury (acute vs. overuse), the availability of medical care, and the extent of insurance coverage will influence reported injury rates in predictable ways.

"Severe" injuries are generally defined as those requiring hospital care or injuries associated with extensive and/or prolonged disability (van Mechelin et al., 1992). Current surveillance methods favor detection of more severe injuries. However, traditional definitions of severity do not always reflect the impact an injury has on a given sport. For example, a sprain of the great toe would normally not be considered a severe injury. However, in a ballet dancer who must perform on pointe, a sprain to the great toe may disrupt an entire season. The same injury in a swimmer is unlikely to warrant a medical evaluation or require time loss from their sport. Similarly, elbow tendinitis may not be considered severe unless it occurs in a baseball pitcher. Conversely, a fracture of the hand may be considered a severe injury in a gymnast but have minimal impact on a soccer player. Hence, the context of the injury is critical in determining severity.

The term "injury" connotes a traumatic incident or event. Acute injuries occur at a specific time, have an identifiable mechanism, and have obvious symptoms and signs. Acute injuries fit the traditional definition of injury and, by their very nature, are more easily recognized. Alternatively, overuse injuries develop over time and do not have a specific injury-producing event. The symptoms, signs, and level of disability with overuse injuries may be subtle and variable. Hence, the diagnosis of overuse injury or even the recognition that an injury has occurred may be difficult. In some cases, overuse injuries are not included under the definition of injury.

Medical conditions such as dehydration, heat illness, or eating disorders are even more likely to escape detection as "injuries." A definition of injury that fails to account for the full spectrum of sports-related morbidity will lead to an incomplete view of the true risks.

The nature and frequency of reported injuries will also vary with the criteria used to diagnose injuries (Linder et al., 1981). When the definition of injury is not clear or uniform, different investigators surveying the same population may come up with different results.

Another factor that contributes to variable injury reporting is diagnostic terminology and accuracy.

Skeletally immature athletes are susceptible to unique injuries that are not always recognized as such (Anderson, 1991). Similar injury mechanisms may produce different responses depending on the maturity of the athlete. A valgus stress to the knee may cause a medial collateral ligament sprain in an adult and a distal femoral epiphyseal fracture in a skeletally immature athlete. Knee pain with swelling and locking may be due to a torn meniscus in an adult while the possibility of osteochondritis dissecans needs to be considered in a younger patient. Infrapatellar pain in an adult is usually due to patellar tendinitis whereas a younger patient is more likely to have Sindig-Larson-Johanssen syndrome or Osgood-Schlatter disease. When unique pediatric conditions are confused with the adult counterpart, the true injury risks for young athletes will be misrepresented.

Many individuals have growth and/or developmental conditions that can become symptomatic as a result of sports participation. An accessory navicular in the foot may become painful as a result of running or jumping. A congenital pars interarticularis defect may become symptomatic from forceful or repetitive lumbar extension. Since sports participation generally commences in the pediatric age group, the "unmasking" of these previously asymptomatic conditions is usually reflected in tallies of youth sports injuries. There is no clear consensus as to whether such occurrences should be classified as a sports injury or a pre-existing condition. However, when this category of problems is not segregated, it is impossible to know if they should be added or subtracted from reported injury totals.

Observer biases

Information about youth sports injuries is also documented in case reports or case series. Such studies tend to focus on specific injuries and/or specific treatment regimens. A case series usually has biases related to selection for the study and often lacks sufficient information for comparison with the remainder of the at risk population. There are also biases stemming from who is most likely to publish a case series. In general, specialists or sub-specialists have greater opportunity to gather sufficient numbers of specific cases for a series and may be more inclined to publish their experience.

The patients recruited for a case series are most likely to be patients whose problem required care by the specialist performing the study. As such, a case series often reflects a narrow subset of the injured population. The majority of sports problems requiring medical attention are cared for by primary care physicians. However, generalists are less likely to see sufficient numbers of a particular problem to publish a case series and may be less inclined to perform research or publish their clinical experience. Ironically, the problems and perspectives most likely to appear in the medical literature are least likely to be relevant to the providers caring for the majority of problems.

Observer bias may also come into play in injury surveillance. It is natural to expect that professional training and personal experience will influence which conditions will be preferentially noted (Atkinson and Nevill, 1998; Linder et al., 1981). Surgeons are accustomed to looking for problems that may need surgery. Rehabilitation specialists may be more attentive to problems that are treated with rehabilitative care. General medical physicians may be more oriented to illnesses or medical conditions. If physical therapists, athletic trainers, podiatrists, chiropractors, or psychologists are asked to survey an athletic population for injury, their reported findings are also likely to say as much about the observer as the population being observed.

Observer bias should be suspected when profiles of similar athletic populations appear inexplicably dissimilar. Observer bias may also account for apparent gaps in the medical literature or when familiar problems are discussed in unfamiliar terms.

Consequences/implications

It is difficult to carry out or even propose an injury surveillance method without biases or shortcomings. The limitations of the particular surveillance method employed must be understood when interpreting any study of youth sports injury. Many of the important questions posed for youth sports injury surveillance remain unanswered including information on overall injury risk, relative risk, individual risk, and efficacy of safety measures.

The answers to basic questions such as, "what are the chances that a given individual will sustain a sports injury?" are not always straightforward. To properly respond to this question requires information that is not always included in injury studies. "Injury" must be clearly defined before injury risk can be discussed. The definition of injury should accurately reflect the risks and morbidity of the sport in question. With proper injury definitions, the number of acute and overuse injuries that occur in a sport should be reflected proportionately in the injury report. Developmental conditions or anatomic variants that become symptomatic with sport should be distinguished from *de novo* injuries. Injury risk cannot be measured or implied without quantification of the population at risk and measurement of injury exposure. Injury rates should not be affected by access to medical care or by the diagnostic capabilities of the recorder.

To accurately determine relative risk, the same definitions and population measures discussed above must be applied to all sports in the comparison group. With proper methodology, injury rates can be compared between different sports. However, differences in the total number of injuries does not always reflect differences in safety. A sport such as football may have a relatively high number of injuries when compared to a sport such as cross country running. However, football injuries are predominantly acute and rarely require more than a week away from play. Conversely, the majority of injuries in cross country are overuse in nature. Recovery times of less than a week are rare; time losses ranging from 3-6 months are not rare. Even when injury definitions allow for equal recognition of acute and overuse injuries, comparing the risk of sports with different types of injuries requires looking beyond the simple injury rates.

Sports injury studies that examine overall risk or relative risk often fail to define the specific risk for an individual. Current statistics can provide rough estimates as to which sports are most dangerous and which injuries are most likely to occur. For these statistics to be meaningful to a given individual, that person would have to have the same age, gender, maturation, fitness, and physical make-up of the study population as well as the same training, rules, equipment, fields, surfaces, coaching, and environmental conditions. Given the improbability of satisfying these conditions, alternative methods for study of specific risk factors should be considered.

Individual risk factors for sports injury have been proposed (Lysens et al., 1984; Lysens et al., 1989; Meeuwisse, 1991). They include factors such as age, gender, maturation, flexibility, strength, fitness, alignment, psychologic make-up, health and injury history. Unfortunately, most injury studies fail to correlate injury with any of these factors. Because of the multifactoral nature of injury pathogenesis, studies that look at injuries in relation to flexibility, strength, alignment, or other physical characteristics are difficult to design and execute. Therefore, while experts may agree that individual characteristics are important in determining injury risk, proving these relationships scientifically remains problematic.

Similar concerns apply to the role of equipment and the role of environmental factors in sports injury. In selected situations such as heat injury, a clear relationship between the risk factor (high temperature) and the injury (heat injury) has been shown. However, for most environmental and equipment risks, a sound scientific foundation for safety and injury prevention has not been established. The lack of a better understanding of individual, environmental, and equipment-related risk factors will thwart any safety measures predicated on this understanding.

Conclusions/recommendations

Injury surveillance and profiling of young athletes serves as the foundation for sport safety and injury prevention programs. Analysis of current sport injury data reveals many areas where critical information is incomplete, inaccurate, or unavailable. The challenge to obtain higher quality and more complete youth injury data remains. To respond to this challenge, the following recommendations are offered:

1. Current information on youth sports injuries should be interpreted in light of methodologic biases and limitations.

Total injuries and injury risk must be interpreted in a context where injury is clearly defined as well as exposure time and the at-risk population. Total injuries should include both the high profile acute injuries as well as the more subtle overuse injuries and medical problems. Comparing risk between different sports or populations requires comparable data. Comparing injury rates between different sports may be misleading if the types of injury are different. The types of injuries reported may vary with the recording method and may reflect the biases of the investigator. Unique pediatric conditions should be distinguished from similar appearing adult counterparts. Symptomatic growth and developmental variants should be distinguished from injuries more directly attributable to skeletal immaturity.

2. Further studies on injury rates and injury risk factors are needed.

In order to reduce the biases and limitations found with current studies, a standard definition of sports injury is needed (van Mechelin et al., 1992). To encompass the full spectrum of sports-related morbidity, injury definitions must be sensitive to both acute injuries as well as overuse injuries, medical injuries, and conditions unique to the skeletally immature athlete. Definitions of injury severity should reflect disability with respect to the demands of the sport.

The connection between injuries and risk factors should be clarified by correlating injuries with injury mechanisms, use of equipment, elements of the sports environment, and individual risk factors. Ideally, injuries would be characterized in a manner that is meaningful and clinically relevant to the needs of both general medical providers as well as specialists.

3. Continue efforts to enhance safety and reduce injuries.

Better information on injury mechanisms, individual risk factors, and risks of the sports environment can foster more specific safety and risk management programs (American College of Sports Medicine, 1993; Rome, 1995; van Mechelin et al., 1992). Correlation between injury mechanisms and injuries can have meaningful implications for changes in rules or training regimens. The connection between individual risk factors and injury can facilitate better matching between individuals and sports. Appreciating these same correlations can enhance the yield of the preparticipation examination.

The sports environment and sports equipment can be factors in injury as well as factors in injury prevention. Further research is needed to clarify how these extrinsic risks can be modified or controlled to enhance safety. Coaches can be a link between a safe sports environment, safe equipment, and a safe sports experience. Educating and training youth coaches to be agents of sports safety should be a priority.

To reduce injuries that are recurrent or result from prior injury, prevention programs must also address the level of medical care available to young athletes. Early recognition and appropriate treatment of injuries can help reduce the number of mild injuries that become severe and reduce the number of re-injuries that occur because the original injury was not properly treated. In order to enhance available care, further research is need to better understand the barriers to existing care and to improve the training and preparation of those in a position to provide the care (Stirling and Landry, 1996).

REFERENCES

American College of Sports Medicine, (1993). Current comment: The prevention of sport injuries of children and adolescents. *Medicine and Science in Sports and Exercise* 25: 1-7.

Anderson, S.J. (1991). Health problems in adolescent athletes. *Current Opinion in Pediatrics* 3: 592-601.

Atkinson, G. & Nevill, A.M. (1998). Statistical methods for assessing measurement error (reliability) in variables relevant to sports medicine. *Sports Medicine* 26: 217-238.

Backx, F.J.G.; Erich, W.B.; Kemper, A.B.A.; & Verbeek, A.L.M. (1989). Sports injuries in school-aged children: An epidemiologic study. *American Journal of Sports Medicine* 17: 234-240.

Backx, F.J.G.; Beijer, H.J.M.; Bol, E.; & Erich, W.B. (1991). Injuries in high-risk persons and high-risk sports: A longitudinal study of 1818 school children. *American Journal of Sports Medicine* 19: 124-130.

Baxter-Jones, A.; Maffuli, N.; & Helms, P. (1992). Low injury rates in elite athletes. *Archives of Disease in Childhood* 68: 130-132.

Bijur, P.E.; Trumble, A.; Harel. Y.; Overpeck, M.D.; Jones, D.; & Scheidt, P.C. (1995). Sports and recreation injuries in US children and adolescents. *Archieves of Pediatric Adolescent Medicine* 149: 1009-1016.

Blyth, C.S. & Mueller, F.O. (1974). Injury rates vary with coaching. *Physician and Sportsmedicine* 1(11): 45-50.

Caine, D.J.; Caine, C.G.; & Lindner, K.J. (1996). *Epidemiology of Sports Injuries.* Champaign, IL: Human Kinetics.

Garrick, J.G. & Requa, R. (1981). Medical care and injury surveillance in the high school setting. *Physician and Sportsmedicine* 9(2): 115-120.

Kujala, U.M.; Taimela, S.; Antti-Poika, I.; Ovara, S.; Tuominen, R.; & Myllynen, P. (1995). Acute injuries in soccer, ice hockey, volleyball, basketball, judo, and karate: Analysis of national registry data. *British Medical Journal* 311: 1465-1468.

Kvist, M.; Kujala, U.M.; Heinonen, O.J.; Vuori, I.; Aho, A.J.; Pajulo, O.; Hintsa, A.; & Parvinen, T. (1989). Sports-related injuries in children. *International Journal of Sports Medicine* 10: 81-86.

Linder, C.W.; DuRant, R.; Seklecki, R.M.; & Strong, W.B. (1981). Preparticipation health screening of young athletes: Results of 1268 examinations. *American Journal of Sports Medicine* 9: 187-193.

Lysens, R.; Steverlynck, A.; van den Auwelle, Y.; Lefevre, J.; Renson, L.; Claessens, A.; & Ostyn, M. (1984). The predictability of sports injuries. *Sports Medicine* 1: 6-10.

Lysens, R.J.; Ostyn, M.S.; Auweele, Y.V.; Lefevre, J.; Vuylsteke, M.; & Renson, L. (1989). The accident-prone and overuse-prone profiles of the young athlete. *American Journal of Sports Medicine* 17: 612-619.

Maehlum, S.; Dahl, E.; & Daljord, O. (1986). Frequency of injuries in a youth soccer tournament. *Physician and Sportsmedicine* 14: 73-79.

Meeuwisse, W.H. (1991). Predictability of sports injuries. What is the epidemiological evidence? *Sports Medicine* 12: 8-15

Mueller, F. & Blyth, C. (1982). Epidemiology of sports injuries in children. *Clinical Sports Medicine* 1: 343-352.

Rome, E.S. (1995). Sports-related injuries among adolescents: When do they occur and how can we prevent them? *Pediatric Review* 16: 185-187.

Stirling, J.M. & Landry, G.L. (1996). Sports medicine training during pediatric residency. *Archives of Pediatrics and Adolescent Medicine* 150: 211-5.

Tursz, A. & Crost, M. (1986). Sports-related injuries in children: A study of their characteristics, frequency, and severity with comparison to other types of accidental injuries. *American Journal of Sports Medicine* 14: 294-299.

van Mechelin, W.; Hlobil, H.; & Kemper, H.C. (1992). Incidence, severity, aetiology and prevention of sports injuries. A review of concepts. *Sports Medicine* 14: 82-99.

Zaricznyj, B.; Shattuck, L.J.M.; Mast, T.A.; Robertson, R.V.; & D'Elia, G. (1980). Sports-related injuries in school-aged children. *American Journal of Sports Medicine* 8: 318-324.

CHAPTER 8

Genetic Advances and Their Implications for Sports Performance

Claude Bouchard
Pennington Biomedical Research Center
Louisiana State University

INTRODUCTION

Progress in molecular biology has given an extraordinary impetus to the study of the human genome. The availability of new technologies has extended the range of questions that can be contemplated in genetic investigations. Problems can now be defined in terms of molecular epidemiology, molecular nutrition, molecular medicine, and even molecular exercise science. And, there is no indication that the pace of progress is slowing as major advances are being reported at an increasing frequency.

Single gene diseases are being elucidated at the DNA and biochemical levels. Complex entities such as atherosclerosis, diabetes mellitus, obesity or hypertension are scrutinized in a search for single gene effects and susceptibility genes. The availability of literally tens of thousands of polymorphic markers distributed across the 22 pairs of autosomes and the sex chromosomes makes it possible to undertake genomic scans with a view to identify chromosomal positions of importance and to undertake positional cloning. Further, a large number of candidate genes for a particular phenotype can now be tested. Such candidate genes are generally identified on the basis of the current understanding of the biology or the physiopathology of the trait or from the evidence gathered in gene expression studies in relevant tissues. The use of these methods in the genetic dissection of complex traits is greatly favored by the high degree of homology between the rodent and human genomes.

It is increasingly feasible to begin genetic studies with a phenotype about which nothing or little is known about the genes involved. Indeed, it has become possible to identify a gene or isolate a specific chromosomal region encoding a gene associated or linked with a phenotype without having any knowledge about its functions. This is analogous to reverse genetics that was initially described in experimental organisms. However, these advances have not yet translated into significant progress in the understanding of sports performance.

GENETIC EPIDEMIOLOGY

Over the last thirty years or so, studies have been reported on the contributions of genetic and nongenetic factors to the population variance in endurance performance phenotypes, particularly on maximal oxygen uptake (VO₂max). It is not possible to review here all the evidence pertaining to the role of genetic differences in endurance performance related phenotypes. Rather, the evidence from key genetic epidemiology studies of VO_2max will be highlighted.

The heritability of VO_2max has been estimated from twin and family studies. Three family studies have measured VO_2max (Bouchard et al., 1998; Bouchard et al., 1986; Lesage et al., 1985). The most comprehensive of these is the HERITAGE Family Study, which is a multicenter study designed to investigate the role of the genotype in cardiovascular, metabolic and hormonal responses to aerobic exercise training (Bouchard et al., 1995). In 429 healthy but sedentary Caucasian subjects form 86 nuclear families, two maximal ergometer exercise tests were performed on separate days, with at least 48 hours between the tests (Bouchard et al., 1998). The average VO_2max was used in the analyses if both values were within 5% of each other. If the difference was greater than 5%, the higher value was used. An analysis of variance revealed a clear familial aggregation of VO_2max in the sedentary state. The variance for VO_2max (adjusted for age, sex, body mass and body composition) was 2.72 times greater between families than within families and about 40% of the variance in VO_2max was accounted for by family lines. Maximum likelihood estimation of familial correlations revealed a maximal heritability (i.e. combined effect of genetic factors and nongenetic transmission) of 51% for VO_2max. However, the significant spouse correlation indicated that the genetic heritability was less than 50 % (Bouchard et al., 1998). The concept of family lines with low and high VO_2max phenotypes in the sedentary state is illustrated in Figure 1.

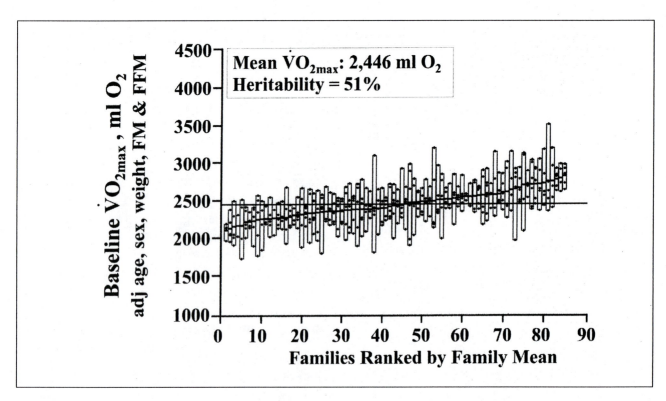

Figure 1. VO_2max adjusted for age, sex, body weight, fat mass and fat-free mass plotted by family rank. Each family is enclosed in a box, with individual data points plotted as dots and each family mean as a dash. The horizontal reference line is the group mean. Reproduced with permission from Bouchard et al. (1998).

Table 1 summarizes intraclass correlations in pairs of dizygous (DZ) and monozygous (MZ) twins from 7 studies. The data vary in test protocol (measured or predicted aerobic power, maximal or submaximal tests), the number of twin pairs, adjustment of data (uncontrolled age or sex effects), and differences in means or variances between twin types. The intraclass correlations for MZ twins ranged from about 0.6 to 0.9, whereas correlations for DZ twins with one exception ranged from 0.3 to 0.5. The largest of the twin studies (Sundet et al., 1994) was derived from a population-based twin panel of conscripts. The data were based on predicted VO_2max values, which were subsequently transformed to categorical scores, from low to high maximal aerobic power, but intraclass correlations for the categorical scores were similar to those found in other twin studies (Sundet et al., 1994).

In our own study involving 27 pairs of brothers, 33 pairs of dizygotic twins and 53 pairs of monozygotic twins (Bouchard et al., 1986), heritability was about 40% for VO_2max per kg of body mass. However, since the correlation in

Source	N pairs		Test	MZ	DZ
	MZ	DZ			
Klissouras (1971) Males	15	10	VO_2max/kg	0.91	0.44
Klissouras et al. (1973) Males and Females	23	16	VO_2max/kg	0.95	0.36
Bouchard et al. (1986) Males and Females	53	33	VO_2max/kg	0.71	0.51
Fagard et al. (1991)	29	19	VO_2max/kg	0.77	0.04
Maes et al. (1993) Males and Females	41	50	VO_2max/kg	0.85	0.56
Sundet et al. (1994) Males	436	622	VO_2max/kg Predicted [A]	0.62	0.29
Maes et al. (1996) 10-year-old boys and girls	43	61	VO2max/kg [B]	0.75	0.32

[A] Maximal aerobic power was predicted from a nomogram and the predicted VO2max was subsequently transformed to a categorical score from 1 to 9. The intraclass correlations are based upon the categorical scores.
[B] VO2max not adjusted for body mass.

Table 1. Intraclass correlations from twin studies of maximal oxygen intake

dizygotic twins (intraclass=0.51) was high in comparison to the brothers (intraclass=0.41), we hypothesized that the 40% estimate was probably inflated by common environmental factors, and that the true heritability of VO_2max per kg of mass was more likely to lie between 25 and 40% of the adjusted phenotypic variance.

Two familial studies have suggested the likelihood of a specific maternal effect for VO_2max (Lesage et al., 1985; Bouchard et al., 1998). This hypothesis was prompted by the observation that correlations reached 0.20 and above in mother-child pairs, but were about zero in father-child pairs for VO_2max per kg of mass or per kg of fat-free mass (Lesage et al., 1985). More recently, the HERITAGE Family Study (Bouchard et al., 1998) has also provided evidence for a substantial maternal heritability in VO_2max adjusted for age, sex, body mass and body composition. About half of the maximal heritability of VO_2max observed in the sedentary state was compatible with a maternal, and possibly a mitochondrial, transmission.

GENETICS AND RESPONSIVENESS TO EXERCISE TRAINING

Several exercise training studies have shown that there are marked interindividual differences in the trainability of cardiorespiratory endurance phenotypes after exposure to an identical training program (Bouchard, 1983). Results from these twin studies and data from the HERITAGE Family Study suggest that the trainability of cardiorespiratory fitness phenotypes is, to some extent, genetically determined.

In pairs of MZ twins, the VO_2max response to standardized training in a series of experiments showed 6 to 9 times more variance between genotypes (between pairs of twins) than within genotypes (within pairs of twins) (Bouchard et al., 1992). In one particular experiment, 10 pairs of

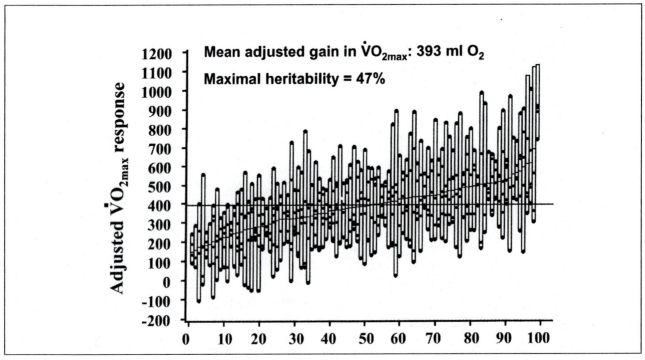

Figure 2. VO_2max response to a 20-week endurance training program. Data are adjusted for age, sex and pre-training VO_2max plotted by family rank. Each family is enclosed in a box, with individual data points plotted as dots and each family mean as a dash. The horizontal reference line is the group mean. Reproduced with permission from Bouchard et al. (1999).

male MZ twins were submitted to a standardized endurance-training program for 20 weeks. Gains in absolute VO_2max showed almost 8 times more variance between than within pairs of twins. The intrapair resemblance for changes in VO_2max were significant with an intraclass correlation reaching 0.77 (Prud'homme et al., 1984; Bouchard et al., 1992).

The most convincing evidence for the presence of family lines in the trainability of VO_2max comes from the HERITAGE Family Study. The adjusted (age, sex and baseline VO_2max) VO_2max response showed 2.6 times more variance between families than within families, and the model-fitting analytical procedure yielded a maximal heritability estimate of 47% (Bouchard et al., 1999). The familial aggregation of the VO_2max response phenotype is illustrated in Figure 2.

MOLECULAR STUDIES

Based on the evidence gathered in twin and family studies, it is justified to search for chromosomal regions, genes and mutations pertaining to VO_2max in the sedentary state and its responsiveness to training. The genetic dissection of these two phenotypes and their determinants requires a wide array of designs and technologies. A handful of studies have focused on candidate genes encoded in the nuclear DNA and on a few mitochondrial DNA sequences. However, it must be recognized that it is unlikely that a single gene or very few loci will be sufficient to define the genetic component of VO_2max and its trainability. To illustrate the underlying concept behind these candidate gene studies and their limitations as well, we will consider one example here.

Skeletal muscle-specific creatine kinase (CKMM) is a legitimate candidate gene (chromosomal mapping on 19q13.22) to investigate in relation to endurance performance. CKMM activity level is two times greater in type II (fast-twitch) than in type I fibers (Yamashita and Yoshioka, 1991), and a low CKMM activity level is typical of the skeletal muscle of endurance athletes. An early study indicated that a CKMM protein charge variant was weakly associated with the ability to perform a 90-min endurance test (Bouchard et al., 1989). In addition, research on transgenic mice indicates that a low CKMM activity is associated with improved skeletal muscle resistance to fatigue (van Deursen et al., 1993). More recently, a sib-pair linkage study has shown a weak genetic linkage between the CKMM locus and changes in VO2max (age, sex, and pre-training VO2max adjusted) in the HERITAGE Family Study (Rivera et al., 1999). Moreover, we have reported a significant association between the CKMM genotype and the VO_2max response to 20-weeks of endurance training in both parents and adult offspring of the HERITAGE Family Study (Rivera et al., 1997). One-third of all homozygotes for the less frequent allele (CKMM Ncol polymorphism in the 3' untranslated region) were observed in the low responder group (lowest decile of response), whereas this genotype was not seen in any high responders (upper decile of response). The CKMM genotype accounted for about 10% of the variance of VO_2max response.

The results of a genomic scan based on 289 polymorphic markers covering all 22 pairs of autosomes performed on the Caucasian families of the HERITAGE Family Study were recently reported. The mean spacing of the markers was 11 cM and a total of 99 families and 415 pairs of sibs were available for the study. VO_2max in the sedentary state was adjusted for the effects of age, sex, body mass, fat mass and fat-free mass while the VO_2max response was adjusted for age and baseline level of the phenotype. Two analytical strategies were used: a single point linkage procedure using all available pairs of sibs (SIBPAL) and a multipoint variance components approach using all the family data (SEGPATH). Linkages at p values of 0.01 and better were observed with markers on 4q, 8q, 11p and 14q for VO_2max before training and with markers on 1p, 2p, 4q, 6p and 11p for the change in VO_2max in response to 20 weeks of a standardized endurance training program (Bouchard et al., 2000). These chromosomal regions harbor many genes that may qualify as candidate genes for these quantitative traits and the research should now focus on these genomic regions.

IMPLICATIONS FOR SPORTS

A more detailed discussion of the implications for the world of sport and sport sciences has been presented in a book that we published recently together with L. Perusse and R. M. Malina (Bouchard et al., 1997). World class athletes in any sport are not only talented for a particular sport activity, but they have also been willing to train and compete until world class status was attained. The price for such prominence is very high in terms of human dedication and financial involvement.

It was possible up until about the middle of this century to become a national or a world class athlete in a given athletic event without being among the most talented individuals of a nation or the world at the time. The selection process was less stringent and the level of competition was not as demanding as today. With the continuous expansion of the pool of young participants and competitors, and with the growing sophistication of training, psychological preparation, equipment and facilities, the level of competition has increased to the point that only those individuals who are highly gifted can expect to reach elite status. Moreover, with the growth in the number of participants in developing countries, an expanded pool of talented individuals and, therefore, a larger array of genotypes is bound to be active on the sport fields. This should contribute to the overall progress in sports performance at the world level.

Two views are commonly encountered concerning the identification of the gifted performer (Bouchard, 1991; Malina, 1993). The first holds that the talented athletes emerge from the sport pyramid. A large number of participants (the base of the pyramid) have the opportunity to take part in the activity, engage in competition, and if they perform well and are interested, get the chance to reach higher levels depending on talent, interest, motivation and economic circumstances. In this approach, a large base of recreational participants, particularly among children and adolescents, is a desirable characteristic. This has been the dominant approach up until the late 1960s and is still the basic philosophy of sport governing bodies in many countries.

The second view is based on the notion that there are individuals who are more endowed than others in terms of the basic skills and physique characteristics commonly associated with success in a given competitive sport. The goal is then to try to identify the children who exhibit these favorable traits. In practice, large numbers of children and adolescents are measured and tested with a battery of tests that tend to be sport specific. The most talented subjects, as defined by these tests, are then typically offered the opportunity to be part of a special school curriculum in which time as well as human and physical resources are available to learn the skills of the particular sport and to train at a high level. The youth who succeed are then nurtured in the developmental system of the particular sport (Bouchard, 1991).

Both approaches are obviously not mutually exclusive, particularly in a democratic society in which anyone who can meet the standards or attain the performance levels of the elite can expect to be invited to join and be offered training conditions conducive to the development of his or her talent.

With progress in the biological sciences, such as those briefly discussed above, the present talent detection practices will eventually be altered, perhaps in a dramatic manner. While specific "athletic genotypes" will never be sufficient by themselves to predict who will become an elite athlete, since there are many other variables that must be considered, it is probably safe to assume that there will be few elite performers in the future who will not enjoy favorable genetic characteristics. It is, therefore, likely that probes will be eventually used to identify the carriers of DNA sequence variations desirable for sport performance, particularly if a small number of genes are found to have a substantial influence. This is likely to happen first for endurance performance activities.

It has been suggested that nothing will prevent parents, sport leaders, coaches or entrepreneurs to use genetic probes in children and then in infants for the purpose of identifying potentially talented individuals (Bouchard, 1991). There is also the possibility that athletic-minded and overly ambitious parents, with the help of forceful entrepreneurs, may later take advantage of the progress made in the biology of reproduction to advocate embryo selection based on specific athletic probes to allow parents or surrogate parents to fulfill their dreams. On the surface, this scenario may appear like science fiction; however, it is not. All of the technologies necessary to make this possible are presently available and are commonly used in a number of specialized centers around the world in a variety of circumstances. The only misssing element for the application of these advanced technologies in the context of sport is knowledge about the important genes upon which athletic genotypes can be defined and embryo selection be designed.

It is likely that this phenomenon will occur within the next 10 to 15 years. The world of high performance sport is so competitive and, for some nations, the stakes are so high, that the use of such technologies will simply constitute a means to attain a goal. The determination of some ambitious parents who would like to see one of their offspring on the olympic podium, should also not be underestimated.

Needless to say, systems for identifying talented individuals for high performance sport will experience a major revolution in decades to come. This will in all likelihood begin when the first key genes, with large effects on performance, or trainability are uncovered. When this happens, the world of sport will be faced with the daunting task of addressing the ethical issues associated with the new opportunities and the ensuing changing environment of sport.

RESEARCH NEEDS

So much remains to be investigated in the field of molecular biology and genetics applied to the field of physical activity and sports performance that it would take a whole treatise to list the research needs. I will mention only two here. It is obvious that we need to understand if differences in the level of habitual physical activity are influenced in part by one or a few genes. If so, finding the nature of these genes and of the pathways involved as well as the role of DNA sequence variation in these genes on physical activity level should be a research priority.

The research agenda should also include studies designed to identify the genes and mutations responsible for the considerable heterogeneity in trainability. These studies should not be limited to the responsiveness to endurance training but should rather incorporate other types of performance such as those placing heavy demands on muscle strength or power as well as motor learning.

REFERENCES

Bouchard, C. (1983). Human adaptability may have a genetic basis. In: Landry, F. (Ed.), *Health Risk Estimation, Risk Reduction and Health Promotion*. Ottawa: Canadian Public Health Association.

Bouchard, C. (1991). Quelques réflexions sur l'avèvement des biotechnologies dans le sport. In: Landry, F.; Landry, M.; & Yerlès, M. (Eds.) *Proceedings of the International Symposium on Sport...The Third Millennium*. Québec: Les Presses de l'Université Laval (pp. 455-464).

Bouchard, C.; Chagnon, M.; Thibault, M.C.; Boulay, M.R.; Marcotte, M.; Cote, C.; & Simoneau, J.A. (1989). Muscle genetic variants and relationship with performance and trainability. *Medicine and Science in Sports and Exercise* 21: 71-77.

Bouchard, C.; Daw, E.W.; Rice, T.; Pérusse, L.; Gagnon, J.; Province, M.A.; Leon, A.S.; Rao, D.C.; Skinner, J.S.; & Wilmore, J.H. (1998). Familial resemblance for VO$_2$max in the sedentary state: The HERITAGE family study. *Medicine and Science in Sports and Exercise* 30: 252-258.

Bouchard, C.; Dionne, F.T.; Simoneau, J.A.; & Boulay, M.R. (1992). Genetics of aerobic and anaerobic performances. *Exercise and Sport Sciences Reviews* 20: 27-58.

Bouchard, C.; Leon, A.S.; Rao, D.C.; Skinner, J.S.; Wilmore, J.H.; & Gagnon, J. (1995). The HERITAGE family study: Aims, design, and measurement protocol. *Medicine and Science in Sports and Exercise* 27: 721-729.

Bouchard, C.; Lesage, R.; Lortie, G.; Simoneau, J.-A.; Hamel, P.; Boulay, M.R.; Perusse, L.; & Theriault, G. (1986). Aerobic performance in brothers, dizygotic and monozygotic twins. *Medicine and Science in Sports and Exercise* 18: 639-646.

Bouchard, C.; Malina, R.M.; & Pérusse, L. (1997). *Genetics of Fitness and Physical Performance*. Champaign, IL: Human Kinetics.

Bouchard, C.; Ping, A.; Rice, T.; Skinner, J.S.; Wilmore, J.H.; Gagnon, J.; Perusse, L.; Leon, A.S.; & Rao, D.C. (1999). Familial aggregation of VO$_2$max response to exercise training: Results from the HERITAGE Family Study. *Journal of Applied Physiology* 87: 1003-1008.

Bouchard, C.; Rankinen, T.; Chagnon, Y.; Rice, T.; Perusse, L.; Gagnon, J.; Borecki, I.; An, P.; Leon, A.; Skinner, J.; Wilmore, J.; Province, M.; & Rao, D.C. (In press). Genomic scan for maximal oxygen uptake and its response to training in the HERITAGE family study. *Journal of Applied Physiology*.

Fagard, R.; Bielen, E.; & Amery, A (1991). Heritability of aerobic power and anaerobic energy generation during exercise. *Journal of Applied Physiology* 70: 357-362.

Klissouras, V. (1971). Heritability of adaptive variation. Journal of Applied Physiology 31: 338-344.

Klissouras, V.; Pirnay, F.; & Petit, J.M. (1973). Adaptation to maximal effort: Genetics and age. *Journal of Applied Physiology* 35: 288-293.

Lesage, R.; Simoneau, J.A.; Jobin, J.; Leblanc, J.; & Bouchard, C. (1985). Familial resemblance in maximal heart rate, blood lactate and aerobic power. *Human Heredity* 35: 182-189.

Maes, H.; Beunen, G.; Vlietinck, R.; Lefevre, J.; van den Bossche, C.; Claessens, A.; Derom, R.; Lysens, R.; Renson, R.; Simons, J.; & Vanden Eynde, B. (1993).

Heritability of health- and performance-related fitness: Data from the Leuven Longitudinal Twin Study. In: Duquet, W. & Day, J.A.P. (Eds.), *Kinanthropometry IV*. London: E & FN Spon. (pp. 140-149).

Maes, H.H.; Beunen, G.P.; Vlietinck, R.F.; Neale, M.C.; Thomis, M.; Vanden Eynde, B.; Lysens, R.; Simons, J.; Derom, C.; & Derom, R. (1996). Inheritance of physical fitness in 10-yr-old twins and their parents. *Medicine and Science in Sports and Exercise* 28: 1479-1491.

Malina, R.M. (1993). Youth sports: Readiness, selection and trainability. In: Duquet, W. & Day, J.A.P. (Eds.), *Kinanthropometry IV*. London: E & FN Spon (pp. 285-301).

Prud'homme, D.; Bouchard, C.; Leblanc, C.; Landry, F.; & Fontaine, E. (1984). Sensitivity of maximal aerobic power to training is genotype-dependent. *Medicine and Science in Sports and Exercise* 16: 489-493.

Rivera, M.A.; Dionne, F.T.; Simoneau, J.A.; Pérusse, L.; Chagnon, M.; Chagnon, Y.C.; Gagnon, J.; Leon, A.S.; Rao, D.C.; Skinner, J.S.; Wilmore, J.H.; & Bouchard, C. (1997). Muscle-specific creatine kinase gene polymorphism and VO$_2$max in the HERITAGE family study. *Medicine and Science in Sports and Exercise* 29: 1311-1317.

Rivera, M.A.; Pérusse, L.; Simoneau, J.A.; Gagnon, J.; Dionne, F.T.; Leon, A.S.; Skinner, J.S.; Wilmore, J.H.; Province, M.; Rao, D.C.; & Bouchard, C. (1999). Linkage between a muscle-specific CK gene marker and VO$_2$max in the HERITAGE family study. *Medicine and Science in Sports and Exercise* 31: 698-701.

Sundet, J.M.; Magnus, P.; & Tambs, K. (1994). The heritability of maximal aerobic power: A study of Norwegian twins. *Scandinavian Journal of Medical Science in Sports* 4: 181-185.

van Deursen, J.; Heerschap, A.; Oerlemans, F.; Ruitenbeek, W.; Jap, P.; ter Laak, H.; & Wieringa, B. (1993). Skeletal muscles of mice deficient in muscle creatine kinase lack burst activity. *Cell* 74: 621-631.

Yamashita, K. & Yoshioka, T. (1991). Profiles of creatine kinase isoenzyme compositions in single muscle fibres of different types. *Journal of Muscle Research and Cell Motility* 12: 37-44.

CHAPTER 9

Social Influences on Children's Psychosocial Development in Youth Sports

Maureen R. Weiss
University of Virginia

Significant adults and peers play a central role in children's psychosocial development through sport participation. Key areas of psychosocial development include self-perceptions (self-esteem, perceived competence), affective responses to physical activity (enjoyment, anxiety), and motivation to continue involvement (effort, persistence). These areas of development, in turn, are crucial to maintaining and enhancing sport and physical activity participation so that youth are able to accrue the physical and psychosocial benefits of activity. A considerable amount of research shows that parents are especially important socializing agents in early and middle childhood, while peers escalate in salience in later childhood and adolescence. However, research also shows that significant adults (parents, teachers, coaches) and peers (classmates, close friends) both make a huge impact on cognitive, affective, and behavioral outcomes throughout childhood and adolescence (Brustad, 1996a; Harter, 1990; Horn, 1987; Weiss et al., 1996). This paper thus focuses upon children's and adolescents' social networks and supports in the domain of sport and physical activity, and the mechanisms by which interactions with significant adults and peers influence self-perceptions, affect, and motivation.

Social influences are central to every theory of motivation that has been applied to the physical domain (Weiss, Ferrer-Caja, 2002). In theories or models such as the sport commitment model (Scanlan et al., 1993), competence motivation theory (Harter, 1978), and cognitive evaluation theory (Deci and Ryan, 1985), influence in the form of social support and constraints, and modeling, informational feedback, and reinforcement by parents, coaches, and peers dominate. In the expectancy-value model (Eccles et al., 1998), socializers' beliefs about a child's competence and the value of being good in sport, and provision of experiences and expression of behaviors that reflect such beliefs are implicated in children's motivated behavior. In achievement goal theory (Ames, 1992; Nicholls, 1989), the motivational or psychological climate shaped by adults and peers emphasizes what is recognized, valued, and evaluated in sport environments. Whether the process of learning or performance outcome is more highly valued and rewarded is what influences children's competence perceptions, feelings of enjoyment, and subsequent motivation. Given the attention that significant others and motivational climate play in these theories, it is fitting that these social influences be given primary attention.

First, a conceptual framework based upon Harter's (1987) model of self-worth is presented to depict the network of relationships among social influence, self-perceptions, affect, and motivation in youth sport. This model is used to answer three questions related to parent, coach, and peer influence in the physical domain: (a) What do we know? (theory and research); (b) What does this knowledge mean? (application); and (c) What do we need to know? (future directions). Second, a model that encompasses motivational climate, individual differences (perceived competence, goal orientations), and affective and motivational outcomes is used to synthesize the research emanating primarily from achievement goal theory. The same three questions – what do we know, what does this knowledge mean, and what do we need to know – are also addressed with this model.

Social Influences: The Role of Parents, Coaches, and Peers

Theories of motivation highlight the role of significant others in shaping children's self-perceptions, affect, and motivation. Harter (1985, 1987) developed a comprehensive model of global self-worth that considers perceived social regard or support from adults and peers as key determinants of self-esteem, affect, and motivation (Figure 1). Perceived competence or adequacy (e.g., athletic competence, physical appearance) is identified as another antecedent of these psychosocial variables. Because parents, coaches, and peers serve as salient sources of physical competence information for children and adolescents, a link between these two constructs is included in the model (dotted line from social support to perceived competence). Harter's model is an appealing framework for

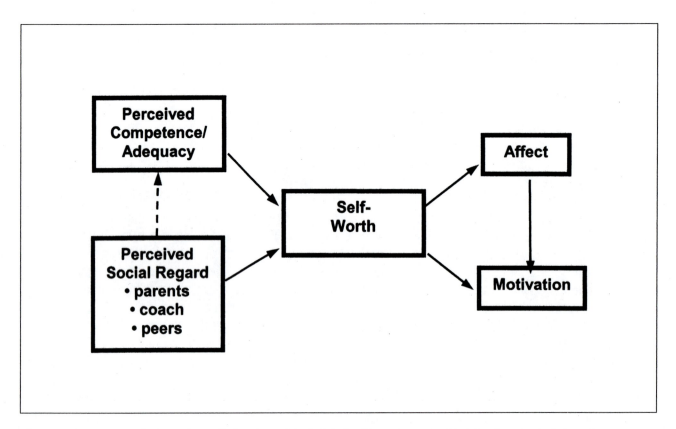

Figure 1. Susan Harter's (1987) mediational model of global self-worth customized for the physical domain.

understanding social influences in youth sport (Weiss and Ebbeck, 1996; Weiss and Ferrer-Caja, 2002).

Harter's emphasis on significant others' influence was inspired by the work of Cooley (1902) who felt that self-esteem was heavily steeped in social origins. His notion of the "looking-glass self" conveys the message that children view parents, coaches, and peers as social mirrors through which they evaluate their competencies and worth as a person. Harter (1990, 1999) has shown that social regard or support is a powerful predictor of self-conceptions in children through older adults, but the source of support that is most salient varies developmentally. For young children and adolescents, parents and other adults (teacher, coach) are salient and strong influences, while perceived social acceptance and support by general peers (i.e., classmates, teammates) and close

friends are key determinants of psychosocial development in childhood through adulthood. A variation of Harter's model is depicted in Figure 2, which emphasizes the central role of parents, coaches, and peers in the physical domain. This model is used to systematically present research and practical applications of significant adult influence in the form of parents and coaches, and the child's peer group as a source of social regard.

Parents: What do we know?

A number of studies have illustrated a strong link between parental beliefs, expectancies, and behaviors with children's psychosocial responses to participation and levels of activity involvement (see Brustad, 1992, 1996a, this volume, for major reviews). Moreover, parental feedback and interactions are sources of children's physical competence judgments and enjoyment of sport

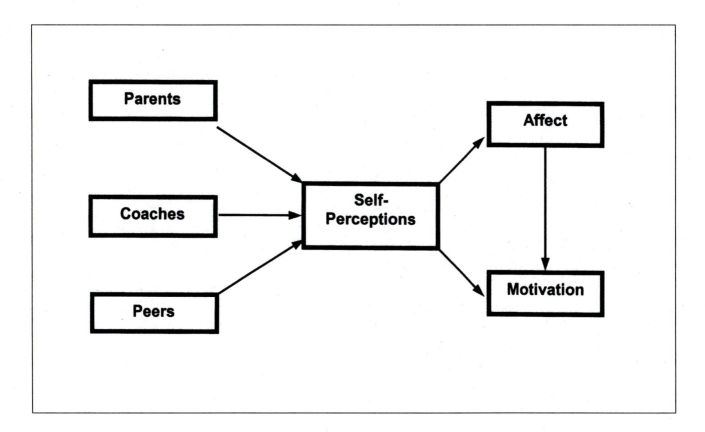

Figure 2. Model of parent, coach, and peer influence on psychosocial development.

(Horn and Harris, 1996; Scanlan and Simons, 1992). Parents are especially important as transmitters of information about their child's competence and the value about the importance of physical activity through the mechanisms of modeling and reinforcement behaviors. In youth sport, these beliefs and behaviors are readily observed between parents and children in positive (e.g., unconditional support, encouragement, positive expectancies) *and* negative (e.g., pressure to perform, stereotypic beliefs, negative competency beliefs) ways.

Brustad (1988, 1993, 1996b) conducted a series of studies on the influence of parental attitudes and behaviors on children's physical competence perceptions and affective responses to physical activity. Children who perceived less pressure from parents to perform well reported higher levels of enjoyment over the course of a basketball season (Brustad, 1988). Further, children who were higher in competitive trait anxiety reported more frequent worries about negative evaluation from important others, including parents than those lower in anxiety. Weiss et al. (1989) corroborated these findings with youth gymnasts, who disclosed that "what my parents will say" and "letting my parents down" were the two most frequently cited worries they experienced prior to competitive events.

In Brustad (1993), parents rated their fitness level, and enjoyment of and value toward physical activity. They also indicated how frequently they encourage their child to be physically active and how often they participate with their child. Results revealed that parents who reported greater enjoyment of physical activity were more encouraging of their children to be active. Greater parental enjoyment and encouragement were associated with higher levels of children's perceived competence and attraction to physical activity. The findings were also moderated by gender: parents gave more encouragement to sons than daughters, and girls reported lower perceived physical competence and positive affect toward physical activity than did boys. The study of parental

influence was extended to lower socioeconomic youth in a large urban area (Brustad, 1996b). Children rated parents' encouragement of their participation, parents' enjoyment of their own physical activity, and degree to which parents exercise. Perceptions of greater parental encouragement and enjoyment were associated with children's perceived competence and intrinsic interest for participating in physical activity and sport. Gender again emerged as a moderating variable with boys reporting greater parental encouragement, enjoyment, and role modeling, as well as higher perceived physical competence and attraction toward physical activity.

The studies of Kimiecik and colleagues (Dempsey et al., 1993; Kimiecik and Horn, 1998; Kimiecik et al., 1996) have contributed substantially to the understanding of determinants of children's psychosocial development and physical activity involvement. Dempsey et al. (1993) examined the relation between parent beliefs and behaviors and children's moderate-to-vigorous physical activity (MVPA. Children whose parents held higher competency beliefs for them recorded higher MVPA levels. Kimiecik et al. (1996) examined the relationship between children's fitness-related beliefs, children's perceptions of parental beliefs about them, and MVPA. Children who perceived that their parents valued fitness, held high competency beliefs for them, and endorsed both task and ego goals reported higher fitness competence and task and ego goals for MVPA. Perceptions of parental value, expectancies, perceived competence, and goal orientations about MVPA were not *directly* associated with children's MVPA; rather they were mediated by the relationship between perceptions of parental beliefs and children's MVPA. Finally, Kimiecik and Horn (1998) assessed parental beliefs about their child's MVPA, whether these beliefs were differentiated by their own or their child's gender, the link between parents' and child's MVPA level, and the relation between parent-reported beliefs and their child's MVPA. Mothers and fathers did not differ on perceived competence, value, or goal orientations for their daughters or sons. Parent-reported MVPA was not related to child's MVPA (i.e., no support for role modeling effects). And, parents' competency beliefs for their child, and to a lesser extent mother's task orientation, were significantly related to the child's MVPA.

Babkes and Weiss (1999) examined parental influence on perceived competence, emotional responses, and motivational orientation in 9-12 year-old soccer players. Three key relationships were pursued: (a) children's perceptions of parent influence and psychosocial responses; (b) parent-reported attitudes and behaviors for these psychosocial outcomes; and, (c) congruency between child and parent perceptions of parental attitudes and behaviors. Athletes who reported more positive perceptions of their mother's and father's competency beliefs, responses to soccer performance, and role modeling behavior reported higher perceived soccer competence, enjoyment, and intrinsic motivation. Positive perceptions of father's involvement in soccer, and less pressure to perform well were also associated with positive psychosocial responses. There was a nonsignificant relationship between parent-reported beliefs and behaviors and children's self-perceptions, affect, and motivation. Finally, correlations between children's perceived and parents' reported influence were low to moderate, indicating a discrepancy between how parents think they act and feel and how children view these same beliefs and behaviors.

Parents: What does this knowledge mean?

The preceding studies provide rather consistent findings about parental influence in youth sport. First, children's perceptions of parental beliefs (e.g., perceived competence, enjoyment) and behaviors (e.g., encouragement, responses to performance) are strongly related to children's own competency beliefs, attraction to physical activity, intrinsic motivation, and levels of MVPA. Parents who are seen as confident about their child's abilities, supportive of physical activity involvement, and experience enjoyment in their own activity are associated with young participants who report greater ability perceptions, positive affect, motivation, and frequency and intensity of physical

activity. Moreover, children's perceptions of parents' beliefs and behaviors are more importantly related to their psychosocial development and physical activity behaviors than *parent-reported* beliefs and behaviors.

Second, children's beliefs about their competence and value placed on physical activity involvement mediate the relationship between parental influence and children's MVPA. Parents' beliefs and behaviors are not directly related to MVPA levels or motivation to continue involvement. Rather, children's perceived competence, goal orientations, and value toward physical activity serve as a mediator for parental influences on motivation and MVPA. Thus, parental influence exerts its strongest effects on children's self and activity beliefs that in turn have an impact upon motivational and participatory outcomes.

Finally, there is a discrepancy between how parents think they act and feel with respect to their child's participation and how children view these same beliefs and behaviors. Thus, there is a fine line between perceptions of support versus pressure, and encouragement versus expectations, depending on whose viewpoint is considered. This finding highlights the importance of child and parent communication about participatory experiences to ensure that multiple perspectives are understood.

In sum, studies based on motivational theory pinpoint the *mechanisms* by which parents socialize their children's attitudes and behaviors in sport and physical activity. These mechanisms include conveying beliefs about the child's physical competencies and the value placed on the importance of being successful in sport. They also include behaviors in the form of providing experiences, modeling behavior such as enjoyment of physical activity, and reinforcing and supporting their child's interest in being involved in sport. Understanding the mechanisms that influence children's involvement in physical activity is more insightful than earlier descriptive studies that solely considered the match between parental and child physical activity levels (Brustad, 1996a).

Parents: What do we need to know?

Recently, Eccles et al. (1998) forwarded a model of parental influence on children's motivation using a family systems approach (Figure 3). In this model, family demographics such as parent characteristics (e.g., single-parent, socioeconomic status), child and sibling characteristics (e.g., birth order, gender), parents' general- and child-specific beliefs and behaviors (e.g., gender- and activity-stereotypes), and the child's psychosocial outcomes (i.e., self-perceptions, values, goals) interact as a reciprocal and dynamic process. Not only do family characteristics and parental beliefs exert influence on the child's behavior (e.g., activity choices), but the child's ability beliefs and behaviors also may impact parental beliefs and behaviors in a bi-directional way.

This model is an appealing framework for understanding not only parental influence but also the institution of the family on children's involvement in the physical domain. First, the model specifies potential *sources* of parental beliefs and behaviors such as family, child, sibling, and neighborhood characteristics. Second, parental behaviors mediate the influence of parents' competency and value beliefs about their child on psychological and achievement outcomes. Third, the model affords importance to siblings as a potential moderator of parental beliefs and behaviors toward the target child. How do parents' reactions toward and involvement in an older sibling's sport participation affect the younger child? Is he or she attracted to the same sport? Is she or he attracted to sport at all or instead a unique achievement domain? Does this differ depending on whether the sibling is male or female? These particular features of the model and others are salient considerations in understanding children's beliefs and behaviors about participating in sport and physical activity.

Coaches: What do we know?

Coaches can make a significant impact on children's perceptions of physical competence, affect, motivation, and participatory behaviors in how they structure practices and respond to performance efforts. Coaches' feedback and reinforcement comprise *informational* (i.e., instruction) or *evaluative* (i.e., praise, criticism) responses to

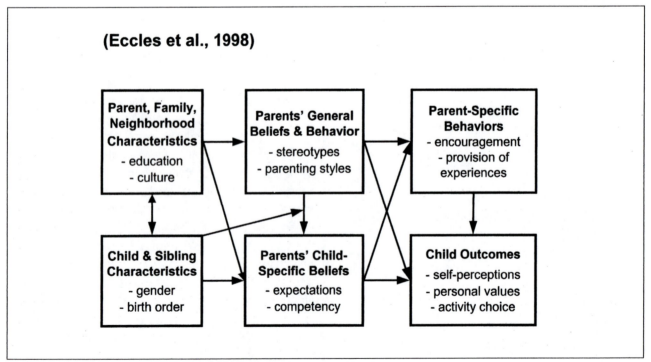

(Eccles et al., 1998)

Figure 3. Schematic of Eccles' et al. (1998) model of parental influence on children's motivation and achievement.

performance. The "gold standard" studies by Smith and Smoll (see Smoll and Smith, 1989, for a review) demonstrated that the quantity and quality of coaches' feedback results in positive outcomes for youth baseball players. Employing a Coach Effectiveness Training (CET) intervention program, coaches were taught to employ the "positive approach" that consisted of praise for desirable behaviors (effort, technique, sportsmanship), encouragement following skill errors, and instruction following performance attempts that merit future improvement. When players who played for CET coaches were compared to those who did not

Recently, Amorose and Weiss (1998) examined age differences in children's perceptions of the meaning of coaches' feedback. Sport participants 6-8 and 12-14 years of age watched videotapes of same-age athletes hitting a baseball or softball, and then rated the athletes' ability after they received either evaluative, informational, or neutral feedback following performance. For both age groups, athletes receiving praise following success were rated higher in ability than those receiving neutral or informational feedback. For unsuccessful performance, both age groups rated athletes higher in ability if they received informational feedback and

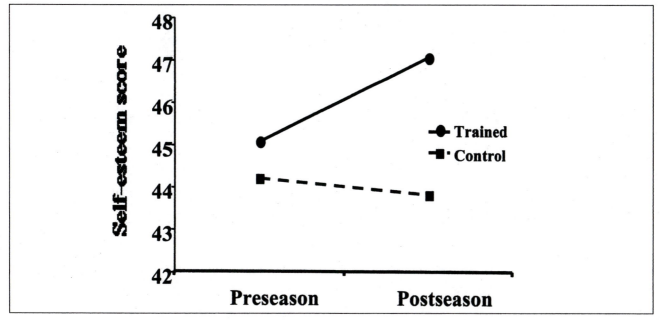

Figure 4. Pre-post season self-esteem change for low self-esteem children who played for CET and untrained coaches (from Smoll et al., 1993).

participate in CET, players of CET coaches were higher in perceived baseball ability, enjoyment, and intention to continue playing, and lower in anxiety and attrition rates (Barnett et al., 1992; Smith et al., 1979a, 1995). Perhaps one of the most powerful findings was the significant pre-post season increase in global self-esteem for children who began the season with low self-esteem and who played for CET coaches (see Figure 4; Smoll et al., 1993).

lowest in ability if they received criticism. Open-ended questions revealed some age-related trends in sources of ability information. Older youth cited form/technique (54% of responses) more than coach's feedback (22%) as a source of determining ability level, while younger children used both of these sources equally (35% coach feedback, 32% form/technique). Older youth who had more sport experience may have been able to draw upon their knowledge about the game of baseball/softball to make ability judgments using cues other than the coach's feedback.

Several studies have examined the role of the coach on children's psychosocial development from the perspective of motivational theory. Horn (1985) studied the influence of coaches' behaviors on 13-15 year-old players' perceptions of softball competence over the course of a season. Players who received more frequent praise following successful performances scored *lower* in perceived competence, while players who received greater frequencies of criticism in response to errors reported *higher* competence perceptions. These paradoxical results were explained in terms of the *contingent* nature of the feedback that was provided. Specifically, praise was not given for *specific and challenging* skills, but was offered for mastering easy skills or exhibiting mediocre performance. In contrast, criticism was given based on specific performance levels and combined with information on how to improve on subsequent mastery attempts. To further support this inference, Horn (1984) reported that lower skilled players were given more praise, while more talented athletes received more criticism for their efforts.

Black and Weiss (1992) extended Horn's (1985) study by assessing age-group swimmers' perceptions of *contingent* coaching praise, information, and criticism following swim performances. For the 12-14 and 15-18 year-old swimmers, greater perceived praise combined with information following successful swims, and greater encouragement combined with information following poor swims, were associated with higher levels of perceived swimming competence, intrinsic motivation, and enjoyment. For 15-18 year-olds, more frequent criticism following poor performances was also associated with lower values on these variables. The results help to explain the contradictory findings by Horn (1985) – when coaching behaviors are contingent to performance efforts and outcomes, praise is positively and criticism negatively related to perceived athletic competence.

Finally, Allen and Howe (1998) evaluated the relationship between contingent coaching behaviors and self-perceptions in highly skilled 14-18 year-old field hockey players. More frequent praise plus instruction was associated with *higher* perceived competence, while more frequent encouragement plus instruction following skill errors was related to lower perceived competence. The authors explained that negative feelings might accompany encouragement given after a skill error, especially if it is given in a team setting. In such contexts, encouragement may conspicuously highlight the error made and, in the public appraisal of her teammates, may lower perceptions of competence. Nevertheless, this finding contrasts that found in other studies (Black and Weiss, 1992; Smoll et al., 1993) where encouragement plus instruction following skill errors was positively related to perceived ability, enjoyment, and motivation. It is possible that the age and skill level of the field hockey players plays a role in these findings.

Coaches: What does this knowledge mean?

Several implications emerge from these studies. First, coaching behaviors contribute above and beyond skill improvement as a source of information about physical competence for young athletes. However, the influence of coaches on children's psychosocial development is not as straightforward as meets the eye. Higher frequency of praise is not always associated with higher ability perceptions and criticism is not always associated with lower feelings of competence. Rather, feedback that is *contingent* and *appropriate* to demonstrated skill levels is most likely to have an impact on children's self-perceptions of competence, enjoyment, and motivation (Horn, 1987). This means that praise should be provided when young athletes master skills that are challenging, meet performance goals, and satisfy specific criteria set for performance. It also means rewarding desirable behaviors that do not necessarily result in successful *outcome* but show successful learning such as effort, technique, form, and personal skill improvement. Finally, if criticism is to be used it should be constructive in nature, containing instructional information on how to improve on subsequent performance attempts.

Second, evaluative and informational feedback affects both sport skill improvement and psychological development. Contingent praise combined with instruction following successful attempts, and encouragement combined with instruction following errors (except for Allen and Howe, 1998) have a positive impact on sport skill improvement *and* physical self-esteem, attraction toward sport, and motivation to continue involvement. Criticism is associated with lower ability perceptions, except in Horn's (1985) study where *constructive* criticism that contained important information for improving performance increased perceptions of competence.

Finally, similar to parental influence reported in the previous section, children's *perceptions* of coaching behaviors, rather than objective behaviors per se, are most important for driving psychosocial outcomes. Smoll and Smith (1989) proposed a mediational model of coaching behaviors, one in which young athletes' perceptions of their coaches' use of evaluative and informational feedback mediates the influence of objective assessments of coaching behaviors on sport skill and psychosocial outcomes. Children's behaviors in turn may exert a reciprocal influence on their perceptions *and* coaches' subsequent behaviors toward them. Thus it is important to consider the child's construction of meaning in their sport experiences, and not simply infer positive and negative outcomes on the basis of objective indicators of praise, instruction, encouragement, and criticism.

Coaches: What do we need to know?

One of the prevalent phenomena of North American culture is the parent-coach dual role. It is common for parents to complain about coaches, for coaches to complain about parents, and for administrators to express concerns about both parents and coaches. Yet, invariably the coach of competitive youth sport teams is a parent of one of the players. Typically parent and coach influence are examined independently of one another. Several anecdotal accounts exist of the positive or negative reasons for why parents should coach their own

children, but there is little empirical research. It is important to assess the dual influence of the parent-coach in order to support or refute anecdotal accounts. This might best be accomplished through interview or naturalistic studies that include observation of parent/coach-child interactions in the athletic and home contexts.

The type of attributional feedback provided by coaches is an important direction for future research. Research in the academic (e.g., Mueller and Dweck, 1998) and sport (Horn, 1987) domains have documented the influence of effort versus ability attributions given for success and failure. An ability attribution for successful outcomes, because it is characteristic of the individual, should signal that future success is imminent and is accompanied by positive affect such as pride, happiness, and satisfaction. However, assigning lack of ability as a reason for performance failure is associated with expected future failure and negative emotions such as shame, embarrassment, and guilt. Effort, in contrast, is changeable and controllable by the child, and can be used to motivate young athletes to try harder, adopt an alternative strategy, or pay selective attention to important elements of the skill to change future performance. These are theoretical applications that have not been empirically tested in real sporting contexts to verify if attributional feedback does indeed carry implications for motivation and self-esteem outcomes in youth sport. The situation becomes more complex in that young children view ability and effort as identical or similar constructs, i.e., if a child tries hard he or she must be athletically talented (Fry and Duda, 1997). Not until about 11-12 years do children understand that greater effort by one child to achieve the same performance must mean that he or she is less skilled than one who required less effort to perform equally.

Finally, the compatibility of child-perceived, observed, and coach-reported behaviors should be investigated in particular sport social contexts. Various studies have typically assessed coaching behaviors in only one of these ways. Smith et al. (1979b) assessed frequency of coaching behaviors using several modes: an observation system, coaches' self-report, and players' perceptions. Correlations between observed and coach-reported measures revealed low and nonsignificant relationships, as did correlations between coach- and player-reported assessments. Interestingly, player perceptions of coaching behaviors were more highly correlated with observed frequencies, suggesting that players were more accurate in their perceptions than were coaches of their own behaviors. Given Smoll and Smith's (1989) model of coaching behaviors that suggests child perceptions mediate the influence of objective assessments on psychosocial and skill outcomes, it is important that any discrepancy among viewpoints be documented and used to enhance coaches' awareness so that positive child outcomes are maximized.

Peers: What do we know?

One's peer group and close friends are powerful socializing agents who contribute beyond the influence of adults to children's psychosocial development in school and sports (Bukowski et al., 1996; Weiss et al., 1996). Both peer acceptance and close friendship are salient aspects of peer relationships and interactions. *Peer acceptance* refers to one's popularity and status within one's peer group. Research conducted in organized sport and physical education settings consistently shows that children and teenagers identify "being good at sports" as an important quality for being popular with one's peers, especially among boys (e.g., Chase and Dummer, 1992; Evans and Roberts, 1987). Youth sport research also specifies a strong linkage between physical competence and peer acceptance. Youth who are rated by instructors and see themselves as popular are those who are similarly rated as and perceive themselves as good in sports (Weiss and Duncan, 1992).

Perceived peer acceptance is also related to reasons for participating in sport, attributions for performance, emotional responses to participation, and motivation to continue involvement (e.g., Klint and Weiss, 1987; Kunesh et al., 1992; Weiss et al.,

1990). For example, children who feel that they are popular with their peer group are motivated to continue participation to maintain friendships, attribute their social competence to stable and personally controllable factors, experience greater enjoyment of physical activity, and report higher levels of motivation.

Friendship refers to specific aspects of a dyadic peer relationship, such as similarity, esteem enhancement, loyalty, and emotional support. Developmental psychologists implore that friendship must be studied within the specific social context in which relationships and interactions take place (Newcomb and Bagwell, 1995; Zarbatany et al., 1992). Thus, friendship findings from school contexts do not necessarily apply to physical activity contexts. Recently, close friendships in sport have been studied to understand their significance to children's and adolescents' psychological development.

Weiss and Smith (1999; see also Weiss et al., 1996, 2002) conducted a series of studies to understand the nature of sport friendships and their role in children's psychosocial development through sport participation. In the first study (Weiss et al., 1996), several positive dimensions of best sport friendships emerged for 8-16 year-old participants such as self-esteem enhancement, companionship, pleasant play and association, intimacy, loyalty, emotional support, and conflict resolution. A few negative dimensions, such as conflict, betrayal, and inaccessibility, were also identified.

A sport friendship quality measure was subsequently developed and validated based on data collected from three youth sport samples (Weiss and Smith, 1999). Several friendship features were established—companionship and pleasant play, self-esteem enhancement and supportiveness, things in common, loyalty and intimacy, conflict resolution, and conflict. In the third study (Weiss et al., 2002), age and gender variations emerged on friendship quality dimensions that were consistent with developmental theory. Younger children cited companionship and pleasant play more frequently, while older youth rated loyalty and intimacy, things in common, and conflict higher. Girls rated self-esteem enhancement and supportiveness, loyalty and intimacy, and things in common higher, and boys rated conflict higher. Finally, companionship and pleasant play was significantly correlated with enjoyment and sport commitment. Children who reported higher friendship quality on this dimension reported greater sport enjoyment and a stronger desire to stay involved in their participation. With a valid measure of sport friendship quality, questions such as the relative influence of parents and peers at varying age levels, and the relation between friendship quality and self-perceptions, affect, and motivation can be pursued.

Two studies have focused upon the influence of close friendship on children's psychosocial development and physical activity involvement. Duncan (1993) examined the influence of esteem support and companionship dimensions of friendship on emotional and motivational outcomes among 12-15 year-old middle school youth. Youths who perceived greater friendship quality in these two areas reported greater enjoyment doing physical activities and interest in choosing activities outside of the school setting. A.L. Smith (1999) found that middle school girls' and boys' perceptions of close friendship were significantly related to physical self-worth, positive affect, intrinsic motivation, and physical activity levels. Specifically, youths who reported they had a close friend in sports felt better about themselves physically, liked physical activity and sports more, were motivated by challenging activities, and were more physically active.

Peers: What does this knowledge mean?

While parents are especially important socializers during early and middle childhood, peers become important sources of social support during later childhood and adolescence, a time when youths seek autonomy from adults. Thus, peer interactions, relationships, and networks are essential to psychosocial development, and sport contexts offer an outstanding opportunity for such development.

Research on peer acceptance indicates that being good in sports is an important quality for being popular with one's peers, and that athletically-skilled boys and girls are afforded greater peer status than those less skilled. Sport educators should be aware of the strong link between perceptions of peer acceptance, physical competence, and participation behaviors, and exploit opportunities in physical activity contexts for positively impacting peer relations and interactions.

Children describe many positive and few negative dimensions of their close sport friendships. They view these friendships as supportive relationships, ones that provide self-esteem enhancement, emotional support, loyalty, companionship, intimacy, and things in common such as values, interests, and activities. Moreover, friendship quality dimensions such as esteem support and companionship are related to feelings of self-worth, positive affect related to physical activity, and motivation to continue. Parents, teachers, and coaches should encourage and help children develop close, supportive friendships within the sport context to accrue these benefits of peer interactions and relationships.

Peers: What do we need to know?

Relatively less research has been conducted on peer influence in youth sport than for coach or parent influence. Thus, there is a need for investigations to further the knowledge base in this area. The network of social relationships that exists in youth sport contexts is important to pursue. For example, how can coaching behaviors influence children's ability to develop and maintain peer relationships? How does the quality of the parent-child relationship affect a child's ability to form close and meaningful sport friendships? What is the relative and interactive influence of adults and peers on children's cognitive, affective, and behavioral outcomes at varying ages, in varying contexts, and across gender?

Contextual issues related to sport friendships include a number of avenues. Children usually have multiple friendships, but little is known about how friendships vary depending on the context in which they occur. For example, do children's friendships differ in individual versus team sport contexts? Do friendships differ depending upon the domain in which they occur such as sport, music, and school?

Interventions to enhance peer acceptance and friendship quality are necessary to determine effective ways in which to nurture such relationships in the sport setting. Structuring a mastery motivational climate in the sport setting is one means of facilitating supportive sport friendships.

Motivational Climate

In the larger social context of sport and physical activity, coaches and teachers influence children's psychosocial development by shaping the psychological or motivational *climate* in which

interactions and activities take place. An emphasis on the climate existing within the sport context

Ames' (1992) intervention research in school classrooms has illuminated the appeal of shaping a mastery motivational climate for promoting positive psychosocial development in youth. She adopted organizational and teaching strategies advocated by Epstein (1988) that revolve around the dimensions of task, authority, recognition, grouping, evaluation, and time (i.e., TARGET). Specifically, task variety and optimal challenges, opportunities for choice and shared decision-making, recognition of effort and self-improvement, partner and small-group problem-solving tasks, evaluation criteria focused on self-referenced standards, and adequate time for learning define the ingredients for a mastery motivational climate. The findings support the notion that such an environment fosters positive

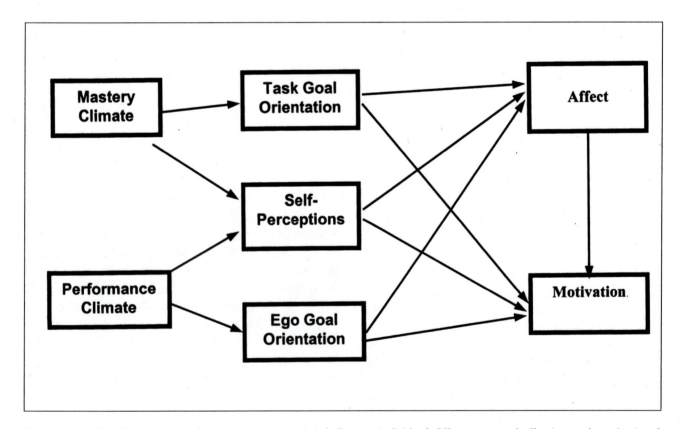

Figure 5. Model of interrelationships among motivational climate, individual differences, and affective and motivational outcomes.

self-perceptions, attitudes, and motivation in elementary and secondary school students. Ames (1992) also points out structural similarities between classroom and sport environments such as definitions of success, extent of adult control, and type of evaluative practices. Thus, concepts of a motivational climate are as relevant to sport settings as in classroom settings.

In recent years, considerable research has explored relationships among motivational climate, goal orientations, self-perceptions, and motivation in the sport and physical activity domains. In general, findings endorse Ames' (1992) observation that sport and academic classrooms share many similarities and thus offer important opportunities for psychosocial growth in children and teenagers. Several linkages shown in Figure 5 are subsequently reviewed: (a) motivational climate and goal orientations; (b) motivational climate, affect, and motivation; and, (c) motivational climate, individual differences, and psychosocial outcomes. For each linkage, the core questions of what we know, what this knowledge means, and what we need to know will be weaved throughout the discussion.

Motivational climate and goal orientations

Mastery and performance climates are expected to promote task- and ego-involved goals, respectively. A mastery motivational climate with its emphasis on learning and improvement encourages participants to adopt a self-referenced definition of success and criteria for judging self-abilities, while a performance motivational climate should facilitate a preference for a normative definition and criteria for success. Several studies indicate a linkage between a mastery motivational climate and task-involved goals (Ebbeck and Becker, 1994; Ferrer-Caja and Weiss, 2000; Treasure and Roberts, 1998; Williams, 1998). Perceptions of a performance climate are positively or unrelated to ego-involved goals. Williams (1998), in fact, found that perceptions of a mastery *and* a performance climate were related to end-of-season task goal orientations, confirming that both task- and ego-involving reward structures exist in the context of competitive sport.

The results suggest that when coaches structure practices and games that color an atmosphere of learning, self-improvement, and optimal challenges, young athletes are likely to adopt goals for success that are defined by the same internal standards. Because competitive sport has an inherent emphasis on performance outcomes and normative criteria for success, it is important that coaches try to reduce the temptation to solely focus on winning and peer comparison by recognizing, valuing, and teaching for optimal skill learning, technique improvement, and strategy development.

Motivational climate, affect, and motivation

A number of studies have examined the association between motivational climate and affective outcomes and intrinsic motivation in sport contexts (Goudas and Biddle, 1994; Papaioannou, 1994; Seifriz et al., 1992; Treasure, 1997; Walling et al., 1993). There is, in general, a relationship between a mastery motivational climate and higher positive affect (e.g., enjoyment, satisfaction, interest), lower negative affect (e.g., anxiety, boredom), and stronger intrinsic motivation. Relationships among performance climate, affect, and motivation are less consistent—the hypothesized negative relationship occasionally emerged, whereas lack of relationship also emerges.

Theeboom et al. (1995) conducted one of the few intervention studies that demonstrated the attractiveness of adopting a mastery motivational climate. They employed organizational and teaching strategies (TARGET) defining mastery and performance climates with 8-12 year-old children participating in a martial arts program for 3 weeks. Post-intervention assessment indicated that children in the mastery climate group reported greater enjoyment and demonstrated better motor skills than the performance climate group. Brief interviews revealed that mastery group participants were unanimous in reporting high ability perceptions and intrinsic motivation, while responses from the performance group were less pronounced. The results highlight the efficacy of a mastery climate curriculum in sport skill programs for youth.

Overall, available data suggest that a learning environment that highlights and rewards effort, self-improvement, and adoption of problem-solving strategies is linked with children's positive self-beliefs, enjoyment of their activity involvement, and interest in sustaining their participation in the future. In contrast, climates that emphasize comparison to peers and performance outcomes, rather than learning and improvement, are usually associated with less positive self-perceptions, affective responses, and motivated behavior.

Motivational climate, individual differences, and psychosocial outcomes

Several studies have investigated relationships among all of the linkages shown in Figure 5 (Biddle et al., 1995; Cury et al., 1996; Goudas et al., 1995; Ferrer-Caja and Weiss, 2000; Ntoumanis and Biddle, 1998). Models specifying associations among motivational climate, goal orientations, perceived ability, and psychosocial outcomes have been tested for goodness of fit to data obtained from sport and physical activity samples. For example, Ferrer-Caja and Weiss (2000) found that adolescents' perceptions of a mastery motivational climate were related to higher task-involved goals, perceived athletic ability, intrinsic motivation, and effort and persistence in physical activity classes.

Findings from the studies suggest that psychosocial and achievement outcomes are best predicted by a *combination* of perceived motivational climate and individual differences such as goal orientations and perceived ability. Moreover, goal orientations and self-perceptions mediate the relationship between climate and motivational outcomes. Thus, young athletes' perceptions of whether the environment is mastery- or performance-oriented directly influences their definition of success and self-judgments of ability, which in turn impact affect, intrinsic motivation, and achievement behaviors.

What do we need to know?

Although task and ego goals are predominant in the achievement goal literature, social goals should also

be considered (Urdan and Maehr, 1995). Social goals converge with findings of participation motivation studies. Developing and affirming friendships, approval from parents and coaches, and team cohesion are important reasons for staying involved in sports (in Weiss and Ferrer-Caja, in 2002).

Urdan and Maehr (1995) define social goals as the perceived social purposes for achievement in a particular domain. Goals include social welfare goals (e.g., become a productive member of society), social solidarity goals (e.g., bring honor to one's family or in-group), social approval goals (e.g., please parents, develop friendships, enhance peer acceptance), and social compliance goals (e.g., become a good person). Hayashi's (1996) observations of in-group pride and harmony goals for physical activity participants socialized in the Hawaiian culture are consistent with social solidarity goals. The linkage between perceptions of peer acceptance and friendship with group affiliation participation motives (Klint and Weiss, 1987) represents an example of social approval goals. Social goals are valued as reasons for participating in youth sport. They merit further consideration along with task and ego goals in future research and applications to practice.

According to achievement goal theory individuals who are primarily task-involved will be high in achievement motivation regardless of level of perceived ability. This is expected because the definition of success revolves around personal mastery, skill improvement, and effective problem-solving—self-referenced forms of success. Individuals high in ego involvement but high in ability perceptions should show the same pattern of behaviors. Although they define success in normative terms, their high ability perceptions lead them to prefer challenging tasks that maximize their chances for demonstrating high skill compared to peers. The child high in ego orientation but low in perceived ability, however, has been designated as at-risk for dropping out of sport (Duda, 1987; Treasure and Roberts, 1995). These children are expected to have low success expectancies, avoid achievement situations, exert low effort, and make external attributions for mastery attempts. Because normative goals are salient, such children have little faith in achieving better performance than others, these strategies help to protect self-worth and judgments of low ability by significant others.

Despite these hypotheses, few studies have considered the interaction between goal orientations and perceived ability in the physical domain. Williams and Gill (1995) and Goudas et al. (1994) specified perceived competence as a mediating variable in the effect of goal orientations on intrinsic motivation. However, theoretical predictions would specify an interaction between ego goal orientation and perceived competence in the model of interrelationships. If the interaction term is significant, then intrinsic motivation scores based on higher/lower ego and higher/lower perceived competence could be graphed and examined. One would expect to find individuals with high ego/high perceived competence associated with higher intrinsic motivation than those with high ego/low perceived competence characteristics. Future studies should consider children's level of perceived ability in combination with ego goal orientation to understand and explain cognitive, affective, and behavioral outcomes in sport.

Concluding Remarks

Social influences in youth sport include parents, coaches, peers, and the motivational climate in which interactions, relationships, and activities occur. From a motivational perspective, significant adults and peers and the nature of the learning environment are strong determinants of children's competency beliefs, affective responses to sport experiences, and desire to continue and sustain their involvement in sport activities. As such, researchers and practitioners alike seek to understand the specific mechanisms by which positive psychosocial outcomes are likely in children and adolescents. The research to date is promising and conveys take-home messages that can be applied in parent and coach education programs in youth sport leagues. These take-home messages include the nature of adult evaluative and informational feedback, the importance of close sport friendships as supportive relationships, and the appeal of a mastery motivational climate for skill learning, perceived competence, enjoyment, and intrinsic interest to remain physically active over one's lifespan.

REFERENCES

Allen, J.B. & Howe, B. (1998). Player ability, coach feedback, and female adolescent athletes' perceived competence and satisfaction. *Journal of Sport and Exercise Psychology* 20: 280-299.

Ames, C. (1992). Achievement goals, motivational climate, and motivational processes. In: Roberts, G.C. (Ed.), *Motivation in Sport and Exercise*. Champaign, IL: Human Kinetics (pp. 161-176).

Amorose, A.J. & Weiss, M.R. (1998). Coaching feedback as a source of information about perceptions of ability: a developmental examination. *Journal of Sport and Exercise Psychology* 20: 395-420.

Babkes, M.L. & Weiss, M.R. (1999). Parental influence on cognitive and affective responses in children's competitive soccer participation. *Pediatric Exercise Science* 11: 44-62.

Barnett, N.P; Smoll, F.L.; & Smith, R.E. (1992). Effects of enhancing coach-athlete relationships on youth sport attrition. *The Sport Psychologist* 6: 111-127.

Biddle, S.; Cury, F.; Goudas, M.; Sarrazin, P.; Famose, J.P.; & Durand, M. (1995). Development of scales to measure perceived physical education class climate: A cross-national project. *British Journal of Educational Psychology* 65: 341-358.

Black, S.J. & Weiss, M.R. (1992). The relationship among perceived coaching behaviors, perceptions of ability, and motivation in competitive age-group swimmers. *Journal of Sport and Exercise Psychology* 14: 309-325.

Brustad, R.J. (1988). Affective outcomes in competitive youth sport: The influence of intrapersonal and socialization factors. *Journal of Sport and Exercise Psychology* 10: 307-321.

Brustad, R.J. (1992). Integrating socialization influences into the study of children's motivation in sport. Journal of Sport and Exercise Psychology 14: 59-77.

Brustad, R.J. (1993). Who will go out and play? Parental and psychological influences on children's attraction to physical activity. *Pediatric Exercise Science* 5: 210-223.

Brustad, R.J. (1996a). Parental and peer influence on children's psychological development through sport. In: Smoll, F.L. & Smith, R.E. (Eds.), *Children and Youth in Sport: A Biopsychosocial Perspective*. Madison, WI: Brown & Benchmark (pp. 112-124).

Brustad, R.J. (1996b). Attraction to physical activity in urban schoolchildren: Parental socialization and gender influences. *Research Quarterly for Exercise and Sport* 67: 316-323.

Brustad, R.J. (This volume). Parental roles and involvement in youth sports: psychosocial outcomes for children.

Bukowski, W.M.; Newcomb, A.; & Hartup, W.W. (1996). *The Company They Keep: Friendship in Childhood and Adolescence*. New York: Cambridge University Press.

Chase, M.A. & Dummer, G.M. (1992). The role of sports as a social status determinant for children. *Research Quarterly for Exercise and Sport* 63: 418-424.

Cooley, C.H. (1902). *Human Nature and the Social Order*. New York: Scribner.

Cury, F.; Biddle, S.; Famose, J.P.; Goudas, M.; Sarrazin, P.; & Durand, M. (1996). Personal and situational factors influencing intrinsic interest of adolescent girls in school physical education: A structural equation analysis. *Educational Psychology* 16: 305-315.

Deci, E.L. & Ryan, R.M. (1985). *Intrinsic Motivation and Self-Determination in Human Behavior*. New York: Plenum.

Dempsey, J.M.; Kimiecik, J.C.; & Horn, T.S. (1993). Parental influence on children's moderate to vigorous physical activity participation: An expectancy-value approach. *Pediatric Exercise Science* 5: 151-167.

Duda, J.L. (1987). Toward a developmental theory of motivation in sport. *Journal of Sport and Exercise Psychology* 9: 130-145.

Duncan, S.C. (1993). The role of cognitive appraisal and friendship provisions in adolescents' affect and motivation toward activity in physical education. *Research Quarterly for Exercise and Sport* 64: 314-323.

Ebbeck, V. & Becker, S.L. (1994). Psychosocial predictors of goal orientations in youth soccer. *Research Quarterly for Exercise and Sport* 65: 355-362.

Eccles, J.S.; Wigfield, A.W.; & Schiefele, U. (1998). Motivation to succeed. In: Eisenberg, N. (Ed.), *Handbook of Child Psychology (5th ed., Volume 3): Social, Emotional, and Personality Development*. New York: Wiley (pp. 1017-1095).

Epstein, J. (1988). Effective schools or effective students? Dealing with diversity. In: Haskins, R. & MacRae, D. (Eds.), *Policies for America's Public Schools: Teacher Equity Indicators*. Norwood, NJ: Ablex (pp. 89-126).

Evans, J. & Roberts, G.C. (1987). Physical competence and the development of children's peer relations. *Quest* 39: 23-35.

Ferrer-Caja, E. & Weiss, M.R. (2000). Predictors of intrinsic motivation among adolescent students in physical education. *Research Quarterly for Exercise and Sport* 72: 267-279.

Fry, M.D. & Duda, J.L. (1997). A developmental examination of children's understanding of effort and ability in the physical and academic domains. *Research Quarterly for Exercise and Sport* 68: 331-344.

Goudas, M. & Biddle, S. (1994). Perceived motivational climate and intrinsic motivation in school physical education classes. *European Journal of Psychology in Education* 9: 241-250.

Goudas, M.; Biddle, S.; & Fox, K. (1994). Perceived locus of causality, goal orientations, and perceived competence in school physical education classes. *British Journal of Educational Psychology* 64: 453-463.

Goudas, M.; Biddle, S.; Fox, K.; & Underwood, M. (1995). It ain't what you do, it's the way that you do it! Teaching style affects children's motivation in track and field lessons. *The Sport Psychologist* 9: 254-264.

Harter, S. (1978). Effectance motivation reconsidered. *Human Development* 21: 34-64.

Harter, S. (1985). Competence as a dimension of self-evaluation: Toward a comprehensive model of self-worth. In: Leahy, R. (Ed.), *The Development of the Self*. New York: Academic Press (pp. 55-118).

Harter, S. (1987). The determinants and mediational role of global self-worth in children. In: Eisenberg, N. (Ed.), *Contemporary Topics in Developmental Psychology*. New York: Wiley (pp. 219-242).

Harter, S. (1990). Causes, correlates, and the functional role of global self-worth: a life-span perspective. In: Sternberg, R.J. & Kolligan, J. Jr. (Eds.), *Competence Considered*. New Haven, CT: Yale University Press (pp. 67-97).

Harter, S. (1999). *The Construction of the Self: A Developmental Perspective*. New York: Guilford.

Hayashi, C.T. (1996). Achievement motivation among Anglo-American and Hawaiian male physical activity participants: Individual differences and social contextual factors. *Journal of Sport and Exercise Psychology* 18: 194-215.

Horn, T.S. (1984). Expectancy effects in the interscholastic athletic setting: Methodological considerations. *Journal of Sport Psychology* 6: 60-76.

Horn, T.S. (1985). Coaches' feedback and changes in children's perceptions of their physical competence. *Journal of Sport and Exercise Psychology* 77: 174-186.

Horn, T.S. (1987). The influence of teacher-coach behavior on the psychological development of children. In: Gould, D. & Weiss, M.R. (Eds.), *Advances in Pediatric Sport Sciences, Volume 2: Behavioral Issues*. Champaign, IL: Human Kinetics (pp. 121-142).

Horn, T.S. & Harris, A. (1996). Perceived competence in young athletes: Research findings and recommendations for coaches and parents. In: Smoll, F.L. & Smith, R.E. (Eds.), *Children and Youth in Sport: A Biopsychosocial Perspective*. Madison, WI: Brown & Benchmark (pp. 309-329).

Kimiecik, J.C. & Horn, T.S. (1998). Parental beliefs and children's moderate-to-vigorous physical activity. *Research Quarterly for Exercise and Sport* 69: 163-175.

Kimiecik, J.C.; Horn, T.S.; & Shurin, C.S. (1996). Relationships among children's beliefs, perceptions of their parents' beliefs, and their moderate-to-vigorous physical activity. *Research Quarterly for Exercise and Sport* 67: 324-336.

Klint, K.A. & Weiss, M.R. (1987). Perceived competence and motives for participating in youth sports: A test of

Harter's competence motivation theory. *Journal of Sport Psychology* 9: 55-65.

Kunesh, M.; Hasbrook, C.A.; & Lewthwaite, R. (1992). Physical activity socialization: Peer interactions and affective responses among a sample of sixth grade girls. *Sociology of Sport Journal* 9: 385-396.

Mueller, C.M. & Dweck, C.S. (1998). Praise for intelligence can undermine children's motivation and performance. *Journal of Personal and Social Psychology* 75: 33-52.

Newcomb, A.F. & Bagwell, C.L. (1995). Children's friendship relations: A meta-analytic review. *Psychology Bulletin* 117: 306-347.

Nicholls, J.G. (1989). *The Competitive Ethos and Democratic Education*. Cambridge, MA: Harvard University Press.

Ntoumanis, N. & Biddle, S. (1997). The relationship between competitive anxiety, achievement goals, and motivational climates. *Research Quarterly for Exercise and Sport* 69: 176-187.

Papaioannou, A. (1994). Development of a questionnaire to measure achievement orientations in physical education. *Research Quarterly for Exercise and Sport* 65: 11-20.

Scanlan, T.K.; Carpenter, P.J.; Schmidt, G.W.; Simons, J.P.; & Keeler, B. (1993). An introduction to the sport commitment model. *Journal of Sport and Exercise Psychology* 15: 1-15.

Scanlan, T.K. & Simons, J.P. (1992). The construct of sport enjoyment. In: Roberts, G.C. (Ed.), *Motivation in Sport and Exercise*. Champaign, IL: Human Kinetics (pp. 199-215).

Seifriz, J.J.; Duda, J.L.; & Chi, L. (1992). The relationship of perceived motivational climate to intrinsic motivation and beliefs about success in basketball. *Journal of Sport and Exercise Psychology* 14: 375-391.

Smith, A.L. (1999). Perceptions of peer relationships and physical activity participation in early adolescence. *Journal of Sport and Exercise Psychology* 21:329-350.

Smith, R.E.; Smoll, F.L.; & Barnett, N.P. (1995). Reduction of children's sport performance anxiety through social support and stress-reduction training for coaches. *Journal of Applied Developmental Psychology* 16: 125-142.

Smith, R.E.; Smoll, F.L.; & Curtis, B. (1979). Coaching effectiveness training: A cognitive-behavioral approach to enhancing relationship skills in youth sport coaches. *Journal of Sport Psychology* 1: 59-75.

Smith, R.E.; Smoll, F.L.; Hunt, E.; Curtis, B.; & Coppel, D. (1979). Psychology and the bad news bears. In: Roberts, G.C. & Newell, K.M. (Eds.), *Psychology of Motor Behavior and Sport—1978*. Champaign, IL: Human Kinetics (pp. 109-130).

Smoll, F.L. & Smith, R.E. (1989). Leadership behaviors in sport: A theoretical model and research paradigm. *Journal of Applied Social Psychology* 19: 1522-1551.

Smith, R.E.; Smoll, F.L.; Barnett, N.P.; & Everett, J.J. (1993). Enhancement of children's self-esteem through social support training for youth sport coaches. *Journal of Applied Psychology* 78: 602-610.

Theeboom, M.; De Knop, P.; & Weiss, M.R. (1995). Motivational climate, psychosocial responses, and motor skill development in children's sport: A field based-intervention study. *Journal of Sport and Exercise Psychology* 17: 294-311.

Treasure, D.C. & Roberts, G.C. (1995). Achievement goals, motivational climate, and achievement strategies and behaviors in sport. *International Journal of Sport Psychology* 26: 64-80.

Treasure, D.C. & Roberts, G.C. (1998). Relationship between female adolescents' achievement goal orientations, perceptions of the motivational climate, belief about success and sources of satisfaction in basketball. *International Journal of Sport Psychology* 29: 211-230.

Urdan, T.C. & Maehr, M.L. (1995). Beyond a two-goal theory of motivation and achievement: A case for social goals. *Review of Educational Research* 65: 213-243.

Walling, M.D.; Duda, J.L.; & Chi, L. (1993). The perceived motivational climate in sport questionnaire: construct and predictive validity. *Journal of Sport and Exercise Psychology* 15: 172-183.

Weiss, M.R. & Duncan, S.C. (1992). The relation between physical competence and peer acceptance in the context of children's sport participation. *Journal of Sport and Exercise Psychology* 14: 177-191.

Weiss, M.R. & Ebbeck, V. (1996). Self-esteem and perceptions of competence in youth sport: Theory, research, and enhancement strategies. In: Bar-Or, O. (Ed.), *The Encyclopaedia of Sports Medicine, Volume VI: The Child and Adolescent Athlete*. Oxford: Blackwell Science Ltd. (pp. 364-382).

Weiss, M.R. & Ferrer-Caja, E. (2002). Motivational orientations and sport behavior. In: Horn, T.S. (Ed.), *Advances in Sport Psychology*, 2nd Edition. Champaign, IL: Human Kinetics. (pp. 101-183).

Weiss, M.R.; McAuley, E.; Ebbeck, V.; & Wiese, D.M. (1990). Self-esteem and causal attributions for children's physical and social competence in sport. *Journal of Sport and Exercise Psychology* 12: 21-36.

Weiss, M.R. & Smith, A.L. (1999). Quality of youth sport friendships: Measurement and validation. *Journal of Sport and Exercise Psychology* 21: 145-166.

Weiss, M.R.; Smith, A.L. (2002). Friendship quality in youth sport: Relationship to age, gender, and motivation variables. *Journal of Sport and Exercise Psychology* 24: 420-437.

Weiss, M.R.; Smith, A.L.; & Theeboom, M. (1996). "That's what friends are for": Children's and teenagers' perceptions of peer relationships in the sport domain. *Journal of Sport and Exercise Psychology* 18: 347-379.

Weiss, M.R.; Wiese, D.M.; & Klint, K.A. (1989). Head over heels with success: The relationship between self-efficacy and performance in competitive youth gymnastics. *Journal of Sport and Exercise Psychology* 11: 444-451.

Williams, L. (1998). Contextual influences and goal perspectives among female youth sport participants. *Research Quarterly for Exercise and Sport* 69: 47-57.

Williams, L. & Gill, D.L. (1995). The role of perceived competence in the motivation of physical activity. *Journal of Sport and Exercise Psychology* 17: 363-378.

Zarbatany, L.; Ghesquiere, K.; & Mohr, K. (1992). A context perspective on early adolescents' friendship expectations. Journal of Early Adolescence 12: 111-126.

CHAPTER 10

Parental Roles and Involvement in Youth Sport: Psychosocial Outcomes for Children

Robert J. Brustad
University of Northern Colorado

Few discussions of children's sport participation occur without the simultaneous mention of parental influence in this arena. Parents are recognized as key participants in the environment of youth sport and their behavior is generally considered to impact children's psychological and emotional experiences in this context. Although the belief that parental socialization behaviors shape the quality of the sport experience for young athletes is rarely challenged, understanding the specific means by which parents exert an influence, and the specific psychological and affective consequences of parental involvement for children, are more complex matters for researchers.

It is important to understand the nature of parental influence if we are to maximize the benefits of youth sport participation. Since the general purpose of youth sport programs is to provide a context that will facilitate children's psychosocial and physical development, it is important to identify influences that contribute to the realization of this goal, or that impede the attainment of this outcome. Without question, parents have a fundamental influence upon the environment of youth sport and, thus, the specific nature of their influence is worthy of close examination. Furthermore, intervention programs can be designed to improve the nature of

parental involvement in relation to the knowledge that we gain about parental roles and involvement in this domain.

Quality research on parental influence entails a multidimensional perspective. First, we need to utilize appropriate theoretical frameworks that help us to identify which parenting practices and psychosocial outcomes are of greatest relevance to our research interest. For example, we could potentially examine a great range of parental communication and feedback patterns, expectational characteristics, motivational strategies, or reinforcement and reward systems in relation to varied psychosocial outcomes for children. However, decisions about which parental practices are most important for study, and any interpretation of subsequent findings, should be structured in accordance with theoretical considerations.

Children's developmental status must also be considered in evaluating the strength of parental influence at any one point in the child's participation. The influence of parents relative to other socializing agents (coaches, peers) in sport varies with the child's level of cognitive and social development. During early and middle childhood, parents typically are the most influential sport socializers. Parents have a strong influence during these years because younger children spend a considerable amount of time within the family and, due to cognitive-developmental characteristics, children also rely heavily upon adult informational sources in forming judgments about personal abilities and capacities (Horn and Hasbrook, 1987; Horn and Weiss, 1991). However, as children move through later childhood and into adolescence they form extensive social networks outside of the family and rely more heavily on peer informational feedback sources and social comparison information to make assessments of their personal competency in sport. It is thus important to recognize that the extent of parental influence is not constant throughout the child's sport involvement, but is largely dependent upon the child's developmental status.

A third consideration relates to the dynamic and reciprocal nature of the socialization process. Parental socialization practices continually change in relation to changes in parents' perceptions of children's interests and abilities, and in accordance with children's physical, psychological, and motor development. The dynamic nature of parent-child interactions is difficult to appreciate through isolated research "snapshots". Furthermore, children can influence their parents' interest and sport involvement in a "reciprocal" manner (Snyder and Purdy, 1982; Weiss and Hayashi, 1995). Thus, a more complete understanding of parental influence in youth sport requires consideration of the ongoing, dynamic, and reciprocal nature of the socialization process. This understanding is facilitated by theoretical perspectives that can account for change processes and by longitudinal investigations that extend across developmental and experiential phases.

Despite the challenges implicit to studying parental influence in youth sport, an extensive body of knowledge has been generated over the past two decades that has provided insight into the nature of parental roles in shaping the quality of the sport experience for youngsters. The bulk of this research supports our intuitive belief that parents are highly influential in shaping psychosocial aspects for children in sport. A major purpose of this chapter will be to provide an interpretation of our current knowledge base and to suggest directions for future research that will facilitate the development of further understanding.

This chapter has three major areas of focus. First, the evolution of parental research in youth sport, with particular attention devoted to the types of issues that have been addressed at various stages of knowledge development is discussed. An appreciation for the history and evolution of youth sport research should help to clarify why certain types of questions have received greater or lesser attention from investigators. Subsequently, the current knowledge base in relation to the three major interest areas for researchers is considered. This discussion summarizes current knowledge about the relationship between parenting practices and children's affective experiences in sport, children's sport-related self-perception characteristics, and the motivational outcomes that youngsters experience in this context. Finally, several recommendations for future research in this area of investigation are offered.

Evolution of Research on Parental Influence

Research on parental roles and involvement in youth sport are classified into three phases consistent with the prevailing issues and research concerns that have captured the attention of researchers at various times. An absolute demarcation between phases is not possible as some overlap has been present in the types of questions that have been asked across eras. This historical/evolutionary classification is intended primarily as a heuristic model for understanding the evolution of research on parental influence in youth sport.

The initial phase of parental youth sport research was conducted during the 1970s and through the early 1980s. This research has been characterized as having a "socialization into sport" focus (Brustad, 1992) since the research emphasis at the time was directed to understanding the role of parents in contributing to children's initial and sustained interest in sport. Phase I research also examined the relative importance of parents in relation to other socialization agents, including peers, siblings, and teachers, and further assessed the relative influence of fathers and mothers upon the sport involvement of sons and daughters (Greendorfer and Lewko, 1978; Lewko and Ewing, 1980).

Phase 1 research was an important building block in our knowledge base and strongly supported implicit beliefs that parents are highly influential contributors to youngsters' sport experiences. In sum, this line of research strongly suggested that parents are the primary socializers affecting children's sport involvement, and that fathers are typically the most important sport socializer for both boys and girls (Greendorfer and Ewing, 1981; Greendorfer and Lewko, 1978). Although this line of research represented an essential first step in understanding the nature of parental influence upon children's participatory involvement in sport, it did not have an explicit focus upon parenting practices in relation to psychosocial outcomes for youngsters in this context and a subsequent stage of research was needed to develop a better understanding of parental influence in this regard.

Phase II research was strongly directed toward understanding the nature of the parental socialization influence upon various psychological and affective outcomes for children in sport. This line of investigation began in the early to mid-1980s and continues through to the present. Phase II research questions were developed, at least in part, in relation to concerns expressed by researchers and physicians about the potentially damaging consequences of youth sport participation (Orlick, 1974; Smilkstein, 1980). Thus, Phase II research has addressed parental roles in contributing to children's anxiety levels, children's self-concept development, and motivational outcomes for children through their sport participation. The major findings from this body of knowledge are presented in a subsequent section, as they are essential to understanding the nature of parental influence in the youth sport domain.

A second fundamental characteristic that distinguished Phase II research from the previous research phase is that it has had an explicit focus upon understanding individual differences in various psychological, social, and affective outcomes for children. In contrast, Phase I research was principally concerned with developing a general understanding of the role of parents in the participatory involvement of children in sport without focused consideration for how differences in parental behavior could result in varied outcomes for children. Phase II research has thus helped us to understand, for example, why some young athletes experience high levels of anxiety in sport whereas most youngsters do not share these experiences (Lewthwaite and Scanlan, 1989; Passer, 1983).

A growing amount of contemporary research reflects a third orientation toward gaining knowledge about parental influence in sport. In my heuristic classification system, Phase III research approaches are those that are structured in broader and more complex theoretical models of parenting. Theoretical frameworks that fit this criteria include Harter's (1978, 1981) competence motivation theory, Eccles' expectancy/value model (Eccles et al., 1983; Eccles and Harold, 1991), and the family influence model (Kimiecik et al., 1996). A commonality of these three frameworks for understanding parental influence is that each is comprehensive and each addresses a variety of parental influences in combination rather than directing attention to a few, isolated aspects of parental influence (e.g., parental encouragement levels, parental role modeling behaviors). Furthermore, each model explicitly addresses the means by which parental beliefs and behaviors can impact children's psychological characteristics and affective outcomes. Thus, these models consider the nature of parent-child interactions as these interactions structure the socialization process. Fundamentally, each model is also primarily concerned with parental belief systems as parental beliefs are believed to structure the nature of parent-child interactions. Although much of the parental influence research during the 1980s was stimulated by theory, a growing proportion of investigations in this area currently are designed in the context of theoretically-based models.

The Content of Our Knowledge Base On Parental Influence

Extensive research has been conducted over the past two decades on parental influence in youth sport. Although this area of investigation had some precedent during earlier eras, the growth of this research line can be directly traced to the establishment of Michigan State University's Institute for the Study of Youth Sports in 1978, which sparked research interest on all aspects of youth sport involvement.

Three areas of focus have dominated parental influence research. First, there has been considerable attention toward understanding parental influence upon affective outcomes for children in sport. Second, parental influence upon children's self-concept development has been a major area of research focus. Third, investigators have been interested in assessing sport motivational outcomes for children in relation to parenting practices.

An important methodological consideration to note at the outset of this summary relates to how knowledge of parental influence has been obtained. Virtually all of the research on parental influence has examined children's perceptions of parenting practices or beliefs rather than relying upon parents' own self-reports, or third-party assessments of parental behavior. While this may appear to be a limitation, it is probable that children's interpretations of their parents' beliefs and behaviors are more useful sources of information as children's perceptions of their parents' motives, expectations, beliefs, etc. are likely to be more strongly linked to children's response patterns. In fact, children's perceptions of parental influence have been more strongly linked to psychosocial and affective outcomes for children than have been parents' own

self-reports of their beliefs and behaviors (Babkes and Weiss, 1999; Gecas and Schwalbe, 1986). Thus, it should be recognized that the research summarized herein primarily reflects upon children's interpretations of their parents' beliefs and behaviors, although this does not necessarily constitute a limitation.

Affective Outcomes

This line of research arose from concerns about the extent and frequency of negative affective experiences for children during their participation in organized youth sport programs. A major initial focus was upon stress outcomes, particularly the identification of contributors to high levels of state and trait anxiety in young athletes. Subsequent investigations have also addressed parents' roles in contributing to favorable affective outcomes for children, including sport enjoyment. The study of affective outcomes in youth sport has been of major interest because of the widespread view that the youth sport environment should be an enjoyable, and relatively, stress-free context. In addition, there is an intuitive and theoretically-based view (e.g., Harter, 1978, 1981) linking affective experiences to future motivation for children.

In the examination of sport anxiety, researchers have considered both competitive trait and competitive state anxiety outcomes for children. Competitive trait anxiety represents a rather stable, or enduring, personality characteristic that reflects a person's generalized tendency to perceive competition as threatening (Martens, 1977). Competitive state anxiety represents a situation-specific form of competitive anxiety that relates to feelings of apprehension or stress "right now", or in any given sport context. Competitive trait and competitive state anxiety are related as children with higher trait anxiety tend to perceive more situations as stressful and are more likely to experience greater state anxiety across situations (Gould et al., 1983; Scanlan and Lewthwaite, 1984).

In relation to the effects of parental influence upon trait anxiety levels, research indicates that children with higher levels of competitive trait anxiety have a greater tendency to worry about negative evaluation from parents (Brustad, 1988; Lewthwaite and Scanlan, 1989; Passer, 1983). This finding suggests that children with a chronic, or generalized, tendency toward anxiety in sport do so, at least in part, because they are concerned about incurring negative parental evaluations should they not perform well. These findings in the youth sport domain are consistent with research findings in educational settings on correlates of trait anxiety in academic contexts (Wigfield and Eccles, 1990).

A similar pattern of findings has also been identified in relation to state anxiety outcomes for young athletes in sport. Typically, researchers interested in state anxiety have measured precompetition levels of state anxiety as this index of state anxiety is the most amenable for assessment. Scanlan and Lewthwaite (1984) found that children with higher levels of competitive state anxiety prior to competition were characterized by their tendency to perceive greater levels of parental pressure and by their greater frequency of worry about incurring negative parental and coach evaluation of their performance in comparison to their less anxious peers. The study by Weiss et al. (1989) study provided further support for this belief as these researchers found that the two primary precompetitive worries of young male gymnasts involved youngsters' concerns about "what my parents will think" and "letting my parents down". In an examination of sources of precompetitive anxiety in young wrestlers, perceived parental pressure to wrestle was also significantly related to precompetitive state anxiety for young males (Gould et al., 1991). Thus, it seems evident that parents can contribute to the anxiety responses of their children in sport. This research indicates that children's perceptions of parental pressure and concerns about parental evaluations and judgments are important contributors to children's anxiety response in sport.

Sport burnout represents an additional, potentially negative affective outcome for children in sport. However, parental influence in contributing to burnout has been infrequently examined. In one of the few studies published in this area, Coakley (1992) concluded that burnout was frequently experienced by high ability athletes whose parents had made substantial commitments of time and energy to maintain and facilitate the athletic development of their children. Although this outcome may seem counterintuitive, Coakley attributed this result to young athletes' perceptions that high levels of parental investment resulted in youngsters' perceptions of being "trapped" in a narrowly defined athletic role.

The "flipside" of parental influence on children's affective outcomes relates to attempts to understand parents' contribution to favorable emotional experiences for children in sport. Within this area, understanding correlates of sport enjoyment has been the principal focus of investigation. The first study to consider parental influence upon sport enjoyment for young athletes was conducted by Scanlan and Lewthwaite (1986). These researchers operationalized sport enjoyment as the amount of fun that participants reported over the course of the sport season; this definition has been most commonly used throughout subsequent research. Scanlan and Lewthwaite found that high levels of enjoyment for children were associated with high levels of parental satisfaction with performance, favorable patterns of adult interaction and involvement, and a low frequency of negative maternal interactions. A similar finding was obtained by this author (Brustad, 1988) in research that indicated that low perceived parental pressure was a predictor of high enjoyment for young male and female basketball players. In a related finding, Scanlan et al. (1989) found that bringing pleasure or pride to their families was an important dimension of enjoyment for elite figure skaters' during their years of involvement.

Overall, research on social influences upon children's emotional outcomes in youth sport has found consistent patterns of relationships between children's perceptions of parental practices and the favorability of affective outcomes for children. Although a considerable amount of research has been generated to link parental practices to affective outcomes for children in sport, further research will be needed to explore the mechanisms by which parenting beliefs and practices impact children in this regard.

Self-Concept

For children and adolescents, the formation and refinement of the self-concept is a natural and essential consequence of cognitive development. The self-concept is an important area for study within youth sport because of interest in understanding the effects of sport participation on youngsters' self evaluations of ability and worth. Furthermore, contemporary theories of motivation (Bandura, 1986; Eccles and Harold, 1991; Harter, 1978, 1981) posit strong links between various aspects of the self-concept and subsequent motivation. From these theoretical perspectives, the desire to engage in particular achievement areas, and the extent of motivation while involved, is directly linked to self-perceptions of competence in a particular domain.

In conducting youth sport research in relation to self-concept development, it is important to recognize that the structure of the self-concept changes with development (Brustad, 1998). For example, the nature and number of dimensions that comprise the self-concept are related to the cognitive maturational status of the individual, and a global sense of self-worth, or self-esteem, does not typically emerge until middle childhood (Harter, 1983). With cognitive development, children and adolescents begin to distinguish between an increasing number of ability dimensions and also become increasingly accurate in their perceptions of their ability (Harter, 1988; Horn and Harris, 1996). As a consequence of these developmental considerations, research in relation to the self-concept is problematic prior to middle childhood (roughly ages 7 to 9 years).

Perceived Competence

Perceived sport competence has been the most heavily investigated dimension of the self-concept

for youth sport researchers interested in parental influence. Other dimensions of the self, including perceptions of personal control, and self-esteem, or one's overall sense of value or worth as a person, have received comparatively less attention.

Parents typically have substantial influence upon children's perceptions of competence for at least two reasons. First, a considerable amount of the child's time is spent in interaction with parents and other family members and these interactions provide children with many opportunities for receiving competence-related information and feedback (Brustad, 1996b). Second, due to cognitive-developmental tendencies, youngsters during the early and middle childhood years tend to rely extensively on competence information provided by adults in forming self-judgments, as opposed to utilizing information provided through other sources, such as peers and personal performance evaluations (Horn and Hasbrook, 1987; Horn and Weiss, 1991). As children move into later childhood, and then into adolescence, they become increasingly capable of using peer comparison, peer evaluation, and internal information sources and tend to prefer these sources to adult sources in gaining competence information. Since the middle and late childhood developmental periods correspond with high levels of participatory involvement in organized sport for youngsters, parental influence on children's self-perceptions in this domain should, logically, be of a substantial magnitude.

Research from diverse achievement contexts indicates that parents are important contributors to children's perceptions of competence. For example, (Eccles) Parsons et al. (1992) found that children's perceptions of their math ability, and their perceptions of the difficulty and effort level required to succeed in mathematics, had a stronger relationship to their parents' perceptions of their ability than to objective criteria of their mathematics ability. Felson and Reed (1986) found a strong correspondence between parents' and children's appraisals of the child's ability in both academic and athletic domains, even when levels of actual ability were statistically controlled. These studies suggest that parental beliefs about competence can actually override more objective competence information available to the youngster.

Eccles and Harold (1991) found parental ability appraisals to be significantly related to children's ability perceptions in the sport domain. With a similar focus, Jacobs and Eccles (1992) examined the nature and strength of the relationship between mothers' perceptions of their child's ability with 11- and 12-year old children's competence perceptions in the sport, mathematics, and social domains. Consistent with Eccles' socialization model (Eccles et al., 1983, Eccles and Harold, 1991), children's self-perceptions of ability tended to be congruent with their mothers' appraisals. An important factor mediating the favorability of ability perceptions across domains was mothers' gender-related stereotypes, as such stereotypes appear to influence mothers' beliefs about the likelihood that their child will experience success in various achievement domains.

Research indicates that parents also contribute to children's competence perceptions in sport through specific parenting practices. In two different studies, children's perceptions of physical competence were found to be significantly related to levels of parental encouragement to participate in a given domain (Brustad, 1993, 1996a). These finding were explained in relation to components of Eccles' socialization model, through which high parental expectations for the child in a particular achievement domain are anticipated to be associated with the provision of greater opportunities for children in this domain by parents. From this perspective, parental encouragement is regarded as the behavioral consequence of favorable parental perceptions of children's ability in a particular achievement arena.

Overall, research across varied domains strongly suggests that parents influence children's perceptions of their competence, and implicitly their subsequent motivation. Although research related to social influences upon children's perceived competence is highly important, there is also a need to investigate other dimensions of self-concept formation and refinement through sport, including parental influence upon children's perceptions of control and children's self-esteem development.

Motivation

A third important area of investigation has focused upon parental influence on children's motivation in sport and physical activity. Furthermore, since affective and self-concept dimensions are viewed as important precursors to motivation in contemporary theories, much of the research on affective outcomes and self-concept development for youngsters in sport is implicitly linked to the motivational area.

Studies reveal that children's perceptions of their parents' level of interest in sport are predictive of children's initial, and sustained, interest in sport (Eccles and Harold, 1991; Greendorfer et al., 1996). With regard to children's motivation to participate in less structured physical activity, parental interest, enjoyment, and involvement in physical activity are similarly predictive of children's motivation in these contexts (Brustad, 1993, 1996a; Kimiecik et al., 1996).

In a three-year longitudinal study, Eccles and Harold's (1991) assessed the relationship between parental belief systems and children's intrinsic motivation to participate in free-choice activities, including sport, reading, and mathematics. The influence of parents upon children's perceptions was evident as parents' perceptions of their child's competence, and parental perceptions of the importance and usefulness of each activity, were predictive of children's perceptions in each respect. Children's perceptions, in turn, predicted their intrinsic motivation to participate in the three domains.

In a comprehensive study of parental socialization, Babkes and Weiss (1999) examined the influence of various parental beliefs and behaviors on affective, self-concept, and motivational outcomes in young soccer players, ages 9 to 11 years. These investigators found that children who perceived their parents to be positive exercise role models, perceived that their parents had favorable beliefs about their competence, and reported that their parents responded to their performance with a high frequency of positive, contingent responses, experienced greater enjoyment, had higher perceived soccer competence, and higher levels of intrinsic motivation than did fellow players who had less favorable perceptions of their parents' involvement. Furthermore, those children who also perceived that their fathers were highly involved in their soccer participation, and who perceived that their fathers exerted lower levels of pressure to perform, experienced more favorable psychosocial outcomes.

In a different vein, McCullagh et al. (1993) examined the relationship between parents' perceptions of their children's motives for participating in sport and children's own self-reported motives. They found a high level of correspondence between the motives expressed by children for participating in sport with parents' perceptions of their children's motives. This research suggests that children's motives for participation are likely to be shaped by their parents' views of the primary benefits and opportunities afforded by youth sport participation.

Parental socialization influence upon children's physical activity motivation has also received attention. One study (Brustad, 1993) examined fourth-grade children's attraction to physical activity in relation to four parental dimensions, including parents' self-reported enjoyment of physical activity and fitness levels, their beliefs about the importance of physical activity, and their levels of encouragement of their child's physical activity involvement. Attraction to physical activity is a construct that reflects children's interest in being physically active and is comprised of five different dimensions of interest and motivation. In this study, parental enjoyment of physical activity and the child's gender was predictive of the level of encouragement parents provided for their child to be physically active. As expected, boys received greater physical activity encouragement from parents than did girls. Parental encouragement and gender, in turn, predicted children's perceived competence levels in physical activity. Perceived competence predicted children's attraction to physical activity along all five dimensions. Thus, parental beliefs and behaviors shaped the extent of encouragement provided to children, which was linked to children's own self-related competence beliefs and, subsequently, to the extent of children's physical activity motivation. A follow-up study (Brustad, 1996a) among fourth- through sixth-grade children differing in socioeconomic status from the previous sample, yielded highly similar results. In this study, children's perceptions of their parents' levels of encouragement to be physical activity, as well as children's perceptions of their parents' enjoyment of physical activity, contributed to the explanation of children's physical activity attraction.

Dempsey et al. (1993) considered relationships among parental physical activity behaviors and belief systems in relation to children's participation in moderate-to-vigorous physical activity (MVPA). They found that parents' perceptions of their children's MVPA competence were predictive of children's actual MVPA participation. Thus, these researchers found a relationship between parental expectations of their children's level of success in physical activity with children's actual levels of participation in these activities. In a follow-up study, Kimiecik et al. (1996) examined relationships among various dimensions of parents' beliefs and children's beliefs in relation to children's levels of involvement in moderate-to-vigorous physical activity. They found that the child's perceptions of their parents' beliefs about the value of fitness, and their parents' beliefs about the child's physical fitness, were significantly related to the child's perceived fitness competence, but not to the child's beliefs about the value of physical fitness.

In sum, parents appear to have extensive influence upon children's sport and physical activity motivation. The nature of parental influence extends to both belief systems, including parental values and expectations, and parental behaviors, such as role modeling, encouragement, and feedback.

Future Directions

Research on parental influence upon psychsocial outcomes for youngsters in sport has shown remarkable growth over the past two decades. However, there is much more room for development of this area, and a number of suggestions for the course of future research are offered. Well-designed future research can provide a greater depth of understanding of the mechanisms of parental influence and can also contribute to the design of appropriate intervention programs.

The primary recommendation for future development of the parental influence area pertains to the continued need to utilize comprehensive, theoretical approaches to guide our investigations. Theoretically-based approaches are needed to help direct attention to possible relationships between parental beliefs and behaviors and specific psychological and affective outcomes for children. Three comprehensive models for the study of parental socialization influence in children's sport and physical activity are those provided by Harter (1978, 1981), Eccles (Eccles et al. 1983; Eccles and Harold, 1991) and Kimiecik et al. (1996). These models approach the socialization process in similar and compatible ways, but differ with regard to their primary area of focus with regard to the socialization process.

Harter's theory is a general motivational model that extends across achievement domains. This theory directs considerable attention to the nature of parental feedback and emotional response to children's motivated efforts in relation to children's subsequent tendency toward intrinsic or extrinsic motivation. This model is highly appropriate to the explanation of sport and physical activity socialization of children in sport, particularly during children's initial phases of sport involvement

Eccles' model (Eccles et al., 1991; Eccles and Harold, 1991) focuses primary attention upon parental belief systems, specifically parental values and expectations, as such beliefs shape interactions between parents and children in relation to achievement opportunities. Parental values and expectations may also be influenced by underlying gender stereotypes about various achievement domains and in relation to parental success expectancies in relation to gender and a particular achievement domain (e.g., mathematics involvement for girls). From this perspective, parents are considered to have an instrumental role in shaping children's perceptions of the relative value of various achievement domains, as well as children's perceptions of competence within these domains. To the extent that children internalize parental expectation and value beliefs, children's motivation to participate in various domains, and their success expectancies within these domains, will also be affected. Research following from this theoretical framework has been useful in contributing to our understanding of the role of parental belief systems in shaping children's orientations toward sport and physical activity involvement (Brustad, 1993; Eccles and Harold, 1991).

The model used by Kimiecik et al. (1996) is explicitly designed for the study of physical activity socialization rather than sport socialization. As does Eccles, Kimiecik et al's Family Influence Model highlights the importance of parental belief systems and perceptions as they contribute to shaping children's beliefs and perceptions about physical activity involvement. In addition, this model includes non-psychological factors, including demographic and family influences, that may contribute to the physical activity socialization of the child.

Each model is comprehensive because each explicitly addresses specific, anticipated relationships among parental beliefs and behaviors as they affect parenting practices, which, in turn, shape opportunities provided for children and resulting psychological and affective outcomes for children. Each theory is also explicitly concerned with the motivational implications for children of parental socialization practices, a consideration that seems fundamental to the study of youth sport involvement.

In addition to the primary recommendation to utilize theoretically-based approaches, a second rec-ommendation relates to the need for more research that considers the dynamic aspects of the socialization process. Currently, our understanding is very limited for how parental influence changes over time in relation to children's psychological, physical, and motoric development and in accordance with changes in children's experiences and interest in sport. With the exception of Eccles and Harold's (1991) three year investigation, there are no longitudinal studies that provide insight into how parent-child interaction may change over time and how this change can affect psychosocial aspects of involvement. Such knowledge would be particularly beneficial as we seek to understand changes in children's interest, motivation, or participation patterns (e.g., dropout) in relation to family influence.

In general, research on the nature of psychosocial outcomes for youngsters in sport has focused on children, and largely ignored the adolescent sporting population (Greendorfer et al., 1996). Consequently, a third recommendation is to examine parental influence upon psychosocial outcomes for adolescents in sport much more closely. Adolescents represent an important group for study because the meaning and importance of sport involvement to youngsters is likely to change in relation to the increasing competitiveness and selectivity of sport involvement during the adolescent years, as well as in relation to the youngster's physical, social, and cognitive development. Although the magnitude of parental influence during the adolescent phase typically declines, the nature and form of parental influence during these years is not yet well understood.

In addition to these three general recommendations for conducting youth sport research in the future, there are numerous avenues of investigation that have been relatively overlooked. For example, minimal research has examined the effects of sport participation upon the functioning of the family (Weiss and Hayashi, 1995). This is an interesting area of investigation, particularly for families with children with extensive sport involvement. Within the family, the relative influence of fathers and mothers in shaping the psychological and affective consequences of sport participation for youth has also been an understudied area. Very few investigations (Babkes and Weiss, 1999) have examined the manner in which mothers and fathers may exert distinct forms of influence upon psychosocial outcomes for youngsters in sport and further investigation in this area holds much promise. Parental gender-based stereotypes are another potentially insightful area for investigation. With the exception of Eccles' and colleagues' work (Eccles and Harold, 1991; Jacobs and Eccles, 1992), gender-based influences on the sport socialization processes have hardly been investigated within Phase II or Phase III research orientations.

In sum, our knowledge base on parental influence on psychosocial outcomes for youngsters in sport is fairly extensive given the relatively recent nature of systematic research in this area. This is an important area for study because our knowledge base informs us that parents can have a profound impact upon the psychological and affective outcomes that children experience through their sport participation. Thus, well-designed future research will help us to better understand parental roles and involvement and allow us to design effective strategies for intervention.

REFERENCES

Babkes, M. & Weiss M. (1999). Parental influence on children's cognitive and affective responses to competitive soccer participation. *Pediatric Exercise Science* 11: 44-62.

Bandura, A. (1986). *Social Foundations of Thought and Action: A Social Cognitive Theory*. Englewood Cliffs, NJ: Prentice-Hall.

Brustad, R. (1988). Affective outcomes in competitive youth sport: The influence of intrapersonal and socialization factors. *Journal of Sport and Exercise Psychology* 10: 307-321.

Brustad, R. (1992). Integrating socialization influences into the study of children's motivation in sport. *Journal of Sport and Exercise Psychology* 14: 59-77.

Brustad, R. (1993). Who will go out and play? Parental and psychological influences on children's attraction to physical activity. *Pediatric Exercise Science* 5: 210-223.

Brustad, R. (1996a). Attraction to physical activity in urban school children: Parental socialization and gender influences. *Research Quarterly for Exercise and Sport* 67: 316-323.

Brustad, R. (1996b). Parental and peer influence on children's psychological development through sport. In: Smoll, F. & Smith, R. (Eds.), *Children and Youth in Sport: A Biopsychosocial Perspective.* Madison, WI: Brown & Benchmark (pp. 112-124).

Brustad, R. (1998). Developmental considerations in sport and exercise psychology measurement. In: Duda, J. (Ed.), *Advances in Sport and Exercise Psychology Measurement.* Morgantown, WV: Fitness Information Technology (pp. 461-470).

Coakley, J. (1992). Burnout among adolescent athletes: A personal failure or social problem? *Sociology of Sport Journal* 9: 271-285.

Dempsey, J.; Kimiecik, J.; & Horn, T. (1993). Parental influence on children's moderate to vigorous physical activity participation: An expectancy-value approach. *Pediatric Exercise Science* 5: 151-167.

(Eccles) Parsons, J.; Adler, T.; & Kaczala, C. (1982). Socialization of achievement attitudes and beliefs: Parental influences. *Child Development* 53: 310-321.

Eccles (Parsons), J.; Adler, T.; Futterman, R.; Goff, S.; Kaczala, C.; Meece, J.; & Midgley, J. (1983). Expectancies, values, and academic behaviors. In: Spence, J. & Helmreich, R. (Eds.), *Achievement and Achievement Motives: Psychological And Sociological Approaches.* San Francisco: W. H. Freeman (pp. 75-146).

Eccles, J. & Harold, R. (1991). Gender differences in sport involvement: Applying the Eccles' expectancy-value model. *Journal of Applied Sports Psychology* 3: 7-35.

Felson, M. & Reed, M. (1986). The effect of parents on the self-appraisals of children. *Social Psychology Quarterly* 49: 302-308.

Gecas, V. & Schwalbe, M. (1986). Parental behavior and adolescent self-esteem. *Journal of Marriage and the Family* 48: 37-46.

Gould, D.; Eklund, R.; Petlichkoff, L.; Peterson, K.; & Bump, L. (1991). Psychological predictors of state anxiety and performance in age-group wrestlers. *Pediatric Exercise Science* 3: 198-208.

Gould, D.; Horn, T.; & Spreeman, J. (1983). Competitive anxiety in junior elite wrestlers. *Journal of Sport Psychology* 3: 69-81.

Greendorfer, S. & Ewing, M. (1981). Race and gender differences in children's socialization into sport. *Research Quarterly for Exercise and Sport* 52: 301-310.

Greendorfer, S. & Lewko, J. (1978). Role of family members in the sport socialization of children. *Research Quarterly* 49: 146-152.

Greendorfer, S.; Lewko, J.; & Rosengren, K. (1996). Family and gender-based influences in sport socialization of children and adolescents. In: Smoll, F. & Smith, R. (Eds.), *Children and Youth in Sport: A Biopsychosocial Perspective.* Madison, WI: Brown & Benchmark (pp. 89-111).

Harter, S. (1978). Effectance motivation reconsidered. *Human Development* 21: 34-64.

Harter, S. (1981). A model of intrinsic mastery motivation in children: Individual differences and developmental change. In: Collins, W. (Ed.), *Minnesota Symposium on Child Psychology (Volume 14).* Hillsdale, NJ: Lawrence Erlbaum Associates (pp. 215-255).

Harter, S. (1983). Developmental perspectives on the self-system. In: Hetherington, E. (Ed.), *Handbook of Child Psychology, Socialization, Personality, and Social Development.* New York: Wiley (pp. 275-385).

Harter, S. (1988). Causes, correlates, and the functional role of global self-worth: A life-span perspective. In: Kolligan, J. & Sternberg, R. (Eds.), *Perceptions of Competence and Incompetence Across the Life-Span.* New Haven, CT: Yale University Press (pp. 67-98).

Horn, T. & Hasbrook, C. (1987). Psychological characteristics and the criteria children use for self-evaluation. *Journal of Sport Psychology* 9: 208-221.

Horn, T. & Harris, A. (1996). Perceived competence in young athletes: Research findings and recommendations for coaches and parents. In: Smoll, F. & Smith, R. (Eds.), *Children and Youth in Sport: A Biopsychosocial Perspective.* Madison, WI: Brown & Benchmark (pp. 309-329).

Horn, T. & Weiss, M. (1991). A developmental analysis of children's self-ability judgments in the physical domain. *Pediatric Exercise Science* 3: 310-326.

Jacobs, J. & Eccles, J. (1992). The impact of mothers' gender-role stereotypic beliefs on mothers' and children's ability perceptions. *Journal of Personal and Social Psychology* 63: 932-944.

Kimiecik, J.; Horn, T.; & Shurin, C. (1996). Relationships among children's beliefs, perceptions of their parents' beliefs, and their moderate-to-vigorous physical activity. *Research Quarterly of Exercise and Sport* 67: 324-336.

Lewko, J.& Ewing, M. (1980). Sex differences and parental influence in sport involvement of children. *Journal of Sport Psychology* 2: 62-68.

Lewthwaite, R. & Scanlan, T. (1989). Predictors of competitive trait anxiety in male youth sport participants. *Medicine and Science in Sports and Exercise* 21: 221-229.

Martens, R. (1977). *Sport Competition Anxiety Test (SCAT)*. Champaign, IL: Human Kinetics.

McCullagh, P.; Matzkanin, K.; Shaw, S.; & Maldonado, M. (1993). Motivation for participation in physical activity: A comparison of parent child perceived competencies and participation motives. *Pediatric Exercise Science* 5: 224-233.

Orlick, T. (1974). The athletic dropout-a high price of inefficiency. *Canadian Association of Health, Physical Education, and Recreation Journal* Nov/Dec: 21-27.

Passer, M. (1983). Fear of failure, fear of evaluation, perceived competence, and self-esteem in competitive-trait-anxious children. *Journal of Sport Psychology* 5: 172-188.

Scanlan, T. & Lewthwaite, R. (1984). Social psychological aspects of competition for male youth sport participants: Predictors of competitive stress. *Journal of Sport Psychology* 6: 422-429.

Scanlan, T. & Lewthwaite, R. (1986). Social psychological aspects of the competitive sport experience for male youth sport participants: Predictors of enjoyment. *Journal of Sport Psychology* 8: 25-35.

Scanlan, T.; Stein, G.; & Ravizza, K. (1989). An in-depth study of former elite figure skaters: Sources of enjoyment. *Journal of Sport and Exercise Psychology* 11: 65-83.

Smilkstein, G. (1980). Psychological trauma in children and youth in competitive sport. *Journal of Family Practice* 10: 737-739.

Snyder, E. & Purdy, A. (1982). Socialization into sport: Parent and child reverse and reciprocal effects. *Research Quarterly for Exercise and Sport* 53: 263-266.

Weiss, M. & Hayashi, C. (1995). All in the family: Parent-child influences in competitive gymnastics. *Pediatric Exercise Science* 7: 36-48.

Weiss, M.; Weise, D.; & Klint, K. (1989). Head over heels with success: The relationship between self-efficacy and performance in competitive youth gymnastics. *Journal of Sport and Exercise Psychology* 11: 444-451.

Wigfield, A. & Eccles, J. (1990). Test anxiety in elementary and secondary school students. *Educational Psychology* 24: 159-183.

CHAPTER 11

Attrition and Dissatisfaction in Youth Sports

Stuart Biddle
Loughborough University

The apparent natural spontaneity of children's engagement in physical activity may seem an easy way to encourage and maintain the interest of youth in sport. However, it is well known that many children find the sport experience unsatisfactory. The purpose of this paper, therefore, is to summarize evidence on why some children and youth might find sport and physical activity a negative experience. Three main themes will be considered and two will be used to further our understanding of amotivated behavior in sport and physical education (PE). First, the reasons young people give for playing or not playing sport will be summarized. Then, evidence on motivational issues using the Goal Perspective and Self-Determination Theory approaches is presented. Finally, evidence that assists in the understanding of amotivation in sport and PE is discussed.

A Descriptive Approach: Motives and Barriers

The most obvious way to investigate what young people think about the sport experience is to ask them! Typical questions might be 'why do you take part?' 'Why do you not take part?' Or 'why have you stopped playing?' Such approaches are descriptive studies of motives. It has been argued elsewhere

(Biddle, 1995; Biddle, 1999) that this approach is useful but also requires more in-depth theoretical investigations. In other words, it is a good place to start, but not finish!

The results from North America and Europe show that children are motivated for a variety of reasons. Reviews by Biddle (1999) and Gould and Petlichkoff (1988) conclude that children are motivated for diverse reasons, including fun and enjoyment, learning and improving skills, being with friends, success and winning, and physical fitness and health. The latter factor might also include weight control and body appearance for older youth. However, more research is needed to understand the differences in motives across activities, levels of participation, and developmental stages.

Various surveys are available on the reasons children and youth give for non-participation in sport and exercise (HeartbeatWales, 1987; Mason, 1995). As with motives for participation, there appear to be numerous reasons why children and youth cease their involvement. For example, Coakley and White (1992) conducted 60 in-depth interviews with 13-23 year olds in England, half of whom had decided to participate in one of five different sports initiatives in their local town. The others had either ceased involvement or had decided not to participate at all. The decision to participate or not appeared to be influenced by perceptions of competence, by external constraints, such as money and opposite sex friends, by degree of support from significant others, and by past experiences, including school PE. Negative memories of school PE included feelings of boredom and incompetence, lack of choice, and negative evaluation from peers. Mason's (1995) study of over 4000 youth in England provides support for these conclusions. Some children reported feelings of embarrassment in sport settings, mainly due to perceived incompetence or concerns over self-presentation associated with their physique during puberty.

Gould (1987) summarized the reasons for some children having poor adherence as conflicts of interest, lack of playing time, lack of fun, limited improvement in skills, or no success, boredom, and injury. Competitive stress and dislike of the coach have also been cited in sport settings. Children, therefore, appear to have multiple motives for participation or non-participation in sport.

THEORETICAL APPROACHES

The descriptive approach provides useful data in the initial stages of understanding attrition and dissatisfaction. However, theoretical approaches are also required. There are extensive data in the literature using goal perspective approaches, such as the study of goal orientations and motivational climate. In addition, the emerging study of Self-Determination Theory appears to hold considerable promise. Both are considered subsequently.

Goal Perspectives Approach

The goals young people may hold in achievement settings, such as the classroom or in sport, are important motivational factors (Duda, 1993). Research has focused almost exclusively on task and ego goal perspectives. Stemming from educational psychology, Nicholls (1989) proposed that people define success and construe ability in different ways. In certain situations, an individual might emphasize task mastery, self-improvement, and effort, and hence depict a 'task' goal. On the other hand, someone may primarily strive to win and demonstrate high normative ability, even with low effort. This reflects an 'ego' goal in that particular situation. Such situational goals are thought to be a reflection of both individual differences and situational factors. Individual differences associated with goals are the 'goal orientations' held by the individual in a specific life domain, such as sport. These tendencies are usually expressed as 'task' and 'ego' goal orientations, and are assessed typically through self-report items referring to when people feel most successful in the domain of interest. For example, 'I feel most successful in sport/physical education when I do my very best' reflects a task orientation and '...when I'm the best' is an ego orientation item (Duda and Whitehead, 1998). In addition, the 'motivational climate' created by a teacher or coach might also reflect task and ego qualities, and hence affect the situational goals adopted (Ames, 1992; Biddle et al., 1995; Ntoumanis and Biddle, 1999a).

Research predictions typically propose that ego oriented children will be motivationally fragile when they doubt their own competence. This is because they are focused on normative ability. Task oriented children, on the other hand, are interested in self-improvement and thus tend to be motivated regardless of perceived ability or competence. However, research has shown mixed findings in physical activity settings (Cury et al., 1997; Vlachopoulos and Biddle, 1997).

Research has demonstrated, quite clearly, that a high task orientation, either singly or in combination with a high ego orientation, is motivationally adaptive in physical activity for children (Duda, 1993; Treasure and Roberts, 1995). This research has focused on four types of associations with goals: beliefs, affect, motivation, and behavior. Similar findings also emerge from the study of motivational climate.

Correlates of Goal Orientations

The links between goal orientations and beliefs about the causes of success are fundamental to the understanding of motivated achievement behavior in youth. Research in the classroom and PE/sport contexts has shown that task and ego goal orientations are differentially correlated with beliefs about the causes of success. For example, Duda et al. (1992) found for 10-11 year old boys and girls that an ego orientation was strongly correlated with ability beliefs, but rather weakly correlated with effort beliefs—beliefs deemed controllable and motivational. These findings have been replicated on many occasions.

While ability and effort beliefs are important and highly salient in sport, research has suggested (Dweck and Leggett, 1988; Elliott and Dweck, 1988) that beliefs concerning ability are multidimensional. For example, Dweck and colleagues have discussed conceptions of ability in terms of beliefs about the nature of intelligence. They distinguished between intelligence thought to be relatively fixed and intelligence thought to be changeable. Children believing in a more fixed notion of intelligence (an 'entity theory' of intelligence) were more likely to adopt an ego-oriented achievement goal. Conversely, children believing that intelligence is changeable (an 'incremental theory' of intelligence) were more likely to adopt a task goal. There is also evidence showing that self-efficacy and perceptual-motor performance are more positively affected by conceptions of ability associated with acquirable skill than when ability is viewed as inherent aptitude (Jourden et al., 1991).

Whether beliefs concerning the fixed or incremental nature of sport ability were related to achievement goal orientations in 11-12 year old children were examined by Sarrazin et al. (1996). Goals were assessed using the Task and Ego Orientation in Sport Questionnaire (TEOSQ) and asking the children to choose their preferred goal in the same way as Dweck and Leggett (1988) had done. Children choosing a task goal were more likely to be represented in the incremental beliefs group.

This provided support for the propositions of Dweck and Leggett (1988) and showed that such notions could be extended into the domain of sport.

Further, using both scientific and lay conceptions of ability, Sarrazin et al. (1996) developed a questionnaire to assess such beliefs and tested it with 304 French adolescents. This scale was labeled the Conception of the Nature of Athletic Ability Questionnaire (CNAAQ), and it assessed beliefs in the following properties of sport ability:

- *learning*: sport ability is the product of learning

- *incremental*: sport ability can change

- *specific ability*: sport ability is specific to certain sports or types of sports

- *general ability*: sport ability generalizes across many sports

- *stable ability*: sport ability is stable across time

- *gift-induced*: sport ability is a 'gift', i.e. 'God-given.'

Correlations were in the predicted directions with task orientation being associated with beliefs that sport ability is incremental, the product of learning, and unstable. Beliefs that sport ability is a gift and general were associated with an ego goal orientation. The latter beliefs are more likely to be associated with sport dissatisfaction or at least the belief that improvement is difficult.

The CNAAQ has been refined such that two higher order dimensions—entity and incremental beliefs—have been shown to be underpinned by learning and improvement beliefs (incremental), and beliefs in stability and gift (entity). Results using the latest version of the CNAAQ (CNAAQ-2) are discussed later in the prediction of amotivated behavior.

When goal orientations have been studied in respect to their relationships with motivational indices, one popular index has involved the assessment of intrinsic motivation. Achievement goals and 'intrinsic interest' of children have been studied in three physical education classes, specifically boys in football (soccer), girls in netball, and both boys and girls in gymnastics (Goudas et al., 1994b). (Netball is a game popular in Britain; it is played in schools by girls and has similar properties to basketball). Intrinsic interest was assessed by using the effort and enjoyment subscales from the Intrinsic Motivation Inventory (IMI) as well as a boredom scale. A task orientation was directly related to intrinsic interest for the soccer and netball lessons, whereas the relationship between ego orientation and intrinsic interest was mediated by perceptions of competence. For gymnastics lessons, only a task orientation was related to intrinsic interest.

In addition to studying generalized perceptions of intrinsic motivation, Goudas et al. (1994a) assessed 255 adolescents performing an aerobic shuttle endurance run 'test' in normal physical education lessons. Prior to the test, the students completed the TEOSQ and immediately after the run they completed the IMI with reference to their current motivational state. For the less objectively successful runners (lower half of the group), IMI enjoyment scores were higher for those in the high task/low ego group compared to the low task/low ego and high ego/low task groups. Similarly, high task/low ego children had higher IMI effort scores than those classified as high ego/low task. Results suggest that a high task orientation, even for those performing below the group average, preserved some form of intrinsic motivation and may help in preventing attrition and dissatisfaction.

It is surprising that so few studies have investigated behavioral correlates of goals. Little is still known about how goals may affect behaviors such as choice or persistence. One application of goal orientations was to study whether goals predicted voluntary participation in school physical education (Spray and Biddle, 1997). Since physical education classes are compulsory until the age of 16 years in England, students 16-18 years were sampled. These students could choose to take physical education as part of a wider program of study options. The results showed clearly that participation was highest for students with a high task and high ego orientation, and lowest for those low in both goals.

Most people involved in youth sport agree that it is essential that children have fun. Are goal orientations related to positive and negative affect in sport? A recent meta-analysis (Ntoumanis and Biddle, 1999b) provides a clear answer: 'Yes!' Specifically, correlations from 41 independent samples of both adult and youth were collated and corrected for both sampling and measurement error. Results showed that task orientation and positive affect were moderately-to-highly correlated ($r = 0.55$) and in a positive direction, whereas the relationship between task orientation and negative affect was negative and moderate-to-low ($r = -0.18$). The relationships between ego orientation and positive ($r = 0.10$) and negative affect ($r = 0.04$) were positive but very low.

Implications for Attrition and Dissatisfaction

Research using goal orientations is now extensive. The results show that attrition and dissatisfaction in youth sport are less likely if the child adopts a task goal, either by itself or in combination with a high ego goal. If they do this, the evidence suggests they will have higher intrinsic interest in the task, more positive affect, more adaptive beliefs concerning improvement and the role of effort, and will be more likely to choose to take part in sport.

Motivational Climate

In addition to individual goals, some have emphasized the importance of the achievement environment, or climate. Two main climates have been identified. A 'mastery' (task) climate is perceived by class or team members when they are directed towards self-improvement, the teacher/coach emphasizes learning and personal progress, effort is rewarded, mistakes are seen as part of learning, and choice is allowed. On the other hand, a 'performance' (ego) climate is one that encourages interindividual comparison, where mistakes are punished, and high normative ability is rewarded (Ames, 1992; Biddle et al., 1995). Effect sizes for physical activity climate studies of adults and youth have been calculated to indicate the strength of relationships between motivational climate and selected cognitive and affective variables (Ntoumanis and Biddle, 1999a).

From a quantitative synthesis of 14 studies with a total sample size of almost 4,500, the correlation, corrected for both sampling and measurement error, between mastery climate and positive motivational outcomes (e.g. satisfaction, positive attitudes towards lessons, intrinsic motivation) was 0.71, indicating a large effect. By contrast, performance climate correlated negatively in a small-to-moderate way with positive outcomes (ES = -0.30). Negative outcomes were also assessed, these comprised factors such as worry and boredom. The effect for mastery climate on negative outcomes was low-to-moderate and negative (ES = -0.26), and for performance climate was moderate and positive (ES = 0.46). Results, overall, indicate the importance of a mastery climate in promoting positive psychological outcomes in physical activity and reducing the likelihood of attrition and dissatisfaction.

Self-Determination Theory

Intrinsic and extrinsic motivation are well known constructs in psychology and are thought to be central to any discussion on motivation in youth sport. Intrinsic motivation is motivation to do something for its own sake in the absence of external (extrinsic) rewards, and involves fun, enjoyment and satisfaction. The enjoyment is in the activity itself rather than any extrinsic reward such as money, prizes or prestige from others, and participation is free of constraints and pressure. Extrinsic motivation, on the other hand, refers to motivation directed by rewards, money, pressure or other external factors. This suggests that if these rewards or external pressures were removed, motivation would decline in the absence of any intrinsic interest.

Deci and Ryan (1985) propose that three key psychological needs are related to intrinsically motivated behavior, the needs for competence, autonomy, and relatedness. Competence refers to striving to control outcomes and to experience mastery. Autonomy is related to self-determination. It is a feeling of freedom and to feel that actions emanate from the self. Finally, relatedness refers to striving to relate to, and care for, others, and to feel that others can relate to oneself. People seek to satisfy these needs, but of more importance from the point of view of enhancing intrinsic motivation and avoiding youth sport attrition, they predict the circumstances in which intrinsically motivated behavior can be promoted.

Extending traditional notions of intrinsic and extrinsic motivation, and including the psychological needs for competence, autonomy and relatedness, Deci and Ryan (1985) have proposed a 'Self-Determination Theory' (SDT) approach to intrinsic motivation. The nature of motivated behavior, according to Deci and Ryan, is based on striving to satisfy these three basic needs. This, in turn, leads to a process of 'internalization'—'taking in' behaviors not initially intrinsically motivating.

Deci and Ryan (1985) have linked the internalization concept to that of extrinsic and intrinsic motivation. In contrast to earlier formulations in which these two motivational types were regarded as mutually exclusive, they proposed that a continuum is formed whereby different types of extrinsically regulated behavior can be located. Deci and Ryan (1991, p. 254) refer to the continuum as one representing "the degree to which the regulation of a nonintrinsically motivated behavior has been internalized."

The four main types of extrinsic motivation are external, introjected, identified, and integrated regulation. External regulation might be illustrated by a child saying 'OK, I'll go to the physical education lesson if I really must.' This is an example of where behavior is controlled by rewards and threats, such as in the case of coercion of children in school.

Introjected regulation might be when one says 'I feel guilty if I don't play for the school team.' This is more internal in the sense that the individual internalizes the reasons for acting, but is not truly self-determined. The individual is acting out of avoidance of negative feelings, such as guilt, or to seek approval from others for their performance or behavior. The term introjection refers to someone 'taking in' a value but, at the same time, not really identifying with it; it is not accepted as one's own.

Identified regulation might be illustrated by the adolescent who says 'I want to train hard to improve my sport.' This is further towards the self-determined end of the motivation continuum where action is motivated by an appreciation of the outcomes of participation, such as fitness improvement. Although this is a more internalized perspective, and is correlated with future intentions, it is still focused on a product or outcome. In physical activity it is often the most strongly endorsed reason for participation (Chatzisarantis et al., 1997; Li, 1999), and has been identified by Whitehead (1993) as the 'threshold of autonomy.' It is behavior acted out of choice where the behavior is highly valued and important to the individual. It is illustrated by feelings of "I want to…" Values associated with this behavior are now accepted.

Integrated regulation is illustrated by Whitehead (1993) through the phrase 'I exercise because it is important to me and it symbolizes who and what I am.' Integrated regulation is a self-determined form of behavioral regulation and the behavior is volitional "because of its utility or importance for one's personal goals" (Deci et al., 1994, p. 121). However, is has not been assessed in all studies (Vallerand and Losier, 1999).

In contrast to these forms of extrinsic motivation, intrinsic motivation is shown when a child says 'I go swimming because I enjoy it.' The individual participates for fun and for the activity itself. Clearly, moving towards intrinsically, or identified and integrated, motivated forms of behavioral regulation are advised for higher levels of intention and sustained involvement in sport since they are likely to involve stronger feelings of personal investment, autonomy and self-identity.

The autonomy continuum, and the Relative Autonomy Index (RAI; a composite index of scores from the continuum reflecting the degree of self-determination) have been used in analyses of children's motivation within the domain of physical activity. Perceptions of autonomy, assessed with the RAI, are predictive of intrinsic interest in physical activity (Goudas et al., 1994b). In a study of 11-15 year olds in England, intentions to participate in leisure-time exercise in terms of both 'autonomous' and 'controlling' forms were considered (Chatzisarantis et al., 1997). Specifically, the children were asked to rate the degree to which they intended to exercise because they "have to" (controlling) or because they "want to" (autonomous). Intentions predicted physical activity when they were autonomous rather than controlling, lending support to SDT. In a study of over 700 Hungarian youth, more self-determined forms of motivation predicted intentions to be active in the future (Biddle et al., 1999). Extrinsic regulations predicted intentions very weakly and in a negative direction.

Implications for Attrition and Dissatisfaction

To reduce the possibility of youth sport attrition and dissatisfaction, it is important to promote self-determined forms of behavior. This requires providing environments where children can satisfy their needs for competence, autonomy and relatedness. In practical terms, this means that they be allowed opportunities for choice, mastery (competence), and social connections. Coaches, teachers, parents and others in youth sport will help this process by creating an autonomy-supportive environment where they understand the perspective of the child, and avoid behaviors and communication that are coercive and controlling.

UNDERSTANDING AMOTIVATION IN SPORT AND PHYSICAL EDUCATION

To further understand youth sport attrition and dissatisfaction we need to look at the construct of amotivation that has been used in the intrinsic motivation field. Amotivation is an important construct to study as an outcome variable in the context of youth sport. Vallerand and Fortier (1998,

p. 85) suggest that the study of amotivation "may prove helpful in predicting lack of persistence in sport and physical activity."

Amotivation refers to the relative absence of motivation where a lack of contingency between actions and outcomes is perceived and reasons for continuing involvement cannot be found (Pelletier et al., 1995; Vallerand and Fortier, 1998). This lack of perception of control over environmental forces is what Deci and Ryan (1985) refer to as amotivation at the 'external boundary' and is viewed similar to feelings of helplessness.

In a recent study based on a review of pertinent literature, unpublished results of Biddle et al. proposed that amotivation will be related to both goal orientations and SDT variables. First, in a model based on the relationships between entity and incremental beliefs and goal orientations, it hypothesized that amotivation in children's sport and PE will be directly related to achievement goals and entity beliefs. In addition, task and ego goal orientations will be predicted by incremental and entity beliefs (see Figure 1). From a large data set of 12-15 year olds, the lowest quartile on the variable of perceived sport competence was selected, giving a sample size of over 500. Nearly 40% of the variance in amotivation was explained by the model. Path coefficients showed that task orientation (negatively) and entity beliefs (positively) were strong predictors of amotivation.

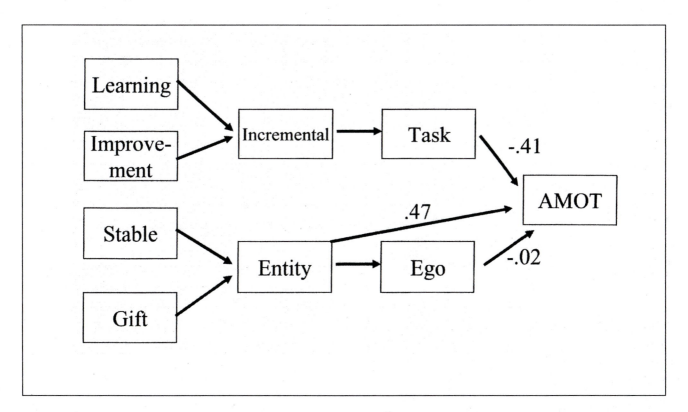

Figure 1. Structural equation modelling analysis and standarized colution, using a full latent model for the proposed model of the relationships between conceptions of sport ability, goal orientations and amotivation for those low in perceived competence.

In a second study (Biddle, unpublished results), nearly 3000 adolescents were classified into 'amotivated' and 'non amotivated' groups on the basis of scores on a measure of amotivation (Goudas et al., 1994b). Discriminant analysis was computed to test for group discrimination on the basis of scores on extrinsic, introjected, identified, and intrinsic forms of behavioral regulation with respect to physical education and sport. A clear discrimination was found, accounting for 25% of the variance with 83% of the participants being correctly classified into groups. Compared to those not amotivated, amotivated youth were characterized by higher scores on extrinsic regulation and lower scores on identified and intrinsic regulation.

Implications for Attrition and Dissatisfaction

Amotivated youth are clearly those we must study further to understand youth sport attrition and dissatisfaction. Preliminary evidence on amotivation suggests that it is associated with a low task orientation, strong entity beliefs, and high extrinsic and low identified and intrinsic behavioral regulations.

CONCLUSIONS

Children and youth drop-out of sport for many reasons, many of which will not be psychological in nature. Indeed, more needs to be known about the interaction between intra-individual, social, and environmental variables in predicting participation. Ecological models of health behavior may prove instructive in this regard (Sallis and Owen, 1996).

Using a psychological approach, however, provides valuable insight into the motivational factors associated with attrition and dissatisfaction. Goal orientations and motivational climate remain important influences. In addition, the Self-Determination Theory approach has been shown to provide further understanding of the motivational dynamics of youth sport. Finally, it is recommended that more research and program development be invested in the study of amotivation and helping those children who find sport unpleasant.

More specifically, more information is needed on how a self-determination theory approach—which asks why people participate—is applicable in contexts where physical activity is not compulsory. It is possible to study amotivation and other forms behavioral regulation in the school context, but the study of youth who have opted out altogether is more difficult. Related to this, better measures are needed for the assessment of amotivation. Finally, research is required where motivational profiles of young people in physical activity are identified on the basis of their psychological responses. This is likely to have high practical value.

REFERENCES

Ames, C. (1992). Achievement goals, motivational climate, and motivational processes. In: Roberts, G.C. (Ed.), *Motivation in Sport and Exercise*. Champaign, IL: Human Kinetics (pp. 161-176).

Biddle, S.; Cury, F.; Goudas, M.; Sarrazin, P.; Famose, J.P.; & Durand, M. (1995). Development of scales to measure perceived physical education class climate: A cross-national project. *British Journal of Educational Psychology* 65: 341-358.

Biddle, S.; Soos, I.; & Chatzisarantis, N. (1999). Predicting physical activity intentions using goal perspectives and self-determination theory approaches. *European Psychology* 4: 83-89.

Biddle, S.J.H. (1995). Exercise motivation across the lifespan. In: Biddle, S.J.H. (Ed.), *European Perspectives on Exercise and Sport Psychology*. Champaign, IL: Human Kinetics (pp. 5-25).

Biddle, S.J.H. (1999). Adherence to sport and physical activity in children and youth. In: Bull, S.J. (Ed.), *Adherence Issues in Exercise and Sport*. Chichester, England: John Wiley (pp. 111-144).

Chatzisarantis, N.; Biddle, S.J.H.; & Meek, G.A. (1997). A self-determination theory approach to the study of intentions and the intention-behaviour relationship in children's physical activity. *British Journal of Health Psychology* 2: 343-360.

Coakley, J. & White, A. (1992). Making decisions: Gender and sport participation among British adolescents. *Sociology of Sport Journal* 9: 20-35.

Cury, F.; Biddle, S.; Sarrazin, P.; & Famose, J.P. (1997). Achievement goals and perceived ability predict investment in learning a sport task. *British Journal of Educational Psychology* 67: 292-309.

Deci, E.; Eghrari, H.; Patrick, B.C.; & Leone, D.R. (1994). Facilitating internalisation: The self-determination theory perspective. *Journal of Perspective* 62: 119-142.

Deci, E.L. & Ryan, R.M. (1985). *Intrinsic Motivation and Self-Determination in Human Behavior*. New York: Plenum Press.

Deci, E.L. & Ryan, R.M. (1991). A motivational approach to self: Integration in personality. In: Dienstbier, R.A. (Ed.), *Nebraska Symposium on Motivation: Perspectives on Motivation (Volume 38)*. Lincoln, NE: University of Nebraska Press (pp. 237-288).

Duda, J.L. (1993). Goals: A social cognitive approach to the study of achievement motivation in sport. In: Singer, R.N.; Murphey, M.; & Tennant, L.K. (Eds.), *Handbook of Research on Sport Psychology*. New York: Macmillan (pp. 421-436).

Duda, J.L.; Fox, K.R.; Biddle, S.J.H.; & Armstrong, N. (1992). Children's achievement goals and beliefs about success in sport. *British Journal of Educational Psychology* 62: 313-323.

Duda, J.L. & Whitehead, J. (1998). Measurement of goal perspectives in the physical domain. In Duda, J.L. (Ed.), *Advances in Sport and Exercise Psychology Measurement*. Morgantown, WV: Fitness Information Technology (pp. 21-48).

Dweck, C. & Leggett, E. (1988). A social-cognitive approach to motivation and personality. *Psychology Review* 95: 256-273.

Elliott, E.S. & Dweck, C.S. (1988). Goals: An approach to motivation and achievement. *Journal of Personal and Social Psychology* 54: 5-12.

Goudas, M.; Biddle, S.; & Fox, K. (1994a). Achievement goal orientations and intrinsic motivation in physical fitness testing with children. *Pediatric Exercise Science* 6: 159-167.

Goudas, M.; Biddle, S.; & Fox, K. (1994b). Perceved locus of causality, goal orientations, and perceived competence in school physical education classes. *British Journal of Educational Psychology* 64: 453-463.

Gould, D. (1987). Understanding attrition in children's sport. In: Gould, D & Weiss, M. (Eds.), *Advances in Pediatric Sport Sciences: II Behavioural Issues*. Champaign, IL: Human Kinetics (pp. 61-85).

Gould, D. & Petlichkoff, L. (1988). Participation motivation and attrition in young athletes. In: Smoll, F.L.; Magill, R.A.; & Ash, M.J. (Eds.), *Children in Sport*. Champaign, IL: Human Kinetics (pp. 161-178).

HeartbeatWales. (1987). Exercise for health: Health-related fitness in Wales. *Heartbeat Report 23*. Cardiff: Heartbeat Wales.

Jourden, F.; Bandura, A.; & Banfield, J. T. (1991). The impact of conceptions of ability on self-regulatory factors and motor skill acquisition. *Journal of Sport and Exercise Psychology* 13: 213-226.

Li, F. (1999). The exercise motivation scale: Its multifaceted structure and construct validity. *Journal of Applied Sport Psychology* 11: 97-115.

Mason, V. (1995). *Young People and Sport in England, 1994*. London: Sports Council.

Nicholls, J. G. (1989). *The Competitive Ethos and Democratic Education*. Cambridge, Mass: Harvard University Press.

Ntoumanis, N. & Biddle, S. (1999a). A review of motivational climate in physical activity. *Journal of Sports Science* 17: 643-665.

Ntoumanis, N. & Biddle, S.J.H. (1999b). Affect and achievement goals in physical activity: A meta-analysis. *Scandinavian Journal of Medicine and Science in Sports*, 9: 315-332.

Pelletier, L.G.; Fortier, M.S.; Vallerand, R.J.; Tuson, K.M.; Briere, N.M.; & Blais, M.R. (1995). Toward a new measure of intrinsic motivation, extrinsic motivation, and amotivation in sports: The sport motivation scale (SMS). *Journal of Sport and Exercise Psychology* 17: 35-53.

Sallis, J. & Owen, N. (1996). Ecological models. In: Glanz, K.; Lewis, F.; & Rimer, B. (Eds.), *Health Behavior and Health Education: Theory, Research and Practice*. San Francisco: Jossey-Bass (pp. 403-424).

Sarrazin, P.; Biddle, S.; Famose, J.P.; Cury, F.; Fox, K.; & Durand, M. (1996). Goal orientations and conceptions of the nature of sport ability in children:

A social cognitive approach. *British Journal of Social Psychology* 35: 399-414.

Spray, C.M. & Biddle, S.J.H. (1997). Achievement goal orientations and participation in physical education among male and female sixth form students. *European Physical Education Review* 3: 83-90.

Treasure, D. & Roberts, G. C. (1995). Applications of achievement goal theory to physical education: Implications for enhancing motivation. *Quest* 47: 475-489.

Vallerand, R.J. & Fortier, M.S. (1998). Measures of intrinsic and extrinsic motivation in sport and physical activity: A review and critique. In: Duda, J.L. (Ed.), *Advances in Sport and Exercise Psychology Measurement*. Morgantown, WV: Fitness Information Technology (pp. 81-101).

Vallerand, R.J. & Losier, G.F. (1999). An integrative analysis of intrinsic and extrinsic motivation in sport. *Journal of Applied Sport Psychology* 11: 142-169.

Vlachopoulos, S. & Biddle, S.J.H. (1997). Modeling the relation of goal orientations to achievement-related affect in physical education: Does perceived ability matter? *Journal of Sport and Exercise Psychology* 19: 169-187.

Whitehead, J. R. (1993). Physical activity and intrinsic motivation. *President's Council for Physical Fitness, Sports, and Physical Activity—Fitness Research Digest* 1(2): 1-8.

CHAPTER 12

Psychological Issues in Youth Sports: Competitive Anxiety, Overtraining, and Burnout

Daniel Gould and Kristen Dieffenbach
Unversity of North Carolina Greensboro

"The intensive training and pressure heaped on by coaches, parents and federation officials often result in eating disorders, weakened bones, stunted growth, debilitating injuries and damaged psyches" (Ryan, 1995, p. 7).

"Overuse injuries occur because young athletes train too hard. When stress on the developing body is too great, breakdowns occur" (Murphy, 1999, p. 25).

"Parents take an unhealthy interest that results in severe pressure on the (young) athlete...Parent support and interest may also yield subtle pressure, creating a sense of obligation and making it difficult for the athlete to quit" (Donnelly, 1993, p. 102).

"In the dark troughs along the road to the Olympics lay bodies of the girls who stumbled on the way, broken by the work, pressure, and humiliation" (Ryan, 1995, p. 4).

As the above excerpts show, competitive anxiety, overtraining and burnout are psychological issues of concern for those interested in youth sports. Opinions on the psychological benefits versus detriments of youth sport involvement range widely from calls to eliminate programs because of excessive demands placed on young performers to

notions that youth sports are excellent training grounds for desirable life skills. Fortunately, over three decades of psychological research on youth sports has shed considerable light on many of these psychological issues of concern.

This review is designed to summarize and discuss the existing research on psychological issues of concern in children's sports, particularly competitive anxiety, overtraining, and burnout. To accomplish this objective, the review is organized around four critical psychological issues of concern.

- Are young athletes placed under too much psychological stress?

- What types of children, in what specific sport situations experience high levels of psychological stress?

- Are young athletes overtraining and burning out of sport?

- What types of young athletes and in what particular sport situations burnout of sport?

- Based on the research, implications for guiding practice and future research is also discussed. Before addressing these issues, however, it is important to understand the stress, anxiety, and burnout nomenclature. Psychological researchers have precise meanings for these terms which, at times, differ from common everyday usage.

Understanding Stress and Anxiety Terminology

Although many people use the terms arousal, stress, and anxiety interchangeably, sport and exercise psychologists find it important to distinguish among them. The use of precise definitions for the phenomena promotes a common language, reduces confusion, and diminishes the need for long explanations.

Stress is a process, a sequence of events that leads to a particular end. It is defined as "a substantial imbalance between demand [physical and/or psychological demands] and response capability, under conditions where failure to meet that demand has important consequences" (McGrath, 1970, p. 20). According to a simple model that McGrath proposed, stress consists of four interrelated stages.

- environmental demand,

- perception of demands,

- physical and psychological response, and

- behavioral consequences.

In the "environmental demand" stage of the stress process, some type of demand is placed on an individual, in this case the young athlete. The demand might be physical or psychological, such as a child having to make a critical free throw at the end of a basketball game or parents pressuring a young athlete to win the race.

People do not perceive demands in exactly the same way. This is reflected in the second stage of the stress process, the child's "perception of the physical or psychological demand." For instance, two youth basketball players might view having to make an important free throw at the end of a game quite differently. One may enjoy the challenge and attention of shooting in a clutch situation, whereas the other may feel threatened, i.e., perceives an imbalance between the demands placed on him

(having to make the free throw with time running out) and his ability to meet those demands. The former example perceives no such imbalance, or perceives it only to a nonthreatening degree.

A person's level of trait anxiety (a personality disposition that shapes the way one interprets situations) greatly influences how a person perceives the world. High trait-anxious children tend to perceive more situations (especially evaluative and competitive ones) as threatening than low trait-anxious children do. For this reason, trait anxiety is an important influence in stage two of the stress process.

The third stage of the stress process is the individual's physical and psychological response to a perception of the situation. If someone's perception of an imbalance between demands and response capability causes him or her to feel threatened, then increased state anxiety (a feeling of nervousness and apprehension) results, bringing with it increased worries, heightened physiological activation, or both. Other reactions, such as changes in concentration and increased muscle tension, accompany increased state anxiety.

Finally, the fourth stage is the actual behavior of the individual under stress. If the basketball player discussed earlier perceives an imbalance between capability and demands and feels increased state anxiety, does his behavior or performance deteriorate? Or, does the increased state anxiety increase intensity, thereby improving performance? These are the questions the final stage of the process addresses. Moreover, the final stage of the stress process also feeds back into the first. If a player becomes overly threatened and misses the shot, the other children may make negative comments, and this negative social evaluation would become an additional demand on the child (stage one). The stress process, then, is cyclical.

When exploring stress, the stress process, and ramifications of stress, it is also important to define state and trait anxiety, terminology frequently used in connection to stress. State anxiety is the proposed byproduct of the stress process and the construct with which negative connotations of stress are most often associated. Specifically, state anxiety is defined as "an existing or current emotional state characterized by feelings of apprehension and tension and associated with activation of the organism" (Martens, 1977, p. 9). Essentially, state anxiety is a negative feeling experienced at a particular moment in time. Everyone has experienced state anxiety in one form or another. State anxiety might be experienced before or during events such as an important speech, an onstage performance, or an athletic competition, and can take many forms such as uncontrollable thoughts, shaky knees, or a nervous stomach.

Trait anxiety is closely associated with state anxiety. However, unlike state anxiety, trait anxiety is considered to be an enduring attribute or part of one's personality. Trait anxiety is defined as "a predisposition to perceive certain environmental stimuli as threatening or nonthreatening and to respond to these stimuli with varying levels of state anxiety" (Martens, 1977, p. 9). Trait anxiety is important because it has been consistently shown to influence one's level of state anxiety. For example, a high trait anxious child will tend to perceive evaluative environments, such as competition, as more threatening than would a child with lower trait anxiety. Consequently, the high trait anxious child is more likely to experience a higher level of state anxiety. This means that the level of state anxiety a child experiences in evaluative environments is directly related to his or her level of trait anxiety.

The term overtrained is another commonly used word in sports to describe an athlete who turns in a below par practice or performance thought to be the result of training too hard or too much. Unfortunately, confusion still exists regarding the definition and causes of overtraining (Kreider et al., 1998). The science of physical training provides a structured method for reaching peak performances at a specific time known as periodized training. This type of training systematically exposes athletes to high volume, high intensity loads followed by a taper to a lower training load/intensity to maximize both recovery and physical gains. Periodized training

intentionally taxes the athlete's physical system to produce optimal muscular and cardiovascular adaptations that maximize both recovery and physical gains. Unfortunately, when periodized training is incorrectly implemented (e.g., the training load is greater than an athlete can handle), negative training effects occur, manifesting themselves in a progression moving from staleness to overtraining, and finally burnout. Overtraining, then, is "an accumulation of training or nontraining stress resulting in long-term decrements in performance capacity...in which restoration of performance capacity may take several weeks or months" (Kreider et al., 1998, p. viii).

In the general psychology literature, burnout is typically viewed as "a state of emotional exhaustion caused by excessive psychological and emotional demands placed on people in helping professions" (Jackson et al., 1986, p. 630). It is composed of three conceptually distinct but interrelated components (Maslach, 1976) including (a) emotional exhaustion, (b) depersonalization or the tendency to become detached from others in one's activity, and (c) feelings of low personal accomplishment (Jackson et al., 1986). Burnout is thought to be caused by a variety of both personal (e.g., personal dedication and commitment) and situational factors (e.g., role conflict), and manifests itself via physical (e.g., headaches, sleeplessness) and behavioral signs (e.g., rigid, inflexible behavior).

Due to the similarities between human service professionals traditionally studied in general burnout research, and sport and exercise professionals such as physical educators, athletic trainers, and coaches, sport psychologists have extended the concept of burnout into the athletic arena. For example, Kelley (1994) has shown that today's coaches are likely candidates for burnout because of the demands and stressors facing them, such as pressure to win, overwhelming time demands, and role ambiguity. Smith (1986) took the burnout concept further by relating it to athletes themselves. Although research into athlete burnout is a recent development, it has been a much discussed topic in the media over the last 20 years, as exemplified by accounts of highly visible athletes (e.g., Tracy Austin, Bjorn Borg, Michael Jordan) who have dropped out of their sport at the peak of their careers.

Athlete burnout from sport is defined as a psychological, emotional, and physical withdrawal from a formerly pursued and enjoyable sport due to excessive chronic stress (Smith, 1986). Situational, cognitive, physiological, and behavioral components of chronic stress can all contribute to athlete burnout. Athlete burnout is the manifestation or consequence of the situational, cognitive, physiological, and behavioral components of excessive stress. Hence, athlete burnout is not viewed solely as a component of one's personality. Instead, it is viewed as the results of a reciprocal interaction of personal and situational factors.

It is important to note that not everyone who discontinues participation in sport does so due to burnout. In fact, the extensive research on children's participation motivation for sports involvement has shown that children who discontinue participation do so because of a change of interests, conflicting interests, lack of fun, and/or low perceptions of competence (see Weiss and Chaumeton, 1992, for an extensive review). An athlete's perception of excessive stress has also been theorized to be a driving factor in discontinued participation due to burnout. Athletes, then, discontinue sport participation for any number of reasons (e.g., sport conflicts with another activity such as music, one would rather play another sport at which he or she is more successful), but those who burnout discontinue because of excessive long-term stress (Gould, 1993). Thus, not everyone who discontinues or drops out of sport burns out; only those who discontinue as a result have prolonged stress burnout of sport.

Are Young Athletes Placed Under Too Much Stress?

A fundamental question at issue surrounding youth sport regards the desirability of levels of state anxiety experienced by young athletes as a consequence of competition. Critics of youth sport have suggested that competitive stress generates excessive levels of state anxiety that can negatively affect the mental health of the young athlete (Martens, 1978). Conversely, youth sport proponents have argued that the very beauty of youth sport is that young athletes do experience stress but not at excessive levels and in a 'safe' environment that allows children to learn how to successfully cope with stress.

Sport psychology researchers have studied this issue focusing on two questions. First, what levels of state anxiety do young athletes experience in competitive sports participation? Second, do young athletes experience higher levels of trait anxiety than their nonsport counterparts?

Levels Of State Anxiety Experienced by Young Athletes

The levels of state anxiety experienced by young athletes have been examined at length to address the question of whether or not competitive stress is excessive in youth sport. Studies examining levels of state anxiety can be classified into three major types: (1) psychophysiological assessments of state anxiety experienced before, during, and immediately after athletic competitions; (2) assessments using nonvalidated surveys of state anxiety and anxiety-related symptoms associated with athletic competition; and (3) assessments of state anxiety occurring before, during and immediately after athletic competition using validated self-report state anxiety inventories.

Psychophysiological Assessments

Several investigators (Skubic, 1955; Hanson 1967; Lowe and McGrath, 1971) have used physiological indices of stress such as heart rate or galvanic skin response to examine levels of state anxiety experienced by young athletes and peers in nonsport settings. For example, Skubic (1955) employed galvanic skin response assessments in young boys, who participated in Little League baseball games and physical education softball competitions. Few differences were found between the groups, and it was concluded that the state anxiety experienced during competitive youth baseball was not greater than that experienced in a physical education class competition.

In another youth baseball study, Lowe and McGrath (1971) examined respiration and heart rates prior to batting under conditions of varying game importance (e.g., based on league standings, won-loss records) and situation critically (e.g., score, number of outs, position of runners on base). Physiological state anxiety was positively related to game importance and increased situation criticality. Unfortunately, assessments did not extend to non-evaluative or other forms of competition.

These two investigations of psychophysiological assessments of state anxiety associated with youth sports competition illustrate typical findings in the area. Specifically, the studies suggest that overall either few differences in state anxiety exist between youth sport and other competitive environments (physical education class competitions), or that high but short-lived elevations in state anxiety occur during events. However, such results must be interpreted with some caution because Dishman (1989) has cited evidence suggesting that elevated physiological state anxiety as assessed by heart rate during youth sport competition may not result from the competitive setting per se, but from the physical activity itself. Not withstanding this caution, it is important to take note of evidence of a relationship between heightened state anxiety during events and game importance and situation criticality.

Nonvalidated Survey Assessments

Taking the survey assessment approach, a number of investigators (Skubic, 1955; Hale, 1961; McPherson et al., 1980; Purdy et al., 1981, Ralio, 1982; Gould et al., 1983a; Feltz and Albrecht, 1986; Tierney, 1988) have asked either young athletes or their parents to rate the degree of anxiety-related symptoms associated with or as a consequence of athletic competition. In most cases one or two questions pertaining to this issue were posed as part of a larger youth sport survey project and hence the findings are somewhat superficial and difficult to interpret. However, the results of the studies provide clues as to the levels of state anxiety experienced by youth sport participants.

Among findings emerging in survey investigations, Skubic (1955) found that approximately one-third of Little League baseball players interviewed reported contest-related sleeping difficulties. Among swimmers, 33% of males and 56% of females surveyed by McPherson et al. (1977) reported experiencing some emotional stress. Feltz and Albrect (1986) reported that 41% of a sample of elite young distance runners reported becoming nervous and worried in races, but one-half of these young athletes indicated that this nervousness helped their performance. Interestingly, Hale (1961) reported that 97% of the fathers of Little League baseball participants indicated that their sons were not affected by participation. Despite problems with non-validated instruments and superficiality, the results suggest that some, but clearly not the majority, of young athletes engaged in competition experience high levels of competitive state anxiety and associated symptoms.

Validated State Anxiety Instrument Assessments

A number of investigators (Scanlan and Passer 1978, 1979; Simon and Martens, 1979; Bump et al., 1985) have used validated self-report state anxiety instruments to assess levels of state anxiety experienced before, during and after competitive youth sport events. For example, Simon and Martens (1979) conducted an extensive survey of state anxiety experienced in competitive and noncompetitive sport settings. State anxiety levels of 749 boys, 9-14 years of age, were assessed in practice settings and just prior to required school activities (e.g., classroom tests and physical education class competitions), non-required nonsport competitive activities (band solos and band group competitions) and non-school sports (baseball, basketball, tackle football, gymnastics, ice hockey, swimming and wrestling) using the competitive state anxiety inventory for children (CSAIC) (Martens, 1977). Differences between practice and competitive state anxiety levels were examined as well as comparisons among the various competitive activities.

Not surprisingly, precompetitive state anxiety was elevated over practice levels although the overall change was not excessive. For example, the mean precompetitive state anxiety score for the entire sample was 16.9 (possible scores on the CSAIC range from 10 to 30). Of particular interest in the study by Simon and Martens (1979) was the comparison of state anxiety levels of boys participating in sport to boys participating in other competitive activities not typically the focus of parental concern (band solos, band group competition, etc.) Band solo participation elicited the greatest state anxiety ($\underline{M}$= 21.5) followed by individual sport participation (for wrestling $\underline{M}$= 19.5; for gymnastics $\underline{M}$ = 18.5) while physical education competition elicited the lowest levels of anxiety ($\underline{M}$= 14.5). However, there were substantial individual differences. Relatively few boys experienced what could be considered extremely high levels of competitive state anxiety (scoring in the upper quartile of possible CSAIC scores or above 25 out of 30), while the vast majority (82%) reported scores between 10 and 20, or the lower half of the scale.

Bump et al. (1985) also examined state anxiety levels of young athletes by administering the CSAIC to 13 and 14-year-old boys prior to competitive wrestling tournament matches. Among the 112 participants, similar to the findings of Simon and Martens (1979) for wrestlers, prematch state anxiety levels averaged 18.9 (out of a possible of 30). Again, relatively few of the boys reported experiencing extremely high levels of state anxiety, with only 9% scoring in the upper quartile of possible CSAIC scores (>25). These results are consistent with other studies (Scanlan and Passer, 1978, 1979) and reveal that the majority of children participating in competitive youth sports do not experience excessive levels of state anxiety as a result of their competitive experience.

Summary

Studies of levels of state anxiety and associated symptoms in young athletes demonstrates that the vast majority of children involved in competitive sport do not experience high levels of stress. Hence, it is premature and perhaps incorrect to criticize competitive youth sport programs as placing excessive stress on young athletes. Concerns about excessive stress should not prevent parents from encouraging their children to become involved in sport activities.

Not withstanding this conclusion, the evidence also shows that a small, but significant, minority of young athletes experience high levels of stress which may be manifested in such psychological and physical symptoms as insomnia and a loss of appetite. If, for example, only 5-10% of the estimated 1 million children in Australia (Robertson, 1986), 18 million children in Brazil (Ferreira, 1986), 2.5 million children in Canada (Valeriote and Hanson, 1986), 40 million children in the USA (Ewing et al., 1996; Martens, 1988), and 23 million children in the former USSR (Jefferies, 1986) involved in organized sport experience excessive stress, this alone would involve about 4.2-8.4 million youngsters. Efforts are needed to identify young athletes who are susceptible to heightened state anxiety, and the specific sport situations related to heightened anxiety states in young athletes.

Levels of Trait Anxiety in Young Athletes

Although the research on state anxiety experienced by young athletes shows that most children do not experience excessive levels of state anxiety, the question still remains as to how competitive sport participation influences a child's trait anxiety. It is important that trait anxiety be examined, because it is a component of child's personality. Hence, if competitive sport influences a child's trait anxiety negatively, the change may become more enduring and stable.

Unfortunately, few studies have examined the trait anxiety of youth sport participants and nonparticipants. In one of the few studies conducted with children, Magill and Ash (1979) found no competitive trait anxiety differences between fourth-grade youth sport participants and nonparticipants. Nonparticipant fifth graders, however, were higher in trait anxiety than 28 elite youth distance runners, 10 to 15 years of age, and the runners had competitive trait anxiety levels that were slightly higher than norms for comparable age and gender groups. Finally, a one-year longitudinal study by Raviv (1981) in Israel revealed that 37 children from sports clubs and 37 matched control nonparticipants did not significantly differ in competitive trait anxiety.

The equivocal and limited nature of the trait anxiety-sport participation research prevents definitive conclusions regarding effects of competitive youth sport participation on trait anxiety. However, the presently available research suggests that at most participants have only slightly elevated levels of trait anxiety compared to nonparticipants, and in one-half of the studies no differences were evident. More longitudinal data are needed before more definitive conclusions can be derived. Further, potential moderator variables (e.g., extent of involvement, success level) that may influence the relationship between participation status and competitive trait anxiety must be assessed.

What Types Of Children In What Situations Experience High Levels of Stress?

Since most young athletes do not experience excessive stress or competitive state anxiety while participating in sport, but a significant minority do, researchers (Scanlan and Passer, 1978; 1979; Gould et al., 1983; Scanlan and Lethwaite, 1984) turned their attention to identifying what types of children (in terms of personal characteristics) in what particular athletic situations experience the most competitive state anxiety. Still other investigators (e.g., Passer, 1983; Brustad and Weiss, 1987; Brustad, 1988; Newton and Duda, 1992) have examined factors associated with heightened trait anxiety in young athletes.

The typical study in this area consists of taking state anxiety assessments in young athletes immediately prior to and following competition and administering trait anxiety, personality and/or demographic measures in a noncompetitive setting such as a practice. Personal factor assessments (e.g., self-esteem, trait anxiety), demographic (e.g., years of sport participation experience, gender), and situational (e.g., event importance, game criticality) factors are then correlated with the pre- and post-game state anxiety or trait anxiety scores.

Personal and Situational Predictors of Competitive State Anxiety: Personal Predictors

Scanlan (1986) has summarized the research in this area and identified a number of personal and situational factors associated with competitive state anxiety in young athletes. Specifically, the following characteristics appear to predict state anxiety in young athletes: trait anxiety; self-esteem; performance expectations relative to one's team; self-performance expectations; worries about failure; worries about adult expectations and social evaluation by others; perceived fun; satisfaction with performance (regardless of winning or losing); perceiving participation to be important for parents; and goal orientations. Each of these predictors needs closer examination.

Trait anxiety (a personality characteristic that predisposes children to perceive evaluative settings, such as athletic competition, as threatening or nonthreating) has consistently been shown to be a strong predictor of competitive state anxiety. Young athletes with high levels of competitive trait anxiety more often perceive sport competition as "psychologically threatening," and because of this, respond with more state anxiety than their low trait anxious counterparts. Similarly, self-esteem has also been associated with state anxiety reactions; in children with lower self-esteem experience higher levels of state anxiety in youth sports. Their higher self-esteem peers, however, find the youth sport competitive experience to be less state anxiety producing.

Young athletes' expectations have also been shown to predict levels of state anxiety experienced. Children with low "team" performance expectations, as well as those with low "personal or self" performance expectations experience more competitive state anxiety.

As expected, children who experience more state anxiety in competitive youth sports also worry more than children who do not experience as much state anxiety. In particular, frequent worries about failure, adult expectations, and social evaluation by others differentiated young athletes who experienced more state anxiety from less state anxious teammates. It also is no surprise to parents and youth sport leaders that children in youth sport who win experience less state anxiety than children who lose.

Especially thought provoking is the finding that satisfaction with performance predicts state anxiety, with higher levels of child satisfaction associated with lower state anxiety. This finding has occurred after co-varying out winning or losing a particular contest.

Children who perceive that it is important to their parents that they participate in sport experience more state anxiety than children who do not perceive such parental pressure. Similarly, young athletes who have an outcome (focus on judging the ability based on comparing their performance to others) versus task or mastery goal orientation (focus on judging their ability based on comparing their performance to their own previous performances) experience more state anxiety, especially if they have low perceptions of their ability.

Finally, Hall and colleagues (Hall and Kerr, 1997; Hall et al., 1998) have recently shown that young athletes who were high in perfectionism and who were characterized by certain motivational goal orientations experienced more state anxiety in competitive sport. Scoring high on the perfectionism subscales of concern over mistakes, doubts about one's actions, and personal standards were consistently related to anxiety in high school runners (Hall et al., 1998). Relative to goal orientations,

adopting an ego goal orientation (where a young athlete judges his or her ability based on comparing performance against others) was related to increased anxiety in youth runners and fencers, whereas adopting a task orientation (where an athlete judges his or her ability based on improvements in his or her own performance) was negatively related to anxiety in these children (Hall and Kerr, 1997; Hall et al., 1998). These goal orientation findings were especially salient in children who had low perceptions of ability.

Situational Predictors

In addition to personal characteristics of children which are predictors of competitive state anxiety in sport, there are several situational factors that are associated with increased state anxiety in young athletes. These include victory versus defeat, the importance placed on a particular athletic event, and sport type. Young athletes who win in competition experience less state anxiety than those young athletes who lose (Scanlan and Passer, 1979). As noted earlier, Lowe and McGrath (1971) in a study of youth baseball players found that the greater the importance placed on a particular game or situation within a game (getting a hit with bases loaded), the greater the anxiety experienced. Finally, in a classic study comparing levels of state anxiety experienced in youth sport versus other socially evaluative activities such as band and school tests, Simon and Martens (1979) found that individual sport participants (e.g., gymnastics and wrestling) experienced more state anxiety than team sport participants (e.g., basketball, ice hockey).

There are unique personal characteristics of young athletes who experience heightened state anxiety in the competitive youth sport setting. Situational factors of victory versus defeat, event importance, and sport type also influence the amount of stress experienced by young athletes.

Predictors of Trait Anxiety

In addition to examining factors associated with state anxiety in young athletes, several researchers

(Brustad, 1988; Brustad and Weiss, 1987; Newton and Duda, 1992) have begun to identify factors that predict trait anxiety in children. This research is important because, as previously shown, the personality variable of trait anxiety is one of the most consistent predictors of state anxiety that a child experiences in sport. Moreover, it helps to answer the question of how sport participation may influence personality development of children.

An example of these studies is one conducted by Brustad (1988). Participants included 207 male and female youth basketball players. Trait anxiety was assessed, as well as a variety of additional psychological measures such as self-esteem and performance-related concerns. High competitive trait anxious players had lower self-esteem and demonstrated more frequent worries about performance and being evaluated than those lower in trait anxiety. The results suggest that the high-trait anxious child athlete perceives negative social evaluation, especially failure, as emotionally aversive. Adult leaders are faced then with finding ways to reduce the degree to which these children feel openly evaluated.

Most interesting in regard to the above is the recent work of Smith et al. (1995) who, as part of their research on coaching relationships, studied the effects of positive coaching on the development of trait anxiety in young athletes. In this field experiment, youth baseball coaches were assigned to an intervention group and were taught to use a positive coaching style (emphasizing the use of positive reinforcement and instruction while downplaying punishment and criticism), while an equivalent group of coaches served as controls, coaching baseball as they normally did. When preseason versus post-season trait anxiety scores for the players were compared, there was a significant decrease in trait anxiety in players who played for group coaches with a positive style. No changes occurred for children who played for the control coaches. Thus, positive coaching is associated with a decrease in trait anxiety.

The Interaction of Personal and Situational Predictors of State and Trait Anxiety

Lastly, it is important to note that when considering the stress process, neither the particular objective competitive situation that a young athlete encounters (e.g., participating in a championship game, playing in front of one's parents) nor the personal or environmental resources available (e.g., the child's sport skill level and social support network) are as important as the interaction between these two sets of factors (Smith and Smoll, 1982). Whenever demands are encountered in the competitive environment, resources are mobilized to meet these demands, and stress is experienced as a consequence of the relative balance or imbalance between demands and resources. Further, the relative balance between demands and resources determines whether the stress is positive, negative, or neutral.

Stress will likely be insignificant, or unlikely to be perceived at all, when there is little imbalance between resources available and the demands of the situation (e.g., two evenly matched wrestlers in a practice match). A young athlete will probably view a situation as challenging if demands slightly exceed resources (e.g., a highly skilled swimmer participating in the city finals). However, a situation featuring a substantial imbalance between demands and resources will likely be regarded as stressful. In the case of a substantial imbalance favoring demands (e.g., a back-up hockey goalkeeper facing league-leading scorers in a championship game), stress will likely have the effective consequences of high levels of nervousness or anxiety states. By contrast, stress in the form of boredom and stagnation is a likely consequence of a substantial imbalance favoring resources (e.g., an internationally ranked tennis player confined to local high school competition).

Although stress may result from excessive external demands (e.g., opponent superiority), Smith and Smoll (1982) emphasize that situational demands may also emanate from within the individual. Personal or motivational factors such as desired goals, personal performance standard, or even unconscious motives or conflicts contribute to the perception of the competitive situation and influence the environmental demands. For example, a young athlete obsessed with perfectionism may experience a great deal of stress, without any reference to an opponent, purely as a consequence of his or her expectations of self. Additionally, memories of past performance as well as anticipation of future consequences may interact with the current situation to influence the young athlete's perception of the setting.

Are Young Athletes Overtraining and Burning Out Of Sport

As children's sports have become more adult organized and professionalized, concern has grown over whether children are burning out of sport or discontinuing involvement because of the emotional costs and pressures involved. Critics contend that young athletes train too many hours, participate in too many competitions, focus too much attention on one sport, and must constantly deal with pressure from parents and coaches to win. One would think, then, that with all this controversy, burnout and overtraining would be much studied topics in youth sports. While sport sociologists and psychologists have developed four different theories to help explain why children burnout out of sport, empirical studies on the topic are sparse. At the time of this review, only four empirical studies were identified. Similarly, while the related topic of physical overtraining has been much studied in elite adult athletes (Raglin, 1993), not a single study has been conducted on young athletes.

Although the literature on burnout in youth sports is sparse, the available data has shed important light on the topic. Similarly, adult studies on overtraining permit inferences to young athletes. The four current theoretical models of burnout are initially discussed, followed by a summary of burnout research on young athletes and overtraining in elite adult athletes.

Burnout Models

Over the last decade, four theoretical models of burnout have been developed. These include: Smith's (1986) cognitive-affective stress model, Silva's (1990) negative training stress model, Coakley's (1992) unidimensional identity and control model, and Schmidt and Stein's (1991) and Raedeke's (1997) sport commitment perspective. Each of these models is reviewed.

Smith's (1986) Cognitive-Affective Stress Model

Based on his general cognitive-affective stress model (Smith, 1986) and burnout research in the helping professions (e.g., Freudenberger, 1980), Smith (1986) has proposed a stress-based interpretation of burnout in sport. According to this model, which is similar to the McGrath (1970) model discussed earlier, burnout is hypothesized to occur via a four-stage process. First, a demand is placed on the athlete (e.g., excessive expectations, high volumes of physical practice and training, pressure to win by significant others). Second, that demand is not perceived equally by all participants; some athletes will cognitively appraise it as more threatening or overwhelming than others. Third, if the demand is appraised as threatening, a physiological response occurs (e.g., anxiety, fatigue). Finally, the physiological response leads to some type of coping and task behavior such as decreased performance, interpersonal difficulties, or withdrawal from the activity.

Smith's model also proposes that all four stages of the burnout process are influenced by personality and motivational factors such as self-esteem and trait anxiety. Additionally, Smith (1986) considers the model circular and continuous, where the coping and task behavior stage feeds back to the situational demand and resources stage. Reciprocal relationships also exist between all four stages of the model.

As previously indicated, although some individuals discontinue sport participation because of burnout, burnout is not the primary cause of sport withdrawal for most individuals (Smith, 1986). Rather, based on Thibaut and Kelly's (1959) social exchange theory and current youth sports research, Smith (1986) hypothesized that individuals withdraw from sport when costs are perceived to outweigh benefits relative to alternative activities. For most children this means that they discontinue because of changing interests, conflicting time demands between activities, low perceived competence, and a lack of fun (Gould and Petlichkoff, 1987; Weiss and Chaumenton, 1992). Thus, burnout only occurs when costs outweigh rewards and when the costs are stress-induced.

Despite its intuitive appeal and identified relationships among variables, Smith's model has failed to generate much burnout research on athletes. It does, however, provide a useful framework for conceptualizing and understanding the topic.

Silva's (1990) Negative Training Stress Response Model

Silva's (1990) model to explain burnout focuses more attention on responses to physical training in addition to recognizing the importance of psychological factors. In particular, Silva suggested that training physically and psychologically stresses the athlete and can have both positive and negative effects. Positive adaptation is a desirable outcome and the main purpose of training (e.g., in weight training the body is purposely overloaded, and adapts, becoming stronger). However, too much training may result in negative adaptation, which is hypothesized to lead to negative responses, moving on a continuum from staleness ("an initial failure of the body's adaptive mechanisms to cope with psychophysiological stress" Silva, 1990, p. 10), to overtraining ("detectable psychophysiological malfunctions characterized by easily observed changes in the athletes mental orientation and physical performance," Silva, 1990, p. 10), and finally to burnout ("an exhaustive psychophysiological response exhibited as a result of frequent, sometimes extreme, but generally

ineffective efforts to meet excessive training and sometimes competitive demands," Silva, 1990, p.11). Thus, burnout primarily occurs when the physical training process becomes too demanding. It is also important to note that like individual perceptual differences, each individual responds differently to different training loads. Thus, what might be optimal for one athlete may be an overload that causes a negative training response for another.

Coakley's (1992) Unidimensional Identity Development and External Control Model

The Smith (1986) and Silva (1990) burnout models place a primary focus on stress; however, Coakley (1992) has developed an alternative view. Agreeing that stress is definitely involved in burnout, Coakley argued, however, that stress is not the cause of burnout, but is only a symptom. According to Coakley (1992), the cause of burnout in young athletes is tied to the social organization of high performance sport and its effects on identity and control issues in young athletes.

In terms of the identity of the young athlete, Coakley proposed that burnout occurs because the structure of high performance sport (e.g., time demands) does not allow the young athlete to develop a normal multifaceted identity (e.g., no time to spend with peers or in other nonsport activities). Instead, identity foreclosure occurs in which the young athletes' identity is solely focused on sport success. Consequently, in many cases (e.g., when injury or performance failure occurs), this sole identity focus on being an athlete causes stress that can ultimately lead to burnout.

Coakley (1992) also contends that in high performance sport the social worlds of young athletes are organized in such a way that their control and decision making is inhibited. In particular, young athletes' social environments "are organized in ways that leave them powerless to control events and make decisions about the nature of their experiences and the direction of their own development" (Coakley, 1992, p. 282). This lack of control and power also leads to stress and ultimately burnout.

The Coakley model was developed as an alternative to the stress-based models of burnout and is important for the emphasis it places on the social environment of the young athlete. Based on this model specific recommendations for preventing burnout include changing the social structure of high performance sport for children, changing the manner in which the sport experience is integrated in children's lives, and structuring the relationships between significant others and child athletes in differing ways.

The Coakely model has yet to be empirically tested. It was formulated from interviews with 15 young athletes who had discontinued their sport involvement. Unfortunately the quotes given by these young athletes to support his contentions throughout the paper, are not presented in a systematic and detailed enough fashion to judge the work's scientific merit.

Schmidt and Stein's (1991) and Raedeke's (1997) Sport Commitment Perspective

Like Coakley's (1992) unidimensional identity development and external control model, the sport commitment model of burnout recognizes that stress is involved in the burnout process, but contends that other variables need to be examined if we are to better understand when and why burnout occurs. Raedeke (1997, p. 398), for example, contends that "everyone can experience stress, but not everyone who experiences stress burns out." Hence, sport commitment perspective theorists suggest that young athletes burnout out of sport because their reasons for being involved differ from athletes who do not burnout. Those children who burnout do so because they are committed to sport for solely entrapment-related reasons, i.e., young athletes burnout out when they feel that they "have to" maintain their involvement versus "want to" maintain their involvement.

Raedeke (1997) indicates that children become entrapped in sport when they do not enjoy participation because of high perceived costs of involvement and low rewards (e.g., must practice many hours and have few friends involved). However, they maintain their involvement because they feel they have too much invested in sport to discontinue, e.g., have committed much time and effort to their training or that their parents have invested much time, effort and financial resources in their training. They also see a lack of alternative activities available to invest their efforts.

Only one study (Raedeke, 1997) has been conducted to test the sport commitment model of burnout. Results of this initial investigation were encouraging in that young swimmers who exhibited psychological characteristics reflecting entrapment experienced higher levels of burnout than swimmers who were not characterized by entrapment characteristics. However, little support was found for the prediction that young athletes who evidenced higher levels of burnout would have few alternative activities that they judged as attractive. It was concluded that a sport commitment perspective can contribute to the burnout knowledge base by going beyond the notion that burnout is a simple consequence of chronic stress. Additional research is needed to verify and test the model's predictions.

Overtraining and Staleness Research

Given the scarcity of athlete burnout research, it is helpful to examine sport psychology research in a related area – studies conducted on overtraining and staleness. Morgan et al. (1987), for example, conducted an impressive 10-year longitudinal study of overtraining, staleness, and mood states (as measured by the McNair et al.[1971] Profile of Mood States-POMS) in competitive adult swimmers. The results showed that as training loads (meters swum) increased, so did mood-state disturbances; and when training loads decreased, mood states returned to normal or baseline levels. These findings fit well with previous research in which Morgan and Pollock (1977) found that more (versus less) successful elite athletes exhibit a positive mood profile on the POMS (higher than average score on vigor and lower than average score on tension, depression, anger, fatigue, and confusion), which they labeled the "iceberg" profile. Less successful athletes, however, did not exhibit the positive iceberg mood pattern. Based on these findings, it is suggested that when athletes become overtrained and stale they shift from the positive iceberg profile to more negative mood patterns and perform poorly. Monitoring of mood states may thus be a means to prevent overtraining and staleness precursors to burnout.

In a follow-up to the previous series, Morgan et al. (1988) did psychological assessments of 12 male collegiate swimmers before, during, and after 10 days of increased training volume. Significant increases in depression, anger, fatigue, global mood disturbance, ratings of exercise intensity, and general sense of well being were associated with increased training loads. As in the previous research, it was concluded that significant changes in psychological mood and feeling states were associated with increased training.

Finally, Murphy et al. (1990) conducted an interdisciplinary investigation of elite adult judo athletes in which training volume was systematically controlled over a 10-week period. Unlike Morgan et al. (1987, 1988), a lack of overall mood disturbance was associated with increased training. However, POMS anger scores were higher at the end of 10 weeks of training. Additionally, significant increases on somatic anxiety, confidence, and effort were associated with increased training. Markers of psychological and physiological overtraining were also related to performance.

Although not directly examining burnout and not involving young athletes, these studies show that significant changes in psychological states are associated with increases and decreases in training volume in the form of overtraining and staleness. This fits well with Silva's (1990) notion that excessive training leads to staleness and overtraining, which cause both negative physical and psychological states and can inhibit athlete performance. It also suggests that monitoring

psychological markers may be of some value in preventing overtraining, staleness, and in turn, burnout.

These findings need to be interpreted carefully. The POMS research conducted by Morgan and his colleagues has recently come under criticism because it has confounded the identification of personality factors discriminating athletes from nonathletes with those differentiating athletes of different levels of ability (Renger, 1993). In addition, results of a meta-analysis conducted by Rowley et al. (1995) suggest that the POMS-performance relationship, though significant, accounts for less than 1% of performance variance. Finally, none of the overtraining research has been conducted with children; hence, it can only be postulated that young athletes have similar overtraining psychological reactions as their adults, which is a major assumption since developmental research has repeatedly demonstrated that children are unique and not just miniature adults.

Athlete Burnout Research

The first youth sport study on athlete burnout (Cohn, 1990) reported the results of interviews with 10 active high school golfers. Cohn (1990, p. 98) defined burnout as "a negative reaction to physical or psychological stress leading to withdrawal form activity" and asked these adolescent golfers (M age = 16.4 years) if they had ever burned out on golf. All 10 youth golfers said they had burned out of golf at some time during their careers, which resulted in 5 to 14 days (M = 10 days) of discontinued participation. Golfers identified factors including too much practice or playing, lack of enjoyment, no new goals to strive for, going into a slump, and pressure from self and others as causes of their burnout. The initial results were interesting and showed that the young athletes experienced some degree of burnout; however, it was unfortunate that distinctions were not made between overtraining, staleness, and burnout because the active golfers interviewed discontinued play for relatively short periods of time. They may not have experienced true burnout, but only initial stages of overtraining and staleness. The investigation was also characterized by a small sample, and the selection criteria for inclusion of golfers in the study were not clearly specified.

In a second youth sport study on burnout, Coakley (1992) reported preliminary findings to support his model of burnout. Results from informal interviews with 15 youth (6 girls, 9 boys) between the ages of 15 and 18 years old who had burned out of predominantly individual sports were reported. Pressure and stress were mentioned by the participants as primary reasons for discontinuing participation. However, Coakley indicated that this pressure was typically tied to a lack of control over their lives (e.g., they wanted to do things with friends, but instead had to practice or participate in competitions). The results also showed that sport participation was closely tied to the young athletes' self-definition, supporting Coakley's notion of unidimensional development of self-identity being related to burnout. Unfortunately, these results must be viewed cautiously because the children were not sampled in any orderly way ("a sample of convenience"), and results were not reported in enough detail to judge their scientific merit. They, however, offer an interesting perspective on burnout.

Recently, Gould and colleagues (Gould et al., 1996a, 1996b, 1997) conducted a three part investigation of burnout in junior tennis. The first phase of the study involved a retrospective survey that was administered to a national sample of 30 male and female junior tennis players identified by US Tennis Association as having burned out and 32 comparison players. All players completed a battery of psychological tests. A series of discriminant function and univariate t-tests were conducted to compare the two groups. Compared to the comparison players, the burned out players had significantly higher burnout scores, had less input into their tennis training and tennis-related decisions, were more likely to play up in an older age division, practiced fewer days (lessened their involvement), were higher in amotivation, were lower in external motivation, reported being more withdrawn, differed in perfectionism (especially relative to concern over mistakes, personal standards, parental criticism, parental expectations, and higher need for organization), were less likely to use planning coping strategies, and were lower on positive interpretation and growth coping. The burned out players did not differ from the comparison players relative to the number of hours trained. Both groups trained, on average, 2.3 hours per day. Hence, the results suggest that in this group of young athletes burnout was more psychologically than physically driven. It was also concluded that in addition to a variety of personal and situational factors, perfectionism played a particularly important role in predicting burnout in junior tennis.

The second part of the investigation (Gould et al., 1996b) involved extensive interviews with the 10 most burned out players identified in the quantitative part of the project. The interviews focused on signs and symptoms of burnout, how players dealt with their burned out feelings, factors perceived to lead to burnout, suggestions for preventing burnout, involvement of significant others in tennis, and advice to others. Content analysis of the 10 interviews revealed two major categories of burned out feelings; "physical" symptoms which included injuries, illness, and/or being physically asymptomatic; and "mental" symptoms which consisted of staying motivated, lacking energy/motivation, negative feelings, feelings of isolation, concentration problems, and high and low moods. Reasons for burning out included physical concerns such as being sick and not being satisfied with performance, logistical concerns like time demands and too much travel, social interpersonal concerns such as dissatisfaction with social life and negative parental influence, and the largest category, psychological concerns which included such things as unfulfilled and unrealistic expectations and pressure. Recommendations for preventing and dealing with burnout for other players included playing for one's own reasons, balancing tennis with other activities such as school clubs or socializing with friends, stopping participation if playing tennis is no fun, focusing on making tennis fun, doing things to relax, and taking time off. The players recommended that parents recognize that some parent push is needed, but it must be an optimal amount as too much contributes to burnout. Additionally, players suggested that parents reduce importance on event and game outcome, have parent-coach role clarification, and solicit input from their junior player. The results were examined in light of the burnout models of Silva (1990), Coakley (1992), and Smith (1986), with all three receiving some support. However, Smith's (1986) cognitive-affective stress model seemed to be most consistent with the data.

In the third part of the study of young tennis players (Gould et al., 1997), individual differences in burnout were highlighted by discussing idiographic profiles of three players who represented different forms of burnout. The cases included: (1) a player characterized by high levels of perfectionism and overtraining who burned out because of her personality orientation; (2) a player who experienced pressure from others and felt a strong need for a social life outside of tennis and burned out due to social psychological factors; and (3) a player who was physically overtrained, failed to get enough sleep, and burned out due to physical factors. Based on these three cases and the earlier phases of the study, it was concluded that burnout might best be viewed within a stress-related strain model (Figure 1), with a "physically-driven" strain resulting from physical overtraining and a "psychologically-driven" strain comprised of two additional substrains. One of the psychological substrains results from a young athlete having an "at risk" perfectionistic personality—a personality that predisposes them to burnout, even in non-pressure situations. The second psychological substrain focuses on burnout results from a situational stress, such as coach or parent pressure to participate and perform. These substrains are not totally independent.

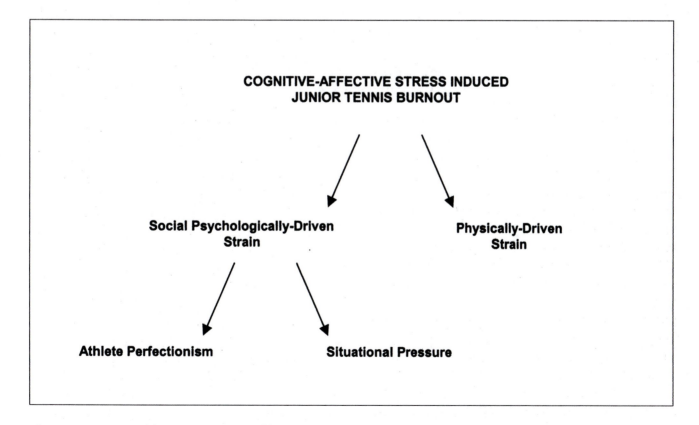

Figure 1. Burnout and burnout strains in athletes. (Adapted from Gould et al., 1996b)

In the most recent study of burnout in young athletes, Raedeke (1997) tested the sport commitment model predictions in a study of 236 age-group swimmers. The investigation was designed to examine whether athletes with motivation profiles representing sport entrapment, sport attraction, and low commitment experience varying levels of burnout. The swimmers with a mean age of 15.5 years and a training load of 40,000 meters a week, completed a 21-item athletic burnout scale, as well as assessments of the benefits and costs of swimming, swimming enjoyment, personal investment in swimming, alternative activity attraction, social constraints, swim identity, and perceived control. Cluster analysis was used to partition the swimmers into profile groups (e.g., enthusiastic, indifferent) based on their psychological characteristics. Swimmers who were characterized by an entrapment profile (e.g., swam because they had to) exhibited significantly higher burnout scores than swimmers who were characterized by an attraction profile (e.g., swam because they wanted to). Moreover, these swimmers were found to be entrapped because of their low perceived control (e.g., not having a say in what they do in swimming) and high social constraints (e.g., social norms and expectations that cause feelings of obligation to swim such as parental pressure). Other entrapment sources, such as the attractiveness of alternative activities, received only scant support. The results are consistent with many of the sport commitment model predictions.

The Incidence of Burnout in Young Athletes

One of the most frequent questions for practitioners is the frequency of burnout. Unfortunately, there is at present no way to estimate its prevalence. However, Raedeke's (1997) youth swimming data can be used to arrive at a preliminary estimate for young swimmers. A burnout inventory assessing burnout, emotional and physical exhaustion, devaluation of involvement and reduced accomplishment was administered to 145 male and 84 female competitive youth swimmers. The number of young swimmers who Raedeke (1997) found scored two standard deviations above the mean on the various measures, as well as all swimmers who indicated an absolute score of 4 or higher on each five-point Likert scale are summarized in Table 1. Between 1 and 5% of the swimmers reported very high levels of burnout. Hence, approximately 3% of young competitive swimmers experience high levels of burnout.

Burnout Assessment	Mean (SD)	# (%) > 2 SD	# (%) of Athletes Exhibiting a Score ≥ 4
Emotional/ Physical Exhaustion	2.47 (.83)	8 (3.3%)	13 (5.5%)
Devaluation	2.02 (.84)	13 (5.5%)	8 (3.4%)
Reduced Accomplishment	2.32 (.74)	5 (2.1%)	3 (1.3%)
Total Burnout	2.27 (.66)	12 (5.1%)	3 (1.2%)

Table 1. The Incidence of burnout In age-group swimmers (based on data from Raedeke, 1997).

In summary, initial burnout research on young athletes, though limited, reveals that some children do indeed experience burnout in sport. An initial estimate places the number of youth experiencing burnout in swimming around 3%. Those suffering from burnout also experience decreased personal motivation, poor concentration, deteriorated performance and feelings of entrapment. Causes of burnout vary, but typically involve a combination of personal (e.g., perfectionism) and situational (e.g., parental expectations, physical overtraining) factors. It also appears that burnout may at times be more psychologically driven and at other times more physically driven. Hence, it is inappropriate to associate burnout with only physical overtraining. Finally, all four existing sport-specific models of burnout models appear to have some merit and should be further explored.

What Types of Young Athletes in What Situations Burnout of Sport?

Having a general idea of the incidence of burnout, the next logical question focuses on identifying personal and situational factors related to burnout in young athletes. Because of the scarcity of original burnout research on young athletes, few studies have addressed this issue. Because stress is central to burnout process, all of the previously discussed personal and situational factors making children susceptible to heightened stress in sport, such as high trait anxiety, low self-esteem, and importance placed on performance, are relevant. Yet, burnout results from chronic or long-term stress, so that it is the accumulation of stress over time and not a single stressful episode that is important in predicting burnout.

In a different regard, youth who burnout of swimming exhibit a specific entrapment motivational pattern (Raedeke, 1997). These young athletes perceived little control over their swimming destinies and high social constraints or pressures from others to participate.

Finally, based on a review of anecdotal reports and applied writings, Weinberg and Gould (1999) have summarized a range of factors that have been proposed as causes of burnout. These are organized with Smith's (1988) cognitive-affective stress management model and are presented in Table 2. A number of personal and situational factors are likely to interact to cause burnout in young athletes.

Practical Implications and Future Directions

This review has summarized current research on overtraining, stress, and burnout in young athletes. Although the literature is far from complete in the area, enough investigations have been conducted that a number of practical implications and directions for future research can be identified.

Practical Implications

- Competitive stress and burnout effects result from a complex interplay of situational factors and personal characteristics of the young athlete. Hence, adult leaders must consider both types of factors and their unique interactions and not attribute stress to the child or the environment alone.

- Youth should not be discouraged from taking part in competitive sport because of excessive stress and burnout concerns. Findings in this area are very clear—the vast majority of youth sport participants do not experience high levels of state or trait anxiety in sport, and best estimates show that burnout afflicts only a very small number of young athletes.

- Even though the absolute numbers of young athletes who experience excessive stress and burnout of sport are small, a significant minority of children suffer from high levels of competitive stress and burnout. It is essential that efforts be made to identify these children who are "at-risk" for stress and burnout.

- Coaches and parents must learn to identify the profile of young athletes who are likely to suffer from high levels of stress and burnout in sport. Familiarity with the personal and situational predictors of stress and anxiety is essential.

Situational Demands	Cognitive Appraisal of the Situation	Physiological/Psychological Responses	Behavioral Responses	Personality and Motivational Factors
High conflicting demands	Perceived overload	Decreased motivation	Physical withdrawal	High trait anxiety
Lack of control/powerlessness; dependency	Few meaningful	Fatigue	Emotional withdrawal	Low self-esteem and low perceived competence
High expectations by self and others	Lack of meaning and devaluation of activity	Decreased concentration	Psychological withdrawal	Competitive orientation: fear of failure, fear of poor evaluation
Low social support	Lack of enjoyment	Weight gain or loss	Decreased performance	Unidimensional self-concept
Excessive demands on time	Chronic stress	Illness or injury susceptibility	Giving up during play, tanking	High need to please others
Limited social relationships	Learned helplessness	Moodiness and impatience	Rigid, inappropriate behavior	Low assertiveness
Parental involvement: inconsistent feedback, negative feedback.	Decreased life satisfaction	Poor sleep	Interpersonal difficulties	Self-critical
Coach involvement: feedback, negative feedback	Identity crisis	Anger; irritability	Lowered school performance	Perfectionism
Injuries	Stifled; trapped	Muscle soreness		Low perceived control
Training loads, repetitive, volume, number of competitions.		Boredom		Low frustration

Table 2. Factors related to athlete burnout (adapted from Gould et al., 1996a).

- Young athletes should be taught stress management strategies to help them learn to manage stress, as well as avoid and/or alleviate burnout. Additionally, educating coaches regarding methods of teaching stress management strategies can help decrease young athletes' inappropriate social evaluation and the resulting stress.

Future Research Directions

- Studies examining stress and burnout in young athletes involved in intensive competitions are needed. Interestingly, much of the debate regarding the desirability of athletic competition for children revolves around "intensive" participation (e.g., women's professional tennis, Olympic figure skating and gymnastics, traveling ice hockey where children play more games than adult professional teams). Yet, to date, participants in these programs have not been studied to any degree. Specific issues which might be examined include optimal and non-optimal levels of parental "push" relative to stress and burnout effects, comparing local versus traveling and seasonal versus year-round sport-specific programs for the stress and burnout levels they might produce, and examination of the interaction of athlete age and program intensity on stress and burnout.

- The long-term effects of competitive stress on all levels of youth sport participants are needed, especially studies using prospective longitudinal designs. In addition, to examining potential negative effects of chronic stress, researchers should also begin to examine positive consequences such as the notion that experiencing small dosages of manageable stress "vaccinates" the young athlete from later full-blown stress.

- Although preliminary evidence was presented as to the number of children who burnout of sport, more complete data are needed. Tracking large groups of young athletes across time may be the best approach in this regard.

- Intervention studies designed to prevent and alleviate stress and burnout in young athletes are needed. The Smith et al. (1995) investigation provides an excellent model in this regard.

- Further evaluation of all existing models of burnout are needed to determine when and in what situations they explain the behavior of young athletes. Moreover, additional sport commitment model studies into potential explanations for the burnout phenomena would be useful.

- Gould et al. (1997) have proposed that all burnout is stress-related and can be classified into several strains and substrains. Further studies of this notion are needed, especially investigations that examine young athletes taking part in intensive physical training (e.g., overtraining). Moreover, further looking at the role that perfectionism plays in burnout and competitive stress responses is warranted.

Summary-Conclusions

This review has shown that three decades of sport psychological research has greatly enhanced our understanding of stress and burnout in young athletes. This research, however, will do little good unless it is disseminated to those working in youth sports programs. Researchers have an obligation to facilitate such dissemination efforts. Moreover, efforts must be made to further our understanding of stress and burnout in young athletes, especially relative to evaluating intervention efforts designed to help children better deal with stress and avoid burnout.

Acknowledgement

We would like to thank Tomas Raedeke for making his youth swimming data available so that an estimate of the frequency of burnout could be made in this review.

Appreciation is also extended to Christy Greenleaf for her helpful comments on the manuscript.

REFERENCES

Brustad, R.J. (1988). Affective outcomes in competitive youth sports: The influence of intrapersonal and socialization factors. *Journal of Sport and Exercise Psychology* 10: 307-321.

Brustad, R.J. & Weiss, M.R. (1987). Competence perceptions and sources of worry in high, medium, and low competitive trait anxious young athletes. *Journal of Sport Psychology* 9: 97-105.

Bump, L.; Gould, D.; Petlichkoff, L.; Peterson, K.; & Levin, R. (1985). *The Relationship Between Achievement Orientations and State Anxiety in Youth Wrestlers.* Paper presented at the North American Society for Psychology of Sport and Physical Activity Conference, Gulfpark, MS.

Coakley, J. (1992). Burnout among adolescent athletes: A personal failure or a social problem? *Sociology of Sport Journal* 9: 271-285.

Cohn, P.J. (1990). An exploratory study of sources of stress and burnout in youth golf. *The Sport Psychologist* 4: 95-106.

Dishman, R.K. (1989). Exercise and sport psychology in youth 6 to 18 years of age. In: Gisolfi, C.V. & Lamb, D.R. (Eds.), *Perspectives in Exercise and Sports Medicine, Volume 2. Youth, Exercise, and Sport.* Indianapolis, IN: Benchmark Press (pp 47-97).

Donnelly, P. (1993). Problems associated with youth involvement in high-performance sport. In: Cahill, B.R. & Pearl, A.J. (Eds.), *Intensive Participation in Children's Sports.* Champaign, IL: Human Kinetics (pp. 95-106).

Ewing, M.E.; Seefeldt, V.D.; & Brown, T.P. (1966). *Role of Organized Sport in the Education and Health of American Children and Youth. Background Report on the Role of Sports in Youth Development.* New York: Carnegie Corporation of New York.

Feltz, D.L. & Albrecht, R.R. (1986). Psychological implications of competitive running. In: Weiss, M.R. & Gould, D. (Eds.), *Sports for Children and Youth.* Champaign, IL: Human Kinetics (pp. 225-230).

Ferreira, M.B.R. (1986). Youth sport in Brazil. In: Weiss, M.R. & Gould, D. (Eds.), *Sports for Children and Youth.* Champaign, IL: Human Kinetics (pp. 11-15).

Freudenberger, H.J. (1980). *Burnout.* NY: Doubleday.

Gould, D.; Wilson, C.G.; Tuffey, S.; & Lochbaum, M. (1983). Stress in the young athlete: The child's perspective. *Pediatric Exercise Science* 5: 286-297.

Gould, D. (1993). Intensive sport participation and prepubescent athlete: Competitive stress and burnout effects. In: Cahill, B. & Pearl, A.J. (Eds.), *Intensive Training and Participation in Youth Sports.* Champaign, IL: Human Kinetics (pp. 19-38).

Gould, D. & Petlichkoff, L. (1987). Participation motivation and attrition in young athletes. In: Smoll, F.L.; Magill, R.A.; & Ash, M. (Eds.), *Children in Sport (3rd Edition).* Champaign, IL: Human Kinetics (pp. 161-178).

Gould, D.; Tuffey, S.; Udry, E.; & Loehr, J. (1996a). Burnout in competitive junior tennis players: I. A quantitative psychological assessment. *The Sport Psychologist.* 10: 322-340.

Gould, D.; Tuffey, S.; Udry, E.; & Loehr, J. (1996b). Burnout in competitive junior tennis players: II. Qualitative analysis. *The Sport Psychologist.* 10: 341-366.

Hale, C.J. (1961). Injuries among 771,810 Little League baseball players. *Journal of Sports Medicine and Physical Fitness* 1(2): 80-83.

Hall, H.K.J.; Kerr, A.W.; & Matthews, J. (1998). Precompetitive anxiety in sport: The contribution of achievement goals and perfectionism. *Journal of Sport and Exercise Psychology* 20: 194-217.

Hall, H.K.J. & Kerr, A.W. (1997). Motivational antecedents of precompetitive anxiety in youth sports. *The Sport Psychologist* 11: 24-42.

Hanson, D.L. (1967). Cardiac response to participation in Little League baseball competition as determined by telemetry. *Research Quarterly* 38: 384-388.

Jackson, S.E.; Schwab, R.L.; & Schuler, R.S. (1986). Toward an understanding of the burnout phenomenon. *Journal of Applied Psychology* 71: 630-640.

Jefferies, S.C. (1986). Youth sport in the USSR. In: Weiss, M.R. & Gould, D. (Eds.), *Sports for Children and Youth.* Champaign, IL: Human Kinetics (pp. 21-26).

Kelley, B.C. (1994). A model of stress and burnout in collegiate coaches: Effects of gender and time of season. *Research Quarterly for Exercise and Sport* 65: 48-58.

Kreider, R.B.; Fry, A.C.; & O'Toole, M.L. (Eds.), (1998) *Overtraining in Sport*. Champaign, IL: Human Kinetics.

Lowe, R. & McGrath, J.E. (1971). *Stress, Arousal, and Performance: Some Findings Calling for A New Theory*. Report No. AF1161-67. Washington, D.C.: Air Force Office of Strategic Research.

Magill, R.A. & Ash, M.J. (1979). Academic, psychosocial, and motor characteristics of participants and nonparticipants in children's sports. *Research Quarterly* 50: 230-240.

Martens, R. (1977). *Sports Competition Anxiety Test (SCAT)*. Champaign, IL: Human Kinetics.

Martens, R. (1978). *Joy and Sadness in Children's Sports*. Champaign, IL: Human Kinetics.

Maslach, C. (1976). Burned-out. *Human Behavior* 5: 50-53,74.

McGrath, J.E. (1970). A conceptual formulation for research on stress. In: McGrath, J.E. (Ed.), *Social and Psychological Factors in Stress*. New York: Hold, Rinehart & Winston (pp. 19-49).

McNair, D.M.; Lorr, M.; & Droppleman, L.F. (1971). *Profile of Mood States Manual*. San Diego, CA: Educational and Industrial Testing Service.

McPherson, B.; Marteniuk, R.; Tihanyi, J.; & Clark, W. (1980). The social system of age group swimmers, parents and coaches. *Canadian Journal of Applied Sport Sciences* 4: 142-145.

Morgan, W.P.; Brown, D.R.; Raglin, J.S.; O'Conner, P.J.; & Ellickson, K.A. (1987). Psychological monitoring of overtraining and staleness. *British Journal of Sports Medicine* 21: 107-114.

Morgan, W.P.; Costill, D.L.; Flynn, M.G.; Raglin, J.S.; & O'Connor, P.J. (1988). Mood disturbance following increased training in swimmers. *Medicine and Science in Sports and Exercise* 20: 408-414.

Morgan, W.P. & Pollock, M. (1977). Psychological characterization of the elite distance runner. *Annals of the New York Academy of Sciences* 301: 382-403.

Murphy, S. (1999). *The Cheers and the Tears: A Healthy Alternative to the Dark Side of Youth Sports Today*. San Francisco, CA: Jossey-Bass Publications.

Murphy, S.M.; Fleck, S.J.; Dudley, G.; & Callister, R. (1990). Psychological and performance concomitants of increased volume training in elite athletes. *Journal of Applied Sport Psychology* 2: 34-50.

Newton, M.L. & Duda J.L. (1992). *The Relationship of Goal Perspectives to Multi-Dimensional Trait Anxiety in Adolescent Tennis Players*. Paper presented at the Meeting of the North American Society for the Psychology of Sport and Physical Activity, Pittsburgh, PA.

Passer, M.W. (1983). Fear of failure, fear of evaluation, perceived competence and self-esteem in competitive trait anxious children. *Journal of Sport Psychology* 5: 172-188.

Purdy, D.A.; Haufler, S.E.; & Eitzen, D.S. (1981). Stress among child athletes: Perceptions by parents and athletes. *Journal of Sports Behavior* 4: 32-44.

Raedeke, T.D. (1997). Is athlete burnout more than just stress? A sport commitment perspective. *Journal of Sport and Exercise Psychology* 19: 396-417.

Raglin, J. (1993). Overtraining and staleness: Psychometric monitoring of endurance athletes. In: Singer, R.N.; Murphey, M.; & Tennant, L.K. (Eds.), *Handbook of Research in Sport Psychology*. New York: Macmillan (pp. 840-850).

Ralio, W.S. (1982). The relationship of sport in childhood and adolescence to mental and social health. *Scandinavian Journal of Sports Medicine Supplement* 29: 135-145.

Raviv, S. (1981). Reactions to frustration, level of anxiety and loss of control of children participating in competitive sports. In: Geron, E.; Mashiach, A.; Dunkelman, N.; Raviv, S.; Levin, Z.; & Nakash, E. (Eds.), *Children in Sport: Psychosociological Characteristics*. Netanya, Israel: Wingate Institute (pp. 72-94).

Renger, R. (1993). A review of the profile of mood states (POMS) in the prediction of athletic stress. *Journal of Applied Sport Psychology* 5: 78-84.

Robertson, I. (1986). Youth sport in Australia. In: Weiss, M.R. & Gould, D. (Eds.), *Sports for Children and Youth*. Champaign, IL: Human Kinetics (pp. 5-10).

Rowley, A.J.; Launders, D.M.; Blaine Kyllo, L.; & Etnier, J.L. (1995). Does the iceberg profile discriminate between successful and less successful athletes? A meta analysis. *Journal of Sport and Exercise Psychology* 17: 185-199.

Ryan, J. (1995). *Little Girls in Pretty Boxes: The Making and Breaking of Elite Gymnastics and Figure Skaters*. New York: Doubleday.

Scanlan, T. (1986). Competitive stress in children. In: Weiss, M.R. & Gould, D. (Eds.), *Sports for Children and Youth*. Champaign, IL: Human Kinetics (pp. 113-118).

Scanlan, T.K. & Passer, M. (1978). Factors related to competitive stress among male youth sports participants. *Medicine and Science in Sport* 10: 103-108.

Scanlan, T.K. & Passer, M. (1979). Sources of competitive stress in young female athletes. *Journal of Sport Psychology* 1: 151-159.

Scanlan, T.K. & Lethwaite, R. (1984). Social psychological aspects of competition for male youth sport participants: Predictors of performance outcomes. *Journal of Sport Psychology* 6: 422-429.

Schmidt, G.W. & Stein, G.L. (1991). Sport commitment: A model integrating enjoyment, dropout, and burnout. *Journal of Sport and Exercise Psychology* 13: 254-265.

Silva, J.M. (1990). An analysis of the training stress syndrome in competitive athletics. *Journal of Applied Sport Psychology* 2: 5-20.

Simon, J. & Martens, R. (1979). Children's anxiety in sport and nonsport evaluative activities. *Journal of Sport Psychology* 1: 160-169.

Skubic, E. (1955). Emotional responses of boys to Little League and Middle League competitive baseball. *Research Quarterly* 26: 342-352.

Smith, R.E.; Smoll, F.L.; & Barnett, N.P. (1995). Reduction of children's sport performance anxiety and social support and stress-reduction training for coaches. *Journal of Applied Developmental Psychology* 16: 125-142.

Smith, R.E. & Smoll, F.L. (1982). Psychological stress: A conceptual model and some intervention strategies in youth sports. In: Magill, R.A.; Ash, M.J.; & Smoll, F.L. (Eds.), *Children in Sports*, 2nd Edition. Champaign, IL: Human Kinetics (pp. 178-195).

Smith, R.E. (1986). Toward a cognitive-affective model of athletic burnout. *Journal of Sport Psychology* 8: 36-50.

Thibaut, J.W. & Kelly, H.H. (1959). *The Social Psychology of Groups*. New York: Wiley.

Tierney, J. (1988). Stress in age-group swimmers. *Swim Technology* 24: 9-14.

Valeriote, T. & Hanson, L. (1986). Youth sport in Canada. In: Weiss, M.R. & Gould, D. (Eds.), *Sports for Children and Youth*. Champaign, IL: Human Kinetics (pp. 17-20).

Weinberg, R.S. & Gould, D. (1999). *Foundations of Sport and Exercise Psychology (2nd Edition)*. Champaign, IL: Human Kinetics.

Weiss, M.R. & Chaumenton, N. (1992). Motivational orientations in sport. In: Horn, T.S. (Ed.) Advances in Sport Psychology. Champaign, IL: Human Kinetics (pp. 61-90).

CHAPTER 13

Moral Community and Youth Sport in the New Millennium

Brenda Light Bredemeier
Center for Sport, Character, and Culture
University of Notre Dame

As we look back on the expiring millennium, it is difficult to draw conclusions about features that characterized youth sports. The expanse of time is so great, and the diversity of cultures so wide, that few conclusions can be drawn. But on one point, most commentators would agree. The closing century of the millennium has been characterized by a truly revolutionary change in the play activities of children. Increasingly, children's play time has become routinized under the rubric of formal youth sports. Moreover, youth sports have increasingly assumed much of the flavor, style, and norms of the professional sports after which they have been modeled (Time, July 1999).

Particularly in the United States, one major justification for the transformation of childhood play into formalized sports has been the belief that sport builds character. If sport enables participants to develop determination, endurance, teamwork, leadership, and other admired traits, then why not provide this experience to the young? Still, questions have lingered over whether and how youth sport builds character in young participants. Certainly, if repeating a slogan could make it true, budding athletes would be walking around with their feet six inches off the ground and little gold circles hovering above their heads. But the assumption that sport builds character continues to be challenged, both in the realm of scholarship and in everyday lives.

Recognizing that context shapes perception, it may be important to inform the reader that parts of this paper were written in the immediate aftermath of the shootings at Columbine High School in Littleton, Colorado. This major tragedy has caused much reflection, dialogue, soul-searching, and political posturing. But two facts struck me as particularly relevant to the topic of this paper. First, both Eric and Dylan—the young men who committed the Columbine massacre—had, in their earlier years, played Little League baseball. The second fact that struck me was how much of their rage was directed at the athletes of their school.

I'm not suggesting that playing Little League, or any other sport, predisposes one to violent actions; nor do I want to do a post hoc "pop psych" analysis of the young men's motivations. Still, I believe that the seemingly random carnage raises important questions for those of us who care deeply about the youth in youth sport. I will not try to answer my questions—I wish that I were so wise!—but I will identify some considerations that will help frame the body of the paper.

First, the tragedy at Columbine raises difficult questions about the very nature and identity of today's youth. There are a number of trends that are quite disturbing. Teenagers today are 300 times more likely to be victims of violence than were youth of my generation. Many youth are suicidal as well as homicidal. Many seem to have developed a callousness and cynicism about the future. William Pollack says children today are "crying bullets instead of tears" (CNN News, April 21, 1999). Of course, these are broad generalizations, but they are trends that are all too pervasive.

There is no single or simple explanation for these trends. They are deeply rooted in economic and demographic changes, as well as cultural shifts and political decisions. But there is an odd paradox that places our youth in a nearly untenable position. As several commentators have observed, the line between childhood and adulthood has become increasingly blurred. A couple of examples will suffice. The U.S. justice system gradually has eroded the once pervasive distinction between juvenile and adult offenders. Schools today employ standardized testing of children's academic abilities and achievement as early as preschool. Advertizers and other media interests now often cater simultaneously to children and adults.

Of special interest to us, youth sports have increasingly modeled themselves after the norms, values, and practices of the "big leagues." As a result, many young sport competitors have gone public with the loss of their childhood. Other youth have suffered from eating disorders, have sustained permanent bodily damage and even have lost their lives in the pursuit of adult-defined success.

The other side of the paradox is this: despite the blurring of childhood and adulthood, little is often expected of our children. Unseemly emotional outbursts are tolerated as self-expression; unruly behavior is accepted in the name of protecting creativity; a lack of respect for others is pardoned because demanding respect is confused requiring outmoded forms of etiquette. But children are often given little responsibility, and as a result, they develop little responsibility. Children who haven't developed a sense of responsibility are ill-prepared for the demands of adulthood, demands which are placed on them from an early age.

These observations underscore the importance of a developmentally-based youth sport model. A developmental model neither confuses children with adults, seeking to mold their experience to the norms and values of adult society, nor confuses childhood with some fantasy realm of unrestrained freedom. A developmental model seeks to balance expectations with sensitivity to the unique qualities and perspectives of youth; it seek to balance responsibility with freedom.

One of the implications for this developmental emphasis is the need to incorporate into coaches' education programs information about age-related developmental issues. Coaches need to learn more than they generally have about children's understandings of competition and success, and age-appropriate norms for thoughts, feelings, and behaviors. For example, anger in a four year-old looks very different from anger in a 14 year-old. Also, what a seven year-old wants out of her sport experience is likely to be very different from what a 17 year-old may want out of her sport experience.

This brings me back to the two young Little League players who later went on to terrorize Columbine High School. I'm obviously not suggesting that their coach was responsible for their later behavior. But I would suggest, as a general principle, that when coaches better understand the development of their athletes, they are in a much better position to identify youth who are withdrawn socially, those who may be teased or ostrasized, or youth who may threaten or lash out against others.

Even if coaches are able to identify such youth, what should they do about it? How far should an adult go in intervening in "kid culture?" How can coaches structure their relationships with youth in a way that promotes their development into healthy, competent, responsible adults?

Both Eric and Dylan were described by their coaches as being quiet and respectful players.

Neither was known for impulsive behavior or angry outbursts. And yet as high school students, both boys saw themselves as isolated. They were angry, hurting young men with access to guns and other weapons. Did Eric and Dylan isolate themselves by their hostile attitudes and behaviors, or were they isolated by adults and peers? Clearly, one thing we have learned from this tragedy is that we must reach out to those youth who feel isolated and alienated. But, can adults reach out with empathy and understanding, while maintaining authority, without their exercise of authority further alienating the youth they seek to help? When and where should adults intervene in youth culture?

Nucci's (1999) recent cross-cultural study with high school students in Japan and the U.S. provides some clues. He found that adolescents in both countries view certain actions as properly personal and appropriately within their own control. In these areas, adult exercise of authority is viewed as intrusive. For example, most teens would not think it reasonable for coaches to dictate the length of a player's hair or the style of their clothes. In fact, when the youth in this study perceived adult intrusion into their areas of personal choice, they self-reported symptoms of depression and hostility. Yet, the study participants wanted and expected adults to exert authority over behaviors outside the personal domain, particularly actions that could involve harm to themselves or others, or violations of basic conventions and norms. The adolescents strongly agreed that adults have an obligation to intervene in any circumstance in order to protect youth. In fact, Nucci (1999) found that youth pathology was much more closely tied to adult undercontrol than overcontrol.

How can adults exert "appropriate" control in youth sport to promote character development? Surely, more must be done than punish rule violations and reward desirable conduct with "good sport" awards, though these efforts are laudable. The answer to this question may lie in another question: How can we promote a sense of moral community in sport teams that is characterized by values of compassion, fairness, and integrity? This question frames the remainder of this chapter.

Rather than focus solely on the character development of individual athletes, I would like us to focus equally on the collective, the team. By asking us to focus on the collective, I do not mean to encourage an increased use of coaching cliches that ask the individual to subjugate personal self-interest to the instrumental goals of the team (i.e. the kind where the coach tells the players that there's no "I" in the word "team"). Rather, the focus is on team character-building, where all participants are asked to take responsibility for the collective norms and values of the team, so that the whole, the team, comes to embody a way of living that affirms the most core values of the participants. In other words, we should think about how we can move beyond a concept of team as a collection of more-and-less skilled athletes united primarily by their common quest for competitive superiority. We should think, instead, about a concept of team that is at once an expression of physical competence and moral community.

The etymology of the word community, to unite with, suggests diversity united by shared values. Within an instrumental community, the shared value is dedication to a pragmatic outcome like winning. When that instrumental community is also a moral community, the shared values go broader and deeper. Moral community requires mutual respect and just relationships. Underlying a moral community is a commitment to promote life, to affirm human dignity, and to resist violence and injustice.

Three character virtues are key to the development of moral community in the context of youth sports: compassion, fairness, and integrity. Briefly, compassion enables us to feel with others; it requires us to listen to one another, and to open our hearts to another's pain and joy. Fairness guards against the tendency to be compassionate only toward those who in some way are like ourselves; it pushes us beyond our world of affiliations to an equal valuing of all. And integrity is that virtue which, when prized, helps resist the temptation to sacrifice morality for lesser values. Each of the three virtues will be discussed, first by identifying the fundamental competencies or characteristics on which each rests, then by suggesting ways that the concept of sport teams as moral communities can help devise strategies to promote them.

Compassion

Compassion does not mean a disposition to charity or sentimentality. Such tendencies reflect a self-other dichotomy and an element of paternalism. Rather, compassion is a virtue akin to moral sensitivity and responsiveness. Compassion opens us up, it puts a hearing aid on our hearts. Yet, compassion is not in opposition to reason; it engages both intellect and emotion. In fact, it demands the cooperation of the intellect, because our reasoning capacities help us to be more fully engaged with another.

Compassion is as relevant in sport as in other arenas of life. It is interesting to note that sport participants often play "with passion," that is compassionately. One cannot have compassion without passion; yet compassion connotes more than intense feeling.

Underlying the moral virtue of compassion is the psychological competency of empathy, and it is important to distinguish the two. Empathy is the ability to "feel with" another. It is a cognitive-affective skill that develops through an orderly sequence of stages or phases. Empathy, in and of itself, is not necessarily moral. A coach, for example, may use empathy to win an undecided recruit's commitment to her university. Compassion is empathy put to the service of moral ends. It is empathy dedicated to mutual respect and human solidarity.

Empirically, little is known about the relationship between sport experience and empathy. It might be hypothesized that most sport experiences discourage the development of empathy. Many coaches and athletes "depersonalize" opponents, characterizing them as objects to be overcome in the quest for victory. Also, many sport participants (sometimes with the assistance of their sport psychology consultants) cultivate anger toward their opponents, a common "psych-up" strategy designed to motivate aggressive play. Empathizing with opponents may be counterproductive to the goal of winning, especially in contact and combative sports; even empathizing with teammates may interfere with an athlete's concentrated focus on performance.

The ability to foster empathy in sport contexts may also be hampered simply by the competitive structure of sport. Empirical studies conducted in contexts other than sport suggest that competition tends to exert an inhibitory influence on empathy (Barnett et al., 1979; Kalliopuska, 1987). Moreover, social scientists have found that competition typically generates human feelings that pull in the opposite direction from empathy: distrust, hostility, anxiety (Johnson and Johnson, 1989). Competitive interactions tend to result in distorted or inaccurate communication, unidimensional views of competitors, lowered self-esteem, and negative stereotyping. Under such conditions, it is certainly difficult for empathy to flourish.

Despite the obstacles, a coach seeking to nurture moral community in youth sport can find ways to encourage the development of empathy and put it to the service of compassion. The emotional richness of sport provides fertile ground for learning and experiencing empathy. But for these experiences to bear fruit, coaches must encourage children to talk about their experience, to share their perspectives and feelings in a safe environment, and to listen attentively to the experiences of others.

Hoffman's (1976, 1978, 1984, 1987, 1990, 1991) theoretical and empirical work, together with that of his colleagues, confirms that empathy develops in stages. Progress in empathy development is often stimulated by cognitive growth in social perspective-taking ability—the ability to differentiate one's perspective from that of others,' and to relate these different perspectives to each another (Selman, 1980). Team sports, in particular, feature interpersonal interactions predicated on the ability to coordinate one's actions with others. To coordinate effectively, the athlete must comprehend the game through multiple frames of reference. Games and sports are miniature social systems that can provide the growing child with experiences of social rules and roles that need to be coordinated.

Developing social perspective-taking skill and empathy, of course, are just the beginning. It is important that moral communities identify shared values to which young athletes' skills of empathy can be devoted. For example, take the value of inclusivity, a critical value for the existence of sustainable moral community. Inclusivity requires that others not be imaged as "the other." Youth are unlikely to use their developing empathic skills to feel compassion for someone who has been defined as "the other," or, "not us." When youth are encouraged to use a broad definition of "us," an atmosphere more conducive to compassion is created. Schulman and Mekler (1985) contend that there is no more important lesson that we can teach children than that "us" includes all of humankind: all ethnicities, all religions, all sexual orientations. Youth can learn either to appreciate the differences in others or to be threatened by them. They can learn either the beauty of diversity, or the ugly distortions and untruths of prejudice. The sport team as a moral community can be a learning environment nurturing the virtue of compassion.

In an ongoing study of lesbian sportswomen who have been identified as moral exemplars, one of the study participants articulated her sense of compassion in a way that fits well here. She stated: "When I feel like I'm really able to act out of love rather than fear, it's like I can act out of my connection, my sense of a person's humanness rather than what they said or did, or the physical body they present to me...I have to try to strip away my fears and concerns to see that the person under all those layers of identity has a lot of the same fears that I do" (Bredemeier et al., 1995).

Finally, if sport experience is to foster compassion, the common view that competition is the antithesis of cooperation needs to be challenged. Though empirically untested, it seems reasonable to believe that when competition is understood as a form of cooperation, empathy and compassion can be important parts of the competitive experience. The root meaning of competition is "to strive with," not "to strive against." Competition can be seen as a process in which participants depend on one another to perform at their best in order to spur each other on through mutual challenge.

This interpretation of competition is consistent with a task-oriented goal orientation and a mastery-oriented motivational climate, both of which have been linked in recent literature with moral thought and action (Duda et al., 1991; Stephens and Bredemeier, 1996). When youth sport success is defined in self-referenced terms, rather than other-referenced terms, the team can be a place where youth passionately strive to achieve a common goal: optimizing the performance of self and other. Such activity can heighten participants' sense of human solidarity and nurture their mutual commitment to one another; it becomes a way of expanding the passion in sport to include compassion for others.

Fairness

The virtue of fairness helps ensure that compassion is not overly influenced by affiliation. Fairness involves even-handedness, equal consideration. It is not "blind justice," but suspended personal interest. One needs to be both engaged and disengaged to be fair.

The media provides us daily with evidence that sport is a training ground for unfair behavior—cheating, favoritism, unbridled egocentrism. Some of my students frankly acknowledge that sport has taught them that seeking unfair advantage is merely good strategy. It is also true, however, that sport can be an extraordinary context for the nurture of fairness. After all, sports are fundamentally premised on the observance of principles of fairness. They are designed to be fair contests, and the rules of the game are carefully structured to balance offense with defense, penalty with infraction, and challenge with capability. In a sense, sports cannot exist apart from fairness. Imagine that someone said, "let's create a new sport in which those with green eyes are advantaged." Who would play the game? Unless participants believe in the fairness of the contest, sport dissolves.

Just as it would be wrong to assume that sport inherently teaches that the violation of rules pays, it would be equally wrong to assume that just because sport is premised on fairness, participants learn to be fair through sport. So, how can we take advantage of the fairness structure inherent in sport practices to promote the virtue of fairness? Conceiving of sport teams as moral communities may help to accomplish this goal.

Community, as I noted earlier, involves "common unity" or shared commitments. It involves shared responsibility for the maintenance of the norms and practices that make community possible. In the context of sport, the team as moral community involves commitment to the fundamental values that undergird the very possibility of sport being sport, rather than mere spectacle. One of the most critical tasks of the youth sport coach may be to initiate his or her players into the traditions and practices that sustain the fairness of sport.

Again, the approach must be thoroughly developmental. If we are to identify ways to promote fairness in physical activity contexts, we must take into account how children at different developmental levels of moral reasoning conceive of fairness.

Scholars who study the structural aspects of moral reasoning have made some key observations that are relevant to this discussion (Haan et al., 1985; Kohlberg, 1981, 1984; Rest, 1986). First, the research has demonstrated that moral reasoning, like other forms of reasoning, develops. Moral concepts and precepts are not inborn, and their meaning and use develop gradually through experience. Second, development is not a process of simply copying the adult world, but occurs as the growing child constructs increasingly more adequate moral theories. Children are budding moral philosophers, and they actively reason about issues of right and wrong. Third, the organizational structure of children's moral theories can be seen to progress through a fairly regular age-related sequence of stages or levels or phases. As children mature, their

moral reasoning becomes progressively more coherent and comprehensive. Finally, as moral reasoning matures, people are less likely to engage in unjustifiable cheating, lying, stealing, and the like (Kohlberg and Candee, 1984). Moral reasoning competency is by no means the only influence on moral action, but it is certainly one of the more important.

Much of my own research has focused on moral reasoning issues in the context of sport. In one of the first investigations, the relationship between collegiate basketball players' moral reasoning maturity and their aggressive basketball play was studied (Bredemeier and Shields, 1984). The hypotheses were supported in that athletes' moral reasoning patterns were related to their levels of athletic aggression, as assessed by coaches' ratings and rankings. The finding that was somewhat surprising, however, was that both male and female athletes were below reported college norms on moral reasoning maturity. As a result, the question of whether some sport experiences restrain or retard participants' moral growth emerged.

In a more elaborate study, the moral reasoning maturity of basketball players, swimmers, and non-athletes at the high school and college levels was examined (Bredemeier and Shields, 1986a,b,c). Respondents reasoned about four hypothetical moral dilemmas, two set in everyday life contexts and two in sport specific situations, yielding a "life" and a "sport" moral reasoning maturity score. Again, among college students, the nonathletes had significantly more mature moral reasoning than the basketball players. The swimmers' moral reasoning scores fell between the basketball players and the nonathletes. Among high school students, however, no moral reasoning maturity differences between athletes and nonathletes were evident.

These findings, and the results of other descriptive studies demonstrating that, on the average, intercollegiate athletes reason at significantly lower levels than non-athletes, raise questions about the sport involvement-moral development relationship that remain unanswered.

Are athletes with more mature moral reasoning less interested in, or purposefully "selected out" of some college athletic programs? Does sport discourage moral development among its participants? Are there mediating variables that influence this relationship? Some evidence supports the hypothesis that more seasons played in sports featuring higher levels of physical contact are associated with lower moral reasoning scores and greater acceptance and expression of athletic aggression (Bredemeier et al., 1986). But, the cause-effect relationships for these variables have yet to be determined.

What are the implications of this research for the coach who wishes to encourage the development of fairness in his or her athletes? The key may be to start with a direct experience of the moral underpinnings of sport. There are many ways to do this. One strategy is to allow youth to experience violations of the fairness premise, and then encourage them to reflect on that experience. Unfortunately, such violations occur all the time in sport competitions. It is also possible to create such situations artificially; for example, to set up a practice game in soccer with one team allowed an extra player. Another practice strategy is to allow athletes to invent competitive practice drills. When players attempt to define a set of rules for their new activity, they will inevitably wrestle with issues of fairness and moral balance. Coaches can facilitate fairness dialogues by asking team members to discuss the salience of fairness for their team and what it means for team strategies and policies. Peer negotiation around such issues as how to ensure participation for all, how to resolve disputes, and how to deal with rule violations can create an excellent context for linking issues of mutual respect and just relationships.

To examine more fully how sport experiences may influence conceptions of fairness, broader questions about the overall team climate are relevant. For many athletes, doing what is fair depends far less on moral reasoning maturity than on their perceptions of the values and expectations of the coaches and athletes on their team, or more

generally, in the world of sport (Stephens and Bredemeier, 1996).

An important influence on conceptions of fairness is what we have termed "game reasoning." Game reasoning is a sport-specific form of moral reasoning (Bredemeier and Shields, 1986b; Shields and Bredemeier, 1995). Our research suggests that most athletes reason differently about moral issues in sport compared to daily life situations (Bredemeier and Shields, 1986b,c; Shields and Bredemeier, 1989). In structure, game reasoning often parallels the egocentric morality of early childhood. Thus, when some athletes reason about moral issues that arise in everyday life, they may use quite advanced forms of moral reasoning, but when those same individuals reason about moral issues that arise in sport, their reasoning may resemble that of a child who is unable to distinguish "I want" from "it's right."

This discrepancy between life and sport moral reasoning may be one aspect of a larger phenomenon. A number of philosophers, anthropologists, sociologists, and psychologists have suggested that play, and by extension sport, exists in a unique sphere, framed apart from the rest of life, and that entry into that sphere involves cognitive, attitudinal, and value adjustments. Firth (1973), for example, discusses how rituals and conventions serve to mark temporal boundaries and symbolize the reconstitution of people into players and players back into people.

If entry into sport involves a transformation of cognition and affect, then it is reasonable to hypothesize that moral reasoning undergoes some change in its underlying organization when one moves from daily life contexts into the sport domain. Game reasoning influences athletes' thinking about fairness because their actions are judged in a context that is separate from daily life. In fact, athletes often see themselves as temporarily freed from making decisions about fairness; rather, they are taught to comply with the rules, or to get away with as much as the officials will allow, and to follow the dictates of their coaches.

One basketball player explained it this way: "In sports you can do what you want. In life it's more restricted. The pressure is different in sports and life. It's harder to make decisions in life because there are so many people to think about, different people to worry about. In sports you're free to think about yourself" (Bredemeier and Shields, 1986b).

One function of game reasoning in contemporary sport may be to suppress empathy so that victory can be pursued by any means necessary. Consider, for example, a comment by former Heavyweight boxing champion Larry Holmes. He explained that before he enters the ring, "I have to change, I have to let the goodness out and bring all the bad in, like Dr. Jekyll and Mr. Hyde" (quoted in Bredemeier and Shields, 1985, p. 23). The theme of this quote is echoed frequently by sport commentators who note a discrepancy between the on-field athlete who is aggressive and dominant and the off-field athlete who may be gentle and caring.

Game reasoning is only one of many influences on athletes' conceptions of fairness. Another important influence is the shared understandings of appropriate behavior by team members. Stephens and Bredemeier (1996), for example, found that the best predictor that a youth sport soccer player's likelihood to play unfairly (i.e., self-described likelihood to cheat, lie to an official, or aggress against an opponent) was not personal dispositions like moral reasoning maturity or goal orientation. Rather, the best predictor was the athletes' perceptions of their teammates' likelihood to engage in these activities. The second best predictor of unfair play was athletes' perceptions of their coaches' goal orientation. Those athletes who believed that their youth sport coaches were more ego-oriented also described themselves as more likely to play unfairly.

In short, the literature confirms the claim of Power at al. (1989) who state that children's moral development occurs best when nurtured in a communal environment where group norms and values support their development. The moral atmosphere of a youth sport community has a tremendous influence, not only on the compassion and fairness of individual athletes, but especially on their ability to demonstrate integrity, that is, to act in a way that is consistent with their ideals.

Integrity

The virtue of integrity is the cornerstone of character, for when we have integrity we embody our ideals. Integrity is a reflection of the unity of self and moral goals. To better understand what makes integrity possible, it will be helpful to discuss the concept of self-understanding.

Self-understandings reflect the different ways that we conceive of who we are. For example, it includes interpretations of who we are physically and psychologically. Self-understanding also includes images and concepts pertaining to our moral characteristics and values. The totality of our moral self-understanding is what is meant by "moral self."

The dimensions of the self that are at the core of self-understanding appear to vary developmentally and individually. Damon (1984) posits that during some periods of development the moral self operates as a distinct psychological structure from self-understanding. At other times, there is more integration between the two. Damon (1984) conducted a series of investigations and found that, although children have some awareness of all the various dimensions of themselves throughout development, the domain of self-perception that children use to define their core identity changes in a consistent developmental progression.

Young children focus their self-definitions on the physical self. For example, a young child might respond to the question, "What are you like?" by saying, "I am a very big boy." When they get a little older, children define themselves in terms of their activities and physical skills; "I am a great soccer player," might be a response. At the next developmental level, older children typically define themselves in terms of their social networks. And then, finally, adolescents begin to define themselves in terms of psychological and moral characteristics.

According to Damon (1984), children's moral cognitions are only minimally integrated into their concepts of self. One consequence of the split between the peripheral "moral self" and the central "physical or active self" is that children often conceive of their self-interest as in opposition to the demands of morality. What children want for themselves is often experienced as inconsistent with what they believe is morally right. This may help to explain the inconsistencies so common in children's moral thought and action. Since moral concerns are not critical to how they define who they are or what they want for themselves, moral knowledge lacks the motivational force necessary to propel moral action.

By adolescence, however, there is at least the possibility that moral concerns are integrated into self-understanding. Adolescents can define their core identity in terms that include a prominent role for moral self-definition. Blasi (1984) has suggested that the more people define themselves in moral categories, the more committed they become to living morally, and the more likely their moral action will cohere with their moral judgment. Thus, as adolescents move toward moral self-understandings, an increasing tendency to choose moral values over nonmoral ones when there is a conflict among them might be anticipated (Damon, 1977; Gerson and Damon, 1978). When people define themselves morally, less than moral actions are experienced as self-inconsistency (Blasi and Oresick, 1987).

One way to gain insight into integrity is to interview moral exemplars, people who have inspired those around them by their moral conviction and courage. Colby and Damon (1994) have done so, and they have learned much about integrity, or what they call the nature, development, and expression of moral commitment. One of the most striking findings in their on-going investigation fits with the previous discussion—those people who inspire others by their moral character tend to have self-definitions that give a central place to moral ideals. In other words, personal identity is closely integrated with moral values. This enables a fusion of personal and moral goals.

Colby and Damon (1994) found that the close relationship between the personal and the moral was revealed in many ways, including in their exemplars' interpretation of moral choices. The exemplars did not see their moral choices as an exercise in self-sacrifice; rather, they saw pursuing moral goals as a way to achieve their personal goals, and vice versa. These people were highly motivated to live their lives with integrity and to act in ways consistent with their sense of compassion and fairness, because their moral goals were not in opposition to their personal goals. Their moral goals were a significant part of their identity.

It is unfortunate that much of sport experience encourages not a unity but a disjunction between moral and personal goals. Most athletes know that cheating is wrong, for example, but they cheat anyway because it helps them get what they want. Most athletes know that hurting others is wrong, but they aggress anyway because it helps move them toward their goals. Most athletes know that showing disrespect or outright contempt for game officials is wrong, but many do so anyway. Moreover, many athletes feel encouraged by teammates to cheat, aggress, and disregard the dignity of others. And what is true of the athletes, is equally true of coaches, sport administrators, and Olympic Board members.

By creating a sense of moral community on youth sport teams, we can hopefully encourage athletes to act with integrity. In the moral community, compassion and fair play, care and justice, become part of the team's self-definition. If the sense of moral community is successfully built within a team, cheating loses its appeal because it no longer furthers the collective goals of the team. The competitive desire to win becomes defined as genuine winning, winning by the rules.

Athletes do not need to conceive of their personal sport goals and their responsibility to others as antithetical to one another. Coaches may be able to encourage the development of children's moral integrity by emphasizing the potential for "feeding two birds with one piece of bread," for meeting the needs of self and other simultaneously. One illustration of how this might be done is in re-framing the contemporary notion of competition, a strategy discussed earlier.

It is unfortunate that so much of sport encourages a disjunction between moral goals and personal goals. The competitive process itself tends to encourage a certain egocentrism that can run counter to moral ideals, and the heightened emotionally-charged atmosphere of sport only aggravates this characteristic of competition. But this tension is precisely why sport offers such a rich possibility for character formation. Of what significance is integrity without the temptation to deviate from moral ideals? Sport provides an ideal setting for the development of integrity precisely because it joins together, in an emotionally charged environment, a salient moral framework and an alluring temptation to deviate from moral standards. Participants are faced with balancing their moral judgments about what is right and their desire to act on that moral ideal with their desire to achieve apparent success—that is, to win. The athlete who chooses to refrain from seeking advantage through moral default may pay a price, but integrity requires that one act according to personal moral standards and accept the cost of doing so. To develop integrity, young athletes must have the opportunity to practice integrity within the context of moral community.

In conclusion, then, youth sport teams can become, under proper guidance, moral communities, a kind of culture within which young people develop both muscles and morals. Social scientists typically use the term "culture" to refer to a system of symbols and shared meanings and values. But for biological scientists, "culture" is literally a medium in which living things grow. It seems important to acknowledge that youth sport teams are mediums within which children grow. We can nurture that growth by envisioning sport teams as moral communities where young people develop an understanding of the fairness structure of sport and its importance; where they develop within themselves a self-understanding that includes compassion; and where they face the test of temptation, so they can respond with integrity.

Future Directions

In this chapter, I have suggested that promoting a sense of moral community within sport teams may provide an efficacious means for promoting such central moral values as compassion, fairness, and integrity. The moral psychology of sport, however, is in the early stages of development and progress is hampered by a lack of valid and reliable instrumentation. Both quantitative and qualitative research methodologies need to be developed to investigate such critical constructs as "moral community" and "collective norms." We need tools, for example, to assess a team's progress in adopting collective norms for behavior. Future research is also needed to determine strategies that youth sport coaches can use to develop shared norms and a sense of moral community within their teams. We can learn from the related work on "just communities" in schools (Power et al., 1989), but interventions in sport will need to have their own character and quality.

REFERENCES

Barnett, M.A.; Matthews, K.A.; & Howard, J.A. (1979). Relationship between competitiveness and empathy in 6- and 7-year olds. *Developmental Psychology* 15: 221-222.

Blasi, A. (1984). Moral identity: Its role in moral functioning. In: Kurtines, W. & Gewirtz, J. (Eds.), *Morality, Moral Behavior, and Moral Development*. New York: Wiley (pp. 128-139).

Blasi, A. & Oresick, R. (1987). Self-inconsistency and the development of self. In: Young-Nisendrafth, P. & Hall, J. (Eds.), *The Book of the Self: Person, Pretext, and Process*. New York: University Press (pp. 69-87).

Bredemeier, B.L.; Carlton, E.; Hills, L.; & Ogelsby, C. (1995). *The Moral Meaning of Coming Out: An Analysis of the Unique and Common Perspectives of Four Lesbian Sportswomen Exemplars*. Paper presented at the Association for Moral Education conference, New York, NY (November).

Bredemeier, B.J. & Shields, D.L. (1984). The utility of moral stage analysis in the investigation of athletic aggression. *Sociology of Sport Journal* 1: 138-149.

Bredemeier, B.J. & Shields, D.L. (1985). Values and violence in sport. Psychology Today 19: 22-32.

Bredemeier, B.J. & Shields, D.L. (1986a). Athletic aggression: An issue of contextal morality. *Sociology of Sport Journal* 3: 15-28.

Bredemeier, B.J. & Shields, D.L. (1986b). Game reasoning and interactional morality. *Journal of Genetic Psychology* 147: 257-275.

Bredemeier, B.J. & Shields, D.L. (1986c). Moral growth among athletes and nonathletes: A comparative analysis. *Journal of Genetic Psychology* 147: 7-18.

Bredemeier, B.J.; Weiss, M.R.; Shields, D.L.; Cooper, B. (1986). The relationship of sport involvement with children's moral reasoning and aggression tendencies. *Journal of Sport Psychology* 8: 304-318.

Colby, A. & Damon, W. (1994). *Some Do Care: Contemporary Lives of Moral Commitment*. New York: Free Press.

Damon, W. (1977). *The Social World of the Child*. San Francisco: Jossey-Bass.

Damon, W. (1984). Self-understanding and moral development from childhood to adolescence. In: Kurtines, W.M. & Gewirtz, J. (Eds.), *Morality, Moral Behavior, and Moral Development*. New York: Wiley (pp. 109-127).

Gerson, R. & Damon, W. (1978). Moral understanding and children's conduct. In: Damon, W. (Ed.), *New Directions for Child Development, Volume 1*. San Francisco: Jossey-Bass (pp. 41-49).

Haan, N.; Aerts, E.; & Cooper, B.B. (1985). *On Moral Grounds: The Search for a Practical Morality*. New York: New York University Press.

Hoffman, M.L. (1976). Empathy, role-taking, guilt, and development of altruistic motives. In: Lickona, T. (Ed.), *Moral Development and Behavior: Theory, Research and Social Issues*. New York: Holt, Rinehart and Winston (pp. 124-143).

Hoffman, M.L. (1978). Empathy, its development and prosocial implications. In: Keasey, C.B. (Ed.), *Nebraska Symposium on Motivation, Volume 25*. Lincoln, NB: University of Nebraska Press (pp. 169-218).

Hoffman, M.L. (1984). Empathy, its limitations, and its role in a comprehensive moral theory. In: Kurtines, W.M. & Gewirtz, J. (Eds.), *Morality, Moral Behavior, and Moral Development*. New York: Wiley (pp. 283-302).

Hoffman, M.L. (1987). The contribution of empathy to justice and moral judgment. In: Eisenberg, N. & Strayer, J. (Eds.), *Empathy and Its Development*. Cambridge, MA: Cambridge University (pp. 47-80).

Hoffman, M.L. (1990). Empathy and justice motivation. *Motivation and Emotion* 14: 151-171.

Hoffman, M.L. (1991). Empathy, social cognition, and moral action. In: Kurtines, W. & Gewirtz, J. (Eds.), *Handbook of Moral Behavior and Development, Volume 1*. Theory. Hillsdale, NJ: Lawrence Erlbaum (pp. 275-301).

Johnson, D. & Johnson, R. (1989). *Cooperation and Competition: Theory and Research*. Edina, MN: Interaction Books.

Kalliopuska, M. (1987). Relation of empathy and self-esteem to active participation in Finnish baseball. *Perceptual and Motor Skills* 65: 107-113.

Kohlberg, L. (1981). *Essays on Moral Development, Volume 1. The Philosophy of Moral Development*. San Francisco: Harper & Row.

Kohlberg, L. (1984). *Essays on Moral Development, Volume 2. The Psychology of Moral Development.* San Francisco: Harper & Row.

Kohlberg, L. & Candee, D. (1984). The relationship of moral judgment to moral action. In: Kurtines,W. & Gewirtz, J. (Eds.), *Morality, Moral Behavior, and Moral Development.* New York: Wiley (pp. 52-73).

Nucci, L. (1999). Personal communication.

Power, F.C.; Higgins, A.; & Kohlberg, L. (1989). *Lawrence Kohlberg's Approach to Moral Education.* New York: Columbia University Press.

Rest, J.R. (1986). *Moral Development: Advances in Research and Theory.* New York: Praeger.

Selman, R.L. (1980). *The Growth of Interpersonal Understanding.* New York: Academic Press.

Shields, D.L. & Bredemeier, B.J. (1989). Moral reasoning, judgment, and action in sport. In: Goldstein, J. (Ed.), *Sports, Games, and Play: Social and Psychological Viewpoints.* Hillsdale, NJ: Erlbaum Associates (pp. 59-81).

Shields, D.L. & Bredemeier, B.J.L. (1995). *Character Development and Physical Activity.* Champaign, IL: Human Kinetics.

Stephens, D.E. & Bredemeier, B.J.L. (1996). Moral atmosphere and judgments about aggression in girls' soccer: Relationships among moral and motivational variables. *Journal of Sport and Exercise Psychology* 18: 158-173.

CHAPTER 14

Abuse of Power: Potential for Harassment

Jody A. Brylinsky
Western Michigan University

Many athletes will tell you that the special relationship that develops between a coach and athlete is one of the more treasured outcomes of their sport experience. However, this special relationship must be based on the understanding of the power and responsibility entrusted to coaches by the school system, sport organizations, parents, and athletes. Knowing how to nurture this relationship without intentionally or unintentionally violating the rights of the athlete is critical to effective and rewarding coaching. Athletic administrators must be particularly aware that this unique power relationship carries the potential for sexual harassment or the creation of abusive environments, and take a proactive role in creating an affirming sport atmosphere.

The recent heightened awareness about abuse in sport is the result of courageous disclosures from athletes who have experienced emotional, physical, and sexual abuse. Athletes who "couldn't hold it in any longer" or "wanted it to stop so their life could go on," have made such disclosures in spite of what Brackenridge and colleagues (1995, p.85) have concluded as an atmosphere of "collective blindness...compounded by lack of knowledge and lack of political will." Some athletes seek punishment for the perpetrators; others spoke up so that someone else would be spared the pain (Woodhouse, 1997). Organizing bodies must recognize the conduciveness of the sport structure and culture to exploitation by the coach or leader, and that harassment it is not just a matter of individual ethics (Tomlinson and Yorganci, 1997). In addition, the independent status of voluntary sport organizations may prevent appropriate scrutiny of coaches and volunteers, making it an ideal breading ground for abuse (Brackenridge, 1994, 1997). Prevention of abuse will be greatly assisted by the development of an attitude where the entire community takes responsibility for the safety of their children and youth (Woodhouse, 1997).

There are differing degrees of abuse and harassment, all maintaining one common thread in the definition: the behavior is unwanted and disrupting to the progress of the individual acted upon. Abuse of power may be:

- Physical—person is intentionally injured or made to do exercise as punishment, i.e., use unreasonable physical force as punishment, use excessive exercise as punishment, encourage athletes to physically assault one another (Woodhouse, 1997).

- Sexual—a person is exposed to or invited to participate in sexual contact, activity or behavior; this can include both contact and non contact actions, i.e., ridiculing sexual body parts.

- Neglect—a child is not provided an appropriate level of care and supervision, i.e., chronic inattention to the basic necessities of life such as clothing, shelter, diet, etc. (Sport Safe: Coach's Game Plan, 1999). Specific types of neglect include the following:

  ✓ Inadequate nutrition—encouraging unhealthy diets, fasting, not allowing sufficient breaks for meals/nourishment;

  ✓ Inadequate shelter /unsafe environments—lack of maintaining equipment or facility, forcing athletes to participate without proper protective equipment;

  ✓ Inadequate clothing—preventing athletes from dressing adequately for weather conditions or making them stay in wet clothes as punishment following a game;

  ✓ Inadequate supervision—leaving young athletes unsupervised in a facility or on a team trip;

  ✓ Lack of medical/dental care—ignoring or minimizing injuries, ignoring medical advice, not seeking medical attention when warranted;

  ✓ Inadequate education—encouraging athletes to not do homework, to not attend school or to drop out;

  ✓ Inadequate rest—overdoing or increasing workouts as punishments, prohibiting adequate sleeping or resting time

  ✓ Inadequate moral guidance and discipline—not providing adequate supervision during team functions, hiring strippers or pornographic activities (Woodhouse, 1997, p. 4).

- Emotional/verbal abuse—a person is made fun of, criticized, discriminated against, or put under unrealistic pressure to perform. Emotional abuse

is a chronic attack on a child's self-esteem, or psychologically destructive behavior by a person in a position of power, authority, or trust (Sport Safe: Coach's Game Plan, 1999). The following are specific forms of emotional abuse:

✓ Rejecting—refusing to acknowledge, believe, hear, or support the child's worth, or the legitimacy of his /her needs, i.e., humiliation or excessive criticism;

✓ Isolating—unreasonably separating the child from others, cutting a child off from normal social experiences which result in extreme aloneness, i.e., prohibiting interactions with others, preventing participation in other school events or contact with family or friends;

✓ Terrorizing—coercing by intimidation, causing a state or instance of extreme fear, violent dread, or fright, i.e., teasing, scaring, verbal threats of harm, inconsistent demands, changing rules, threatening dismissal from the team, or forcing athletes to participate in unsafe activity;

✓ Corrupting—rendering anti-social or maladjusted behaviors changing from good to bad, encouraging destructive and anti-social behavior, i.e., rewarding socially unacceptable behavior, endorsing athlete's violent behavior or attitude, encouraging substance use and abuse, or reinforcing rituals or habits such as hazing;

✓ Ignoring—failing to provide sensitive, responsive care-giving, depriving youth of essential stimulation and responsiveness, not being psychologically available, i.e., acting cold, withholding responses, showing favoritism, not allowing athletes a voice, or failing to intervene when help is needed;

✓ Exploiting—making use of someone for one's own advantage or profit, making excessive age-inappropriate demands, i.e., giving athletes responsibilities far greater than they can handle for their age, using athletes to meet the adult's needs, treating an athlete as property (Woodhouse, 1997).

While research demonstrates that the athletic world is no better and no worse than other social domains regarding occurrences of sexual harassment and other forms of abuse, there is the need to recognize the abuse of power that occurs behind gymnasium doors. Results from the 1997 Canada Games Research on Harassment and Athletes (Findlay and Corbett, 1997) found that 52% of the 537 Olympic athletes and 72 coaches who responded to the survey reported no harassment experiences. Of those responding "yes," the most likely form of harassment was verbal abuse (25%), followed by sexual orientation (12.6%) and sexual encounters (12.6%). Physical (11%), and racial (6.7%) behaviors were less likely to be reported (Findlay and Corbett, 1997). Kirby and Greaves (1997) also found that sexual harassment was a key complaint for both male and female athletes in nationally organized Canadian teams, as also noted by Volkwein et al. (1997) among American female college student athletes.

The ability to accurately assess the extent of abuse is made difficult by the athlete's sensitivity to the power of the coach. Tomlinson and Yorganci (1997) reported that 69% of the sample denied any knowledge of sexual harassment; yet 25% of the respondents reported experiencing demeaning language, verbal intrusion, physical contact, and even to some degree, fondling and pressure to have sexual intercourse. In other words, the athlete is likely to see the behavior as wrong or unwanted but not as harassment. Athletes simply "coped" with the unwanted behaviors in fear of making matters worse, while the coach did not have to account for his actions. Tominson and Yorgancy (1997) concluded that the normalcy of conditions conducive to harassment and abuse and the culture of coach domination were the most striking findings.

Masteralexis (1995) points out that athletic departments need to address more than just the coach-athlete relationship when dealing with issues of sexual harassment and/or abusive power situations. Harassment may be claimed against athletic department supervisors by their own employees, or even coaches and school employees by other co-coaches or staff. Abusive conditions may be identified against non-school coaches by other coaches and school staff, and even claims against student-athletes by their peers must be addressed by the athletic administrator. In the 1997 Canada Games Research on Harassment and Athletes (Findlay and Corbett, 1997), the most frequent perpetrator of harassment was a teammate (29.6%), followed by a coach (24.7%), a spectator (21.9%), and even parents and officials (14%).

It is not just the conduct itself that makes certain behaviors inappropriate, but the context or manner in which it is delivered, or its repetitive nature. Individuals who have experienced harassment often describe not one or two incidents of harassment, but an environment around them that is cold, hostile, or alienating . The environment is described as "a chilly or poisoned environment" (Findlay and Corbett 1997, p. 3). Hazing, or initiation rights, which single out a person or a group of people and subject them to embarrassing, degrading or secretive behavior, will almost always be viewed as harassment (Findlay and Corbett, 1997). The following information is intended to alert athletic administrators, and/or those involved in youth sport programs, to the heart of the harassment issue, the imbalance of power, and what they can do to be proactive in creating a safe and affirming athletic environment for all involved.

Coach-Athlete Relationships

The coach-athlete relationship can be characterized by clearly identifying and balancing the scope of the coach's authority, responsibility, and power. These concepts can provide a framework for building a trusting relationship between the athlete and coach.

Given that sport by its nature promotes aggressive, dominant behavior, and the exertion of power over others, and that sport has traditions of male domination, it may be a fertile breeding ground for the demonstration of male power over women and men (Aussie Sport Action, 1995).

Authority is the coach's right to make decisions on behalf of others. Authority is best balanced by a well written job description designed and approved by the school administration or youth sport organization. Specific boundaries of the coach's authority should be spelled out, such as to decide who starts or makes the team, what defense or offense will be run, when practice will be held or even who will be the assistant coach. The school or organization may delegate to the coach other aspects of authority in matters that regard the scope and safety of the program within the guidelines of the designated sport association. In all cases the coach's authority should be described in behavioral terms, communicated to all parties involved, and reflect clear acceptable boundaries. A coach who decides to extend their authority beyond stated lines would be clearly judged as harassing or abusive.

Responsibility is the obligation or expectation in carrying out the role of coach. Courts and professional associations have been working to establish a legal sense of these responsibilities or duties, many of which are identified as essential coaching competencies in various coaching certifications. The head coach is also responsible "for" what all coaches should know and be able to do. The coach is expected to be knowledgeable about training and conditioning, nutrition and weight control, injury prevention and care, and skill development (NASPE, 1995), but not to have a say in the athlete's personal life. The range of what a coach is responsible for may differ by specific sport situations. For example, in some programs the coach has the additional responsibility for making sure athletes arrive safely home, from practice, or are given sport instruction framed within a religious atmosphere. Since a majority of athletes want a "close" professional relationship with the coach, school administration should clearly communicate to the coach and parents the scope of professional responsibilities.

It is important to keep in mind that the coach is also responsible "to" the school, and/or sport association in which that organization has chosen to belong, as well as "to" the students and parents, over whom the coach has been given authority. A coach has the obligation to actively seek out and listen to the expectations of parents and athletes, and clearly identify what can and can not be done in fulfilling these expectations. Athletes and even parents often perceive the coach to be simultaneously knowledgeable in all areas of life, e.g., medical expert and psychological concerns, which can translate into an abuse of the coach's responsibility over the life of an athlete (Tomlinson and Yorganci, 1997). Personal requests for attention and special relationships should be denied and discussed in relation to the overall responsibilities of the coach.

Power is the force or actions that allow a coach to use his or her authority in meeting specified responsibilities. How the coach defines power, and how it is used greatly influences the number and nature of conflicts within relationships. Power is the capacity to act effectively and the ability to influence others. Many see power as the ability to make others behave as one wants them to, or to exert control and gain an advantage over someone. "This creates conflicts because the parties in the relationship are, in effect, being disempowered and made dependent on the other person's agenda for the relationship" (Weeks, 1994, p. 50)

Official power includes those actions that are within the specified coaching authority, such as team selection or granting starting status to certain players. A coach has the "official power" to discipline athletes within the scope of school policy and due process (e.g., suspend from practice, drop from team, request additional practice time or out-of-season training or withholding rewards). Coaches even have the official power to physically contact a student athlete in order to control that athlete in potentially violent confrontations (e.g. intervening in a fight, removing a weapon, or restraining an out-of-control student) (Carpenter, 1995). Harassment and abuse are never written into formal lines of power, but are often assumed by omission of clear policy.

Most of the time, the ability to be an effective coach does not rely on official power, but rather on "personal power," or the ability to bring about action using social and personal skills. Personal power is appropriately gained through recognition and respect of the coach's experience, knowledge, physical skills, or positive personal characteristics. Weeks (1994) suggests that positive personal power is developed by the following:

- having a clear self-image, i.e., base our perceptions of ourselves on our own needs, capabilities, priorities, and goals, understanding of our values;

- having a clear understanding of our values and a congruency between values and behavior;

- being in charge of one self, rather than reacting to the negative behavior of others;

- learning and applying effective relationship and conflict resolution skills.

However, using the demonstration of personal or official power to create a hostile or threatening environment is abusive, and if harassing with regard to gender, is illegal.

It does not matter that a person did not mean their behavior to be harassing, or did not intend to abuse their position of power or trust. It is the effect of the behavior that is most critical (Findlay and Corbett, 1997). Negative power disempowers the other party in an attempt to increase one's advantage, focuses on specific attempts to gain advantage, and ignores the negative effects those specific actions have on the relationship. In other words, negative power, focuses on "power over" rather than "power with" relationship (Weeks, 1994).

Imbalance of power—dual relationships

Dual relationships exist when the coach combines incompatible roles, such as friend, counselor, or mentor, with the powerful role of coach (Hornak and Hornak, 1993). It is natural for the coach and athlete to develop strong emotional ties; in fact, this type of trust is necessary for effective athletic achievement. However, the imbalance of power that the coach has over the athlete must be recognized as a limitation in creating other social bonds.

The dual role of coach and friend should be discouraged since the need to be accepted or liked may reduce the coach's need for objectivity or control (Hornak and Hornak, 1993). Social friendships are based on the expectation of mutual considerations and obligations that the coach may not be able to provide, so the athlete is left to carry the weight of maintaining the friendship. The athlete stands to not only lose an effective working relationship with his or her coach, but a friend as well. The coach also may be misled, for as what appears to be a genuine liking on the part of the athlete may actually be a ploy by the athlete for favors and special attention.

The dual role of counselor and coach becomes one of conflict when the athlete's need for emotional support goes beyond that of the normal disclosure of feelings that is inevitable in the sport environment (Hornak and Hornak, 1993). Even if the coach was trained to deal with professional counseling issues, the emotional intimacies and confidentiality necessary in a professional mental health relationship is not possible with the other assumed duties of a coach. Since most coaches are not trained to deal with the diagnosis and intervention of emotional disorders, coaches should only act to refer the athlete to available counseling services. It is important that the coach let the athlete know that they are not abandoning him or her, but instead will work "with" the athlete in solving the problem through the assistance of a trained mental health professional or counselor.

The dual role of coach and *mentor* can also be abusive if the coach becomes an agent of what is called "positive deviance." In this case, athletes find themselves worshipping the ground the coach walks on as he or she "beats them to death." Coaches who use extreme, rigid, command styles of control build dependency relationships similar to those found in abused children and spouses. Athletes in such an environment will often make excuses for those who control and abuse them, believing that they deserve the inhumane treatment they receive (Coakley, 1993). In many ways a coach is just adopting the social myths about pain and suffering in relation to sport achievement. The athlete is led to believe that if playing in pain is noble, then being in agony is even better and is warranted if summoned by the coach (Nelson, 1994). In such situations coaches may create environments where athletes are asked to become violent (e.g., spear in football), play with chronic injuries, or engage in negative heath behaviors (e.g., use diuretics for weight loss or allowing themselves to be "run into the ground" for the sake of approval and image).

The negative power relationship of the coach over the athlete's self can translate into an athlete's over dependence on the coach. Athletes report that the dependence was not the result of intimidation, but rather a long-standing relationship in which the imbalance of power was dominated by an autocratic coach, and reflect regret over the extent of the dependent relationship between self and the coach (Tomlinson and Yorganci, 1997). This was especially true of young female athletes coached by men. Lenskyj (1992) notes that female athletes may be more vulnerable to sexual harassment than non athlete counterparts. While athletes spend time training rather than socializing, non athletes are developing important interpersonal skills and strategies of adolescence. This may be exacerbated by feelings that to reject a coach's behavior may result in losing favor with the coach, may leave the athlete out in the cold, out of team selections or without opportunities to train competitively (Aussie Sport Action, 1995).

The athlete who complains of harassment may also be seen as having a poor sense of humor, being uptight about innocent casual sexual comments, or failing to be able to hack the pace or be one of the boys. There may even be the subconscious belief that she does not really belong in a man's world anyway, (Aussie Sport Action, 1995).

Attempts to control a female athlete's body weight is a frequent part of the domination in male coach-female athlete relationships (Donnelly, 1993). Having to demonstrate commitment or "prove" yourself through self-destructive behavior is contrary to the goals of athletic participation.

Coaches who attempt to enhance their personal power through such a relationship should be considered abusive.

Clearly coaches need to continually be aware of the impact of the personal ties that they build with their athletes and assistant coaches. Recognizing that dual power relationships do exist allows the coach to maximize an appropriate emotional attachment within ethical limits. Openly communicating about relationship dilemmas can be the first step in dealing with the situation before it becomes harassment (Hornak and Hornak, 1993).

Sexual Harassment

The most sensitive power relationship issues deal with sexual harassment. Most of the time, sexual harassment is not founded on romantic or physical attraction between the coach and athlete, but rather a display of power. The hostile environment created by the use of sexual innuendoes of the coach or other athletes, or by sexist behaviors permitted by the coach, is not only unethical but illegal. Sexual harassment is the unwanted imposition of sexual advances, request for sexual favors and other verbal or physical conduct of a sexual nature in the context of a relationship of unequal power. This includes displaying a condescending sex-based attitude toward an individual (Women's' Sport Foundation, 1995).

The most overt type of sexual harassment called Quid pro quo ("this for that") exists when benefits are granted or withheld (starting status, camp enrollment) as a result of an athlete's willingness or refusal to submit to the sexual demands of a coach. Romantic and/or sexual behaviors between coach and athletes rarely develop into healthy, long term, mutually beneficial relationships. In the context of athletic programs, these situations lower the athlete's self-esteem and limit the ability of the athlete to develop to his or her full potential (Women's' Sport Foundation, 1995). Because of the debilitating effects that such a relationship has on the athlete and program, it should be clearly identified as unprofessional and unacceptable!

Sexual harassment law has broadened to consider a second, more covert form of harassment termed a hostile environment. A hostile environment exits when a person's conduct or work environment is permeated with "conduct [of a sexual nature that] has the purpose or effect of unreasonably interfering with an individual's work performance or creates an intimidating, hostile, or offensive working environment" (Women's' Sport Foundation, 1995,p. 2). Whether the harasser's behavior is deliberate and purposeful, or simply has the effect of creating an offensive atmosphere does not matter. In fact, a team member who witnesses repeated incidents of sexual harassment may also be considered a victim of sexual harassment (Wolohan, 1995).

Hostile behaviors are often allowed to continue as a part of social customs or tradition. Such beliefs allow the "boys-will-be-boys" attitude to be considered simple flirting or appropriate initiations to a group (Stein, 1995). Regardless of how it appears or is rationalized by tradition or customs, sexual harassment interferes with the right to receive a quality sport opportunity.

A hostile environment may be created by the following conditions or events:

- *Unwelcome and unwarranted verbal expressions of a sexual nature*—e.g., talking about the breast size of the opponents, locker room talk about sexual conquests or prowess, talking about one's clothing such as looking good in a swim suit;

- *Sexually explicit comments and or graphics*—e.g., advertisements that use sexual messages or gender demeaning photographs; or posters that over emphasize display of anatomy such as beach volleyball or bodybuilding;

- *Actions that cause the recipient discomfort or humiliation of a sexual nature*—e.g., referring to the menstrual cycle in disciplining an athlete, using obscene gestures such as whistles, cat calls, facial and hand gestures to motivate or intimidate;

- *Unwelcome use of sexually degrading language, jokes, or innuendoes*—e.g., referring to the athlete as "babe" or "honey," obscene sounds or gestures;

- *Unwelcome and inappropriate touching, patting or pinching*—e.g., hugging an athlete for longer than a few seconds, placing of the hand on the athlete's thigh while talking, contact with the face, and pats on the buttocks.

The bottom line is that actions which can not be utilized with all athletes, and which are reserved for just a few "special relationships" are probably suspect to review.

Risk Management in Regard to Sexual Harassment or Abuse of Power

It is inevitable that athletes will come to idolize their coach and that coaches will build nurturing supportive relationships with their athletes. Many youth will not disclose abuse due to fear (74%), embarrassment (60%), fear of getting into even more trouble (55%), or getting anyone else in trouble (47%). A percentage of athletes also thought that no one would believe them (46%) (Woodhouse, 1997). Coaches who acknowledge the power they have over their athletes and the multiple roles that a coach may play in the athlete's life, will be better prepared to act professionally and ethically when accusations of abuse occur.

Institutional reluctance to report cases of abuse due to a concern about making a false allegation of abuse or neglect is certainly warranted. Individual careers and reputations can be irreversibly affected by false accusations of abuse. Statistics show that 50% of cases are labeled "unfounded" or "unsubstantiated," and never go to court (Yuille, et al., 1995, as cited in Woodouse, 1997). One study in the United States showed that 92% of children accurately reported their sexual abuse, while only 8% were counted as false allegations. Among the 8%, 6% of the false allegations originated with adults, many of whom were involved in a custody dispute; the other 2% came from children who either recanted their accusations or displaced the accusation for safety reasons (Woodhouse, 1997).

The following strategy is a proactive approach to dealing with harassment:

- *Administrators should assure that each coach knows, understands, and appreciates the specific authority, responsibility and official power that accompanies a coaching position.* This should be clearly agreed upon by the administration, parents and athletes at the beginning of the season and, if applicable, be placed in a handbook to be shared by all parties.

- *The athletic administrator should take a lead role in communicating and setting the boundaries of the coach-athlete relationship, and what services or expectations may be requested between the coach and athlete.* The athletic code of conduct for coaches and athletes should be the base of this relationship.

- *Administrators should encourage coaches to explain to the athlete and athlete's parents the anticipated emotional and/or physical contact that he or she might have with the athletes.* This should be done in the normal course of explaining season plans and goals as well as implementation of these plans. Discuss and negotiate physical boundaries, such as touching during new skill development and spotting, but not in the shower. Hugging and high fives are a part of celebrating.

- *Parents, coaches and athletes should understand at the beginning of the season how disciplinary action may be taken during the course of the season as well as how due process of the athletes or coaches will be protected.* State up front that the coach will not use exercise as punishment. Early communication may prevent misunderstanding when disciplinary issues arise. Demonstrate proper planning and evaluation. It is less likely that a coach will be unaware of his or her abusive nature or a parent will perceive a behavior to be abusive if they are within the scope of pre-established standards.

- *Athletes and parents should be provided with an objective means to evaluate the coach on a regular basis.* Through the evaluation the athletes can anonymously report incidents of abuse of power before they escalate and the coach may get a more accurate perspective of how athletes perceive their relationship with the coach.

- *The athletic administrator should present his or her respective sport organization's policy on sexual harassment and procedures to implement the policy to parents, athletes and coaches.* Stopping unfounded or false rumors can save both the coach and the school's reputation. All parties should know:

  ✓ how a complaint is registered,

  ✓ what happens after a complaint is registered,

  ✓ who conducts an investigation,

  ✓ how an investigation is conducted,

  ✓ what disciplinary actions are to be taken.

There are a number of outstanding curricula for coaches' training as well as parent support materials to create a safer environment for youth sports. "Sport Safe" is an initiative of the Recreation and Sport Branch of British Columbia, Canada (1998). Information presented includes material on volunteer screening, guidelines for the coach, and how parents can get involved in preventing harassment and abuse. Another outstanding resource is the Aussie Sport Action series Don't Stand for Harassment (1995) of the Australian Sport Commission. Information on behaviors that contribute to harassment and how to make sport clubs harassment free is based on sound coaching principles and easy to use. The most extensive resource for practitioners can be located on the internet "Harassment and Abuse in Sport" of the Canadian Hockey Association (1997)—*http://harassmentinsport.com*. This site provides an extensive handbook on all aspects of preventing and reducing harassment. Contributing authors provide clear definitions, check-lists for behavior assessments, research findings, and legal issues pertinent to Canadian law.

Summary

Whether a coach's behavior is deliberate or purposeful, or simply creates an offensive atmosphere does not matter; only the outcome of the behavior is relevant in determining whether harassment has occurred. Keep in mind, an institution and administration may be held liable in hiring a coach with a history of sexual harassment (Masteralexis, 1995).

A well-developed policy on coach-athlete relationships is the first step to preventing problems, but only provides a minimum level of expected conduct. Administrators need to go one step further and indicate to the athletes, parents, and coaches that they are eager to create a positive and nurturing environment that will promote the positive benefits of sports participation. Schools and youth sport organizations owe it to their constituents to post the laws and policies against sexual harassment and inform employees and students about their rights under the laws and the grievance procedures available should these rights be violated.

While the topic of power and potential for abuse in the athletic culture seems to be a prominent theme in recent media, systematic inquiry has been primarily exploratory and narrowly focused on aberrant individual behavior. Future research needs to explore the power dynamics between coach and athlete from a wider social context, inclusive of sport culture, gender identity and institutional norms. Understanding the institutionalized nature of harassment, normalization of coach domination, player violence, and over-conformity to a patriarchal and/or macho self-assertion sport ethic, seem critical to moving toward meaningful understanding and intervention. Research should also explore motives for coach involvement as a meaningful assessment of the potential for abuse. Finally, both quantitative and qualitative accounts of abuse at all levels of sport are needed to arrive at a full understanding of the scope and severity of this issue. This will be especially challenging given the voluntary nature of most sport organizations and the political incentive to evade organizational accountability. Research techniques will need to combine qualitative techniques such as covert observations and participant interviews with theoretically based psychometrically sound instruments relative to the construct of abuse and power.

REFERENCES

1995. Don't stand for sexual harassment. *Aussie Sport Action*, 6(4), [Available on line] www.ausport.gov.au/act646.html.

Brackenridge, C.H. (1997). 'He owned me basically...' Women's experience of sexual abuse in sport. *International Review for the Sociology of Sport* 32: 115-130.

Brackenridge, C.H. (1994). Fair play or fair games? Child sexual abuse in sport organizations. *International Review for the Sociology of Sport* 29: 287-299.

Brackenridge, C. & Kirby, S. (1997). Play safe: Assessing risk of sexual abuse to elite child athletes. *International Review for the Sociology of Sport* 32: 407-418.

Brackenridge, C.H.; Summers, D.; & Woodward, D. (1995). Educating for child protection in sport. In: Lawerence, L.; Murdoch, E.; & Parker, S. (Eds.), *Professional and Development Issues in Leisure, Sport and Education*. Eastbourne, UK: Leisure Studies Association (pp. 167-190).

Carpenter, L.J. (1995). *Legal Concepts in Sport: A Primer*. Reston, VA: AAHPERD.

Coakley, J. (1993). Social dimensions of intensive training and participation in youth sports. In: Cahill, B.R. & Pearl, A.J. (Eds.), *Intensive Participation in Children's Sports*. Champaign, IL: Human Kinetics Publishers (pp. 77-94).

Donnelly, P. (1993). Problems associated with youth involvement in high-performance sport. In: Cahill, B.R. & Pearl, A.J. (Eds.), *Intensive Participation in Children's Sports*. Champaign, IL: Human Kinetics Publishers (pp. 95-126).

Findlay, H. & Corbett, R. (1997). *What is harassment? Harassment and Abuse Handbook*. Center for Sport and Law, [Available on Line] http://harassmentinsport.com/Handbook/Sec1ch2.html.

Hornak, N.J. & Hornak, J.E. (1993). Coach and player: Ethics and dangers of dual relationships. *Journal of Physical Education, Recreation and Dance* 64(3): 84-86.

Kirby, S. & Greaves, L. (1997). A forbidden game: Sexual harassment in sport. *Recherches feministes* 10: 5-33.

Lenskyj, H. (1992). Sexual harassment: Female athlete's experiences and coaches responsibilities. *Sport Science Periodical on Research and Technology in Sport* 12(6): (Special Topics B-1 [Coaching Association of Canada]).

Masteralexis, L.P. (1995). Sexual harassment and athletics: Legal and policy implications for athletic departments. *Journal of Sport and Social Issues* 19(2): 141-156.

Nelson, M.B. (1994). *The Stronger Women Get, the More Men Love Football: Sexism and the American Culture*. New York: Harcourt Brace & Company.

Sport Safe (1998). *Protecting BC's Children*. Victoria, B.C.: Recreation and Sport Branch Ministry of Small Business, Tourism and Culture, Province of British Columbia.

Sport Safe (1998). *Coach's Game Plan: Guidelines to Creating a Safer Environment*. Victoria, B.C.: Sport and Community Development Branch of British Columbia in partnership with Sport BC; Coaches Association of BC; Recreation and Sport Branch Ministry of Small Business, Tourism and Culture, Province of British Columbia.

Stein, N. (1995). The definition of sexual harassment applies to schools. In: Swisher, K. (Ed.), *What Is Sexual Harassment?* San Diego, CA: Greenhaven Press, Inc. (pp. 19-24).

Tomlinson, A. & Yorganci, I. (1997). Male coach/female athlete relations: Gender and power relations in competitive sport. *Journal of Sport and Social Issues* 21(2): 134-155.

Volkwein, K.; Schnell, F.; Sherwood, D.; & Livezey, A. (1997). Sexual harassment in sport: Perceptions and experiences of American female student-athletes. *International Review for the Sociology of Sport* 32: 283-295.

Week, D. (1994). *The Eight Essential Steps to Conflict Resolution*. New York: Tarcher/Putnam.

Wolohan, J.T. (1995). Title IX and sexual harassment of student athletes. *Journal of Physical Education, Recreation and Dance* 66(3): 52-55.

Women's Sports Foundation. (1995). *An Educational Resource Kit for Athletic Administrators: Prevention of Sexual Harassment in Athletic Settings*. East Meadow, NY: Author.

Woodhouse, P. (1997). *Abuse and Neglect*. Harassment and Abuse in Sport. Canadian Hockey Association, [Available on Line]. http://harassmentinsport.com/Handbook/Sec1ch3.html.

CHAPTER 15

Challenges for Youth in Urban Areas

Leonard W. Smith, Past President
The Skillman Foundation

INTRODUCTION

The non-school hours, and after-school programs in particular, have moved from the margins to the center of public policy discussions about how to address problems of teen violence and crime. The Carnegie Council on Adolescent Development report, entitled *A Matter of Time: Risk and Opportunity in the Out-Of-School Home* (1992), has been singularly instrumental in creating broader public awareness about how critical the non-school hours are for youth development. The report brought attention to the fact that 40 percent of young adolescents' time is discretionary. This discretionary time, most of it concentrated in the hours after the end of the school day, is when young people engage in health compromising activities and crime.

Fight Crime-Invest in Kids, a national crime prevention group, issued a report (Fox and Newman 1998) based on FBI data that the peak hours for violent juvenile crime are from 3 to 8 p.m. The report also goes on to cite numerous studies that show that quality after-school programs can help prevent crime and delinquency (Sickmund et al., 1997; Fox and Newman, 1997; Jones and Offord, 1989; Tierney et al., 1995).

This revived interest in the out-of-school hours has brought new attention to such local initiatives, such as L.A.'s BEST and the Virtual Y in New York City. Well-established, comprehensive programs such as the Beacons' Schools in New York are being replicated in communities such as Savannah, Oakland, Minneapolis and Denver. The Clinton Administration raised the issue to the level of federal policy with its 21st Century Community Learning Centers initiative, which provided $40 million in 1998 to local school districts to enhance and expand quality after-school programs. Congress has also approved $200 million-the full amount requested by the Administration for the second year of the initiative. The Flint, Michigan-based C.S. Mott Foundation has formed a collaborative partnership with the federal government in this effort, with a pledge of up to $55 million to provide technical assistance, training and support to the program and its grantees.

Another local initiative to address this issue has been the Youth Sports and Recreation Initiative in Detroit, supported by The Skillman Foundation. The initiative, launched in 1992, is a long term, comprehensive effort to increase the participation of urban youth in quality sports and recreational programs and also to increase the numbers of adults and parents involved directly with youth in these programs.

The initiative represents an attempt to address the key barriers—policy, program, infrastructure, financial and social—to improving after-school opportunities for youth in a major American city. Based on an extensive two year needs assessment, the initiative also calls for a new model for providing youth development and recreation services in an urban area,

This chapter will not only attempt to describe what happened specifically in Detroit, but also why Detroit's experience might be instructive for other urban areas, which struggle to foster positive youth development in the face of daunting odds. Although we have certainly not achieved all our aims yet, the progress—as well as the continuing challenges—have provided us with some broadly generalizable lessons about developing quality urban youth programs and bringing them to scale.

As the Skillman program officer responsible for this initiative, I have been directly involved in helping shape and guide the initiative through its planning and early implementation phases. Although this chapter draws on my experience of this process, most of the chapter is based upon the research and analysis of several independent investigators. The Foundation supported these separate studies in order to assemble detailed information about the status of recreational opportunities for youth.

The first and most important of these investigators was the Institute for the Study of Youth Sports at Michigan State University (MSU), led by Vern Seefeldt, who was also one of the principal consultants for the Carnegie Corporation's report, A Matter of Time. The MSU team conducted an initial needs assessment of youth development and sports activities in Detroit, Hamtramck and Highland Park, which was then followed up by an in-depth needs assessment (Seefeldt et al., 1994, 1995). The Citizens Research Council of Michigan, a tax policy analysis organization in Michigan, assessed the current financial and funding status of the recreation departments of the three cities (Lupher,

1996). Finally, Moore & Associates, Inc., a metro Detroit area survey and research firm, conducted a sample assessment of community use of schools policies and practices in the Detroit Public Schools (1998).

Clearly this and other initiatives to improve positive opportunities for youth in the non-school hours are essential to youth development. Community-based after-school youth programs provide opportunities for youth to learn critical life skills, such as goal setting, communication, decision-making and problem solving (Carnegie Council, 1992).

Non-School Hour Programs in Urban Areas

Nowhere is the need for quality after-school programs more evident than in America's inner cities. At the same time urban areas face serious social barriers to increasing such programs. The *City Kids Count* report (O'Hare, 1997) reported that for the largest American cities every indicator of child well-being was on average worse than for children in the nation as a whole. City children are twice as likely as suburban children to grow up in single parent family homes. They are more likely to live in poor families in neighborhoods with high concentrations of poverty. City children are also twice as likely to drop out of school. African American youth are disproportionately reflected in these figures. To make matters worse, safe havens and good programs (which can often spell the difference for a young person between a productive life or a life mired in crime or addiction) are few are far between (McLaughlin et al., 1994).

Although the needs for more quality after-school and organized recreational programs are profound in urban areas, the task of increasing these programs to sufficient scale faces daunting odds. Strained city budgets make it difficult to maintain recreation budgets, much less increase them (Seefeldt, 1995; Lupher, 1996; Rauner et al., 1994). One consequence of this is that the recreational infrastructure parks and playgrounds has deteriorated (Coleman Children and Youth Services,

1995; Seefeldt, 1995). Even successful community based youth serving agencies find it difficult to secure the resources to keep up with the demands for more services (McLaughlin et al., 1994; Seefeldt, 1995).

Despite the renewed public spotlight on after-school programs, the bulk of public dollars spent on youth are still for "specialized" services rather than "primary" services (Wynn et al., 1994). Specialized services are narrowly targeted at youth considered "at-risk," or youth in need of treatment or residential care. Such services are aimed at dealing with problems, instead of fostering youth resiliency and positive youth development. Primary services, those "activities, facilities and events provided by organizations that are part of families' familiar social world (p. 7)," such as recreation, sports, public parks, museums, libraries, culture, arts and music, still get short shrift in tight city budgets. These primary services, however, contribute to an overall quality of life in communities and provide an infrastructure that support a wide array of positive influences in a child's life.

The new interest by policymakers on after-school programs is often remains focused on the problem-preventing aspects of these programs. This occurs despite much stronger and robust research that shows that quality recreational, sports and other organized leisure activities can enhance a host of positive attributes. Among these are social skills, resiliency, academic achievement, self-esteem, career maturity and career efficacy, as well as improved overall health and fitness (Gambone and Arbreton, 1997; Eccles et al., 1993; Csikszentmihalyi, 1982).

Since the mid 1980s, a growing body of research has focused on "protective" factors in a child's environment that engender "resiliency." This refers to an ability to resist negative factors and influences that lead to delinquency, teen pregnancy and drug abuse (Benard, 1987; Benard 1992; Brewer et al., 1994; Smith et al., 1995). This research has investigated specific factors within a child's family, school, peers and community, as well as within the child him or herself (Hawkins and Catalano, 1992; Werner and Smith, 1989) that contribute to resilien-

cy. Communities where strong norms about alcohol and drug use and clear rules and boundaries about public behavior, for example, which are promoted and reinforced have lower incidence of delinquency and drug abuse. Another critical factor is the density of social networks within a community (Gabarino, 1989; Miller and Ohlin, 1985). These are the inter-personal, inter-group and inter-organizational relationships that bind a community together and build social cohesion. Such socially cohesive communities can tap into these networks—their social capital—and solve the problems and meet the challenges that occur in all communities (Coleman, 1987; Benard, 1989). Within such communities, youth find the opportunities for pro-social involvement with other youth and adults. Recreation and leisure programs serve as a prime venue for these activities (Brewer et al., 1994).

Several other policy-related issues, however, stand in the way of improving the social and physical environments for youth. These include lack of commitment to recreation and sports, lack of leadership, poorly managed public systems and low program quality (Rauner et al., 1994). Further, until sports, recreation and other organized programs in the out-of-school hours can be brought to sufficient scale, their effect will continue to be marginal (Schorr, 1988; Karoly et al., 1998).

Further, the question of how programmatically to improve the larger social-environmental context in which youth live is still largely unanswered. It is clear that urban youth, in particular, encounter an environment that is rife with risk factors, and that to affect positive change for large numbers of youth will probably require a significant change in that environment across a broad range of factors and influences. Several large-scale community wide strategies have been launched in recent years to comprehensively address these factors (Connell et al., 1995; Fulbright-Anderson et al., 1998). Some of these efforts have had promising early successes (Schorr, 1997). But the evaluation research still needs to identify how communities change and what works to change them (Fulbright-Anderson et al., 1998).

THE SKILLMAN YOUTH SPORTS AND RECREATION INITIATIVE

The Skillman Foundation is a private, independent foundation, which makes grants mostly in the metropolitan Detroit area, with a focus primarily on children and youth. As noted earlier, it launched the Youth Sports and Recreation Initiative in 1992 to involve significantly more youth, parents and mentors in sports, recreation and leisure activities in Detroit, Highland Park and Hamtramck.[1] (Hamtramck and Highland Park are two encapsulated municipalities within the city boundaries of Detroit). That initiative was announced via a concept paper in 1993. The paper stated that the goal of the initiative "will be accomplished by improving, reorganizing and expanding a wide variety of sports, recreation and youth development activities and opportunities for youth ages six to sixteen. It is important that the goal of the initiative be viewed in the context of developing children and youth to their maximum human potential. (p. 3)" The goal was to be achieved through a three phase process, beginning with a Phase I planning and needs assessment process, followed by implementation and operational phases. The needs assessment was deemed critical, since data on sports and recreation in the cities of Detroit, Highland Park or Hamtramck was scant and unreliable, especially regarding existing programs, facilities, play-fields. Little was known about the effectiveness of the known programs. Unlike specialized programs for troubled and at-risk youth in Detroit, which often have received extensive evaluation, primary programs—those which serve the general youth population—had few thorough or reliable evaluations.

The need for such an initiative was articulated not only by such documents as the Carnegie Council's watershed report, *A Matter of Time*, but also by many local reports and experts. These

groups all cited the drastic loss of recreational and other leisure time activities (University Cultural Center and Zachary Associates, 1991; United Community Services, 1987).

Several specific objectives were set forth in the concept paper:

- Improve access to services and activities and availability of quality programs.

- Increase diversity of recreational offerings.

- Support existing providers and develop new providers

- Provide training and technical assistance to improve program quality.

- Increase numbers of youth in a wide variety of activities.

- Increase numbers of parents and adults in youth sports and recreation.

- Increase awareness of recreation and youth development as critical public issues.

From the outset Skillman envisioned a long term, comprehensive effort to improve opportunities for positive leisure, recreational and other youth development activities. The initiative was not to be narrowly focused on individual programs, but simultaneously moving on several fronts, from improving infrastructure to building grassroots and nonprofit capacity. This was not merely an effort to support a number of model or demonstration programs. From the outset what was envisioned was to bring these programs to scale and laying the ground for their long-term sustainability.

The Skillman Foundation saw the initiative as part of a trio of major initiatives, which dovetailed with each other to improve the overall environment for children. The other two initiatives were major school reform initiatives—Comer Schools and

---

[1] The title for the initiative suggests a sports-oriented effort, but the initiative actually has a much broader scope. The initiative seeks to increase the quantity and quality of positive youth development activities for youth during the non-school hours. These activities include not only sports and recreation, but cultural and arts, academic enrichment, social skills programs, community service, job training and preparation and other activities that contribute to youth development. There was considerable discussion about what to call the initiative, given all that it was meant to address. The decision to use "youth sports and recreation" was based on a sense that the broader public could relate to and easily understand this language and also on the original inspiration for initiative—that the empty play-fields of the city were the sign of something terribly wrong.

Families and Schools of the 21st Century—and the Parenting Matters Initiative.[2] Each of the three initiatives was directed at improving a major environment affecting the development of children and youth: family, school and community. The Parenting Matters Initiative seeks to improve parenting skills of families in Detroit and increase the overall awareness of how good parenting affects child development. The Foundation's education initiatives are comprehensive, whole-school reform efforts, aimed at improving the learning environment for children in the Detroit Public Schools.

Needs Assessment

Phase I of the Initiative was devoted to gathering detailed information about youth and youth participation in sports, recreation and other youth development activities. This was a task that clearly required some expert help, since there was little research to help Skillman determine methodologically how to proceed (Carnegie Council on Adolescent Development, 1992). Through a Request for Proposal process Skillman selected the Institute for the Study of Youth Sports at Michigan State University (MSU), to conduct the assessment. The MSU team was charged to:

- Assess the demography of youth 6-16 and their families in the target area;

- Identify and assess needs, including facilities, access, providers, youth and adult involvement, outreach;

- Assess the environment for improving, reorganizing and expanding programs and activities, including barriers to improvements;

- Make recommendations for meeting needs, including structure, programs and activities; and

- Present an action plan for implementing the recommendations.

Skillman staff also thought it critical that the needs assessment process be guided by local government, civic, community and church leaders, as well as by both professionals and volunteers involved in youth and recreational services.

A Recreation Advisory Committee was formed, which included 58 individuals representing public recreation departments, public and private schools, youth serving agencies, major civic organizations, youth sports associations as well as professional sports teams, a commercial provider of recreation, faith-based organizations, community groups, health and social service agencies, universities and foundations. There were several reasons why convening such a large, representative group was crucial for the initiative. The group included the key providers of recreational and leisure services, who understood the challenges and needs in the city. Ultimately, if the initiative was to have legitimacy within the community, then the community needed to be genuinely involved in the process of developing and shaping the initiative. Looking beyond the needs assessment itself, Skillman realized that its resources alone could neither sustain the initiative over time nor bring the effort to sufficient scale to make a city-wide impact. The future of such an initiative would depend upon marshalling untapped citizen and parent volunteers, influencing public policy and allocation of funds for recreation and youth services, enlisting community leadership to advocate for youth development and bringing other partners and resources to the table.

For three months the MSU project team interviewed the 58 RAC members. Members were questioned specifically on various aspects of non-school youth sports and recreation programs, including the roles programs play in the lives of youth, what makes particular programs successful, ideas for new programs and the barriers to provision of quality programs.

---

[2] The Comer Schools and Family Initiative is a ten year school reform initiative in the Detroit Public Schools, based upon the successful School Development Model of James Comer of Yale University. The Schools of the 21st Century is a $60 million school reform effort aimed at improving the Detroit Public Schools at three separate levels: student-teacher interaction, local school - central administration interaction and community involvement. It has received one of several national Annenberg Challenge grants. The Parenting Matters Initiative is a multi-year effort aimed at promoting good parenting practices through parent education, resource and referral and social marketing.

The MSU team also gathered information from other sectors of the community, The team conducted a series of sample written surveys of public and private schools in the target communities, commercial and non-profit providers of recreational programs, community recreation centers, churches and businesses. The process included conducting 15 focus groups with children and youth, program providers and community leaders on how community residents viewed non-school hours programming. The focus groups were conducted between November 1993 and April 1994. The MSU team also made twelve site visits at neighborhood, community, volunteer, social service and private programs. The agencies visited represented a broad cross-section of the diverse array of youth serving organizations in the tri-city area.

Findings: Demographics

The changes in the population of the city over the past several decades have been profound. Detroit is a city of roughly one million people (1,028,000 according to the 1990 U.S. Census). This is about 44 percent fewer people than resided in the city in 1950. Although many cities of the industrialized "rustbelt" regions of the country have lost population, the decline in Detroit has been steeper (Neithercut, 1993).

The numbers of youth in the city have also declined dramatically. In the last 20 years alone the numbers of youth have dropped from 494,000 in 1970 to 302,000 in 1990 (U.S. Census). Of the 302,000 children and youth, an estimated 184,000 are between the ages of 6-16. These youth represent about 17.3% of the population of Detroit, 14.2% of the population of Hamtramck and 16.3% of the population of Highland Park.

Youth by Race/Ethnicity

Much of the population loss, although not entirely, is due to exodus of whites from the city. The result is that Detroit now is a city that is over 77% African American. The percentages are even higher for youth. In Detroit over 81% of youth, ages 6-16 are African American, while Highland Park is 97.8% African American. Hamtramck—from its origins a destination for immigrants from Poland and Eastern Europe—still is predominantly Caucasian at 77.7% of the population.

Youth by Gender

The percentage of males, ages 6-16, in the tri-city area is slightly over half the population (average of 50.97% for Detroit, Hamtramck and Highland Park). These percentages roughly mirror statistics for the rest of the country. But to be a young African American male carries a particular risk. Nationally, homicide is the leading cause of death among 15-30 year old African American males. In Michigan in 1991, 66% of all deaths for 15-24 year old males occurred in Detroit (Unpublished data, Statistical Services, Michigan Department of Public Health, 1992).

Findings: Families and Poverty

Of Detroit households with children, 56.4% are headed by single females. The percentage of households headed by females is even higher in Highland Park (71 %). In Hamtramck the majority of households with children (52.8%) are married couples, but the percentage of single female headed households is still high (41%).

Detroit has the worst rate of childhood poverty rate of the nation's ten largest cities (46.6%). Most of Detroit's poorest children live in households headed by a single female (82.6%), The rates for Highland Park and Hamtramck are comparable (54.7% and 44% respectively).

For those familiar with data on the urban poor and underclass these statistics are not surprising. It is just that in Detroit the statistics are generally much worse in many categories. The implications for recreation and positive after-school programming are profound. Youth are not only walking into recreation centers and onto playgrounds with more needs, there are fewer adults, especially adult men, to provide supervision, guidance and coaching. The majority of youth come from homes without the constant presence of a father. In many communities, fathers and other adult men traditionally provide the bulk of the volunteer leadership for organized sports. In Detroit it is difficult even to find adequate professional help. During the course of the Initiative, Skillman staff frequently heard complaints from Detroit Recreation Department officials about the difficulties of finding enough competent play-leaders who did not test positively for drugs.

Findings: The Role of Public Recreation

However, the most serious problem confronting the Detroit Recreation Department was not finding enough play-leaders. Although recently rejuvenated with new leadership following the election of a new mayor, the department had already suffered years of steep budget cuts. The study conducted by the Citizens Research Council of Michigan, funded by the Skillman Foundation, estimated that the expenditures for recreation within the department had decreased by over $1 million from 1990 to 1994 (Lupher, 1996). But the Council's investigators could not determine the exact amounts spent for recreation and for youth recreation in particular, because of inadequate record-keeping and cost accounting methods by the department.

The MSU survey of public recreation centers also revealed that most centers required immediate and extensive attention regarding their general maintenance (1995). Only one of the 33 centers reported that conditions were good. Most of the centers reported leaking roofs, loosening plaster or missing windows. Equipment was in generally poor condition.

Many of the 800 parks, play-fields and play-lots in Detroit, Hamtramck and Highland Park were also poorly maintained and in need of major refurbishment. Much of the playground equipment, for example, was built for an earlier time, and rarely met current safety standards. Uncut grass left baseball and football fields unplayable. Not only unplayable, but unsightly too, due to copious litter.

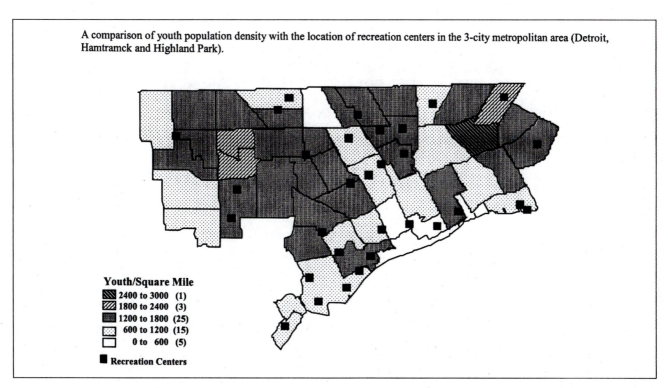

A comparison of youth population density with the location of recreation centers in the 3-city metropolitan area (Detroit, Hamtramck and Highland Park).

Youth/Square Mile
2400 to 3000 (1)
1800 to 2400 (3)
1200 to 1800 (25)
600 to 1200 (15)
0 to 600 (5)
■ Recreation Centers

Figure 1. A comparison of youth population density with the location of recreation centers in the 3-city metropolitan area (Detroit, Hamtramck and Highland Park).

The MSU team compared the current distribution of the youth population in the tri-city area with the availability of recreation centers, using GIS (geographic information systems) technology. The geo-coded mapping showed that there was a serious mismatch in the placement of the centers and areas of the cities with the highest concentrations of youth (see Figure 1). Geo-coding was not only useful in this particular instance, but was an extremely important tool in visually displaying such key information as placement of community based programs, school facilities, churches and many other important community assets.

Interviews with community residents, leaders and youth also surfaced this key issue: the loss of confidence in the Detroit Recreation Department to deliver services that the community itself desires. This issue manifested itself in two ways: first, the Department was simply unable to perform roles expected by the community—such as cutting grass on play-fields or fixing faulty equipment in centers—and secondly, by offering programs without input and feedback from community residents. The MSU needs assessment report was critical of this "top-down" approach, and proposed a more community-based approach to recreational services. Such an approach would involve more community participation, both at the planning and also programmatic stages. It also would generate greater collaboration with neighborhood groups and organizations that may be already providing some form of recreation.

Findings: Schools

Schools may be perhaps the most important community asset as far as children and youth go. They are the places not only where children go to get educated, they also serve as sites for latchkey and other after-school activities. The model after-school programs cited earlier in this chapter—Beacons, L.A.'s BEST—are all school-based. Schools potentially can play a critical role in providing safe havens for children in a city such as Detroit, where recreation centers are not located in areas of highest concentrations of youth.

With this in mind the MSU team developed an extensive survey instrument, which was distributed to every public and private school in the target area. The instrument asked each school to answer questions regarding facilities, types of programs offered, participation rates of youth, program leadership and community resources in the vicinity of the school. With the help of a retired high school principal who served as a consultant, the team was able to garner a 93% rate of return of the surveys from the Detroit Public Schools and 100% return from both Hamtramck and Highland Park Schools. Private school retrieval was the lowest at 47%.

The primary finding of the survey was that a relatively small number of youth participated in after-school programs. A little more than one-third (about 77,500) of children, ages 6-16, were involved in these programs. But this number does not represent an unduplicated count, hence the actual participation was probably much lower. The survey also revealed wide variances in the number of programs offered in different regions of city. One region offered 256 activities, involving 26,649 participants, while another region, with a similar sized youth population, had only 115 activities, involving 2,998 participants almost a ten-fold difference.

Through focus groups of school and community representatives the MSU team uncovered reasons why school facilities were not more frequently used. The key issue here was community use of schools. One hypothesis considered by MSU was that schools would more likely be open for programming in the after-school hours, if they were more accessible to community groups for use. From the focus groups MSU heard that the inability to pay the cost of supportive services, including custodial care, utilities and engineering was the primary reason (27.4%) schools were not used more. School principals, on the other hand, stated that a primary reason was the incompatibility of the building with the intended purpose (20%). Other reasons given by principals were an inability to provide supervision (14.9%) and concerns involving the safety of the potential users (11.8%). A little over 10% of the principals also stated that no one requested to use the building.

Findings: Non-profit Organizations

Neighborhood organizations, usually small non-profit and church-related agencies, often serve not only as safe havens for children in poor, inner city communities, but also places where they find the support and guidance to develop their best selves. (see McLaughlin et al., 1994; Cahill et al., 1993; Gainbone and Arbreton, 1997). These organizations offer programs that teach life skills, such as goal setting and negotiation; they provide opportunities for community service and to develop special interests and nurture talents; they give children an opportunity to engage in constructive, organized activities, such as sports (Carnegie Council on Adolescent Development, 1992).

An MSU look at community agencies revealed that approximately 465 organizations in the tri-city area were providing some form of youth programming. MSU sent an initial survey to randomly selected organizations in 1993 during the first phase needs assessment (54 responses). This was followed by the in-depth survey in 1995, which had 61 responses.

The survey responses showed that these groups offer a comprehensive array of programs, including organized sports and recreation, educational, life skills, culture and arts, aquatics, special events (e.g. field trips) and informal recreation. 43ne of the issues raised by the MSU team, however, was the lack of coordination among the agencies. The team found duplication of services in some areas or gaps in service, "turf protection," lack of focus on areas of greatest need and an ineffective utilization of scarce resources. The Detroit Recreation Department, weakened by budget cuts and loss of staff, was unable to provide coordination or even to ensure that baseball diamonds or football fields would be ready for play by community groups.

These agencies frequently struggle to keep afloat, often competing for these scarce resources. Securing adequate funding is an ongoing effort, None reported that they received adequate funding for their programs. Community groups also must rely more heavily on volunteers. Although volunteers are a valuable asset for youth, they are a "mixed blessing" (to borrow a quote from McLaughlin et al., 1994). They must be recruited, screened, trained, managed and motivated.

Common complaints raised by the community, not only about private agency programs, but also about public sector ones, were centered around the main issue of access: program times, transportation and safety. The MSU team found that there were few programs offered on weekends. The most frequently mentioned barrier was the absence of safe and reliable transportation. Children often reported feeling unsafe traveling to and from recreation programs and mentioned that their parents often had to accompany them. Children and parents described parks as being particularly dangerous because of shootings.

Findings: Faith-Based Organizations

In addition to the 465 community based agencies operating in Detroit, Hamtramck and Highland Park, the researchers counted 871 religious organizations. Their original conjecture was that these organizations—which have historically played a powerful role in African American communities—would also be playing an important role in youth development activities. But of the 871 surveys sent in the first phase of the needs assessment to churches and other faith based organizations, only 27 were returned. The second phase needs assessment of churches was only slightly more successful: 44 organizations responded to the questionnaire.

MSU researchers were able, however, to gather information from third party sources, principally members of the local school community organizations. ("LSCOs" are affiliated with most schools in the Detroit Public Schools system and operate somewhat like Parent Teacher Associations do in other districts). Through the input of LSCO members and school principals, 358 programs in sports, recreation and other youth development offered by faith based organizations were identified.

Although it was possible that there were more programs being offered by religious organizations, the researchers concluded that this was not likely and that churches were probably providing much less youth programming than originally estimated. At the same time, the MSU report highlighted churches as an area of opportunity for expanding the number and distribution of youth programs.

Findings: Organized Sports

The needs assessment also included surveys of organized sports programs, including for-profit commercial providers. The first phase needs assessment yielded a broad picture of organized sports. Agencies reported that funding, facilities and equipment were the major barriers to greater youth participation. The second in-depth needs assessment provided more detail about organized sports programs.

A survey of 44 nonprofit providers showed that programs were available in baseball, basketball, bowling, boxing, cheerleading, figure skating, floor hockey, football, golf, gymnastics, ice hockey, martial arts, skiing, soccer, softball, swimming, track and field and volleyball. In total agencies reported that 20,669 youth were involved in 18 sports, with basketball (N = 5394) and baseball (N = 5219) boasting the highest participation. Male participation was 7,750 and female participation was 4,182.

Recreation departments in Detroit, Hamtramck and Highland Park reported much lower participation numbers. The total number of participants in public recreation programs was 6,257. The number of males participating in these programs was almost three times as much as females (although departments' records frequently did not record gender).

Based on its findings, the MSU team concluded that:

- Private, not-for-profit programs providers support programs in most sports and reach more athletes than programs sponsored by public and private schools and public recreation departments.

- Recreation departments sponsor the most programs but reach relatively fewer youth.

- School-based programs reached the highest average number of athletes.

- Team sports were most common—with traditional sports of baseball, basketball, football and softball dominating.

- Life-long sports (such as swimming, tennis or martial arts) involved barely 16% of the youth.

Findings: Youth Participation

Overall, the results of the needs assessment indicated that the participation of children and youth in organized and supervised out-of school hours programs was relatively low. Exact numbers were hard to come by, given the inconsistent or inadequate record keeping of both public and private agencies. The MSU team estimated that about a third of youth in the tri-city area are involved in sports, recreation and other youth development activities offered by public recreation, private non-profits, community groups and religious organizations.

The unresolved challenge of the overall needs assessment was gathering actual participation data. The largest public provider of services, the Detroit Recreation Department, frequently was unable to provide participation data for its programs and recreation center usage. The survey responses from non-profits and from faith-based organizations, in particular, were disappointing. In retrospect, had the MSU researchers been able to recruit one or more individuals with entrée to the city's churches—as they did with the Detroit Public Schools—they might have had better success. The researchers' conjecture, however, that churches were not providing as many youth recreational programs as originally estimated has so far not been proven incorrect. Since the release of the needs assessment

PROGRAMS, SERVICES AND FACILITIES

- Design programs to meet the needs of all children in the community, increase diversity of programming, and emphasize the comprehensive development of youth and the need to target those who have been under-served.

- Improve safety at neighborhood and program facilities and sites,

- Increase accessibility to programming through increasing availability of transportation and convenient program times.

- Increase opportunities for children and youth to participate in organized sports and recreation activities.

- Locate programs and services in neighborhoods with high concentrations of youth and expand the number of facilities and sites in areas that are not currently served by increasing the use of school and religious facilities for after-school activities, Promote establishment of multi-service centers and programs.

- Improve the condition and maintenance of public recreation facilities and sites.

FUNDING & RESOURCES

- Increase fiscal resources for public and private youth sports and recreation programs and facilities.

IMPLEMENTATION, COOPERATION & COORDINATION

- Establish a broad-based public/private organization as the mechanism to provide leadership in implementing the Skillman Youth Sports & Recreation Initiative recommendations and oversee the planning, development, coordination, maintenance and evaluation of youth sports and recreation programs.

COMMUNITY INVOLVEMENT

- Shift from a "top-down" model to a model involving community-based planning, implementation and evaluation of programs and redefine the roles and responsibility of public and private providers and professionals and volunteers in the delivery of programs and services.

- Increase the involvement of families and citizens as volunteers and mentors in the planning, management and delivery of programs and services. Support and encourage volunteers through professional assistance and training to improve program quality.

PLANNING, EVALUATION & PROFESSIONALISM

- Develop a future plan for sports and recreation utilizing standards for national accreditation as a guide, where appropriate.

- Assess and evaluate sports and recreation programs on an ongoing basis.

- Establish a computer-based Management Information System for public recreation departments to facilitate communication among recreation departments, centers and private youth-serving agencies that may wish to be linked to the information system.

- Assist professional staff to adapt to new roles and responsibilities and program models.

PUBLIC AWARENESS & ADVOCACY

- Educate policymakers and the general public about the importance of youth sports and recreation in the positive development of youth and the prevention of delinquency, crime, educational underachievement, substance abuse and teenage pregnancy

Table 1: Recommendations of *Re-creating Recreation in Detroit, Hamtramck and Highland Park* (1995) to Improve Youth Sports and Recreation Services.

in 1995, the overwhelming majority of programs seeking funding from Skillman or from intermediary organizations which re-grant its dollars have come from public recreation, non-profit youth serving agencies and emerging, grassroots organizations.

Recommendations and Action Plans for the Initiative

The recommendations and action plans for the Skillman initiative were finalized together by the MSU team and Skillman staff (see Table 1). These, together with a summary of the MSU needs assessment, were published by Skillman in 1995 in a report entitled, *Re-creating Recreation* in Detroit, Hamtramck and Highland Park. The recommendations and action plans of the report provide the framework and foundation of the Skillman Youth Sports and Recreation Initiative. The underlying premise upon which the recommendations themselves rest is that the out-of-school hours represent a time of risk and opportunity for children and youth. Increasing opportunities for positive, supervised and constructive activities during this period can foster positive youth development and reduce incidence of health compromising behaviors. The report also calls for the establishment of a coordinating mechanism—the Youth Sports and Recreation Commission—as the key to increasing these opportunities.

The Commission was viewed as an integral component of the entire Skillman initiative. It would be the entity that would drive the implementation of the recommendations of *Re-creating Recreation*. The needs assessment revealed that the whole arena of youth development and recreation lacked the kind of broad public/private leadership demanded to foster greater cooperation and coordination among the public recreation departments and 465 community groups in the tri-city area. The services provided by tri-city organizations were fragmented, sometimes overlapping and weak in reaching certain groups. This was especially true for girls and children with special needs. Smaller, grassroots organizations lacked organizational capacity to sustain programs and were in need of much technical assistance and training. A strong, unified voice was also clearly needed to advocate for greater citizen involvement in and increased public and private resources for youth development. Although the MSU report emphasized the importance of the potential leadership role of public recreation, it recommended that a commission be established to bridge the gaps between public and private providers and also to bring local community groups into the process of community planning.

During late 1994 and early 1995 the Foundation set in motion the process to create such a body from the ground up. Through a consultative process that included the Detroit Mayor's office, it was determined that the commissioners of the new body would be appointees of the mayors of Detroit, Hamtramck and Highland Park. The Commission itself, however, legally would be a 501(c) (3) non-profit organization.

In the fall of 1995 the Commission was officially established with 15 members. An executive, with many years of experience at the YMCA, was hired as executive director.

The Commission and its staff quickly found that their plate was already filled to the brim. There were already several important projects under way that would require the Commission's leadership and involvement. These are briefly summarized:

1. Community Use of Schools Task Force (CUSTF)

The CUSTF, convened by Skillman in 1995, was a sixteen-member body, representing the Detroit Public Schools, the City of Detroit and several community youth serving agencies. The Task Force's charge was to:

- Determine the current status of the community use of schools, based on the MSU survey data;

- Identify issues involved in community use of schools that inhibit such use; and

- Explore and recommend ways to increase and

improve community use of schools; and develop a realistic plan for implementing the recommendations.

The CUSTF is seeking to improve access to schools for community and nonprofit organizations that serve youth. The Task Force has unearthed several major obstacles to community use of schools and sent its recommendations to the Detroit Board of Education (cf. Table 2). The Commission helps to staff this continuing effort.

2. Pistons-Palace Foundation's Partnership Program to Adopt and Renovate Parks for Kids or P.A.R.K. Program.

The Pistons-Palace Foundation, which is the corporate giving arm of the Detroit Pistons Professional Basketball team, developed the program in collaboration with the Detroit Mayor's office. The program, originally an $8 million, is now an $11 million, effort to refurbish and renovate 33 public playgrounds and parks in the city. Foundations, corporations and other businesses were approached for contributions.

In the early stages of the initiative the Pistons-Palace Foundation and its partners determined that the program would not only focus on capital improvements, but also on community building. No park would be selected unless there was a strong local base of community support. Community residents, grass-roots community organizations and churches would have to commit to helping maintain the parks and also help plan and operate programs at the parks. The Commission has partnered with the Pistons-Palace Foundation in the community building component of the P.A.R.K. program.

3. The Re-Capitalization of Recreation Centers project.

This is a joint funder collaborative involving the City of Detroit, W.K. Kellogg, Kresge and Skillman foundations. This initiative is applying $11 million towards the renovation of four recreation centers in Detroit. The Youth Sports & Recreation Commission was handed the responsibility of both fiscal and construction management of the re-capitalization project to the Commission.

4. The Tri-Cities Sports Coalition.

The Commission organized this coalition to improve coordination among teams and leagues involved in diamond sports (baseball, softball and T-ball) and soccer. The coalition has been instrumental in improving scheduling of play-fields with the Detroit Recreation Department and coordinating activities between different leagues. It has also helped create and organize annual, citywide baseball and soccer tournaments.

Each of these four efforts addresses one or more of the recommendations of the report, *Re-creating Recreation*. The Community Use of Schools Task Force seeks to improve access to programs (recommendation #3) and increase the number of after-school programs (#5). The P.A.R.K. program and Re-Capitalization of Recreation Centers project are aimed at improving recreational infrastructure (#6), as well as increase citizen involvement in recreation (#10). The Tri-Cities Sports Coalition also seeks to increase volunteerism (# 1O) and to increase opportunities for organized sports (#4). What is common in all these efforts is that they involve collaborative planning and intensive community involvement. The Commission has been instrumental in helping to organize and staff these activities. But what has given each of these efforts momentum and energy has been the enthusiasm and responsiveness of the other partners.

Other Commission Projects: Grants and Funding

Besides acting as a coordinator, the Commission also acts as a funding resource, both directly and indirectly. As a direct funding source, it provides small grants to community organizations for youth programming in the out-of-school hours. The grants are flexible and are intended to cover a wide range of needs, from equipment and minor capital needs to helping defray program staff expenses. As an indirect source, the Commission acts as an advocate and liaison with

Public Policy

- The school community partners should adopt a policy statement emphasizing the importance of positive youth development, recreation, family support and similar preventive programs as well as the important roles the schools and community play in meeting these program needs.

- DPS and its stakeholders should adopt a policy statement that the community's use of schools during non-school hours is important to the entire community and is a component of "school day."

Access, Operation and Management

- Develop system-wide "guiding principles" for schools and groups to use schools based on successful after-school programs.

- Develop model compacts or user agreements.

- Develop a comprehensive model community use of schools program in one or more schools.

- Develop additional latch-key programs involving parent/adult volunteers from community.

- Explore use of insurance pool that might be available to non-profits and community groups to reduce liability concerns.

- Explore and revise current DPS policies and procedures and make process for community use more "user friendly."

Funding and Costs

- "Piggy-back" concurrent use of schools.

- Assess and make public current funding sources for community use of schools and seek additional resources.

- Assess cost components of community use of schools and seek ways to reduce costs.

Training and Public Awareness

- Inform public through media and forums about importance of after-school programs, extension of school day, guiding principles and community use of schools procedures.

- Train principals, administrators and teachers about community use of schools.

- Involve LSCOs and parents in public information, advocacy and coordination of community use of schools.

- Explore use of ombudsman to assist community.

Table 2: Community Use of Schools Task Force Recommendations

corporate and professional sports funders seeking opportunities to invest in youth programming. The Commission, for example, has worked with Major League Baseball's RBI or Reviving Baseball in Inner Cities program and with the World Cup Host Committee in diverting funds to youth sports.

Other Commission Projects: Technical Assistance

In 1997 the Commission joined with New Detroit, Inc.—one of the city's major civic organizations—and Skillman to establish the Community Grants and Assistance Partnership. New Detroit was invited as a partner, due to its long history of providing technical assistance to grassroots organizations. The Partnership seeks to coordinate technical assistance and training opportunities for these organizations, through workshops, consultants and linking to other technical assistance providers. The need for such a partnership became apparent as the Commission began to fund these small community-based groups, which frequently needed help with grant-writing, program development, evaluation and financial reporting.

Other Commission Projects: Summer Youth Employment

The Commission provides grants to local public and private, non-profit groups grants to provide employment, job-preparation and leadership training for youth during the summer months. This program was initially developed in response to cutbacks in the federal summer jobs funds under the Job Training and Partnership Act (JTPA). But its scope has broadened to support more comprehensive work-readiness, community-service programs that seek to prepare youth for future careers and work.

MEETING THE CHALLENGES OF REPLICATION (SCALE), SUSTAINABILITY AND QUALITY

In the fifth year of implementation the Youth Sports and Recreation Initiative and the Commission have clearly begun to make noticeable changes in Detroit,

Hamtramck and Highland Park. Most obvious, perhaps, are the physical changes at city parks and recreation centers. But more difficult to measure are the human d environmental changes needed to "re-create" recreation in Detroit. An outside evaluation of the initiative is currently in progress to attempt to assess the true impact of these changes.

A Stakeholder Interview Report (Moore and Brown, 1998), an initial assessment of the initiative's progress, notes that many challenges still confront the Initiative. Some of the biggest obstacles are the two major public institutions in Detroit affecting the lives of children: the Detroit Public Schools and the Detroit Recreation Department. Central to Skillman's strategy is a partnership with the Detroit Public Schools to replicate quality, comprehensive after-school programs throughout the district. But the work of the Community Use of Schools Task Force has revealed the numerous barriers to this effort. What has become clear through the process of investigating these barriers is that they are system-wide, embedded in the culture and practice of the district, intertwined with contract issues and often determined by the priorities of the local school principal. Currently, Skillman is involved with members of the district and with leaders from local civic, governmental and community organizations to develop a plan that will not only keep schools open but leverage both public and private funds. This coalition also will facilitate the involvement of community groups in the operations of after-school programs.

The MSU report underlined the important role that public recreation departments can and must make to restore recreation in the city. With fewer resources, however, public recreation is faced with the challenge of trying to maintain a crumbling infrastructure, provide programs to low-income children and families at little or no cost and try to coordinate its programming with the needs and wishes of community residents and youth serving organizations. The Detroit Recreation Department, for example, has historically not coordinated its efforts with community groups. Both the PARK program and Re-Capitalization of Recreation Centers project mentioned earlier are both experiments in a new form of public/private cooperation in recreation. Both programs are seeking to develop a model for future infrastructure improvements to be carried out by the department. But a first year assessment of the Re-capitalization project (Social Program Evaluators and Consultants, Inc., 1999) indicated numerous bureaucratic and personnel barriers within the Recreation Department to accommodating system reforming change.

Without further fundamental change in these two institutions it will be nearly impossible to achieve the overall challenges of scale and sustainability. There is simply not enough capacity in community and faith based organizations to serve the 180,000 children and youth in the tri-cities areas.

Convincing lawmakers, civic leaders and the public that recreation and after-school programs should be considered primary public sector responsibilities, instead of marginal, is one of main objectives of the Skillman initiative. Developing an explicit advocacy plan to move public will in this direction is a step that at the moment lies in the future. The publication of the Re-creating Recreation report itself was a communication event, intended to build a case among community leaders and policy-makers for after-school and other recreational programs. Research and evaluation studies such as this will continue to play an important part in the overall communication strategy.

Skillman also is seeking to play a larger role as a public advocate and champion for children and youth in general. Collaboration with other funders, public and private, is also a means to moving an agenda for children. Skillman's role, for example, in a funders collaboration on community development is helping increase community development organization's roles in providing after-school programs. Similarly, its involvement in a major school reform collaboration is helping to ensure that after-school programs are included in school improvement plans.

Another serious challenge for the initiative is the capacity of neighborhood nonprofit organizations to carry out and sustain quality programs for youth. These organizations are not only constantly in need of more funding, they frequently need considerable technical assistance in areas such as board and staff development, fiscal and program management, volunteer recruitment and training, proposal writing, evaluation and computer technology. Furthermore, there are few sources or providers of technical assistance available for these organizations. The Community Grants and Assistance Partnership, which was mentioned earlier as a Commission project, was created to address these needs.

Ultimately, much of the success of the initiative will depend on the response of the community. As Re-creating Recreation states in its recommendations (The Skillman Foundation, 1995): "Significantly greater numbers of volunteers must be involved in planning, conducting, and evaluating programs and services if community based programming is to have credibility, especially since significantly reduced budgets for public recreation has resulted in reduced services, programs and maintenance." Recruiting and training more volunteers, however, faces considerable obstacles. The MSU needs assessment pointed out that the changes in family composition, the high mortality rate of young African American men, the concentration of poverty in many neighborhoods present daunting challenges to raising the number of volunteers for youth. Even in less distressed communities, as a recent edition of the Search Institute periodical, Assets (Kimball-Baker and Roehlkepartain, 1998), observed, finding good and willing volunteers is often difficult. One of the promising signs in Detroit, as well as in many other cities, is that there is a newfound zeal among faith based organizations to rouse their congregations to work with youth. Community service initiatives, such as AmeriCorps, also are helping to generate grassroots voluntarism.

Skillman has recently approved grants to the Commission to organize local community advisory groups to support programming and maintenance at parks and recreation centers, and to Wayne State University in Detroit to develop a coaching training program for community volunteers.

These most recent grants highlight the third critical challenge for the Initiative: quality. The MSU report has revealed that a significant number of youth in Detroit are not involved in supervised and organized after-school programs. Most of the effort in the first five years of implementation has been directed at increasing the participation levels of youth by increasing program offerings and improving access. Much work has also been expended in laying the foundations for systemic change—particularly in the schools—for large scale expansion of after school programs. But such program expansion cannot be at the cost of program quality (Danish, 1997). This means that programs not only are research based, but have trained program leaders. The success of programs depends upon quality of the staff or volunteers. These are staff who are not only property trained, but who come with the requisite attributes of working with youth, especially at-risk youth (McLaughlin et al., 1994). Poorly implemented programs and unwelcoming staff are prime causes for under-utilization of programs (Rauner et al., 1994). Programs must be responsive to the needs and wants of young adolescents, if they are to attract them (Carnegie Council on Adolescent Development, 1992). Programs must also be of sufficient intensity to affect necessary changes in adolescents. Programs too frequently, for example, do not offer youth opportunity to contribute and be of service, a critical component of healthy youth development (Carnegie Council on Adolescent Development, 1992). Training and technical assistance will clearly have to play a major role for the initiative as it seeks to build the capacity of local groups and organizations to deliver services for youth.

LESSONS LEARNED

Some of the key lessons learned thus far in the initiative are:

- *Providing positive leisure time activities for children and youth in sufficient enough scale will require much greater collaboration, cooperation and coordination among public,* *private non-profit and community groups than ever before.* A corollary to this is that public and private sector agencies will have to learn how to operate differently than they have in the past. This will mean, for example, cooperative planning efforts and willingness to sacrifice turf. It will also mean jettisoning old ideas.

- *After-school programs and youth sports are a critical component of building caring communities for children and youth, but they are only a part.* Resiliency research presents increasingly convincing evidence that children develop best when they are enveloped in protective factors in all domains of their lives, especially home, school, peers and community. The best after school programs cannot by themselves overcome drug abusing parents and dysfunctional schools. But these after-school programs can be even more effective if they can be linked to school reform and family support initiatives.

- *Two of the most serious obstacles to increased participation in after-school activities remain the lack of transportation and fears about safety.* The quality of public transportation, of course, is different from city to city. Detroit, the motor capital of the world, has long relied on the automobile as the dominant mode of transportation. As a result, public transportation has suffered. This situation is unlikely to change. Creating recreational opportunities in nearby schools, parks and other sites will help alleviate some of the travel problems. This will address some of the safety issues as well. But the issue of safety will also need to be squarely addressed. Recreation providers, youth serving agencies and neighborhood groups must forge stronger partnerships with law enforcement to increase safety around recreational sites and programs. Law enforcement must also increase its efforts to reduce firearm violence. The prevalence of guns on city streets has radically changed the nature of urban violence (Canada, 1995; Marshall and Wheeler, 1996).

EPILOGUE

One of the things I have frequently heard throughout the entire process of helping get this initiative on track are the stories from people from every walk of life, about how important non-school hour activities were to their development as children and adolescents. More significantly, each person reminisced how much of these programs were simply taken for granted. They were deeply woven into the fabric of the community. The Foundation's own trustees had their own stories to share. Indeed, from the beginning, this initiative seems to have been one that proceeded from the heart. Although the release of *A Matter of Time* virtually coincided with the inauguration of the Skillman initiative, this was simply fortuitous. The empty play-fields and broken playground equipment in the city of Detroit had been evidence enough that something needed to be done.

One of the very hopeful signs for the future of the initiative is that better recreational opportunities is an issue that residents of Detroit—from young to old—have embraced. Policy-makers and community and civic leaders have also become increasingly persuaded that improving the environment for children during the non-school hours is critical, and probably cost effective.

This is not a matter of bringing back the "good old days." This is a matter of concern to us all, because it is about creating the kinds of environment in which children can grow and develop. It is creating the space for children to play and to experience what childhood should be about.

REFERENCES

Benard, B. (1987). Protective factor research: What we can learn from resilient children. *Illinois Prevention Forum* (73)

Benard, B. (1989). Working together: Principles of effective collaboration. *Illinois Prevention Forum* 10(1).

Benard, B. (1992). Fostering resiliency in kids: protective factors in the family, school and community. *Illinois Prevention Forum* 12(3).

Brewer, D.; Hawkins, J.D.; Catalano, R.F.; & Neckerman, H.J. (1994). *Preventing Serious, Violent and Chronic Juvenile Offending: A Review of Evaluations of Selected Strategies in Childhood, Adolescence and the Community*. Seattle, WA: Developmental Research and Programs, Inc.

Cahill, M.; Perry, J.; Wright, M.; & Rice, A. (1993). *A Documentation Report on the New York City Beacons Initiative*. New York: The Youth Development Institute, Fund for the City of New York.

Canada, G. (1995). *Fist, Stick, Knife, Gun: A Personal History of Violence in America*. Boston: Beacon Press.

Carnegie Council on Adolescent Development. (1992). *A Matter of Time: Risk and Opportunity in the Nonschool Hours*. New York: Carnegie Corporation of New York.

Coleman Children & Youth Services. (1995). *Report Card on San Francisco's Parks*. San Francisco: Coleman Advocates.

Coleman, J. (1987). Families and schools. *Educational Researcher* 16(6): 32-38.

Connell, J.; Kubisch, A.; Schorr, L.; & Weiss, C. (Eds.). (1995). *New Approaches to Evaluating Community Initiatives: Concepts, Methods, and Contexts*. Washington, D.C.: Aspen Institute.

Czikszentmihalyi, M. (1982). The value of sports. In Partington, J.T.; Orlick, T.; & Samela, J.H. (Eds.), *Sport in Perspective*. Ottawa: Coaching Association of Canada (pp. 122-127).

Danish, S.J. (1997). Going for the goal: A life skills program for adolescents. In Albee, G. & Gullotta, T. (Eds.), *Primary Prevention Works*. Beverly Hills, CA: Sage Publications.

Eccles, J.S.; Midgley, C.; Wigfield, A.; Buchanan, C.M.; Reuman, D.; Flanagan, C.; & MacIver, D. (1993).

Development during adolescence: The impact of state-environment fit on young adolescents' experiences in schools and in families. *American Psychologist* 48(2): 90-101.

Fox, J.A. & Newman, S.A. (1998). *Quality Child Care and After-School Programs: Powerful Weapons Against Crime*. Washington, D.C.: Fight Crime: Invest in Kids.

Fox, J. A. & Newman, S. A. (1997). *After-school Crime or After-school Programs: Tuning in to the Prime Time for Violent Juvenile Crime and Implications for National Policy*. Washington, D.C.: Office of the United States Attorney General.

Fulbright-Anderson, K.; Kubisch, A.; & Connell, J. (Eds.). (1998). *New Approaches to Evaluating Community Initiatives*. Washington, D.C.: Aspen Institute.

Gabarino, J. (1989). Preventing child maltreatment. In Price, R. (Ed.), *Prevention in Mental Health: Research, Policy and Practice*. Beverly Hills, CA: Sage (pp. 63-108).

Gambone, M.A. & Arbreton, A. J. (1997). *Safe Havens: The Contributions of Youth Organizations to Healthy Adolescent Development*. Philadelphia: Public/Private Ventures.

Hawkins, J.D.; Catalano, R.F.; & Miller, J.Y. (1992). Risk and protective factors for alcohol and other drug problems in adolescence and early adulthood: Implications for substance abuse prevention. *Psychological Bulletin*, 112(l): 64-105.

Jones, M.A. & Offord, D.R. (1989). Reduction of antisocial behavior in poor children by nonschool skill development. *Journal of Child Psychology and Psychiatry and Allied Disciplines* 30: 737-750.

Karoly, L.; Greenwood, P.W.; Everingham, S.S.; Houbé, J.; Kilburn, M.R.; Rydell, C.P.; Sanders, M.; & Chiesa, J. (1998). *Investing in Our Children: What We Know and Don't Know About the Costs and Benefits of Early Childhood Interventions*. Santa Monica, CA: The RAND Corp.

Kimball-Baker, K. & Roehlkepartain, E.C. (1998). Are Americans afraid of teens? *Assets* Summer: 6-8.

Lewthwaite, R. & Piparo, A. (1993). Goal orientation in youth competitive athletes: Physical achievement, social-relational and experiential concerns. *Journal of Research in Personality* 27: 103-117.

Lupher, E. (1996). *Public Funding of Youth Sports and Recreation in Detroit, Hamtramck and Highland Park, Report #316*, Detroit, MI: Citizens Research Council of Michigan.

McLaughlin, M.W.; Irby, M.A.; & Langman, J. (1994). *Urban Sanctuaries: Neighborhood Organizations in the Lives and Futures of Inner-City Youth*. San Francisco: Jossey-Bass Publishers.

Marshall, J. Jr. & Wheeler, L. (1996). Street Soldier: One Man's Struggle to Save a Generation One Life at a Time. New York: Delacorte Press.

Miller, A. & Ohlin, L. (1985). *Delinquency and Community: Creating Opportunities and Controls*. Beverly Hills, CA: Sage.

Moore, J. & Brown, J. (1998). *Community Use of Schools Process Evaluation*. Detroit, MI: Moore & Associates, Inc.

Neithercut, M.E. (1993). *Status of Detroit Area Youth*. Detroit, MI: Wayne State University.

O'Hare, W.P. (Ed.). (1997). *City Kids Count: Data on the Well-Being of Children in Large Cities*. Baltimore, MD: Annie E. Casey Foundation.

Rauner, D.M.; Stanton, L.; & Wynn, J. (1994). *Sports and Recreation for Chicago Youth*. Chicago: The Chapin Hall Center for Children.

Schorr, L.B. & Schorr, D. (1988). *Within Our Reach: Breaking the Cycle of Disadvantage*. New York: Doubleday.

Schorr, L.B. (1997). *Common Purpose: Strengthening Families and Neighborhoods to Rebuild America*. New York: Doubleday.

Seefeldt, V. (Ed.). (1994). *Reinvesting in Communities: Sports, Recreation and Youth Development in Detroit, Hamtramck and Highland Park: Phase I, An Assessment of Needs*. Detroit, MI: The Skillman Foundation.

Seefeldt, V. (Ed.). (1995). *An Extended Assessment of Needs for the Provision of Sports, Recreation and Youth Development in the Cities of Detroit, Hamtramck and Highland Park*. Detroit, MI: The Skillman Foundation.

Sickmund, M.; Snyder, H.N.; & Poe-Yamagata, E. (1988). *Juvenile Offenders and Victims: 1997 Update on Violence*. Washington, D.C.: National Center for Juvenile Justice, Office of Juvenile Justice and Delinquency Prevention.

Skillman Foundation (The). (1993). *Sports, Recreation and Youth Development Initiative: A Concept Paper*. Detroit, MI: The Skillman Foundation.

Skillman Foundation (The). (1995). *Re-creating Recreation in Detroit, Hamtramck and Highland Park: The Youth Sports and Recreation Initiative*. Detroit, MI: The Skillman Foundation.

Smith, C.A.; Lizotte, A.J.; Thornberry T.P.; & Krohn, M.D. (1995). Resilience to delinquency. In Hagan, J. (Ed.). *Delinquency and Disrepute in the Life Course*. Greenwich, CT: JAI Press.

Social Program Evaluators & Consultants (1999). *Recapitalization of Four Recreation Centers, Year One Evaluation Report*. Detroit, MI: Social Program Evaluators & Consultants.

Tierney, J.P.; Grossman, J.B.; & Resch, N.L. (1995). *Making a Difference: An Impact Study of Big Brothers/Big Sisters*. Philadelphia: Public/Private Ventures.

United Community Services. (1987). *Looking at Leisure: A Study of the Negative Aspects*. Detroit, MI: United Community Services.

United Way for Southeastern Michigan. (1993). *A Closer Look: An Assessment of Major Local Issues Affecting Metropolitan Detroit*. Detroit, MI: United Way for Southeastern Michigan.

University Cultural Center Association and Zachary & Associates. (1991). *Lower Woodward Corridor: Facilities and Programs Analysis*. Detroit, MI: Community Foundation for Southeastern Michigan and the Ford Foundation.

Werner, E. & Smith, R. (1989). *Vulnerable But Invincible: A Longitudinal Study of Resilient Children and Youth*. New York: Adams, Bannister and Cox.

Wynn, J.; Costello, J.; Halpern, R.; & Richman, H. (1994). *Children, Families, and Communities: A New Approach to Social Services*. Chicago: The Chapin Hall Center for Children.

CHAPTER 16

School and Agency-Based Programs in the Inner City

Don Hellison
University of Illinois at Chicago

Children and youth living in America's inner cities and other underserved communities face a number of issues such as poverty and racism, the stress of living in "war zones," the paucity of functional male adults, and the influence of gangs and drug trafficking (Walberg et al., 1997). One issue that has received considerable attention in the media as well as from Carnegie Council on Adolescent Development (1992) is the discretionary or unstructured time in the daily lives of these children and youth. It is during this time that sexual activity, substance abuse, and negative peer pressure escalate (Dwyer et al., 1990; Steinberg, 1986). Yet extended day youth programs in underserved neighborhoods, unlike more affluent communities, are scarce, often underfunded, and in many times in need of reform (Cairnes and Cairnes, 1994). For example, programs that do not exist tend to "blame the victim" rather than unresponsive educational, social and political institutions by attempting to control youth and/or fix their deficiencies (McLaughlin and Heath, 1993). It is no wonder that by the ages of 11 or 12, youth start to drop out, not only of school, but of extended day programs as well (Carnegie Council on Adolescent Development, 1992; McLaughlin et al., 1994).

Programs for Underserved Children and Youth

The discretionary time issue has drawn the attention of the media and politicians, so that it is no longer unusual to read about political debates over the merits of, for example, midnight basketball. In addition, both private (e.g., Nike) and federal funding for extended day programs has increased markedly. More importantly, this issue has contributed to an emerging field of youth development. One important aspect of this development is the professionalization of long-time community program providers such as the YMCA and Boys and Girls Clubs. Fueled by a five year study (DeWitt Wallace-Reader's Digest Fund, 1996), staff training, retention, and in-service education have been analyzed and reforms initiated. In addition, theoretical-philosophical perspectives have been developed. A recent journal, *New Designs in Youth Development*, has further enhanced development of the field. Perhaps the most salient change in youth work programming has been the articulation of two different rationales for extended day youth programs (DeWitt Wallace Readers Digest, 1996; Hudson, 1997, Kahne et al., 2000):

- Rationale #1. Offer safe, structured, enjoyable activities.

- Rationale #2. Offer safe, structured, enjoyable activities that also target youth development— e.g., health/physical, personal/social, cognitive/creative, vocational, civic.

Sport and Youth Development

Typical sports programs in underserved communities have not fared any better than youth programs in general. For example, extended day programs with a loose "gyme and swim" orientation experience the same dropout patter as non-sport extended day programs (McLauglin et al., 1994). In general, traditional school sport programs do not support youth development very well. Kahne and associates (2000) found that organized sports programs in the inner city did not promote youth development (the second rationale) as well as other extended day programs, and two other studies (Larson, 1994; Spady, 1970) supported this conclusion. One reason for this unfavorable comparison is the growing encroachment of the professional sport model, which problematizes the character development claims made by youth sport enthusiasts (Rees, 1998). The recent emergence of inner city "street agents" is one more indicator of the professionalization of youth sport. In-school physical education often includes sport activities, but, while it is sometimes structured and sometimes enjoyable (first rationale), it is rarely developmental (Placek, 1983; Taylor and Chiogiorji, 1987) and this is even more evident in underserved schools.

However, something atypical has occurred in the past few years: an influx of extended day programs in underserved communities that claim to promote holistic youth development, for example, Midnight Basketball, Soccer in the Streets, Revival of Inner City Baseball, PASS (Promoting Achievement in School through Sport), Jesse White's Tumblers (a longstanding Chicago "institution"), and the National Youth Sports Program. Studies of some of these programs have shown crime reduction and less gang involvement (Farrell et al., 1995) as well as

---

- Treat youth as resources to be developed. Build on the strengths they already possess and emphasize their competence and mastery.

- Focus on the whole person—the emotional, social, and cognitive as well as physical dimensions of the self.

- Respect their individuality including cultural differences and developmental needs.

- Empower them.

- Give them clear, demanding (but not unreasonable) expectations based on a strong, explicit set of values.

- Help youth envision possible futures for themselves.

- Provide both a physically and psychologically safe environment.

- Keep program numbers small and encourage participation over a long period of time; emphasize belonging and membership.

- Maintain a local connection.

- Provide courageous and persistent leadership in the face of systemic obstacles.

- Provide significant contact with an adult who cares about them.

Note: From Hellison, D, Cutforth, N. 1997. Extended day programs for urban children and youth: From theory to practice. In: Walberg, HA, Reyes, O, Weissberg, RP, editors. *Children and Youth: Interdisciplinary Perspectives*. Newbury Park, CA: Sage. P 223-249. Copyright 1997 by Sage Publications, Inc.

Table 1. State-of-the-art criteria for state-of-the-art extended day programs in the inner city.

academic improvement (American Sports Institute, unpublished data), although the data are often weak (Derezotes, 1995) and the research methods questionable (Kahne and McLaughlin, 1998).

Perhaps the most promising development has been the recently published 11 state-of-the-art criteria for inner city extended day programs shown in Table 1 (Hellison and Cutforth, 1997), drawn from best practices and scholarly opinion (Ianni, 1993; Heath and McLaughlin, 1993; McLaughlin et al., 1994; Villarruel and Lerner, 1994) and supported by the alternative school (Raywid, 1994) and resiliency (Wang et al., 1994) literature. These criteria, while not specific to youth sport, provide a set of guidelines for program development and evaluation of all extended day programs in underserved communities.

The Urban Youth Leader Project (UYLP)

For the past eleven years, I have directed a project at the University of Illinois at Chicago that builds on some of this past work, especially holistic youth development (the second rationale) in the emerging youth development field and the 11 state-of-the-art criteria. In addition, it builds on field work teaching inner city youth since 1970 which led to the ongoing development of the personal and social responsibility model (Hellison, 1978, 1985, 1995). It also takes its direction from recent interest in a university more relevant to society, one which embraces university-community collaboration, service learning, and applied research. Lawson (1997) and Siedentop (1999) have been leading spokespersons for this movement in Kinesiology and physical education in higher education.

UYLP attempts to integrate the traditional tripartite mission of the university by providing: 1) service in the form of physical activity-based youth programs in its most underserved neighborhoods, 2) service learning and professional preparation programs and field experiences for interested undergraduates and graduate students, and 3) opportunities for applied studies of the processes and outcomes of UYLP youth programs by faculty and students.

Service: UYLP currently offers six extended day clubs, a mentor program, an advanced cross-age teaching program, and a Nike Scholar program to support the post-secondary education of high school graduates who have been involved in these clubs and programs. The processes of all programs adhere to the 11 state-of-the-art criteria, and the intended outcomes are in line with the second youth development rationale. More specifically, all programs follow the guidelines of the responsibility model which emphasize:

- A program leader-student relationship that respects the individuality, voice, and capacity for decision-making of students.

- The movement from physical activity to life skills and values embedded in a loose progression of five student responsibilities: respect for the rights and feelings of others, self-motivation and teamwork, self-direction, helping others and leadership, and trying these things outside the program (Hellison, 1995; Hellison and Cutforth, 1997).

- The gradual shifting of power from the program leader to students.

Teaching: These service programs are developed, led, and taught by faculty and graduate students who receive pre-service and in-service education, and by undergraduate students who become teaching assistants in these programs and occasionally step up to program leadership. (Several undergraduates have been involved in UYLP for four years. Others remain to do graduate work associated with UYLP). Graduate students, in addition to program leadership, also consult with interested schools and social agencies in Chicago and conduct workshops for teachers and youth workers both in and outside Chicago.

To facilitate the service learning education and professional preparation of university students involved in UYLP, two undergraduate courses, a kinesiology master's degree in urban youth development, and a College of Education doctoral program with an emphasis in urban youth development in kinesiology are offered. Further,

UYLP, which is housed in the College of Health and Human Development Sciences, has a relationship with the College of Education, the Jane Addams College of Social Work, and the College of Urban Planning and Public Policy.

Research: Because the fieldwork from 1970 to the present has involved developing and teaching the responsibility model with inner city youth, the work is highly relational, labor-intensive, complex, and to some extent context-specific. As a result, our research has for the most part been a mixture of practical inquiry (Schubert, 1986), case study (Stenhouse, 1988), teacher-as-researcher (Hubbard and Power, 1993), reflective practice (Schon, 1990), and curriculum-as-craft (Kirk, 1993). The specific research process has been forged by trial and error, resulting in something labeled service-bonded inquiry (Martinek and Hellison, 1997). These studies, beginning in 1978 and continuing to the present, include published work by Compagnone (1995), Cutforth and Puckett (1999), DeBusk and Hellison (1989), Hellison (1978), and Williamson and Georgiadis (1992), as well as theses, dissertations, and unpublished papers by Eddy (1998), Herbel and Parker (1997), Lifka (1989), Kallusky (1997), and Lulaudzi (1995). Published program descriptions which do not meet all the case study criteria include Georgiadis (1990), Hellison (1982, 1983, 1986, 1988, 1990), and Hellison and Georgiadis (1992).

Studying program processes resulted in the following findings:

- How completely the responsibility model was implemented had a direct effect on the outcomes of a particular program (no surprise).

- Who did the implementing—that is, the qualities of the program leader, also directly affected outcomes (see Hellison, 1995).

- Studying process has an ongoing effect on the development of the responsibility model's goals and strategies.

Despite some doubts about program outcomes (Hellison, 1990), these studies and program descriptions yielded a number of supportive cross-context outcomes:

- Specific behavioral changes corresponding to program goals were observed during the program.

- Student voluntary attendance, anonymous program evaluations, and interviews were very positive and corresponded to program goals.

- The following outcomes are to some extent context-specific: Adults outside the program—e.g., parents; school and social agency teachers, youth workers, security guards, and administrators—observed changes in students who were involved in responsibility model programs, but the strength of the observations varied from site to site. In the strongest case, the principal stated that our one small club of fifteen students changed the culture of her school (Hellison, 1999).

Although emphasizing the complexities of practice rather than attempting to replicated the controlled settings in other kinds of research is strongly advocated by Schon (1990), it is contested as well, both by those advocating controlled experimental or quasi-experimental studies, e.g., Tolan and Guerra's (1994) review of violence prevention studies, and by Kahne and McLaughlin (1998) who find fault with both case studies and controlled designs in evaluating extended day programs. We had concerns as well, but they focused less on the credibility of our research methods and more on the kinds of data we were not getting from the case studies (Hellison, 1990). Funders, for example, want hard data that show the program's impact on teen pregnancy, court referrals, grades and graduation, drug use, employability, and so on.

We then began a series of mixed methodology (Tashakkori and Teddlie, 1998) studies with the intention of using more controlled designs to collect quantitive data. At the same time, we conducted interviews and used other qualitative techniques to better explain the reasons for the findings—e.g., reported changes in drug use. To date, these studies include the following:

Cummings (1998) followed 6th-8th grade responsibility model club participants into high school in order to longitudinally compare the grades, attendance, and dropout rates with cohorts who were in the same K-8 school grade and class, but did not participate in the club. She found no difference between groups in absenteeism or repeating grades. However the non-club students had a dropout rate of 34% (including freshmen, sophomores, and juniors), which is typical of the neighborhood, whereas no former club members had dropped out. Follow-up interviews are currently being analyzed to help understand why a sport club, even with the infusion of the responsibility model, could influence dropout to such an extent, or whether other factors were involved.

Martinek and associates (1999) devised a quantitative technique to determine the extent of transfer of responsibility from the club to the classroom. Students were evaluated by program leaders in the club, and teachers in the school, according to a simple classification system for the specific responsibilities of the model. The study showed strongest transfer in effort and some transfer in self-control and helping others, but less in goal-setting and conflict resolution. Overall, transferability from club to classroom was "medium" (vs. high or low).

Wright (1998) studied the effects of a responsibility model martial arts club on violence prevention by categorizing club participants according to a combination of in-school referrals for fighting and student interviews. He found that students whose attendance and commitment to the club were strong were less violence-prone than dropouts. Although causation was not established, non-violence was reinforced for club members who attended regularly. In addition, the leadership skills that were an integral part of the martial arts curriculum could make a future contribution to violence prevention in the community.

Walsh (1999) compared the youth development supports of a responsibility model club to youth development supports in the club

members' school experience based on an instrument developed by Kahne and associates (2000) that builds on the second rationale for youth development programs. He followed up with interviews of all club members for their explanations and interpretations. There were statistically significant differences in favor of the club in enjoyment, belonging and trust, guidance, support, and leadership opportunities, whereas the school scored higher in valuable content and high expectation. Interviews revealed that club members were positive about both the club and school, but that they could think of more club examples to support their opinions.

Urban Youth Leader Project Partnership

Over the past few years, several kinesiology/physical education faculty members from other universities began to implement UYLP components in underserved communities near universities. All provide service programs for youth based on the responsibility model. Figure 1 shows the range of programs currently being conducted by one or more partners as well as a map for future development at individual sites. All involve university students in this work. All engage in applied research. Nick Cutforth at the University of Denver and James Kallusky at the California State University-Los Angeles are former students and worked in the UYLP programs. Tom Martinek at the University of North Carolina at Greensboro and Missy Parker, now at Slippery Rock University, took leaves of absence (at different times) to study with me in Chicago. Jim Stiehl, University of Northern Colorado, is a long-time friend who has incorporated the responsibility model into his outdoor/adventure education work with underserved youth.

In 1997-98, thanks to support from the Great Cities institute and the Center for Urban Educational Research and Development at University of Illinois at Chicago, a formal partnership was formed, and the first meeting was held in Chicago (also attended by three faculty members interested in becoming involved in the partnership). The second meeting was held in Reno at the national AAHPERD

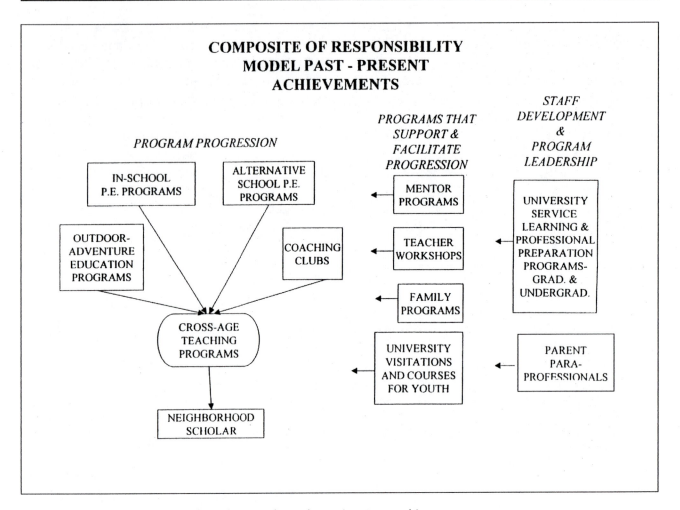

**COMPOSITE OF RESPONSIBILITY
MODEL PAST - PRESENT
ACHIEVEMENTS**

PROGRAM PROGRESSION

PROGRAMS THAT SUPPORT & FACILITATE PROGRESSION

STAFF DEVELOPMENT & PROGRAM LEADERSHIP

IN-SCHOOL P.E. PROGRAMS

ALTERNATIVE SCHOOL P.E. PROGRAMS

MENTOR PROGRAMS

UNIVERSITY SERVICE LEARNING & PROFESSIONAL PREPARATION PROGRAMS- GRAD. & UNDERGRAD.

OUTDOOR-ADVENTURE EDUCATION PROGRAMS

COACHING CLUBS

TEACHER WORKSHOPS

FAMILY PROGRAMS

CROSS-AGE TEACHING PROGRAMS

UNIVERSITY VISITATIONS AND COURSES FOR YOUTH

PARENT PARA-PROFESSIONALS

NEIGHBORHOOD SCHOLAR

Figure 1. Range of programs in the Urban Youth Leader Project Partnership.

Convention that year, and the third meeting was held at the University of Denver 1998-99 (funded by the university). The results of this partnership so far include a book (Hellison & Cutforth, 1997), several joint presentations and workshops, idea sharing, and grant-writing.

Future Research Needs

It is probably evident that this work involves a lifetime journey. It started with sixteen years of fieldwork with little assistance, expanded to student and occasional faculty involvement in the past eleven years, and has culminated, at least so far, in a partnership. Next steps include addressing the following research needs:

- Continuation of mixed methodology studies which have begun to shed light on youth program outcomes overlooked in earlier studies.

- Studies of the impact of dissemination (i.e., in-service workshops and publications) on professionals who work with underserved youth. Such dissemination has been a component of the UYLP since its inception, but systematic studies focused on implementation have yet to be conducted.

Studies of the community barriers to university-community collaboration in youth work and how to overcome these barriers. UYLP faculty and students routinely encounter such barriers, but strategies to counteract these forces have been limited to anecdotal incidents communicated informally among staff.

The developmental, implementation, and evaluation of collaborative models. UYLP currently holds membership in a variety of collaborative arrangements with both community and university partners in addition to the Urban Youth Leader Partnership described above. While it is often argued that youth will benefit more from integrated services and more holistic approaches, collaborations involving UYLP have not been systematically evaluated, nor has UYLP initiated such collaborative arrangements, except for the UYLP Partnership.

Closing Thought

Perhaps the best summary of this work is an often quoted statement attributed to Arthur Ashe when he taught tennis to inner city children in New York: "Tennis is a way to reach kids and teach them things that are much more important than tennis."

REFERENCES

Cairns, R.B.; Cairns, BD. 1994. *Lifelines and risks: Pathways of Youth in Our Time.* New York: Cambridge University Press.

Carnegie Council on Adolescent Development. 1992. *A Matter of Time: Risk and Opportunity in the Non-school Hours. Report of the Task Force on Youth Development and Community Programs.* New York: Carnegie Corporation of New York.

Compagnone, N. 1995. Teaching responsibility to rural elementary youth: Going beyond the urban at-risk boundaries. *Journal of Physical Education, Recreation and Dance* 66 (8):58-63.

Cummings, T.K. 1998. *Testing the Effectiveness of Hellison's Personal and Social Responsibility Model: A Dropout, Repeated Grade, and Absentee Rate Comparison.* Master's thesis. Chico, CA. California State University, Chico.

Cutforth, N.J.; Puckett, K. 1999. A qualitative evaluation of an urban cross-age teaching Program. *Urban Review* 31: 153-172.

DeBusk, M.; Hellison, D. 1989. Implementing a physical education self-responsibility model for delinquency-prone youth. *Journal of Teaching Physical Education* 8: 104-112.

Derezotes, D. 1995. Evaluation of the late nite basketball project. *Child and Adolescent Social Work Journal* 12: 33-50.

DeWitt Wallace-Reader's Digest Fund. 1996. *Strengthening the Youth Work Profession.* New York: DeWitt Wallace-Reader's Digest Fund.

Dwyer, K.M.; Richardson, J.L.,; Danley, K.L.; Hansen, W.B.; Sussman, S.Y.; Brannon, B.; Dent, C.W.; Johnson, C.A.; Flay, B.R. 1990. Characteristics of eighth grade students who initiate self-care in elementary and junior high school. *Pediatrics* 86: 448-454.

Eddy, M.H. 1998. *The Role of Physical Activity in Educational Violence Prevention Programs for Youth.* Doctoral dissertation, New York: Teachers College, Columbia University.

Farrell, W.; Johnson, J.; Sapp, M.; Pumphrey, R.; Freeman, S. 1995. Redirecting the lives of urban black males: An assessment of Milwaukee's midnight basketball league. *Journal of Community Practice* 2: 91-107.

Garbarino, J.; Dubrow, N.; Kostelny, K.; Pardo, C. (1992). *Children in Danger: Coping with the Consequences of Community Violence.* San Francisco: Jossey-Bass.

Georgiadis, N. 1992. *Practical Inquiry in Physical Education: The Case of Hellison's Personal and Social Responsibility Model.* Doctoral dissertation. Chicago: University of Illinois at Chicago.

Gordon, E.W.,; Song, L.D. 1994. Variations in the experience of resilience. In Wang, MC, Gordon, EW (Eds.), *Educational Resilience in Inner-City America: Challenges and Prospects.* Hillsdale, NJ: Lawrence Erlbaum Associates, (pp. 27-43).

Heath, S.B.; McLaughlin, M.W., (Eds.), 1993. *Identity and Inner-City Youth: Beyond Ethnicity and Gender*. New York: Teachers College Press.

Hellison, D. 1978. *Beyond Balls and Bats: Alienated (and Other) Youth in the Gym*. Washington, DC., American Association for Health, Physical Education and Recreation.

Hellison, D. 1982. Attitude and behavior change in the gym: The Oregon story. *Physical Educator* 39 (2): 67-70.

Hellison, D. Teaching self-responsibility (and more). *Journal of Physical Education, Recreation and Dance* 53 (7):23-25.

Hellison, D. 1985. *Goals and Strategies for Teaching Physical Education*. Champaign, IL: Human Kinetics.

Hellison, D. 1986. Cause of death: Physical education. *Journal of Physical Education, Recreation and Dance* 57 (4): 27-28.

Hellison, D. (1990). Making a difference: Reflections on teaching urban at-risk youth. *Journal of Physical Education, Recreation and Dance*, 61 (6): 44-45.

Hellison, D. 1995. *Teaching Personal and Social Responsibility Through Physical Activity*. Champaign, IL: Human Kinetics.

Hellison, D. 1998. Cause of death: Physical education—a sequel. *Journal of Physical Education, Recreation and Dance* 59 (4): 18-21

Hellison, D. 1999. Promoting character development through sport: Rhetoric or reality? *New Designs for Youth Development* 15 (1): 23-27.

Hellison, D., Cutforth, N., (Eds.), 1997. *Serving Underserved Youth Through Physical Activity: Toward a Model of University-Community Collaboration*. Thousand Oaks, CA: Sage. (pp. 223-249).

Hellison, D.; Georgiadis, N. 1992. Basketball as a vehicle for teaching values. *Strategies* 4 (1): 1-4.

Herbel, K.; Parker M. 1997. Youth, basketball, and responsibility: A fairy tale ending? Presentation at National Convention of the American Alliance of Health, Physical Education, Recreation, and Dance. St. Louis, MO.

Hubbard, R.S.; Power, B.M. 1993. *The Art of Classroom Inquiry: A Handbook for Teacher-Researchers*. Portsmouth, NJ: Heinemann.

Hudson, S.D. 1997. Helping youth grow. *Journal of Physical Education, Recreation and Dance* 68 (9): 16-17.

Ianni, F.A.J., 1993. *Joining Youth Needs and Program Services*. Urban Diversity Series No. 104. ERIC Clearinghouse on Urban Education. Institute for Urban and Minority Education.

Kahne, J.; Nagaoka, J.; Brown, A.; O'Brien, J.; Quinn, T.; & Thuede, K. 2000. School and after-school programs as contexts for youth development: A quantitative and qualitative assessment. In M.C. Wang & W.L. Boyd (Eds.). Improving Results for Children and Families: Services with School Reform Efforts (pp. 121-152). Greenwich, CT: Information Age Publishing.

Kallusky, J.P. 1997. *Constructing an Urban Sanctuary for At-Risk Youth in Physical Education: An Artistically Crafted Action Research Project in an Inner-City High School*. Doctoral dissertation. Greeley, CO: University of Northern Colorado.

Kirk, D. 1993. Curriculum work in physical education: Beyond the objectives approach? *Journal of Teaching Physical Education* 12: 244-265.

Larson, R. 1994. Youth organizations, hobbies, and sports as developmental contexts. In Silbereisen, RK, Todt, E, editors. *Adolescence in Context: The Interplay of Family, School, Peers, and Work in Adjustment*. New York: Springer-Verlag.

Lawson, H.A. 1997. Children in crisis, the helping professions, and the social responsibilities of universities. *Quest* 49: 8-33.

Lifka, R. 1989. *Implementing an After-School Alternative Wellness/Activities Program for At-Risk Hispanic Youth*. Master's thesis. Chicago: University of Illinois at Chicago.

Martinek, T.; Hellison, D. 1997. Service-bonded inquiry: The road less traveled. *Journal of Teaching Physical Education* 17: 107-121.

Martinek, T.; McLaughlin, D.,; Schilling, T. 1999. Project effort: Teaching responsibility in the gym. *Journal of Physical Education, Recreation and Dance* 70: 59-65.

McLaughlin, M.W.; Heath, S.B. 1993. Casting the self: Frames for identity and dilemmas for policy. In: Heath, S.B., McLaughlin, M.W. (Eds.), Identity and inner-city youth: Beyond ethnicity and gender. New York: Teachers College Press, (pp. 210-239).

McLaughlin, M.W.; Irby, M.A.; Langman, J. 1994. Urban sanctuaries: Neighborhood organizations in the lives and futures of inner city youth. San Francisco, CA: Jossey-Bass.

Mulaudzi, L. 1995. A program evaluation of an implementation of a responsibility model for inner-city youth. Master's thesis. Chicago: University of Illinois at Chicago.

Placek, J. 1983. Concepts of success in teaching: Busy, happy, and good? In: Templin, T., Olson, J., (Eds.), *Teaching in Physical Education*. Champaign, IL: Human Kinetics (pp. 45-56).

Raywid, M.A. 1994. Alternative schools: The state of the art. *Educational Leadership* 52 (1): 26-31.

Rees, C.R. 1998. Building character and the globalization of sport. In: Feingold, R.S., Reese, C.R., Barrette, G.T., Fiorentino, L., Virgillio, S., Kowalski, E. (Eds.), *Education for life: Proceedings of the Association Internationale des Escoles Superieures d' Education Physique* (pp. 281-286).

Schon, D.A. 1990. *Educating the Reflective Practitioner*. San Francisco: Jossey-Bass.

Schubert, W.H. 1986. *Curriculum: Perspective, Paradigm, and Possibility*. New York: Macmillan.

Shields, D.L.L.; Bredemeier, B.J.L. 1995. *Moral Development and Action in Physical Activity Contexts*. Champaign, IL: Human Kinetics.

Siedentop, D. 1999. Physical activity programs and policies: Toward an infrastructure for healthy lifestyles. *Journal of Physical Education, Recreation and Dance* 70: 32-35.

Spady, W.G. 1970. Lament of the letterman: Effects of peer status and extracurricular activities on goals and achievement. *American Journal of Sociology* 75: 32-35.

Steinberg, L. 1986. Latchkey children and susceptibility to peer pressure: An ecological analysis. *Developmental Psychology* 22: 433-439.

Stenhouse, L. 1988. Case study methods. In: Keeves, J.P., (Ed.). *Educational research, methodology, and measurement: An international handbook*. Oxford Pergamon. (pp 49-53).

Tashakkori, A.; Teddlie, C. 1988. *Mixed methodology: Combining qualitative and quantitative approaches*. Thousand Oaks, CA: Sage.

Taylor, J.; Chiogioji, E. 1987. Implications of educational reform on high school programs. *Journal of Physical Education, Recreation and Dance* 58 (2):22-23.

Tolan, P., Guerra, N. 1994. *What Works in Reducing Adolescent Violence: An Empirical Review of the Field*. Boulder, CO: Center for the Study and Prevention of Violence.

Villarruel, R.M.; Lerner, R.M. (Eds.), 1994. *Promoting Community-Based Programs for Socialization and Learning*. San Francisco, CA: Jossey-Bass.

Walberg, H.J.; Reyes, O., Weissberg, R.P. (Eds.), 1997. *Children and Youth: Interdisciplinary Perspectives*. Thousand Oaks, CA: Sage

Walsh, D. 1999. *A Comparative Analysis of Extended Day Programs for Inner City Youth*. Masters thesis. Chicago: University of Illinois at Chicago.

Wang, M.C.; Haertel, G.D.; Walberg, H.J. 1994. Educational resilience in inner cities. In: Wang, MC, Gordon, EW, (Eds.), *Educational Resilience in Inner-City America: Challenges and Prospects*. Hillsdale, NJ: Lawrence Erlbaum Associates. (pp. 45-72).

Williamson, KM.; Georgiadis, N. 1992. Teaching an inner-city after-school program. *Journal of Physical Education, Recreation and Dance* 63 (8), 14-18.

Wright, PM. 1998. *The Impact of a Responsibility-Based Martial Arts Program on Violence Prevention*. Master's thesis. Chicago: University of Illinois at Chicago.

CHAPTER 17

Challenges and Issues in Interscholastic Sports

By John E. "Jack" Roberts, Executive Director
Michigan High School Athletic Association

INTRODUCTION

The Michigan High School Athletic Association is a leader in coaches' education among high school athletic associations in the United States, due in part to the Institute for the Study of Youth Sports. This is not because we *require* coaches' education; we cannot. It is because we provide coaches' education. We began before any other state high school association, we continue to reach more people directly than any other state high school association, we invest more time and money, and we take a more hands-on approach. We could not make these claims if the Institute had not been with us in the design and the delivery of coaches' education. The Institute helped get us started when little else existed, and continues to serve us. We have now reached nearly 11,000 high school coaches through our Program of Athletic Coaches' Education (PACE).

We are not satisfied. We need to reach far more coaches, perhaps as many in a single year as we have in the past ten years combined. We need to provide additional levels of training, especially in the areas of coaching for character and equipping students with life skills, and in the areas of health and safety.

We may have done more than most state high school associations in the area of coaches' education, but we have accomplished only a portion of what needs to be done in our state. And this gap is one of the most serious challenges in school sports. If we are among the best at coaches' education, how bad are the worst?

But, I believe that we will be able to reach more coaches and provide more breadth and depth in their education. It will also be done without government mandates and without government money. That is the American way, or at least the MHSAA way.

Twenty-five different countries are represented at this conference, and 65 of 130 guests are from outside the United States. It is only because these 65 are so well traveled and so well informed that I dare talk about school sports in the United States or school sports in Michigan, because school sports in this state and nation are not like school sports in most other countries. In most other countries, schools do not sponsor and conduct interscholastic athletics quite like in the United States.

A major part of youth sports in the United States is school sports. It is the level of youth sports that attracts the most attention, the largest crowds, the most space in sports pages of newspapers, and the most time devoted to youth sports in television and radio sports reports.

Because of the role of school sports in the lives of youth and because of the role of the Institute in the life of the Michigan High School Athletic Association, I am here to discuss challenges and issues in interscholastic athletics. I hope to increase awareness of some critical issues, to identify four core concerns, and convey a passion for keeping them in the forefront of the minds of any who would claim expertise about or responsibility for school sports.

CRITICAL ISSUES

A paragraph of an editorial in the April 5, 1999 *Newsweek* helped me to focus and rearrange the way to present this topic. The writer, Dennis Williams, Director of the Center for Minority Educational Affairs and a teacher of English at Georgetown University, wrote as follows: "...NCAA regulations have nothing to do with either education or the well-being of the young people involved. They have everything to do with competitive balance and public relations." These two sentences stopped me because they caused me to wonder: "Would anyone ever write that about the MHSAA (or any other state organization involved with high school sports)?" After a period of reflection, I determined that what Mr. Williams wrote is not all bad. Some of what he wrote is actually complimentary, although he did not intend it, and some of what he wrote would not be accurate if directed to school sports.

Yes, the MHSAA and most school sports organizations are concerned about "competitive balance." That is not bad. Mr. Williams might have meant it as a criticism of the NCAA; but we claim it as an essential purpose of *high school* associations.

In fact, one of the four parts of the stated purpose in the *MHSAA Handbook* is as follows: "3. Promote uniformity and predictability and competitive equity in the application of eligibility rules for athletic contests." "Competitive equity" is our way of saying "competitive balance." Competitive equity is one of our essential purposes in serving schools. No apologies.

And yes, the MHSAA *is* concerned about "public relations." Again, from our four-part stated purpose is the following: "1. Increase and promote the educational value of interscholastic athletic programs throughout the state." That is public relations. In the sense of promoting the educational value of school sports and doing what we can to increase their educational value, public relations is a purpose we claim, not a criticism we fear.

So, I would take it as a compliment, not a criticism, if Mr. Williams (or anyone) would cite us for preoccupation with competitive equity for schools and students, and promotion of the programs' values. We are guilty and glad of it.

What should not be said about the MHSAA and what stopped me longest in my reading to apply Mr. Williams' criticism to our organization, is his opinion that the NCAA has nothing to do with either education or the well-being of the young people involved. I do not believe that is true about the NCAA, and I know it is not true about the MHSAA.

As I trace the history of high school athletics in the United States, not only competitive equity, but also education and the well-being of the young people involved have guided and continue to guide school sports organizations in general and the MHSAA in particular. One hundred years ago, when athletic programs were first becoming organized well enough in secondary schools to cause people to wonder how the youth of one school might fare against the youth of another school, it took but a very few experiences of interscholastic competition to realize that a common set of understandings was necessary for competition to occur with fair result and without hard feelings. Those who were coordinating these first athletic exchanges quickly discovered that they needed several kinds of rules. The first set of rules needed was to determine *where* and with *what* the competition would be conducted: facility dimensions, ball specifications, net heights, etc. The second set of necessary rules was to determine *how* the competition would proceed: number of balls and strikes and innings, lengths of quarters, halves, etc. These two sets of understandings show that there was concern from the very beginning of school sports for competitive balance. We could not have it without these kinds of rules.

But deciding where and with what and how the competition should be played was not sufficient. Gradually, it became clear to the coordinators of programs at that time that there had to be some understandings, some agreements, some policies, and some rules about *who* could play. Not surprisingly, School A soon objected if School B's participants in an event seemed to be men against School A's boys.

So, the schools coordinating the event agreed that all participants in all contests had to be enrolled in the schools they represented in competition. This is still the first regulation in the *MHSAA Handbook*. They agreed next that all participants had to fall within a certain age range, an age rule, which is still the second regulation in the *MHSAA Handbook*.

It was not fair to have it any other way, i.e., competitive balance. It was not healthy for participants to have it any other way. Not in the 1920s, and not at present. We have not lost our focus. Rules 1 and 2 historically are still rules 1 and 2 in the *Handbook*. It has not been easy to keep these rules. This month alone, we have had to defeat initiatives of the Governor and some legislators to keep Rule 1 and to defend the enrollment rule in a $30 million lawsuit which would have eliminated the enrollment requirement for some young people.

In previous years, we have had to fight in several courts to keep Rule 2, the age rule. We have never lost, although once had to appeal to the Michigan Supreme Court and once to the U.S. Sixth Circuit Court of Appeals to defend the age rule successfully.

The commitment to the enrollment and age rules, Rules 1 and 2, is for the sake of competitive balance and for the sake of the education and well-being of those involved. We are as focused and firm about these objectives as ever.

As interscholastic athletic programs became more sophisticated and assured higher profiles within the school, community and state, pressures mounted for athletic teams to do better and to win more. So some schools would start practices sooner, play more games, and seek more distant and prestigious venues for competition.

Not surprisingly, again, it did not take very long for some schools to complain that other schools, in pursuit of a competitive advantage, were moving toward excesses, were abusing the health and welfare of students, and were interfering with the educational objectives of schools and the pursuits of students. Again, schools agreed among themselves on some limitations, for example, on the lengths of seasons, numbers of contests, and distances of travel.

They did so to keep the program fair (competitive equity, competitive balance). They did so to keep the program healthy for the youth involved. They did so to keep the program consistent with the mission of the sponsors, namely, education by schools.

This brief review of the history of the regulation of high school athletics leaves no doubt that those in charge, teachers at first and then administrators and their voluntary associations, had definite objectives in mind, namely, the physical and educational well-being of students and competitive equity within the programs.

CORE CONCERNS

The objectives with which we began still guide us. Challenges, however, continue to confront us, and in fact increase. The pace of change in education is amazing. The pace of change in technology is mind-boggling. If we were to graph the rate of change, the line is nearly horizontal in 1900 compared to the year 2000 when the line would be almost vertical.

Change surrounds us and greatly affects us more rapidly and more profoundly every year, including in schools and educational processes. But, while many things will change, we must not change the soul, the core values, of school sports.

Students, coaches, athletic directors, principals, superintendents and school boards will come and go. State association staff and officials change. Old schools will be replaced by new ones; leagues will form and dissolve. All are important, but they are not the soul of school sports. What is? What is closer to the heart and soul are four core concerns. They are *scholarship*, *sportsmanship*, *safety* and the *scope of the program*. These are the issues that make school sports educational. These are the issues that define school sports, and make them different than sports on any other level by any other sponsor.

Watching the September 1998 chase to break Babe Ruth's home run record on television, I noticed in the crowd the Hall-of-Famer, Stan Musial. This reminded me of the time when a rookie pitcher faced "Stan the Man" for the first time. The young pitcher looked in for the sign, and the catcher signaled for a slider. The young pitcher shook him off. Next, the catcher signaled for a curve, and the young hurler shook him off. Then the catcher signaled for a fast ball, and again the young pitcher shook him off. Finally the catcher signaled for a change-up, and again his rookie pitcher shook him off. So the catcher called time-out, walked to the mound and said, "Look, kid, you have shaken off every pitch you have. What are you trying to do?" The young pitcher looked at the ball, then looked at Stan the Man, and then looked back at the ball, and said, "I am just trying to hold onto the ball for as long as I can."

Ladies and gentlemen, that is not bad advice. We fact intimidating opposition in school sports, made more imposing by the rapid change in the world around us. We must hold onto what is pure and precious about school sports for as long as we can.

SCHOLARSHIP

By scholarship, we mean scholarship in high school, not scholarships to college. Academics must come first. Athletics must support the educational mission of schools and help to complete the education of many of the students. Interscholastic athletics is educational athletics, not merely recreation and not primarily for entertainment.

Today we are challenged to increase academic standards, to reduce loss of classroom instructional time for sports-related activities, and to maintain the requirement that participants be enrolled in the schools for which they compete. And those who see this differently, those who want to change this, threaten the soul of school sports. They cannot be allowed to change us. We have got to hold onto the ball for as long as we can.

SPORTSMANSHIP

By sportsmanship, we mean the atmosphere that surrounds the events—the conduct of players, coaches and spectators. We have all of the rules we need for high school athletes. In Michigan, the best behaved athletes on any level are the high school athletes.

Right now, the challenge is in the spectator stands. Athletes would be ejected immediately for using once the words and gestures which fans now use routinely, and they threaten the soul of school sports. They cannot be allowed to change us. We have got to hold onto that ball for as long as we can.

The two largest sportsmanship summits in America have been held here in Michigan: 800 people in 1997 and 1,200 people in 1998. We are planning for 2,000 people at our third summit in September 2000, and this year – to demonstrate our belief that the best solutions to problems are the most local solutions – we are going to provide in excess of $20,000 in mini-grants to encourage and equip leagues and local school districts to create or enhance local efforts, especially those addressing adult spectators. We are going to hold onto the sportsmanship ball for as long as we can.

SAFETY

By safety, we mean the health and welfare of sports participants. We mean protecting them from injuries, enforcing the rules intended to protect their physical health, providing first-aid and emergency care, and promoting healthy lifestyles, including the teaching of life skills to help them avoid drug use, including tobacco and alcohol. Challenges in this area for the earliest days of the new century include head protection for skiers, soccer goalkeepers and pole vaulters; neck protection in ice hockey; performance standards for baseball and softball bats; continuation of the wrestling weight monitoring program; expansion of nutrition education to all sports; and avoidance of all kinds of unproven drugs and supplements with unknown consequences for the health of adolescents. And anyone who would put honors before health, or championships before caring for youth, they threaten the soul of school sports. They cannot be allowed to change us. We have got to hold onto that ball for as long as we can.

SCOPE

By scope, we mean the limitations of the program—How many? How long? How early? How late? How far? In school sports, or educational athletics, we address those questions more than on any other level. Without apologies, we put borders around the program to avoid the excesses that have come to other programs. We attempt to avoid the extremes and abuses of other levels. We attempt to avoid directions which inflate egos and turn out athletes who leave us thinking that they are the center of the universe, and that the world should serve them rather than the other way around.

We attempt to promote well-rounded scholar-athletes. We attempt to discourage year-round specialization in a single sport. We believe the best experience is a balanced one: academic and non-academic, athletic and non-athletic, a star in one activity and a substitute in another, to participate in solo and ensemble, on-stage and back-stage, winning and losing.

Those who would fight us on this, like the National Federation of State High School Associations which proposed a summertime national high school basketball tournament last year, and FOX Sports Net which currently is advancing a national high school football championship game, and those who would relax the amateur and awards rules and travel limitations and national championship prohibitions, they threaten the soul of school sports. They cannot be allowed to change us. We have got to hang onto that ball for as long as we can.

I do not have the space to discuss in great detail these dangerous challenges or the courageous responses on the local and state levels, here and across the country. But without addressing the four core concerns – scholarship, sportsmanship, safety and the scope of the programs, one cannot accurately describe the history of school sports and one cannot preserve the future of school sports, one of this nation's richest assets and one of our schools' best tools.

In the face of great change, leaders of state and national high school athletic organizations keep talking about the adaptations these organizations must make to survive in the future. However, if we make some of these adaptations, we will not deserve to survive, for we will have lost our ability to serve. School sports must maintain their requirements, standards and limitations to maintain their soul. I urge you to help the administrators of school sports in America stand up for what is good and right, what is wholesome and pure, for as long as we can.

RESEARCH NEEDS

- Determining if minimum grade point averages for athletic eligibility improve academic performance of student-athletes, increase or decrease participation rates, or discriminate against any groups of students.

- Measuring the success of sportsmanship initiatives and developing models that work best with students, coaches and spectators.

- Determining the health risks to adolescents who ingest various dietary supplements and over-the-counter drugs in large doses or for extended periods.

- Measuring the effect of out-of-season practice and competition expectations on the rate at which students drop out of school sports and adults resign coaching positions.

CHAPTER 18

Enhancing Coaching Effectiveness in Youth Sports: Theory, Research, and Intervention

Frank L. Smoll and Ronald E. Smith
University of Washington

A recent survey of the status of youth sports in 20 countries revealed that athletic competition directly touches the lives of a great many children and adolescents (De Knop et al., 1996). In the United States alone, an estimated 20 to 35 million individuals between the ages of 6 and 18 years participate in nonschool sports, and 10 million 14- to 18-year-olds participate in interscholastic athletics (Seefeldt et al., 1992). Figures indicate that participation has steadily risen over the past several decades (Martens, 1988, Weiss and Hayashi, 1996), and there is no reason to believe that the trend will abate or that a decline is likely to occur. The rising participation by youngsters has been accompanied by a greater degree of adult involvement. Consequently, these programs have become extremely complex social systems that have attracted the attention of researchers interested in studying the impact of sport competition on psychosocial development (see Bredemeier, this volume; Brustad, this volume, 1993; Cahill and Pearl, 1993; Gould, this volume; Smoll and Smith, 1996; Weiss, this volume).

Sport scientists have emphasized that youth sports provide socialization opportunities and place adaptive demands on participants that parallel those of other important life experiences (Coakley, 1993; Ewing et al., 1996; Martens, 1993; Scanlan, 1996; Smoll, 1989). For this reason, organized athletic experiences are regarded as potentially important in child and adolescent development, and participation is believed to have direct relevance to the development of prosocial attitudes and behaviors, such as respect for authority, cooperation, self-discipline, risk-taking, and the abilities to tolerate frustration and delay gratification. Yet, a realistic appraisal indicates that participation does not automatically result in these outcomes. The most important factor determining outcomes is the manner in which this social learning situation is structured and supervised by the adult leaders. It is, therefore, not surprising that the major focus of educational intervention has been the coach.

Most athletes have their first sport experiences in programs staffed by volunteer coaches. These individuals typically know their sport and the skills involved quite well, but they rarely have had any formal training in creating a healthy psychological environment for young athletes. Educational programs have thus been developed for the purpose of positively affecting coaching practices and thereby increasing the likelihood that youngsters will have favorable sport experiences. For example, national coaching associations of many countries have programs that provide training in sport psychology as well as other areas, such as sport pedagogy, exercise physiology, and sports medicine (Australia [Oldenhove, 1996]; Canada [Wankel and Mummery, 1996]; Finland [Laakso et al., 1996]; Portugal [Goncalves, 1996]; the United States [Weiss and Hayashi, 1996]).

In a research program that has spanned two decades, we have focused on interactions between coaches and young athletes. The major thrust of our collaborative work has been to (a) discover how specific coaching styles affect children's reactions to their athletic experiences, and (b) to use this information to develop an intervention program for training coaches in how to create an athletic environment that fosters positive coach-athlete and peer interactions, increases the pleasure of participating, enhances self-esteem, and reduces performance anxiety and attrition from youth sports. This paper begins with an overview of the theoretical model and basic research underlying the development of our coach-training program. Consideration is then given to the content of the program and procedures for its implementation. Next, applied research assessing the efficacy of the intervention is described. The chapter concludes with a discussion of community applications and topics for future research.

Theoretical Model and Basic Research: Coaching Behaviors and Their Effects on Children

What should be included in a psychologically oriented coach-training program? In addressing this question, our work was guided by a fundamental assumption that an intervention should be based on scientific evidence rather than on intuition and/or what we "know" on the basis of informal observation. An empirical foundation for coaching guidelines not only enhances the validity and potential value of the program, but it also increases its credibility in the eyes of consumers.

Theoretical Model and Research Paradigm

Our multi-method approach to generating an empirical database incorporated a simple model having the following components: coach's behaviors —> athletes' perceptions and recall —> athletes' evaluative reactions. This model stipulates that the ultimate effects of coaching behaviors are mediated by the athletes' recall and the meaning they attribute to the coach's actions. In other words, what children remember about their coach's behaviors and how they interpret these actions affects the way that children evaluate their sport experiences. Furthermore, a complex of cognitive and affective processes are involved at this mediational level. These processes are likely to be affected not only by the coach's behaviors, but also by other factors, such as the athlete's age, what he/she expects of coaches, and certain personality variables. Therefore, the basic three-element model was expanded to reflect these factors (Smoll and Smith, 1989). The more comprehensive model, which is presented in Figure 1, specifies a number of situational as well as coach and athlete individual difference variables that are expected to influence the core components and hypothesized relations among them.

In accordance with the model, we have sought to determine how observed coaching behaviors, athletes' perception and recall of the coach's behaviors, and athlete attitudes are interrelated. We have also explored the manner in which athlete and coach individual difference variables might serve as moderator variables and influence the basic behavior-attitude relations. One of these variables, namely, the athlete's level of self-esteem, will be highlighted in this chapter to illustrate important linkages among theory, research, and intervention.

Behavioral Assessment of Coaches

Because coaches play such a vital role in influencing both skill development and psychosocial outcomes, they are a natural focus of behavioral assessment measures. Coding systems have, therefore, been devised for a variety of verbal and nonverbal behaviors (Smith et al., 1996). To measure leadership behaviors, the Coaching Behavior Assessment System (CBAS) was developed to permit the direct observation and coding of coaches' actions during practices and games (Smith et al., 1977). This system allowed the measurement of differences in the use of positive reinforcement, various types of technical instruction, punitive responses to mistakes, encouragement, organizational and order-maintaining behaviors, ignoring athletes' positive behaviors and mistakes, and other coaching behaviors. Use of the CBAS in observing and coding coaching behaviors in a variety of sports indicates that the scoring system is sufficiently comprehensive to incorporate the vast majority of overt leader behaviors, that high interrater reliability can be obtained, and that individual differences in behavioral patterns can be discerned (Chaumeton and Duda, 1988; Cruz et al., 1987; Horn, 1984, 1985; Jones et al., 1997; Krane et al., 1991; Rejeski et al., 1979; Sherman and Hassan, 1986; Wandzilak et al., 1988).

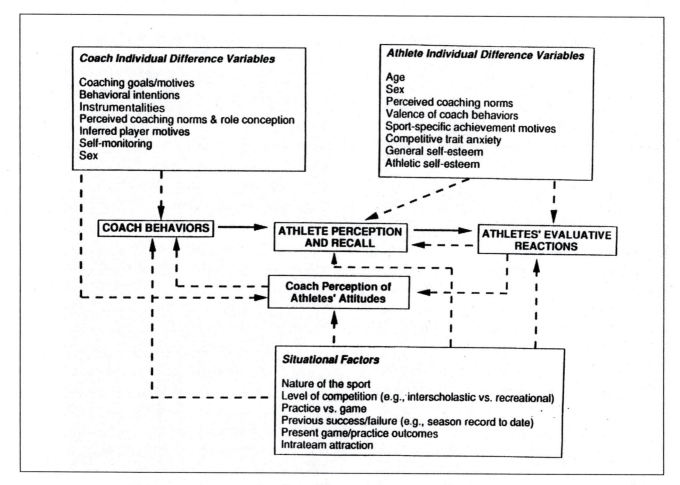

Figure 1. A theoretical model of coaching behaviors, their antecedents, and their effects on athletes, with hypothesized relations among situational and individual difference variables that are thought to influence the base relations (from Smoll and Smith, 1989).

Coaching Behaviors and Children's Evaluative Reactions

Following development of the CBAS, a systematic program of research was carried out over a period of several years (Curtis et al., 1979; Smith and Smoll, 1990; Smith et al., 1978; Smith et al., 1983; Smoll et al., 1978). The research pursued several questions concerning the potential impact of youth coaches on athletes' psychological welfare. For example, how frequently do coaches engage in such behaviors as encouragement, punishment, instruction, and organization, and how are observable coaching behaviors related to children's reactions to their organized athletic experiences? Answers to such questions were not only a first step in describing the behavioral ecology of one aspect of the youth sport setting, but they also provided an empirical basis for the development of a psychologically oriented intervention program.

The results, which are described in greater detail elsewhere (Smith and Smoll, 1996a), indicated that the typical baseball or basketball coach engages in more than 200 codable actions during an average game. We were thus able to generate behavioral profiles of up to several thousand responses over the course of a season. In large-scale observational studies, we coded more than 80,000 behaviors of about 70 male youth coaches, then interviewed and administered questionnaires after the season to nearly 1,000 children in their homes to measure their recall of their coaches' behaviors and their evaluative reactions to the coach, their sport experiences, and themselves. We also obtained coaches' postseason ratings of how frequently they engaged in each of the observed behaviors.

The data provided clear evidence for the crucial role of the coach. Won-loss records had little relation to the psychosocial outcome measures (i.e., reactions to coach, enjoyment, and self-esteem); virtually all of the systematic variance was accounted for by differences in coaching behaviors. Not surprisingly, the most positive outcomes occurred when children played for coaches who engaged in high levels of positive reinforcement for both desirable performance and effort, who responded to mistakes with encouragement and technical instruction, and who emphasized the importance of fun and personal improvement over winning. Not only did the children who had such coaches like their coaches more and have more fun, but they also liked their teammates more.

There were also some surprises in the data. Punitive and hostile actions occurred less frequently but had more devastating effects than anticipated. Although only about 3% of the coded behaviors were punitive and critical in nature, they correlated more strongly (and negatively) than any other behavior with children's attitudes. Second, general encouragement had a curvilinear relation to children's attitudes; either very low or very high levels of encouragement were linked to negative attitudes toward the coach. Finally, coaches were, for the most part, blissfully unaware of how they behaved. The only actions on their self-report measure that correlated significantly ($r = \sim 0.50$) with the observational measures were the punitive behaviors. In all other behavioral categories, the children were more accurate in their perceptions of coach behaviors than were the coaches themselves. This finding clearly indicated the need to increase coaches' self-awareness when developing an intervention program.

Because of our interest in self-esteem as a moderator variable that might influence responses to coaches' behaviors, a self-enhancement model of self-esteem development was tested (Shrauger, 1975; Swann, 1996; Tesser, 1988) against the consistency model (e.g., Rogers, 1951). The self-enhancement model posits that most people have a strong need to enhance their self-evaluations and to feel positively about themselves. People who are low in self-esteem are thought to have particularly strong self-enhancement needs. Therefore, they should value positive feedback and respond very favorably to people with whom they have self-enhancing interactions. A different prediction is derived from the consistency model, which suggests that people with low self-esteem may actually be more comfortable with someone who provides negative feedback that is congruent with their negative self-image, thereby satisfying needs for cognitive consistency.

To test the models, an analysis was conducted of the reactions of children who scored either low, moderate, or high on a measure of general self-esteem to coaches who were either quite high or quite low on a behavioral dimension that we term supportiveness (the tendency of the coach to reinforce desirable performance and effort and to respond to mistakes with encouragement rather than punitiveness). Attraction responses toward the coaches revealed a significant interaction between coach supportiveness and athletes' level of self-esteem. As shown in Figure 2, children with low self-esteem were more responsive than other children to variations in supportiveness, and the pattern of their responses favored the self-enhancement model. Rather than liking the nonsupportive coaches, these children reacted especially negatively to them, presumably because the coaches fustrated their self-enhancement needs by being nonsupportive (Smith and Smoll, 1990). This observation extends to a naturalistic setting a body of results derived from laboratory studies which, collectively, suggest that self-enhancement motivation causes people who are low in self-esteem to be especially responsive to variations in supportiveness (Brown et al., 1988; Swann et al., 1987; Tesser and Campbell, 1983). Indeed, the pattern of results in Figure 2 almost directly parallels those obtained in a laboratory study by Dittes (1959, p. 79, Figure 2), involving college students' responses to accepting or nonaccepting group members, and suggest a notable consistency of findings across differing populations and situations.

A Coaching Effectiveness Intervention

Data from the basic research indicated clear relations between coaching behaviors and the reactions of youngsters to their athletic experiences. These relations provided a soild foundation for developing a set of coaching guidelines (i.e., behavioral dos and don'ts). The data-based

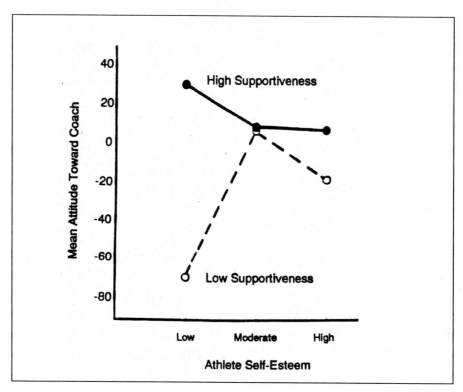

Figure 2. Mean evaluations of coaches by athletes as a function of athletes' self-esteem and supportiveness of the coach (data from Smith and Smoll, 1990).

guidelines served two other functions: (a) they allowed us to structure our coach-training program as an information-sharing rather than speculative enterprise, and (b) the scientific origin of the guidelines increased their credibility with coaches. An overview of the content of the program and procedures for its implementation is presented subsequently. A more comprehensive discussion of cognitive-behavioral principles and techniques used in conducting psychologically oriented coach-training programs appears elsewhere (Smoll and Smith, 1998).

Coach-Training Principles

A set of five core principles underlies the guidelines that are communicated in the program, which is known as Coach Effectiveness Training (CET, Smith and Smoll, 1996b). First, emphasis is given to the important differences between the professional sports model, where winning and financial gain are the bottom line, and a developmental model, where the focus is on providing a positive developmental context for the child. In the latter model, "winning" is defined not in terms of won-loss records, but in terms of giving maximum effort and making improvement. The explicit and primary focus is on having fun, deriving satisfaction from being on the team, learning sport skills, and developing increased self-esteem and lowered fear of failure.

The second principle emphasizes what is termed a "positive approach" to coaching. In such an approach, coach-athlete interactions are characterized by the liberal use of positive reinforcement, encouragement, and sound technical instruction that help create high levels of interpersonal attraction between coaches and athletes. Punitive and hostile responses are strongly discouraged, as they have been shown to create a negative team climate and to promote fear of failure in athletes. It is important to emphasize that reinforcement should not be restricted to the learning and performance of sport skills. Rather, it should also be liberally applied to strengthen prosocial behaviors (e.g., teamwork, leadership,

sportsmanship). Coaches are urged to reinforce effort as much as they do results. This guideline has direct relevance to developing a healthy philosophy of winning and a reduction in performance anxiety. CET also includes several positive-approach guidelines pertaining to the appropriate use of technical instruction. For example, when giving instruction, coaches are encouraged to emphasize the good things that will happen if athletes execute correctly rather than focusing on the negative things that will occur if they do not. This approach is believed to motivate athletes to make desirable things happen (i.e., helps to develop a positive achievement orientation) rather than building fear of making mistakes.

The third coaching principle is to establish norms that emphasize athletes' mutual obligations to help and support one another. Such norms increase social support and attraction among teammates and thereby enhance cohesion and commitment to the team. They are most likely to develop when coaches (a) model supportive behaviors, and (b) reinforce athlete behaviors that promote team unity. Coaches are also instructed in how to develop a "we are in this together" group norm. This norm can play an important role in building team cohesion, particularly if the coach frequently reinforces athletes' demonstrations of mutual supportiveness.

A fourth principle is that compliance with team roles and responsibilities is most effectively achieved by involving athletes in decisions regarding the formulation of team rules and by reinforcing compliance with them rather than by using punitive measures to punish noncompliance. Coaches should recognize that youngsters desire clearly defined limits and structure. By setting explicit rules for athletes' conduct and using positive reinforcement to strengthen desirable behaviors, coaches can often avoid the use of keeping control behaviors and the need to deal with frequent misbehaviors on the part of athletes.

Finally, CET coaches are urged to obtain behavioral feedback and to engage in self-monitoring to increase awareness of their own actions and to encourage compliance with the positive-approach guidelines.

CET Procedures

In a CET workshop, which lasts approximately 2.5 hours, behavioral guidelines are presented both verbally and in written materials (a printed outline and a 24-page manual) given to the coaches. The manual (Smoll and Smith, 1997) supplements the guidelines with concrete suggestions for communicating effectively with young athletes, gaining their respect, and relating effectively to their parents. The importance of sensitivity and being responsive to individual differences among athletes is also emphasized. The written materials keep the workshop organized, facilitate the coaches' understanding of the information, eliminate the need for coaches to take notes, and give coaches a tangible resource to refer to in the future. Visual aids (content slides and cartoons illustrating important points) are also used to clarify and emphasize key ideas and add to the organizational quality of the session.

The most basic objectives of CET are to communicate coaching principles in a manner that is easily comprehended, and to maximize the likelihood that coaches will adopt the information. As part of the approach to creating a positive learning environment, coaches are encouraged to share their own experiences and associated practical knowledge with the group. CET workshops are thus conducted with an interactive format in which coaches are treated as an integral part of the session rather than a mere audience. The open atmosphere for exchange promotes active versus passive learning, and the dialogue serves to enhance interest and involvement in the learning process.

The instructional procedures contain many verbal modeling cues that essentially tell coaches what to do. To supplement the didactic verbal and written materials, coaching guidelines are transmitted via behavioral modeling cues (i.e., actual demonstrations showing coaches how to behave in

desirable ways). In CET, such cues are presented by a live model (the trainer) and by symbolic models (coach cartoons). In addition, modeling is frequently used in conjunction with later role playing of positive behaviors. Coaches are kept actively involved in the training process by presenting critical situations and asking them to role play appropriate ways of responding.

One of the striking findings from the basic research on coach behaviors was that coaches had very limited awareness of their own actions while coaching. Thus, an important goal of CET is to increase awareness, for no change is likely to occur without it. To this end, coaches are taught the use of two proven behavioral change techniques—namely, behavioral feedback and self-monitoring. To obtain feedback, coaches are encouraged to work with their assistants as a team and share descriptions of each others' behaviors. With respect to self-monitoring, CET coaches are given a brief form which they are encouraged to complete immediately after practices and games (see Smoll and Smith, 1998, pp. 58-59). On the form, coaches indicate approximately what percentage of the time they engaged in the recommended behaviors in relevant situations. For example, coaches are asked, "Approximately what percentage of the times they occurred did you respond to mistakes/errors with encouragement?" Coaches report that they find this form very useful in fostering self-awareness and in helping them identify areas for potential improvement.

CET also includes discussion of coach-parent relationships and provides instructions on how to organize and conduct a sport orientation meeting with parents. Some purposes of the meeting are to inform parents about their responsibilities for contributing to the success of the sport program and to guide them toward working cooperatively and productively with the coach (see Smoll, 1998).

Assessing the Efficacy of CET

Three national coaching education programs are currently available in the United States that include curricular components designed to assist coaches in creating a positive and enjoyable athletic environment—the American Coaching Effectiveness Program (ACEP, Martens, 1987), the National Youth Sport Coaches Association program (NYSCA, Brown and Butterfield, 1992), and the Program for Athletic Coaches' Education (PACE, Seefeldt and Brown, 1996). Weiss and Hayashi (1996, p. 53) noted that ACEP, NYSCA, and PACE "have provided coaching workshops to thousands of individuals involved in community-based and school-sponsored sports, but evaluation research is essential to determine the effectiveness of these training programs on increasing sport science knowledge and applications." Indeed, CET is the only program that has been subjected to systematic evaluation to determine its influence on coaches' behaviors and the effects of such behaviors on youngsters' psychosocial development (Brown and Butterfield, 1992). The remainder of this section summarizes the program-evaluation research.

Initial Experimental Field Research

It was important not only to develop an empirical foundation for CET, but also to measure its effects on coaches and the youngsters who play for them. In an initial field experiment (Smith et al., 1979), 31 Little League Baseball coaches were randomly assigned to an experimental (training) or to a no-treatment control group. During a preseason CET workshop, behavioral guidelines were presented and modeled by the trainers. In addition to the information-modeling portion of the program, behavioral feedback and self-monitoring procedures were employed in an attempt to increase the coaches' self-awareness of their behaviors and to encourage them to comply with the coaching guidelines. To provide behavioral feedback, observers trained in the use of the CBAS observed experimental group coaches for two complete games. Behavioral profiles for each coach were derived from these observations and were then mailed to the coaches so that they were able to see the distribution of their own behaviors. Trained coaches were also given brief self-monitoring forms

that they completed immediately after the first 10 games of the season.

To assess the effects of the experimental program, CBAS data were collected throughout the season and behavioral profiles were generated for each coach in the experimental and control groups. Postseason outcome measures were obtained from 325 children in individual data collection sessions in their homes. On both observed behavior and player perception measures, the trained coaches differed from the controls in a manner consistent with the coaching guidelines. The trained coaches gave more reinforcement in response to good performance and effort, and they responded to mistakes with more encouragement and technical instruction and with fewer punitive responses. These behavioral differences were, in turn, reflected in their players' attitudes. Although the average won-loss percentages of the two groups of coaches did not differ, the trained coaches were better liked and were rated as better teachers. Additionally, players on their teams liked one another more and enjoyed their sport experiences more. These results seemingly reflect the more socially supportive environment created by the trained coaches. Finally, children who played for the trained coaches exhibited a significant increase on a measure of general self-esteem compared to scores obtained a year earlier, while those who played for the untrained coaches showed no significant change.

Replication and Extension Studies

Replication of the research on the efficacy of CET has been conducted, with the inclusion of several additional outcomes measures. The subjects were 18 coaches and 152 children who participated in three Little League Baseball programs. Using a quasi-experimental design, one league (8 teams) was designated as the experimental group. The no-treatment control group included 10 teams from two other leagues. Prior to the season, the experimental group coaches participated in CET. The control coaches participated in a technical skills training workshop conducted by the Seattle Mariners baseball team. To assess the effects of CET, preseason and postseason data were collected for 62 and 90 children in the experimental and control groups, respectively.

The study yielded four major results. First, the CET intervention resulted in player-perceived behavioral differences between trained and untrained coaches that were consistent with the behavioral guidelines. Thus, as in previous research (Smith et al., 1979), the experimental manipulation was successful in promoting a more desirable pattern of coaching behaviors. Second, the behavioral differences resulting from the CET program were accompanied by player evaluative responses that favored the trained coaches. The trained coaches were better liked and were rated as better teachers by their players. Moreover, their players reported that they had more fun playing baseball, and a higher level of attraction among teammates was again found, despite the fact that their teams did not differ from controls in won-lost records. Third, the children who played for the CET

coaches decreased in sport performance anxiety over the course of the season, whereas those who played for the control coaches did not change (Smith et al., 1995).

The fourth result is particularly encouraging. The mean preseason and postseason self-esteem scores for subsamples of low self-esteem children are shown in Figure 3. Consistent with a self-esteem enhancement model and with previous findings (Smith and Smoll, 1990), children with low self-esteem who played for the trained coaches exhibited significant increases in general self-esteem; low self-esteem youngsters in the control group did not (Smoll et al., 1993). Although the mean increase was rather modest in absolute terms, it was, nevertheless, meaningful in relative terms. Using the preseason self-esteem distribution as a reference point, the average low self-esteem child who played for a trained coach moved from the 27th percentile of the self-esteem distribution (preseason) to the 44th percentile (postseason). Moreover, by the end of the season, 42% of the

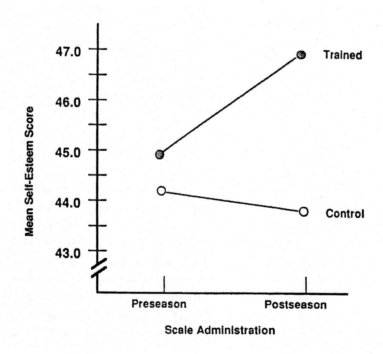

Figure 3. Mean preseason and postseason self-esteem scores of children with low self-esteem who played for trained and control-group coaches (from Smoll et al., 1993).

low-esteem children who played for the trained coaches were above the preseason median, compared with only 24% of similar children who played for the control group coaches. Apparently, the low self-esteem youngster, who is probably most in need of a positive athletic experience, is the one who is most likely to be affected by a coach who gives positive feedback, who is encouraging, and who provides high quality technical instruction that helps the child acquire prized athletic competencies. Thus, our outcome research not only provided support for the efficacy of CET, but also for the broader theoretical model that was in part inspired by the self-enhancement theory of self-esteem.

An extension of the above study was completed one year following the CET intervention. At the beginning of the next baseball season, dropout rates were assessed for youngsters who had played for the two groups of coaches. The results showed a 26% dropout rate among the control group, a figure that was quite consistent with previous reports of 22% to 59% annual attrition rates in youth sport programs (Gould, 1987). In contrast, only 5% of the children who had played for the CET-trained coaches failed to return to the sport program in the next season (Barnett et al., 1992).

In summary, CET has proven to be an effective program that alters coaching behaviors in a desirable fashion and thereby has positive psychosocial effects on the children who play for trained coaches. Five classes of outcome variables have been significantly influenced by the training program—coaching behaviors, children's attitudes, self-esteem, performance anxiety, and attrition. The consistently positive outcomes derived from the relatively brief intervention can be attributed to the fact that basic research helped to identify a set of core principles that are relatively easy for coaches to learn and that have a strong impact on young athletes.

Community Applications and Future Research

Given the ever-expanding nature of youth sports, the need for effective coach-training programs is obvious. Likewise, the large coach turnover from year to year creates a continuing demand for intervention. To this end, CET has been widely applied in the United States and Canada. More than 15,500 youth sport coaches have participated in some 300 workshops to date. Many of the workshops have been sponsored by community-based agencies (e.g., Washington Council for Prevention of Child Abuse and Neglect, Washington Department of Community, Trade and Economic Development), and CET has been included in the coaching certification modules of several youth sport organizations (e.g., Seattle Catholic Youth Organization, Washington State Youth Soccer Association). The principles of CET have also been applied at the high school, college, and professional levels in staff development projects (e.g., Smith and Johnson, 1990). Undoubtedly, a major factor contributing to the acceptance of CET among coaches and administrators alike is the fact that the program is based on scientific evidence rather than armchair psychology and/or athletic folklore. In this regard, CET has received positive reviews in relation to other coach-training programs. For example, in an article comparing CET with ACEP and the NYSCA program, Brown and Butterfield (1992, p. 216) concluded that "CET is the most convincingly documented program in theory and research-proven effectiveness. The CET program guarantees quality instruction because the developers conduct each training session themselves."

The study of coaching behaviors and their effects on children is certain to yield more information in future research. The work suggests at least four lines of investigation that are particularly germane. First, at the basic research level, we have focused primarily on boys' programs and male coaches to this point. Girls' programs clearly need empirical attention, and comparative studies of boys' and girls' reactions to specific relationships with coaches may reveal important gender differences.

Second, although the model of coach-athlete interactions was formulated two decades ago, we have barely scratched the surface in terms of testing it. An initial attempt to test the hypothesis that athletes' perceptions mediate relations between coaching behaviors and athletes' evaluative reactions to the coach provided some supportive evidence, but the analysis was done using a regression methodology that is quite unsophisticated by current standards (Smoll et al., 1978). Advances in statistical techniques have now made it possible to test such models using structural equation modeling. Such an approach would enable testing of the hypothesized causal links in a more powerful and systematic manner.

Third, from an intervention perspective, our evaluation research has indicated that CET produces a range of positive outcomes. However, dismantling studies are needed to assess the relative contributions of the various components of the training program, which include verbal and written instruction, modeling and role playing of desired behaviors, training in self-monitoring of coaching behaviors, and behavioral feedback. Such studies would include experimental conditions in which some of the components were left out. Research of this kind could help to establish the necessary and sufficient components of an effective program and could facilitate the development of improved training programs.

Finally, evaluations of CET have been done with a limited range of samples, mainly White, middle class participants. Extensions of the program to other populations could have notable benefits. For example, the low dropout rates among children who play for trained coaches may have important delinquency-prevention implications. Reducing sport attrition by applying CET within inner city settings, where dropout rates often exceed 50%, may yield significant payoffs by keeping youngsters who are at risk for delinquency involved in sports and out of gangs and other unfavorable activities.

In conclusion, it is appropriate to restate our firm belief that extended efforts to improve the quality and value of coach-training programs are best achieved via well-conceived and properly conducted evaluation research. Future research will not only serve to advance understanding of the effects of competition, but will also provide for enriched opportunities for children and youth in sport.

REFERENCES

Barnett, N.P.; Smoll, F.L.; & Smith, R.E. (1992). Effects of enhancing coach-athlete relationships on youth sport attrition. *The Sport Psychologist* 6: 111-127.

Bredemeier, B.J.L. (This volume). *Moral Community and Youth Sport in the New Millennium*.

Brown, B.R. & Butterfield, S.A. (1992). Coaches: A missing link in the health care system. *American Journal of Diseases in Childhood* 146: 211-217.

Brown, J.D.; Collins, R.L.; & Schmidt, G.W. (1988). Self-esteem and direct versus indirect forms of self-enhancement. *Journal of Personal and Social Psychology* 55: 445-453.

Brustad, R.J. (1993). Youth in sport: Psychological considerations. In: Singer, R.N.; Murphey, M.; & Tennant, L.K. (Eds.), *Handbook of Research on Sport Psychology*. New York: Macmillan (pp. 695-717).

Brustad, R.J. (This volume). *Parental Role and Involvement in Youth Sport: Psychosocial Outcomes for Children*.

Cahill, B.R. & Pearl, A.J. (Eds.), (1993). *Intensive Participation in Children's Sports*. Champaign, IL: Human Kinetics.

Chaumeton, N.R. & Duda, J.L. (1988). Is it how you play the game or whether you win or lose? The effect of competitive level and situation on coaching behaviors. *Journal of Sport Behavior* 11: 157-173.

Coakley, J. (1993). Social dimensions of intensive training and participation in youth sports. In: Cahill, B.R. & Pearl, A.J. (Eds.), *Intensive Participation in Children's Sports*. Champaign, IL: Human Kinetics (pp. 77-94).

Cruz, J.; Bou, A.; Fernandez, J.M.; Martin, M.; Monras, J.; Monfort, N.; & Ruiz, A. (1987). Avaluacio conductual de les interaccions entre entrenadors isjugadors de basquet escolar. *Apunts Med de L'esport* 24: 89-98.

Curtis, B.; Smith, R.E.; & Smoll, F.L. (1979). Scrutinizing the skipper: A study of leadership behaviors in the dugout. *Journal of Applied Psychology* 64: 391-400.

De Knop, P.; Engstrom, L.M.; Skirstad, B.; & Weiss, M.R. (Eds.), (1996). *Worldwide Trends in Youth Sport*. Champaign, IL: Human Kinetics.

Dittes, J. (1959). Attractiveness of a group as a function of self-esteem and acceptance by group. *Journal of Abnormal Social Psychology* 59: 77-82.

Ewing, M.E.; Seefeldt, V.D.; & Brown, T.P. (1996). Role of organized sport in the education and health of American children and youth. In: Poinsett, A. (Ed.), *The Role of Sports in Youth Development*. New York, NY: Carnegie Corporation.

Goncalves, C. (1996). Portugal. In: De Knop, P.; Engstrom, L.M.; Skirstad, B.; & Weiss, M.R. (Eds.), *Worldwide Trends in Youth Sport*. Champaign, IL: Human Kinetics (pp. 193-203).

Gould, D. (1987). Understanding attrition in children's sport. In: Gould, D. & Weiss, M.R. (Eds.), *Advances in Pediatric Sport Sciences. Volume 2. Behavioral Issues.* Champaign, IL: Human Kinetics (pp. 61-85).

Gould, D. (2000). (this volume). *Psychological Issues in Youth Sports: Competitive Anxiety, Overtraining, and Burnout.*

Horn, T.S. (1984). Expectancy effects in the interscholastic athletic setting: Methodological considerations. *Journal of Sport Psychology* 6: 60-76.

Horn, T.S. (1985). Coaches' feedback and changes in children's perceptions of their physical competence. *Journal of Educational Psychology* 77: 174-186.

Jones, D.F.; Housner, L.D.; & Kornspan, A.S. (1997). Interactive decision making and behavior of experienced and inexperienced basketball coaches during practices. *Journal of Teaching Physical Education* 16: 454-468.

Krane, V.; Eklund, R.; & McDermott, M. (1991). Collaborative action research and behavioral coaching intervention: A case study. In: Simpson, W.K.; LeUnes, A.; & Picou, J.S. (Eds.), *The Applied Research in Coaching and Athletics Annual 1991.* Boston, MA: American Press (pp. 119-147).

Laakso, L.; Telama, R.; & Yang, X. (1996). Finland. In: De Knop, P.; Engstrom, L.M.; Skirstad, B.; & Weiss, M.R. (Eds.), *Worldwide Trends in Youth Sport*. Champaign, IL: Human Kinetics (pp. 126-138).

Martens, R. (1987). *American Coaching Effectiveness Program: Level 1 Instructor Guide*, 2nd edition. Champaign, IL: Human Kinetics.

Martens, R. (1988). Youth sport in the USA. In: Smoll, F.L.; Magill, R.A.; & Ash, M.J. (Eds.), *Children in Sport*, 3rd edition. Champaign, IL: Human Kinetics (pp. 17-23).

Martens, R. (1993). Psychological perspectives. In: Cahill, B.R. & Pearl, A.J. (Eds.), *Intensive Participation in Children's Sports*. Champaign, IL: Human Kinetics (pp. 9-17).

Oldenhove, H. (1996). Australia. In: De Knop, P.; Engstrom, L.M.; Skirstad, B.; & Weiss, M.R. (Eds.), *Worldwide Trends in Youth Sport*. Champaign, IL: Human Kinetics (pp. 245-259).

Rejeski, W.; Darracott, C.; & Hutslar, S. (1979). Pygmalion in youth sport: A field study. *Journal of Sport Psychology* 1: 311-319.

Rogers, C.R. (1951). *Client-Centered Therapy*. Boston: Houghton Mifflin.

Scanlan, T.K. (1996). Social evaluation and the competition process: A developmental perspective. In: Smoll, F.L. & Smith, R.E. (Eds.), *Children and Youth in Sport: A Biopsychosocial Perspective*. Dubuque, IA: WCB/McGraw-Hill (pp. 298-308).

Seefeldt, V. & Brown, E.W. (Eds.). (1996). *Program for Athletic Coaches' Education: Reference Manual.* Carmel, IN: Cooper Publishing Group.

Seefledt, V.; Ewing, M.E.; & Walk, S. (1992). *Overview of Youth Sport Programs in the United States.* Washington, DC: Carnegie Council on Adolescent Development.

Sherman, M.A. & Hassan, J.S. (1986). Behavioral studies of youth sport coaches. In: Pieron, M. & Graham, G. (Eds.), *The 1984 Olympic Scientific Congress Proceedings: Volume 6. Sport Pedagogy.* Champaign, IL: Human Kinetics (pp. 103-108).

Shrauger, J.S. (1975). Responses to evaluation as a function of initial self-perceptions. *Psychology Bulletin* 82: 581-596.

Smith, R.E. & Johnson, J.J. (1990). An organizational empowerment approach to consultation in professional baseball. *The Sport Psychologist* 4: 347-357.

Smith, R.E. & Smoll, F.L. (1990). Self-esteem and children's reactions to youth sport coaching behaviors: A field study of self-enhancement processes. *Developmental Psychology* 26: 987-993.

Smith, R.E. & Smoll, F.L. (1996a). The coach as a focus of research and intervention in youth sports. In: Smoll, F.L. & Smith, R.E. (Eds.), *Children and Youth in Sport: A Biopsychosocial Perspective*. Dubuque, IA: WCB/McGraw-Hill (pp. 125-141).

Smith, R.E. & Smoll, F.L. (1996b). *Way To Go, Coach! A Scientifically-Proven Approach to Coaching Effectiveness*. Portola Valley, CA: Warde.

Smith, R.E.; Smoll, F.L.; & Barnett, N.P. (1995). Reduction of children's sport performance anxiety through social support training and stress-reduction training for coaches. *Journal of Applied Developmental Psychology* 16: 125-142.

Smith, R.E.; Smoll, F.L.; & Christensen, D.S. (1996). Behavioral assessment and interventions in youth sports. *Behavior Modification* 20: 3-44.

Smith, R.E.; Smoll, F.L.; & Curtis, B. (1978). Coaching behaviors in Little League Baseball. In: Smoll, F.L. & Smith, R.E. (Eds.), *Psychological Perspectives In Youth Sports*. Washington, DC: Hemisphere (pp. 173-201).

Smith, R.E.; Smoll, F.L.; & Curtis, B. (1979). Coach effectiveness training: A cognitive-behavioral approach to enhancing relationship skills in youth sport coaches. *Journal of Sport Psychology* 1: 59-75.

Smith, R.E.; Smoll, F.L.; & Hunt, E.B. (1977). A system for the behavioral assessment of athletic coaches. *Research Quarterly* 48: 401-407.

Smith, R.E.; Zane, N.W.S.; Smoll, F.L.; & Coppel, D.B. (1983). Behavioral assessment in youth sports: Coaching behaviors and children's attitudes. *Medicine and Science in Sports and Exercise* 15: 208-214.

Smoll, F.L. (1989). Sports and the preadolescent: "Little league" sports. In: Smith, N.J. (Ed.), Common *Problems in Pediatric Sports Medicine*. Chicago: Year Book Medical Publishers (pp. 3-15).

Smoll, F.L. (1998). Improving the quality of coach-parent relationships in youth sports. In: Williams, J.M. (Ed.), *Applied Sport Psychology: Personal Growth to Peak Performance*, 3rd edition. Mountain View, CA: Mayfield (pp. 63-73).

Smoll, F.L. & Smith, R.E. (1989). Leadership behaviors in sport: A theoretical model and research paradigm. *Journal of Applied Social Psychology* 19: 1522-1551.

Smoll, F.L. & Smith, R.E. (Eds.), (1996). *Children and Youth in Sport: A Biopsychosocial Perspective*. Dubuque, IA: WCB/McGraw-Hill.

Smoll, F.L. & Smith, R.E. (1997). *Coaches Who Never Lose: Making Sure Athletes Win, No Matter What the Score*. Portola Valley, CA: Warde.

Smoll, F.L. & Smith, R.E. (1998). Conducting psychologically oriented coach-training programs: Cognitive-behavioral principles and techniques. In: Williams, J.M. (Ed.), *Applied Sport Psychology: Personal Growth to Peak Performance*, 3rd edition. Mountain View, CA: Mayfield (pp. 41-62).

Smoll, F.L.; Smith, R.E.; Barnett, N.P.; & Everett, J.J. (1993). Enhancement of children's self-esteem through social support training for youth sport coaches. *Journal of Applied Psychology* 78: 602-610.

Smoll, F.L.; Smith, R.E.; Curtis, B.; & Hunt, E. (1978). Toward a mediational model of coach-player relationships. *Research Quarterly* 49: 528-541.

Swann, W.B. (1996). *Self-Traps: The Elusive Quest for Higher Self-Esteem*. San Francisco: Freeman.

Swann, W.B.; Griffin, J.J.; Predmore, S.C.; & Gaines, B. (1987). The cognitive-affective crossfire: When self-consistency confronts self-enhancement. *Journal of Personal and Social Psychology* 52: 881-889.

Tesser, A. (1988). Toward a self-evaluative maintenance model of social behavior. In: Berkowitz, L. (Ed.), *Advances in Experimental Social Psychology, Volume 21*. Orlando, FL: Academic Press (pp. 69-92).

Tesser, A. & Campbell, J. (1983). Self-definition and self-evaluation maintenance. In: Suls, J. & Greenwald, A.G. (Eds.), *Psychological Perspectives on the Self*, Volume 2. Hillsdale, NJ: Erlbaum (pp. 1-32).

Wandzilak, T.; Ansorge, C.J.; & Potter, G. (1988). Comparison between selected practice and game behaviors of youth soccer coaches. *Journal of Sport Behavior* 11: 78-88.

Wankel, L.M. & Mummery, W.K. (1996). Canada. In: De Knop, P.; Engstrom, L.M.; Skirstad, B.; & Weiss, M.R. (Eds.), *Worldwide Trends in Youth Sport*. Champaign, IL: Human Kinetics (pp. 27-42).

Weiss, M.R. & Hayashi, C.T. (1996). The United States. In: De Knop, P.; Engstrom, L.M.; Skirstad, B.; & Weiss, M.R. (Eds.), *Worldwide Trends in Youth Sport*. Champaign, IL: Human Kinetics (pp. 43-57).

Weiss, M.R. (2000). (This volume). Social influences on children's psychological development in youth sports.

CHAPTER 19

Youth Sports in the 21st Century: Overview and New Directions

Anthony P. Kontos and Robert M. Malina
University of New Orleans, and
Tarleton State University

The study of youth sports has steadily evolved from its beginnings in the early 20th century. The knowledge base about growth, maturation, physiology, sociology, psychology, and more recently genetics as they relate the participation in organized youth sports has expanded considerably in recent years. However, many of the problems that existed when organized youth sports were initially studied, such as the effects of stress related to competition and intensive training, early specialization and the elite, and risk of injury, among others, are still evident. There is a need for integrated, cross-disciplinary research in youth sports as we move into the next century.

This chapter provides an overview of several pertinent issues in youth sports today. It is based largely on evidence and suggestions offered by the contributors to this volume. The influence of significant others, multiple effects of sport participation youth, maintaining the interest of youth in sport and other forms of physical activity, and other topics are addressed. Goals and future directions for youth sport research and concerns are also suggested.

SIGNIFICANT OTHERS IN THE SOCIALIZATION OF YOUTH SPORT PARTICIPANTS

Youth sport participants are influenced by the actions of individuals who, willingly or unwillingly, act as role models. The impact of significant others on youth (i.e., parents, coaches, peers, siblings) is most prominent in late childhood and the transition into puberty. Significant others influence socialization and behavioral development of all youth, including organized sport participants (Brustad, Chapter 10). As a result, many of the behaviors, perceptions, and outcomes associated with youth sports are influenced by those individuals, usually adults, who are most closely involved in early sport experiences.

The process of socialization into youth sport is complex. Parents, coaches, and peers influence this process to varying degrees. Parents are the most influential socializing agents in the formative stages of a young athlete's development (Weiss, Chapter 9). The influence of coaches and peers is also central, but their importance increases as the young athlete moves from childhood into adolescence and early adulthood. Coaches and parents often believe that they are influencing young athletes in an appropriate or positive manner. However, it is the athlete's perceptions of these influences that are most salient in relation to positive psychosocial outcomes such as increased perceived competence and motivation (Weiss, Chapter 9).

It is historically accepted that female athletes have been socialized by parents away from the aggressive, physical, and leadership behaviors that are considered necessary components for success in sports. Title IX and the ever-evolving societal views of girls and women in sport and as athletes are positive influences that have changed, and will continue to change, the socialization process. However, parental socialization continues to negatively influence girls and to support boys in sport (Brustad, 1993). Still, many of the stereotypical views of females in sport (e.g., uncompetitive, weak) have been modified as a result of the strides made by child, adolescent, and young adult female athletes in the past decades. The recent successes of the U.S. Women's national soccer team have inspired many young female athletes and provided role models that more closely approximate those typically provided for young male athletes, in contrast to the prepubertal, 'girlish' model associated with successful female gymnasts and figure skaters.

Expectations for behavior in sport ideally follow the same moral and behavioral expectations as in other areas of life. However, the context of sports is often used as an arena for inappropriate or immoral behaviors (Bredemeier, Chapter 13). Behaviors of some athletes, parents and coaches are inappropriate from societal and sport perspectives. Of course, sport is a part of society and reflects many of its salient features. Obviously, behavioral expectations for participants and others differ by the

sport. In the context of ice hockey, for instance, it is considered acceptable and it is expected that a young athlete will engage in 'checking' and other physically aggressive behaviors. The same behaviors would be viewed as major fouls and possible grounds for disqualification in sports like soccer or basketball. Hence, some inherent level of aggression or violence is acceptable in certain sport contexts. The behaviors and views of parents often stimuate and reinforce these questionable behaviors. Increasingly, such aggressive tactics in some sports cross the line between legal and illegal, occasionally resulting in severe injury. In Chicago, for example, a 15 year old hockey player was paralyzed after sustaining an illegal, "post-game hit" from an opposing player (Robinson, 1999). Subsequently, felony assault charges were filed against the player who made the "hit".

Measures have been taken to reduce the occurrence of such incidents in youth sports. The American Academy of Pediatrics (2000) recently recommended that body checking be eliminated from youth hockey among participants under 15 years of age. After several altercations among parents, officials, and coaches in West Palm Beach, Florida, administrators of the National Alliance for Youth Sport decided to require parental and coach attendance at a pre-season, sportsmanship meeting (Dreyfus, 1999). The meetings, which are currently being piloted for use on a national scale, require all parents and coaches to view a video, receive a handbook, and sign a code of ethics for sport behaviors. Should parents or coaches violate the code, they face the possibility of being discharged from the organization and being restricted from attending youth sport contests. This is a positive initial step in dealing with this problem, but is a sad commentary on parental behavior at youth sport events. Attendance at a single meeting or viewing a video is unlikely to bring about anything more than awareness in parents and coaches. What is needed is to build what Bredemeier (Chapter 13) describes as 'moral sport communities'. To do so, the values that we want young athletes to learn must be communicated and modeled (Brustad, Chapter 10). In the heat of competition, it is easy to sacrifice morality for the sake of success, but it is more difficult to sacrifice success for the sake of doing what is right.

EFFECTS OF YOUTH SPORT PARTICIPATION: WHAT DO WE REALLY KNOW?

In spite of numerous advances in the study of organized youth sports, many misconceptions concerning the effects of participation persist. In some cases, researchers unwittingly perpetuate these myths by providing readers with an incomplete or uni-dimensional interpretation of findings. More often, it is an issue of coaches and parents being misinformed regarding the effects of youth sports. Potential effects of participation in youth sports are considered in the context of several areas: training, injuries, athlete's heart, dehydration and nutrition, psychological concerns, and interactional effects.

Training

Many assumptions have been made regarding potentially negative effects of intensive training on the growth and maturation of young athletes. Evidence from cross-sectional and longitudinal studies suggests that physical training of varying intensities in young athletes does not produce deleterious effects on growth and maturation (Beunen and Claessens, Chapter 2). More extensive longitudinal studies that integrate nutritional, personality, and hormonal factors, in addition to training need to be conducted to enhance knowledge in this area. An essential requisite is a more accurate means of specifying and quantifying training in its many contexts. Hours spent in a gymnasium is not an adequate definition of training; it is more appropriately an indicator of time spent in the gymnasium.

It is also important to keep in mind that factors related to training are influenced by the cultural context per se and the traditions of a given sport. From a practical perspective, coaches play an important role in monitoring and encouraging safe and effective approaches to training. Coaches,

particularly in aesthetic sports like artistic gymnastics, figure skating and diving, should be cautious in their focus on intensive training and dietary modifications as means to maintain body mass or appearance among young athletes. Overemphasis on training and dietary restrictions to maintain body appearance may provide the impetus for disordered eating and body image distortion, and may contribute to chronic undernutrition in "presumably healthy" young athletes.

Researchers and practitioners have traditionally been uncertain of the effects of specific training programs on young athletes. Resistance strength training was, until the last two decades, considered inappropriate and ineffective for prepubertal youth (American Academy of Pediatrics, 1983). However, children do in fact demonstrate gains in muscular strength with consistently applied and supervised resistance training (Blimkie et al., 1989; Weltman et al., 1986). As with any youth sport activity, unsupervised or overly intensive training may be potentially detrimental to the young athlete, and may result in injury.

The notion of "critical periods" for the trainability of youth has been suggested as a key factor in enhancing the development of sport abilities (Malina and Eisenmann, Chapter 6). The suggested "critical periods" differ in timing and duration for motor skills, strength, and anaerobic and aerobic power, and are in part influenced by characteristics associated with sex and maturity timing and progress. One of the problems in studying "critical periods" for training is the partitioning of the effects of different factors and confounders from those presumably associated with training. More recent methods, such as multilevel modeling and allometric scaling, may help to understand the interactions among training, sex, growth status, and maturity in an effort to partition the specific contributions of training to the responses of young athletes.

Risk of Injury

The lack of a consistently applied definition of an injury limits the comparability and interpretation of findings of many studies of injuries in youth sports (Anderson, Chapter 7). An initial concern in studies of injuries among youth sport participants is, therefore, the development of consensus on a definition of injury. Delineating among severe, overuse and nuisance injuries significantly impacts the sensitivity and specificity of a study, and thus the results and implications. In particular, overuse injuries tend to be ignored because of the inherent difficulty in assessing them. Another concern in injury research is the determination of mechanisms, which are often not assessed or are indeterminable.

Studies of injuries in youth sports are largely descriptive and often focus on overall risk or relative risk, at the expense of assessing specific risk for the individual athlete (Anderson, Chapter 7). As a result, understanding of the contribution of subject-related risk factors to injury occurrence is limited. Controlled, subject-related, risk factor studies examining psychological, growth and maturity, environmental, and biomechanical variables are needed. Further, youth specific models of injury need to be developed and assessed, in contrast to the application of traditional adult-based models (Williams and Andersen, 1998) to youth sport participants. Beyond these operational issues, researchers in sport injury have reported trends concerning the types and consequences of injuries sustained in several youth sports.

One concern is the hypothesized increased susceptibility of the growth plates (particularly of the tibia, radius and ulna) to injury during the adolescent growth spurt. Although there may be an increase in these injuries related to the adolescent growth spurt, treatment and correction of these injuries is ordinarily effective and common. However, the long-term effects of epiphyseal injuries are largely unknown, and deserve further study. Researchers have examined, for example, the interactions of maturity and participation in the prevalence of ulnar variance, a potentially injurious condition thought to be related to intensive training and competition in gymnastics. Among a large sample of internationally elite female gymnasts, ulnar variance is related primarily to skeletal maturity status (Beunen et al.,1999). The results of this study highlight the need to consider interactions among growth status, maturity progress and timing, and intensive training in understanding the etiology of injuries observed among young athletes.

The early recognition and treatment of injuries among youth sport participants is an additional concern (Anderson, Chapter 7). This is especially important in the case of mild or nuisance injuries that may, if untreated or if treated improperly, evolve into more serious injuries. Hence, it is important that injuries be attended to appropriately and in a timely and consistent manner. This has and continues to be a problem in youth sports at the local or community level, as coaches and parents are the primary managers of injuries. This is likely not to change as a result of resource limitations in youth sports. Efforts should be focused on educating coaches and parents on the recognition, primary treatment (e.g., rest-ice-compression-elevation [RICE], basic first-aid), monitoring, and referral of injuries. Programs such as the Coach Effectiveness Training (CET: Smith and Smoll, Chapter 18), and first-aid/CPR training offered by the American Red Cross are excellent sources for educating coaches on a variety of important issues (see American Red Cross, 1997).

Athlete's Heart

Ventricular enlargement, bradycardia and specific electrocardiographic changes, more commonly referred to as "athlete's heart," are recognized as being related to high levels of cardiac capacity in adult endurance athletes (Rowland, Chapter 4). These characteristics have been variously attributed to genotype and physiological adaptations to systematic endurance exercise, alone or in combination. In regard to the presence of 'athlete's heart' in young athletes, equivocal findings have been reported (Obert et al., 1998; Rowland et al., 1987, 1994, 1998). Factors such as testosterone level and sport specific training may influence the presence of 'athlete's heart'. The equivocal findings and the potential implication of understanding this phenomenon necessitate further studies of heart functioning in the young athlete.

Dehydration and Nutrition

Two often-overlooked issues in youth sports are dehydration and nutrition. Maintaining a consistent and appropriate level of fluid intake before, during, and after participation in sports is essential not only for performance, but also to mitigate potential health-related concerns. The effects of dehydration are magnified in hot, humid climates, and in endurance sports such as running and cycling, or team sports such as soccer and football. Surprisingly, dehydration is often a result of inappropriate fluid intake during or prior to a practice or competition, or 'voluntary hydration' (Rothstein et al., 1947). As a result, one of the key factors in preventing dehydration among youth athletes is the consistent intake of fluids primarily during sport participation. This can be accomplished most easily by providing drinks that are both chilled and flavored (Bar-Or, Chapter 5). Young athletes should also be reminded and encouraged by adult supervisors to take numerous hydration breaks during participation. This is particularly important in tournament settings that often involve multiple games or competitions in a single day or weekend.

Nutritional effects related to sport participation occur along three dimensions: behavioral, biological, and the interactions of behavior and biology. Behavioral effects might include social pressure to eat a certain way, engaging in food 'fads' for performance enhancement, and low self-esteem and confidence related to concerns about body image and weight control. Biological concerns include weight reduction or gain, increased or decreased physical strength, and increased potential for stress-related injuries, especially in young female athletes. Interactional effects may lead to more severe concerns such as eating disorders, which involve a combination of behavioral (social, body image pressures) and biological (weight loss, decreased physical strength) consequences. It is important that coaches and parents encourage good nutritional habits in young athletes, and that emphasis on body image and weight loss, particularly in aesthetic, female sports such as gymnastics and figure skating, be minimized.

Psychological

Many psychological consequences, both positive and negative, are associated with participation in organized youth sports. Involvement in competitive sport at a very young age may result in negative emotional consequences such as frustration and low self-esteem (Brustad, 1996). Some researchers even suggest that youth should not participate in competitive sports prior to age 7 or 8 years (Coakley, 1992; Passer, 1983). Participation in developmental and instructional sports, where learning rather than winning is the focus, is less likely to be detrimental to a young athlete. However, even in sport participation at these levels, parents and coaches often exert undue pressures on youth to perform at unrealistically high levels. As such, parents and coaches play a major role in the development of achievement motivation, self-perception, and confidence in a young athlete (Brustad, 1996).

Potential psychological effects of youth sport participation also include stress, competitive anxiety, and burnout (Gould and Dieffenbach, Chapter 12). Stress in youth sports can be viewed as having negative consequences such as increased anxiety and decreased mental health (Martens, 1978). Conversely, the stress associated with youth sports can be seen as acceptable and occurring within a safe environment, thereby providing a useful lesson for dealing with future stresses associated with life in general. In either case, stress is present in organized youth sports to varying degrees. Levels of stress and competitive anxiety are related to the importance of the outcome, parental and coach pressure to perform, and personal factors of the athlete. The effect of stress on an individual athlete depends on his/her coping skills, personality, and social support. As a result, the same sport situation or a coach's comment may be interpreted differently by individual athletes.

Although the majority of participants in youth sports do not experience high levels of stress, a significant minority does. It is estimated that 40 million children experience stress related to organized sport participation in the United States (Ewing et al., 1996). A process of identification and intervention for young athletes at risk for stress may be helpful in improving their sport experiences and in reducing potential long-term negative effects associated with high levels of competitive anxiety. On the other hand, stress reported by young athletes in organized sports is usually transient and is not necessarily perceived as negative. Among elite young distance runners, for example, about 50% perceived stress as helping their performances (Feltz and Albrecht, 1986). Perceptions of stress by youth sports participants need to be examined more closely.

Burnout, which is often associated with prolonged competitive anxiety, excessive training, and psychological exhaustion, is a serious concern in highly competitive sports, including some youth sports. Burnout is influenced by parental criticism and "playing up" in competitive levels (Gould et al., 1996). Early sport specialization may also be a contributory factor. Youth should be given the opportunity to experience a variety of sports in an uncritical environment, thus reducing the potential for burnout. Coaches and parents should provide young athletes with 'sandwich' style feedback, and allow athletes time away from competitive sports to recuperate physically and mentally.

Interactional Effects

The processes of growth and biological maturation are influential both as primary contributors and as effects of psychological issues. For instance, the early maturing male may initially be very competent and successful in sport. His relative dominance in a sport compared to peers may draw the attention of parents, coaches, and others at an early age. He may be susceptible to competitive stress and anxiety (Feltz and Albrecht, 1986; Simons and Martens, 1979), in part due to expectations placed upon him in the context of sport. Examining these issues without regard to maturity-associated variation in growth and performance does not provide much insight into the catalyst affecting these interactions. As adolescence and puberty progress, many peers

eventually "catch-up" and pass the early maturing boy in size, ability, speed, and strength. This may lead to frustration, greater competitive pressures, and reduced self-efficacy (Bandura, 1997) that is directly related to factors that are largely biologically driven, specifically the timing and tempo of progress toward maturity that begins with the transition into puberty. Clearly, the assessment of psychological variables alone precludes the determination of interactional or causal effects between psychological and biological variables. The use of a biocultural perspective is beneficial to understanding potential effects of participation in youth sports.

MAINTAINING PARTICIPATION IN YOUTH SPORTS

In today's world of high-tech video games, the internet and cable television, sport participation appears to be besieged from all sides. While absolute numbers of youth sport participants continue to increase, especially at younger age levels (5-12 years), it is becoming more and more difficult to compete for a young child's time. The net result is an increasingly sedentary lifestyle beginning during childhood. With reductions in physical education in schools, organized youth sports are emerging as a major source of regular physical activity for children and adolescents. Indeed, middle school children who are regularly active in sport have a greater daily energy expenditure and spend less time viewing television than students not involved in sport (Katzmarzyk and Malina, 1998). There is a need for further study of the contribution of participation in organized youth sports to the daily energy expenditure in moderate-to-vigorous physical activity among children and adolescents.

Regular participation in sport and physical activity at an early age is presumably beneficial to health later in life from both physiological and lifestyle perspectives. However, numbers of participants in organized youth sports tend to decline with increasing age, particularly in the transition into adolescence and through adolescence (Malina, 1995). The declining trend occurs at about 12-13 years of age. A major challenge facing the youth sport community is the involvement of youth in sports and related physical activities. Several issues affecting the interest of youth in and potential dissatisfaction with sport include appropriate levels of competition, maturity-related considerations, sport specialization, and mastery motivational climates, among others. These are addressed subsequently.

Appropriate Levels of Competition

"Playing-up" in skill level is becoming a more common occurrence in organized youth sports. Youth are often selected or encouraged to play with older or more skilled athletes as a result of their ability and/or physical size. The decision for an athlete to "play-up" should not be based solely on an athlete's skill or body size. Biological maturity and behavioral development must be considered. Among the potential negative effects of "playing-up" are feelings of isolation from one's peer group, excessive pressure to perform at a high level, and burnout. The use of developmentally inappropriate techniques, strategies, and training methods by coaches may also adversely affect a young athlete's potential for injury and lowered self-confidence.

Maturity Matching

Appropriate matching of young athletes is often viewed as important for equalizing competition and reducing the risk of injury. Traditionally, athletes have been matched solely on the basis of chronological age. The issue of matching based on skeletal or sexual maturity, skill, and strength, in contrast to chronological age has been often suggested (Malina and Beunen, 1996). This issue is very salient in collision (e.g., football) and contact (e.g., soccer) sports, where injury rates were reduced after implementation of matching based on sexual maturity status and several other criteria (Caine and Broekhoff, 1987). Potentially negative effects of maturity matching may involve the psychological consequences of the elevation (e.g., increased competitive stress) or demotion (e.g., dropout, lower self-esteem) of young athletes based on factors that are different than those used in other

centrally important areas of life during childhood and adolescence, for example, school (Hergenroeder, 1998). Some athletes, in spite of their maturity and skill, may not want to move up. For instance, an 11 year old early maturing girl may not want to deal with the social and competitive pressures associated with competing against 13 year girls.

While matching based on skeletal or sexual maturity may be a valid tool for equitable matching on biological maturation and physical size characteristics, it is not necessarily accurate in matching participants on behavioral and psychological factors. A physically mature athlete may be "matched" with older athletes who are physically similar, but psychologically more mature and tactically superior. Subsequently, the athlete who was "matched" may become disenchanted with sports and withdraw from further sport activities. Another concern is progress in biological maturation after an athlete has been placed in a competitive category (Malina and Beunen, 1996). How should changes in maturity status during a season be treated? A related factor to consider in matching athletes is level of skill, which is usually assessed by coaches. The potential subjectivity and abuse of such a rating may pose a concern for its use in matching.

The prudent implementation of matching using a combination of psychological, physical size, behavioral, and other factors needs to be more systematically evaluated. In spite of being logistically difficult to implement, a matching system, if implemented properly, may be beneficial to equalizing competition, to maintaining interest in participation, and to reducing the potential for injury.

Sport Specialization

The contemporary youth sports environment is increasingly characterized by more and more young athletes who are specializing in a single sport at relatively young ages. While this may enhance sport specific skill development, there are potentially negative consequences of sport specialization at an early age. Burnout from sport has been linked to excessive participation in a single sport (Gould and Dieffenbach, Chapter 12). Burnout, in turn, may lead to an athlete's decision to drop out from sport. In some cases, the decision to focus on a single sport is determined largely by the parent(s), with little or no input from the young athlete. In such cases, an athlete's level of enjoyment may be compromised, particularly if the athlete is not interested in the sport to the same degree as his/her parents. Specialization in sport also promotes year-round practices and limited time-off from sport-related activities and training. Unfortunately, many coaches and sport organizations encourage and in some cases require athletes to participate in a sport on year-around basis to the exclusion of other sports and activities. This results in a more or less continuous repetition of competition and training, which increases exposure to injury and which may contribute to increased occurrence of overuse injuries. Sport specialization may also foster and create a singular identity based solely on sport participation. This is potentially negative when an athlete is injured, or for some other reason (e.g., financial constraints) cannot maintain his/her identity in the sport.

Mastery Motivational Climates

Youth are more likely to participate in sport opportunities that provide mastery rather than performance climates (Weiss, Chapter 9). A mastery climate emphasizes learning and improvement; mistakes are viewed as part of the learning process. The success of this type of environment depends in part on the coach's ability to provide evaluative and informational feedback that is appropriate both in quantity and quality (Smoll and Smith, 1989). Parents must also reinforce the mastery-based environment by providing both praise and constructive criticism when necessary. Close, supportive relationships among sport participants are also important in fostering mastery environments and enhancing sport enjoyment. All of these factors help to maintain children's enjoyment, interest, and participation in sport.

YOUTH SPORTS INTO THE 21ST CENTURY

Participation in organized youth sports has the potential for both positive and negative experiences and consequences. Many factors in combination contribute to the overall sport experiences of youth. It is the role of future researchers and practitioners to better understand these factors and their potential effects on participation and the participants. The contributors to this volume have provided a comprehensive base from which youth provided sports can be further understood and improved. In promoting the ideas and suggestions of the contributors, researchers and practitioners alike should consider the following goals in the future examination and betterment of youth sports:

- Integration of a variety of approaches into a biocultural perspective for studying youth sports;

- Examination and comparison of organized youth sports in a variety of cultural contexts;

- Development, implementation, and evaluation of programs to educate parents, coaches, and athletes on the values and morals of participation in youth sports; and

- Expansion of multidisciplinary collaborative longitudinal studies of youth sports participants.

Toward a Biocultural Perspective in Youth Sports

Researchers and practitioners have traditionally viewed youth sports in a contextual vacuum, usually focusing exclusively on only one of the following areas: psychological, sociocultural, biological growth and maturation, or physiological. Although these approaches have provided valuable information, there is a need for a more integrated approach. An immediate beneficiary will be the reduction in easily accepted 'truths' for coaches, parents, and athletes. This is the case, for example, in recent progress in genetic research, where individual studies have often been heralded by the media as definitive proof of a specific gene or allele in the prediction of future athletic performance. However, as Bouchard (Chapter 8) suggests, 'athletic genotypes' alone will never be sufficient to predict elite athletic performance: too many other variables, i.e., motivation, opportunity, environment, and culture, must also be considered. Until researchers examine youth sport phenomena from a multivariate perspective, we will continue to see only a part of the total picture. A biocultural perspective is important. It provides an interactional and contextual model for examining issues in youth sports. After all, the individual physically performs sport-related tasks, but does so in the context of the culture within which the sport is played!

Typically, research has focused only on social/psychological, or only on biological factors related to sport. However, it is the interactions of these factors that likely have a major influence on youth sport participants. Age at menarche of adolescent athletes serves as an example. Menarche, or the first menstrual period, is an important maturational landmark in the development of girls. It occurs late in the sequence of events of female adolescence (Malina and Bouchard, 1991). Menarche occurs, on average, later in many (but not all) adolescent athletes, and training for sport is often indicated as the 'causative' factor. Much of the sport-related research, however, focuses on menarche per se to the exclusion of the many factors that are associated with and perhaps influence this maturational landmark. Factors such as physique, the selective or exclusive nature of many sports, nutritional status, family size, strength, among others are excluded or overlooked. More importantly, the interactions among biological and cultural factors as they relate to sport are overlooked. An early maturing girl, for example, may be socialized away from sport as a function of her earliness and related physical characteristics. Conversely, a late maturing girl may not be subjected to the same processes, and may in fact, be socialized into sport in part by being biologically more in synchrony with peers of both sexes (Malina, 1996). Cultural factors related to the significance of menarche and its impact on roles and behavioral expectations are additional considerations in evaluating the association of menarche and sport participation. A biocultural perspective provides for the interactions among such factors.

An issue that merits further study is the psychological correlates of physical characteristics among youth sports participants, especially those in aesthetic sports such as artistic gymnastics and figure skating. It is important to consider the relationships between physical characteristics and psychological constructs that purportedly measure aspects of the physical self such as body image, social physique anxiety, and so on. Among adolescent figure skaters, for example, body weight (controlling for age and height) and self-esteem, global physical self-concept, and perception of body fat correlate negatively but moderately, whereas body weight and social physique anxiety and body dissatisfaction correlate positively and moderately. Further, a combination of psychological and biological factors predict a significant proportion of the variance in dimensions of self-concept. The results suggest an association between low body weight and a linear physique, on one hand, and perceptions of body fat and appearance, drive for thinness and body dissatisfaction, on the other. Smaller and leaner figure skaters who describe their physical attributes positively have a more positive self-concept and lower social physique anxiety (Vadocz, 1999). An issue that merits further study is the role of the figure skating infrastructure (i.e., coaches, judges, and sport officials) in the demands and pressures placed upon adolescent girls. Similar trends are evident among elite female artistic gymnasts. For example, there is a modest relationship between anthropometric variables, largely related to the endomorphic component of somatotype, and performance scores in an international competition (Claessens et al., 1999). The suggests the need to systematically address the perception of fatness, or more specifically, endomorphy, by gymnastics judges. These issues are especially important because elite young female figure skaters and gymnasts are by no means fat. The gymnastics and figure skating infrastructures demand petiteness, leanness and linearity, and these demands can have an important influence on the psychological development of young female participants in these sports.

FUTURE ISSUES IN YOUTH SPORTS

As we move into the new millennium, new and familiar issues will affect the development and promotion of youth sports. Three issues are of particular relevance: talent identification, the potential influence of genetic advances on sport, and the need to meet the sport interests of urban youth. Given national and international interests in success in sport, early talent identification and selection will continue to be an issue in some sports. Genetic advances in the biomedical community will be increasingly applied to sport in the future and will undoubtedly affect subsequent generations of youth sport participants. The needs of urban youth, especially those resident in the impoverished environments of inner cities, are many and organized sport is both a major need and perhaps a part of the solution to some of inner city problems.

Talent Identification

The efficacy of talent identification needs systematic study and evaluation. Can future athletic success be predicted from growth, motor and behavioral traits of children? The necessary morphological and physical characteristics required for future success in specific sports or positions within sports have been described by many (Komadel, 1988; Malina, 1993, 1997; Regnier et al., 1982, 1993). On one end of the spectrum of talent identification is the intuition of coaches, whereas at the other end of the spectrum is the use of validated and reliable assessments. These batteries focus on the assessment of morphological, psychological, and physiological factors in the prediction of future success in sport. The efficacious use of 'detection batteries' or 'screening programs' is partially substantiated in the literature (Bloomfield, 1992; Hebbelinck, 1989; Komadel, 1988), but focus is usually on those who eventually are successful, and in many cases only medal winners in elite competitions. Those who are not successful are

ordinarily not considered.

The use of such 'batteries' is controversial: should young athletes be directed into a single sport to the exclusion of other sports and activities based solely on their performance on such tests? If this is done, the risk of sacrificing the enjoyment of youth for the sake of talent development is real. A related issue is youth who are excluded by the selection process. What is the impact of exclusion on sport participation and other activities of these youth?

Leaving talent identification solely up to the intuition and judgment of a coach or group of coaches is equally controversial and potentially less reliable and objective. Several other important considerations in the process of talent identification and selection are related to decision making. Are parents involved in the process? Do the young athletes have any input in the decision process? Whose interests are being served by talent identification? Clearly, children should have a voice in the process; unfortunately, they often are excluded from the process altogether.

It is important to note that early identification and selection is not necessarily indicative of future sport success in adolescence or adulthood (Malina, 1997). A host of intervening variables related to physical growth, psychological development, socialization, and the sport context interact to affect young athletes' abilities to be successful in sports. Talent identification and selection are exclusionary processes. As a result, the vast majority of young athletes are eliminated from further involvement in a sport, and the subsequent numbers of participants continue to dwindle as the level of competition and selectivity increase. This reduction of opportunity is compounded by the potential for talent identification programs to involve economic discrimination and exploitation (Malina, 1997). The former is particularly prevalent in sports requiring equipment purchases (e.g., ice hockey), expensive team fees (e.g., gymnastics), and extensive travel (e.g., travel soccer teams), whereas the latter is apparent in the intensive recruiting of inner city youth in the United States and the talent scouting of youth in many developing countries for the purposes of elite sport at the university and professional levels.

Talent identification and selection will continue to be an integral part of youth sports, particularly at the more elite levels. Sport organizations, coaches and parents should emphasize opportunities to participate rather than identification of talent. Many youth sports likely lose more talented athletes to exclusionary practices of "cutting" and "tryouts" than are gained through successful talent identification. After all, the important caveat for all talent identification and selection programs is—"Wait and see!"

Genetics

The explosion of genetic research in the biomedical community is spilling over into the athletic arena. The contributions of specific genetic factors to attributes necessary for athletic performance are appearing in the literature with increasing frequency. Studies of familial resemblance in VO_2 max and responses to exercise training (Bouchard et al., 1998; Bouchard et al., 1986) have yielded encouraging results, which have potential implications for this relatively new field of inquiry in the exercise sciences (see Bouchard, Chapter 8). Caution must be used in the application of these findings to potentially controversial issues related to talent identification and premeditated sport specialization, and perhaps prenatal selection for "talent" in sport. The effects of cultural, environmental, and psychological factors must also be recognized and considered. After all, with the same genetic characteristics but in a different environment or culture, Michael Jordan may have never been. This is an important consideration, as the inevitability of cloning and "manufactured" genetic traits pose tremendous ethical and moral dilemmas for the future of youth sports.

Meeting the Sport Needs of Urban Youth

Today's urban youth face a myriad of negative factors including crime, teen pregnancy, and drug abuse. Many of the activities (i.e., sexual activity, substance abuse) leading to these problems are pursued during the over 40% of discretionary time available to today's youth (Carnegie Council on Adolescent Development, 1992). Youth sports provide a healthy and alternative to these activities. However, lack of funding, inappropriate management of programs, and inconsistent community involvement have created a need for better sport alternatives for urban youth. Most programs targeting urban youth tend to focus on 'at-risk' youth rather than fostering youth resiliency and positive youth development (Smith, Chapter 15). Youth sport programs can provide an opportunity for urban children to develop these traits and reap the benefits of a healthy lifestyle.

Effective inner city youth sports programs are scarce and insufficient in scale to engender significant change (Schorr and Schorr, 1988). Programs also tend to suffer from high drop-out rates and a focus on the professional-sports model (Hellison, Chapter 16). Cooperative efforts involving public, non-profit, and community interest groups are best suited to mobilize interest and maintain support of after-school youth sport programs (Smith, Chapter 15). Programs that focus on holistic youth development such as Midnight Basketball, Soccer in the Streets, and the National Youth Sports Program have demonstrated that youth sport programs can be successful in the inner city, given the appropriate financial and community support. After-school programs, however, should not be expected to be a 'save-all' for urban youth sport involvement. Additional activities such as in-school physical education, parental support of organized youth sports, and community-based initiatives must also augment after-school offerings.

SUMMARY

As children are faced with more demands on their time and fewer physical education opportunities in school, youth sports will continue to be an important source of physical, psychological and social development. It is important to minimize risk and negative effects associated with participation in youth sports, and to maximize the potential benefits. Hence, further understanding of the effects of participation in organized youth sports is vital to the enhancement of the youth sport experience. A biocultural approach focusing on the interaction between biological and cultural factors, is important to continued understanding and improvement of youth sports.

Youth sports will continue to be heavily influenced by adult leadership and, therefore, education of parents, coaches, officials and administrators must be a priority. Maintaining youth sport participation will continue to be a challenge as societal reliance on sedentary lifestyles dependent upon computers, the internet and television for information and entertainment increases.

Youth sports are a fact in the daily lives of many children and adolescents. Researchers, coaches, administrators, and parents must address the issues presented in this volume to enable organized youth sports to effectively and consistently reach a wider audience. As we move into the 21st century, researchers and practitioners alike share the burden for improving youth sports so that they can meet the needs of children and adolescents.

REFERENCES

American Academy of Pediatrics. (1983). Weight training and weight lifting: Information for the pediatrician. *Physician and Sportsmedicine* 11: 157-161.

American Academy of Pediatrics. (2000). Safety in youth ice hockey: The effects of body checking. *Pediatrics* 105: 657-658.

American Red Cross. (1997). *Sport Safety Training: Injury Prevention and Care Handbook.* St. Louis, MO: Mosby Lifeline.

Anderson, S.J. (This volume). Injury profiles and surveillance of young athletes.

Bandura, A. (1997). *Self-efficacy: The Exercise of Control.* New York: Freeman.

Bar-Or, O. (This volume). Dehydration and rehydration in the exercising child and adolescent.

Beuenen, G.P. & Claessens, A.L. (This volume). Auxological issues in youth sports.

Beunen, G.P.; Malina, R.M.; & Thomis, M. (1999). Physical growth and maturation of female gymnasts. In Johnston, F.E.; Eveleth, P.B.; & Zemel, B. (Eds), *Human Growth in Context.* London: Smith-Gordon (pp. 281-289).

Blimkie, C.J.R.; Ramsay, J.; Sale, D.; MacDougall, D.; Smith, K.; & Garne, S. (1989). Effects of 10 weeks of resistance training on strength development in prepubertal boys. In Oseid, S. & Carlsen, H.K. (Eds), *Children and Exercise XIII.* Champaign, IL: Human Kinetics (pp. 183-197).

Bloomfield, J. (1992). Talent identification and profiling. In Bloomfield, J.; Fricker, P.A.; & Fitch, K.D. (Eds), *Textbook of Science and Medicine in Sport.* Melbourne: Blackwell Scientific Publications (pp. 187-198).

Bouchard, C. (This volume). Genetic advances and their implications for sport performance.

Bouchard, C.; Daw, E.W.; Rice, T.; Perusse, L.; Gagnon, J.; Province, M.A.; Leon, A.S.; Rao, D.C.; Skinner, J.S.; & Wilmore, J.H. (1998). Familial resemblance for VO_2 max in the sedentary state: The HERITAGE family study. *Medicine and Science in Sports and Exercise* 30: 252-258.

Bouchard, C.; Lesage, R.; Lortie, G.; Simoneau, J.-A.; Hamel, P.; Boulay, M.R.; Peruse, L.; & Theriault, G. (1986). Aerobic performance in brothers, dizygotic, and monozygotic twins. *Medicine and Science in Sports and Exercise* 18: 639-646.

Bredemeier, B.L. (This volume). Moral community and youth sport in the new millennium.

Brustad, R.J. (1993). Who will go out and play? Parental and psychological influences on children's attraction to physical activity. *Pediatric Exercise Science* 5: 210-223.

Brustad, R.J. (1996). Parental and peer influence on children's psychological development through sport. In Smoll, F.L. & Smith, R.E. (Eds), *Children and Youth in Sport: A Biopsychosocial Perspective.* Madison, WI: Brown and Benchmark (pp. 112-124).

Brustad, R.J. (This volume). Parental roles and involvement in youth sport: psychosocial outcomes for children.

Caine, D.J. & Broekhoff, J. (1987). Maturity assessment: A viable preventive measure against physical and psychological insult to the young athlete? *Physician and Sportsmedicine* 15: 67-80.

Carnegie Council on Adolescent Development. (1992). *A Matter of Time: Risk and Opportunity in the Nonschool Hours*. New York: Carnegie Corporation of New York.

Claessens, A.L.; Lefevre, J.; Beunen, G.; & Malina, R.M. (1999). The contribution of anthropometric characteristics to performance scores in elite female gymnasts. *Journal of Sports Medicine and Physical Fitness* 39: 355-360.

Coakley, J. (1992). Burnout among adolescent athletes: a personal failure or a social problem? *Sociology of Sport Journal* 9: 271-285.

Dreyfus, I. (1999). Parents required to study sportsmanship. *Lansing State Journal*, September 6, p 2A.

Ewing, M.E.; Seefeldt, V.D.; & Brown, T.P. (1996). *Role of Organized Sport in the Education and Health of American Children and Youth. Background Report on the Role of Sports in Youth Development*. New York: Carnegie Corporation of New York.

Feltz, D.L. & Albrecht, R.R. (1986). Psychological implications of competitive running. In Weiss, M.R. & Gould, D. (Eds), *Sports for Children and Youth*. Champaign, IL: Human Kinetics (pp. 225-230).

Gould, D. & Dieffenbach, K. (This volume). Psychological issues in youth sports: competitive anxiety, overtraining, and burnout.

Gould, D.; Tuffey, S.; Udry, E.; & Loehr, J. (1996). Burnout in competitive junior tennis players: I. Qualitative analysis. *The Sport Psychologist* 10: 341-366.

Hebbelinck, M. (1989). Detection and development of talent in sports: Kinanthropometric aspects. *Sport (BLOSO, Belgium)* 31: 2-9.

Hellison, D. (This volume). School and agency-based sport programs in the inner city.

Hergenroeder, A.C. (1998). Prevention of sports injuries. *Pediatrics* 101: 1057-1063.

Katzmarzyk, P.T. & Malina, R.M. (1998). Contribution of organized sports participation to estimated daily energy expenditure in youth. *Pediatric Exercise Science* 10: 378-386.

Komadel, L. (1988). The identification of performance potential. In Dirix, A.; Knuttgren, H.G.; & Tittel, K. (Eds.), *The Olympic Book of Sports Medicine*. Oxford: Blackwell Scientific Publications (pp. 275-285).

Malina, R.M. (1993). Youth sports: Readiness, selection, and trainability. In Duquet, W. & Day, J.A.P. (Eds.), *Kinathropometry IV*. London: E & FN Spon (pp. 285-301).

Malina, R.M. (1995). Physical activity and fitness of children and youth: Questions and implications. *Medicine, Exercise, Nutrition, and Health* 4: 123-135.

Malina, R.M. (1996). Tracking of physical activity and physical fitness across the lifespan. *Research Quarterly of Exercise and Sport* 67: 48-57.

Malina, R.M. (1997). Talent identification and selection in sport. *Spotlight on Youth Sports* 20(1): 1-3.

Malina, R.M. & Beunen, G.P. (1996). Matching of opponents in youth sports. In Bar-Or, O. (Ed.), *The Child and Adolescent Athlete*. Oxford: Blackwell Scientific Publications (pp. 202-213).

Malina, R.M. & Bouchard, C. (1991). *Growth, Maturation, and Physical Activity*. Champaign, IL: Human Kinetics.

Malina, R.M. & Eisenmann, J. (This volume). Trainability during childhood and adolescence.

Martens, R. (1978) *Joy and Sadness in Children's Sports*. Champaign, IL: Human Kinetics.

Obert, P.; Steecken, F.; Courteix, D.; Lecog, A.-M.; & Guenon, P. (1998). Effects of long-term intensive endurance training on left ventricular structure and diastolic function in prepubertal children. *International Journal of Sports Medicine* 19: 149-154.

Passer, M.W. (1983). Fear of failure, fear of evaluation, perceived competence, and self-esteem in competitive trait anxious children. *Journal of Sport Psychology* 5: 172-188.

Regnier, G.; Salmela, J.H.; & Russell, S.J. (1993). Talent detection and development in sport. In Singer, R.N.; Murphey, M.; & Tennant, L.K. (Eds.), *Handbook of Research on Sport Psychology*. New York: McMillan (pp. 290-313).

Regnier, G.; Salmela, J.H.; & Alain, C. (1982). Strategie fur die Bestimmung und Entdeckung von Talenten im Sport. *Lesitungssport* 12: 431-440.

Robinson, M. (1999). Youth player paralyzed. *State News (Michigan State University)*, December 9, p 12B.

Rothstein, A.; Adolph, E.F.; & Wills, J.H. (1947). Voluntary dehydration. In Adolph, E.F. (Ed.), *Physiology of Man in the Desert*. New York: Interscience (pp. 254-270).

Rowland, T.W. (This volume). Cardiac characteristics of the child endurance athlete.

Rowland, T.W.; Goff, D.; Popowski, B.; DeLuca, P.; & Ferrone, L. (1998). Cardiac responses to exercise in child distance runners. *International Journal of Sports Medicine* 19: 385-390.

Rowland, T.W.; Unnithan, V.B.; MacFarlane, N.G.; Gibson, N.G.; & Paton, J.Y. (1994). Clinical manifestations of the 'athlete's heart' in prepubertal male runners. *International Journal of Sports Medicine* 15: 515-519.

Rowland, T.W.; Delaney, B.C.; & Siconolfi, S.F. (1987). "Athlete's heart" in prepubertal children. *Pediatrics* 79: 800-804.

Schorr, L.B. & Schorr, D. (1988). *Within Our Reach: Breaking the Cycle of Disadvantage*. New York: Doubleday.

Simon, J. & Martens, R. (1979). Children's anxiety in sport and non-sport evaluative activities. *Journal of Sport Psychology* 1: 160-169.

Smith, L. (This volume). Challenges for youth in urban areas.

Smoll, F.L. & Smith, R.E. (This volume). Enhancing coaching effectiveness in youth sports: theory, research, and intervention.

Smoll, F.L. & Smith, R.E. (1989). Leadership behaviors in sport: A theoretical model and research paradigm. *Journal of Applied Social Psychology* 19: 1522-1551.

Vadocz, E.A. (1999). *The Psychobiological Profile of Competitive Female Figure Skaters*. Doctoral dissertation, Michigan State University, East Lansing, MI.

Weiss, M. (This volume). Social influences on children's psychosocial development in youth sports.

Weltman, A.; Janney, C.; Rians, C.B.; Strand, K.; Berg, B.; Tippitt, S.; Wise, J.; Cahill, B.R.; & Katch, F.I. (1986). The effects of hydraulic resistance strength training in pre-pubertal males. *Medicine and Science in Sports and Exercise* 18: 629-638.

Williams, J.M. & Andersen, M.B. (1998). Psychosocial antecedents of sport injury: Review and critique of the stress and injury model. *Journal of Applied Sport Psychology* 10: 5-25.

ABOUT THE EDITORS

Dr. Robert M. Malina has earned doctoral degrees in physical education (University of Wisconsin, Madison) and anthropology (University of Pennsylvania, Philadelphia), and honorary degrees (doctor honoris causa) from the Catholic University of Leuven, Belgium, and the Academy of Physical Education, Jagiellonian University, Krakow, Poland (2001).

Dr. Michael A. Clark has a doctoral degree in education (Michigan State University).

Both Drs. Malina and Clark have extensive backgrounds in youth sports. Both were participants in youth sports, albeit in a different era, and have been involved in coaching and officiating youth sports. More importantly, perhaps, Drs. Malina and Clark have devoted a significant part of their academic careers to youth sports in the context of research and coach education.

Dr. Malina's research has included detailed studies of the growth and maturation of Olympic athletes less than 18 years of age; participants in youth football, swimming, diving, soccer, skiing, volleyball, and gymnastics; and most recently, elite adolescent Portuguese soccer players.

Dr. Clark's research has included major surveys of recreational and sport needs in Detroit and of injuries in youth baseball. In addition, Dr. Clark has made significant contributions to the development of the Program for Athletic Coaches Education (PACE) of Michigan State University and of the National Standards for Athletic Coaches of the National Association for Sport and Physical Education.

Dr. Malina has an extensive publication record in the sport sciences; recent books include *Growth, Maturation, and Physical Activity* (1991, with Claude Bouchard), and *Genetics of Fitness and Physical Performance* (1997, with Claude Bouchard and Louis Perusse). He is also a co-editor of *Sports Medicine for Specific Ages and Abilities* (2001, with Nicola Maffulli, Kai Ming Chan, Rose Macdonald, and Anthony W. Parker).

Dr. Clark has contributed chapters to *Sporting Dystopies: The Making and Meaning of Urban Sport Cultures*, the second edition of *Children and Youth in Sport, Sports in School: The Future of an Institute*, and *The Epidemiology of Sports Injuries*.